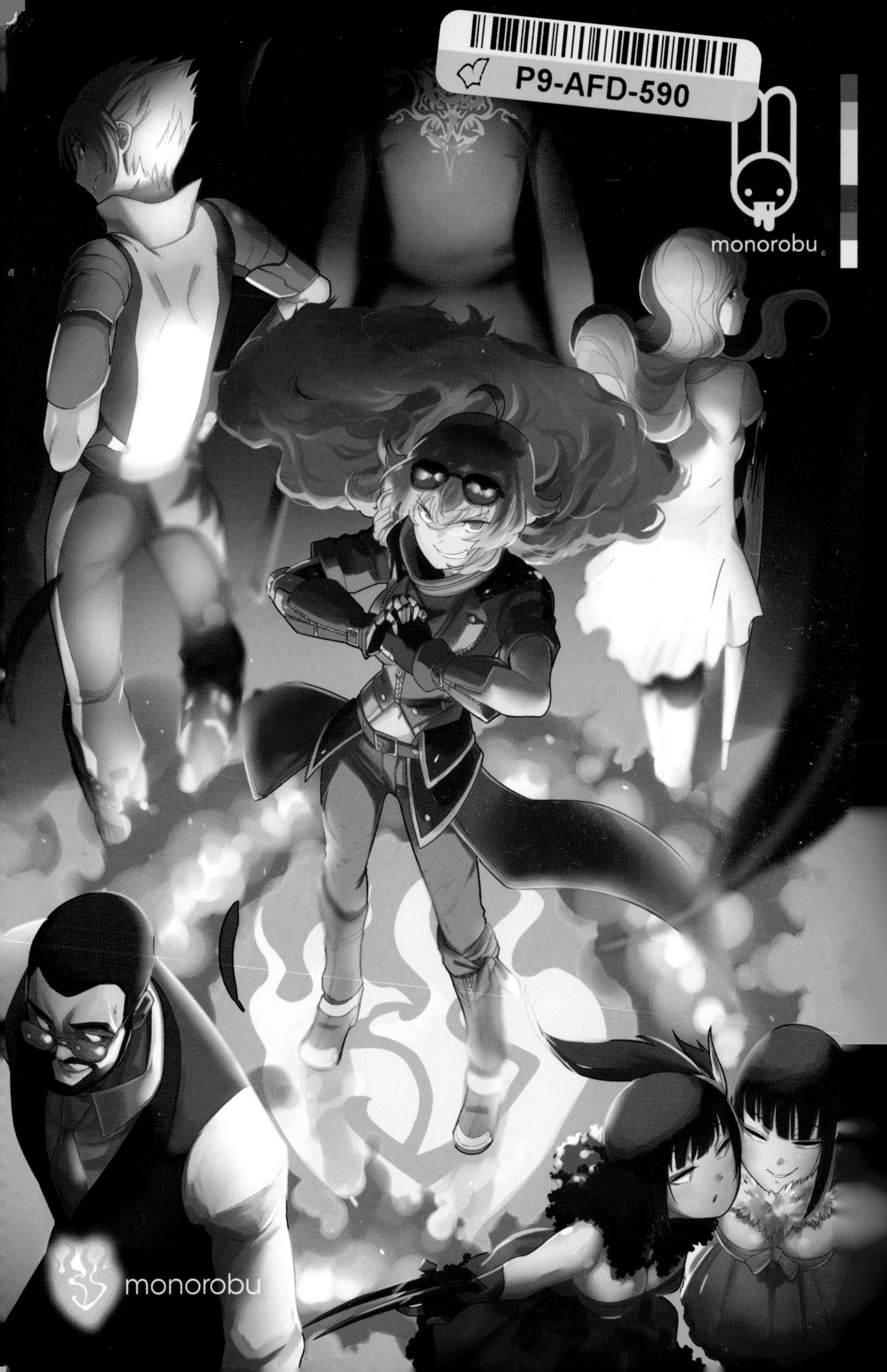
monorobu
monorobu

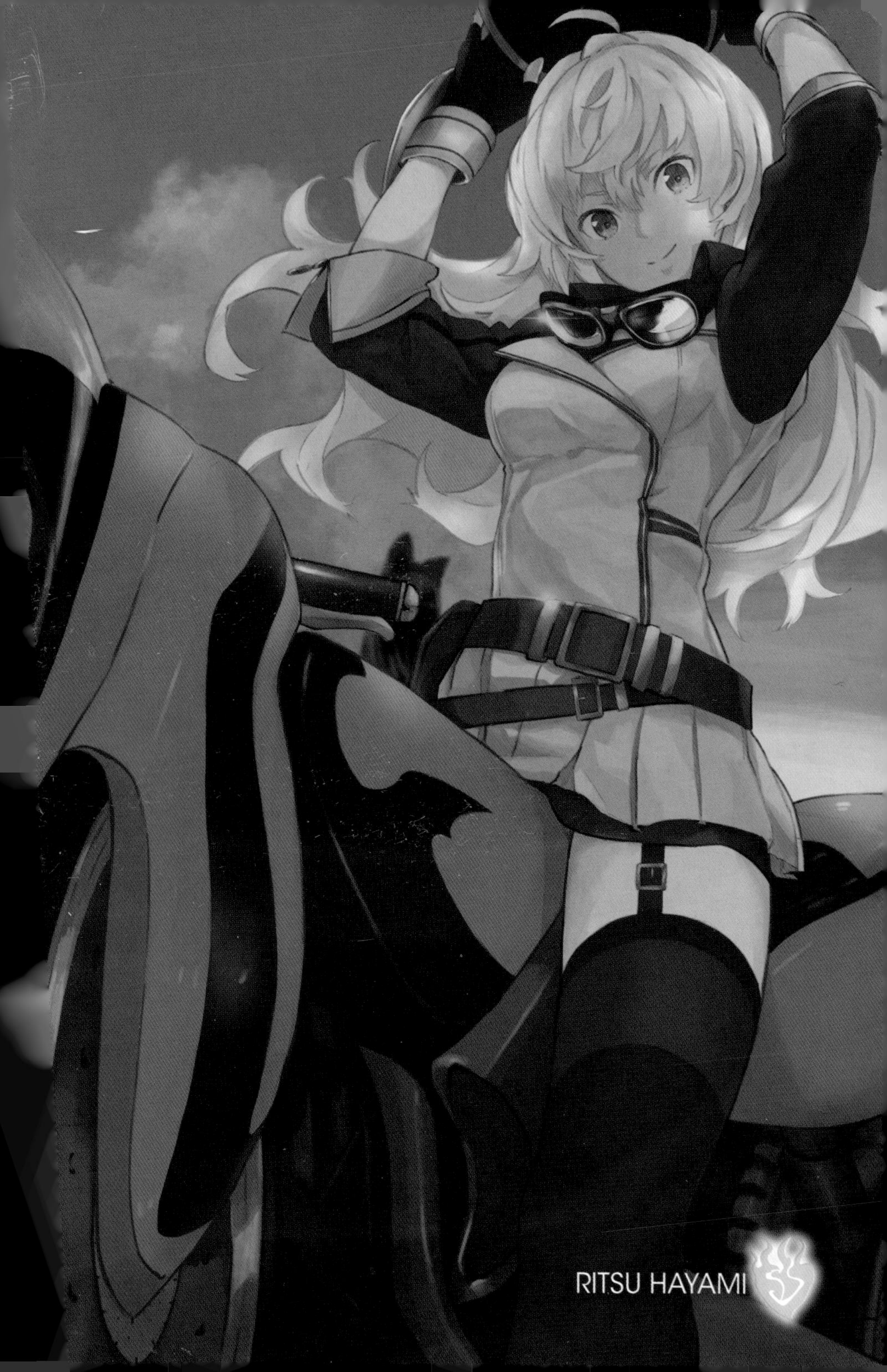
RITSU HAYAMI

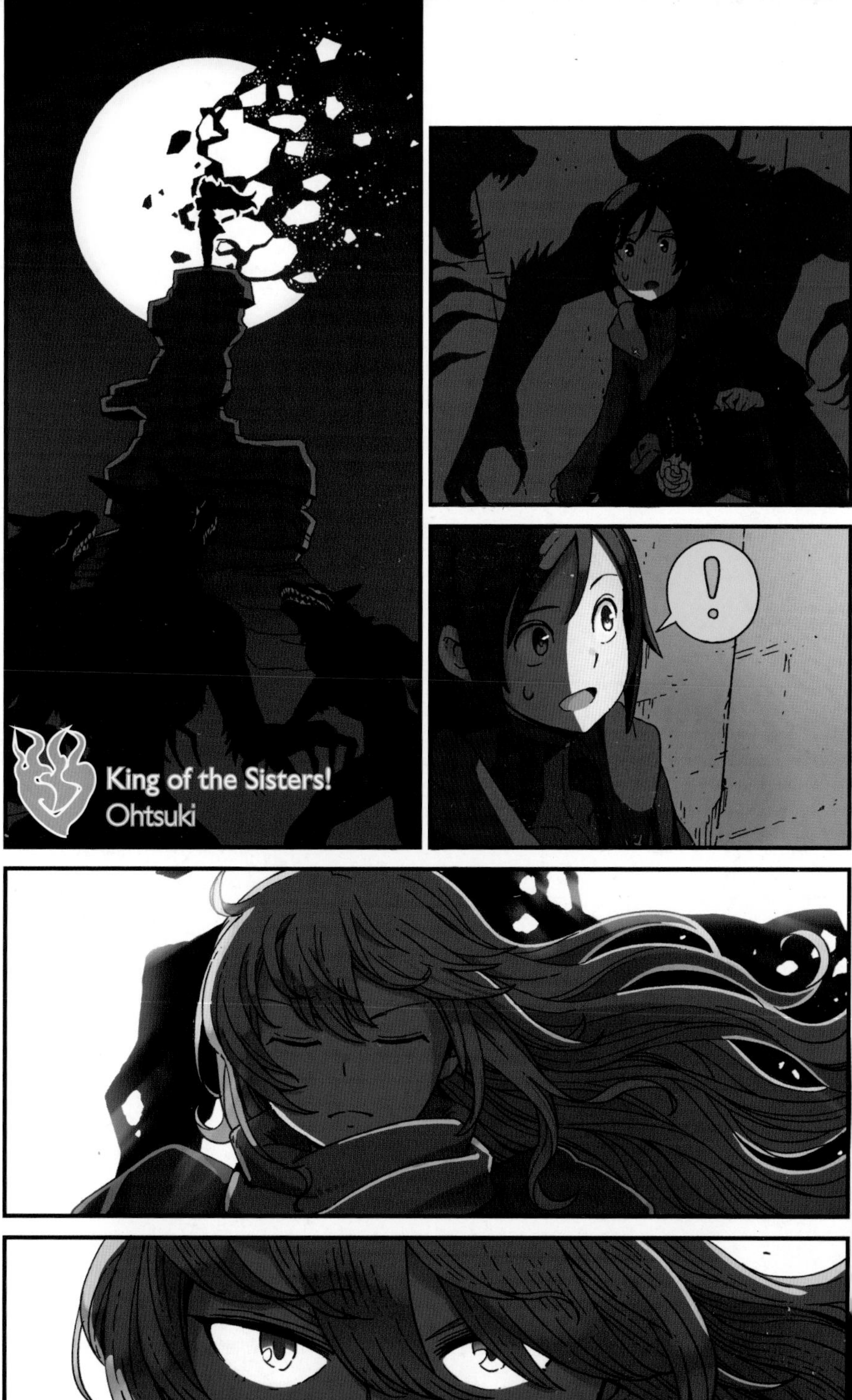
King of the Sisters!
Ohtsuki
!

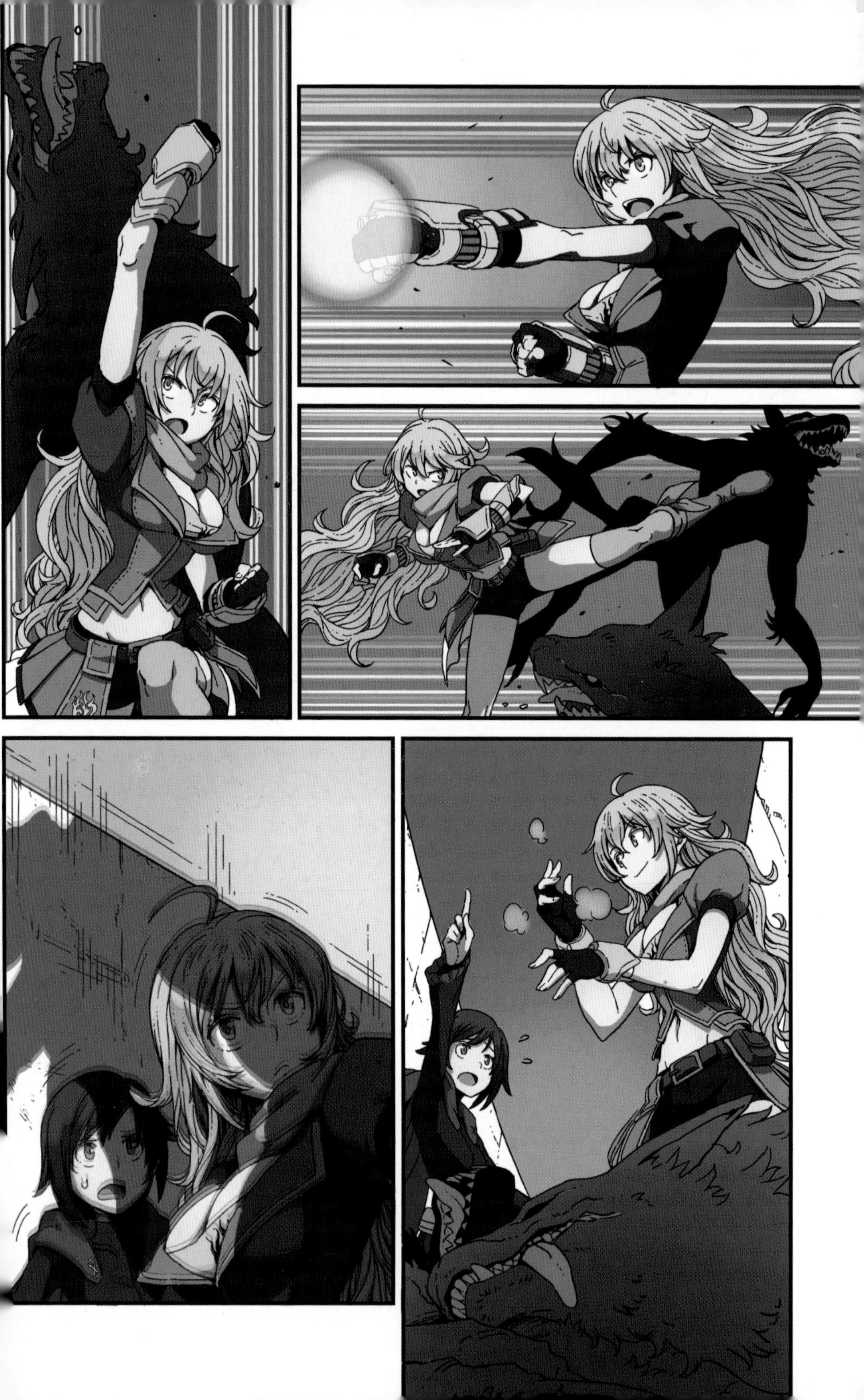

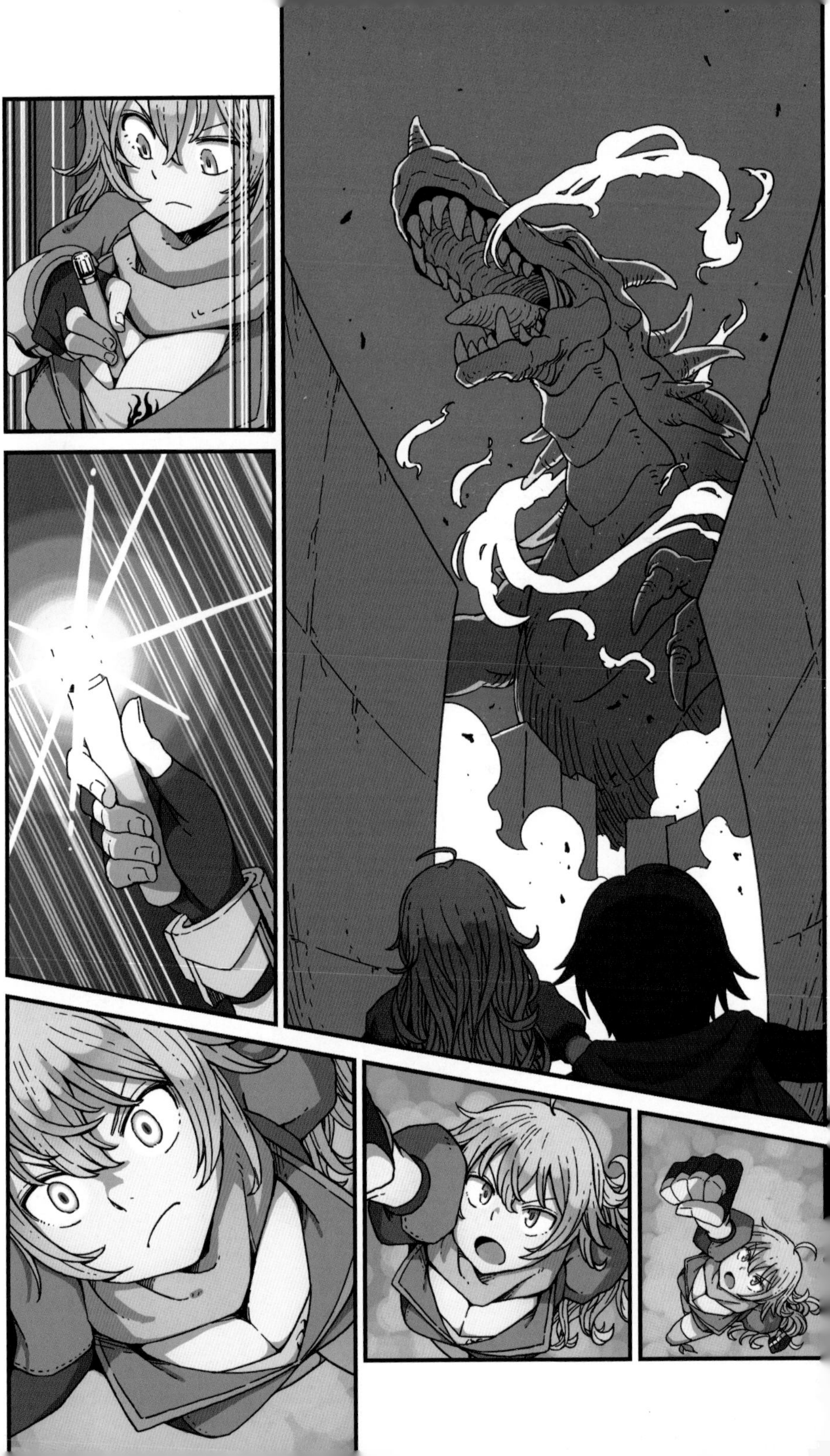

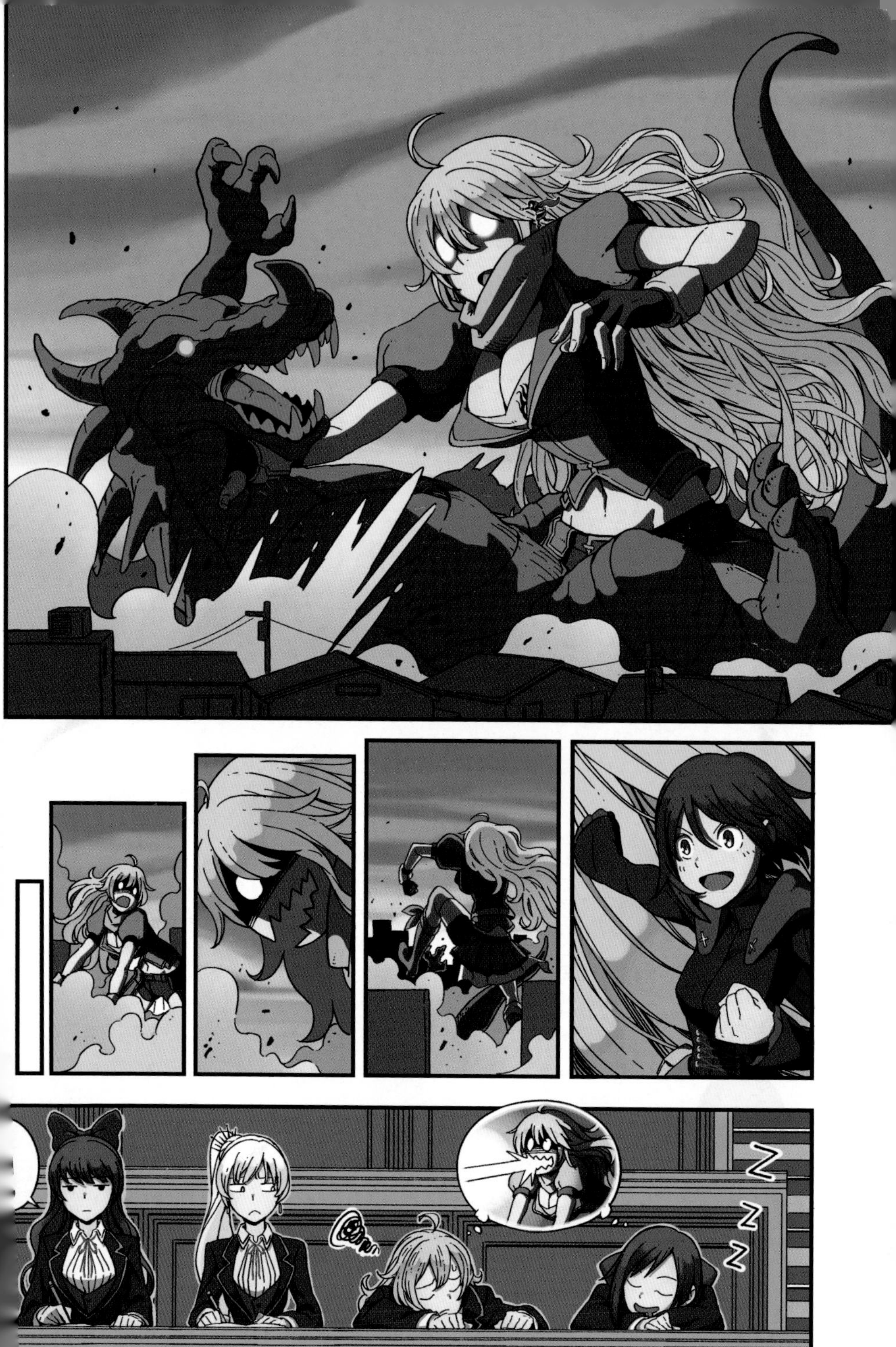
Z
Z
Z

ing of the Sisters!/END

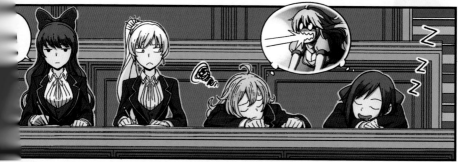

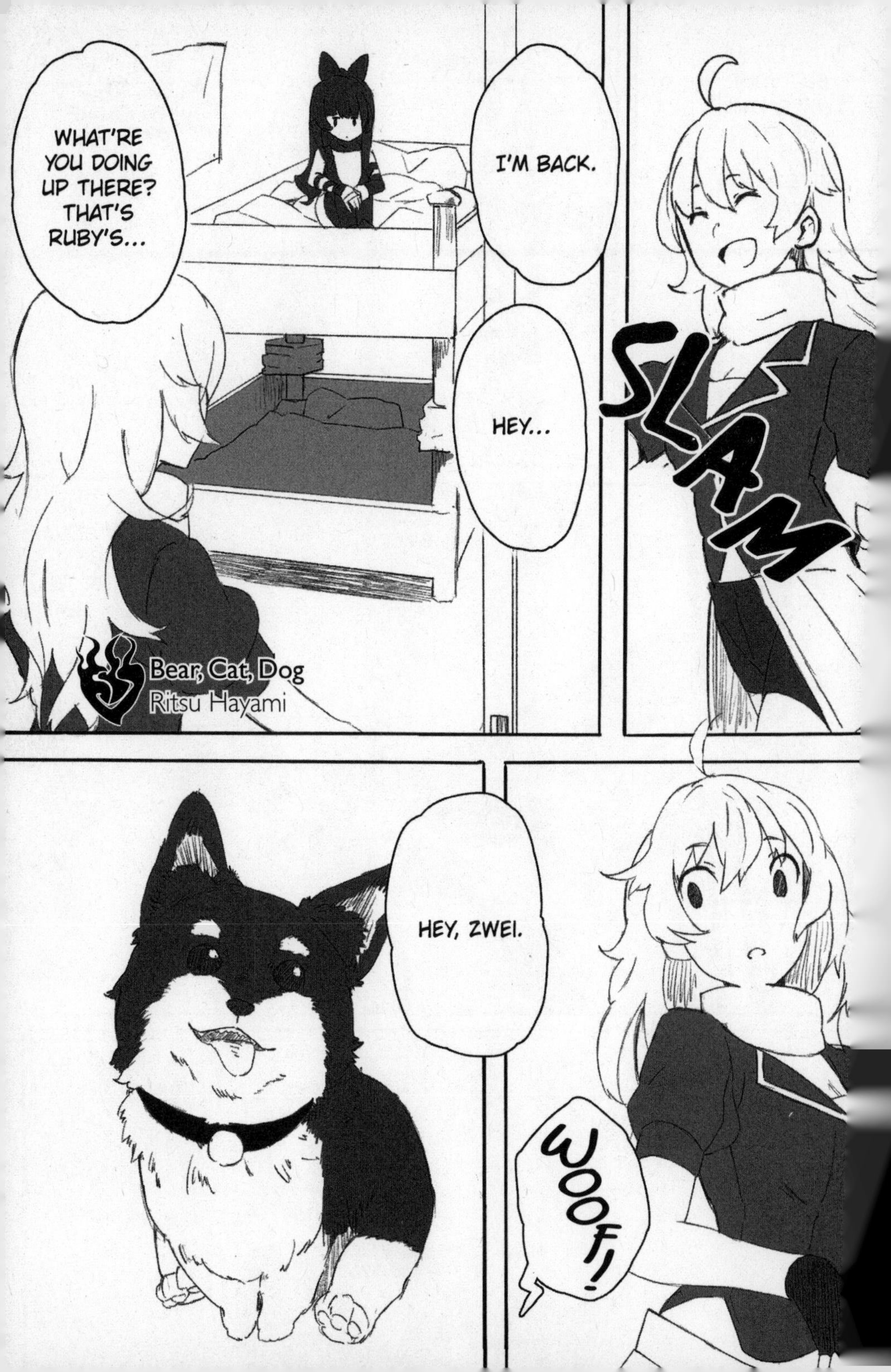
I'M BACK.
SLAM
HEY...
WHAT'RE YOU DOING UP THERE? THAT'S RUBY'S...
Bear, Cat, Dog
Ritsu Hayami
HEY, ZWEI.
WOOF!

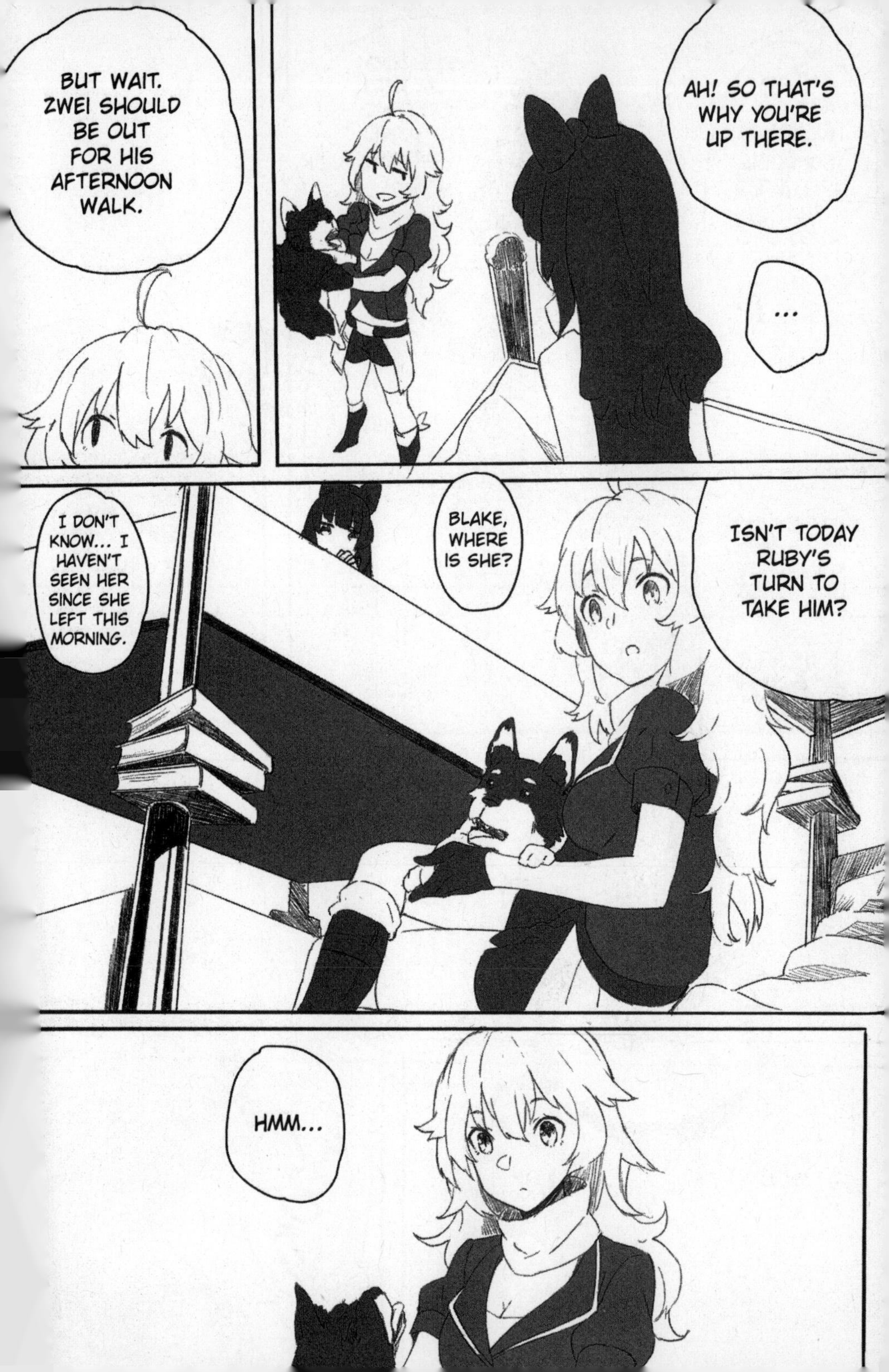
AH! SO THAT'S WHY YOU'RE UP THERE.
...
BUT WAIT. ZWEI SHOULD BE OUT FOR HIS AFTERNOON WALK.
ISN'T TODAY RUBY'S TURN TO TAKE HIM?
BLAKE, WHERE IS SHE?
I DON'T KNOW... I HAVEN'T SEEN HER SINCE SHE LEFT THIS MORNING.
HMM...

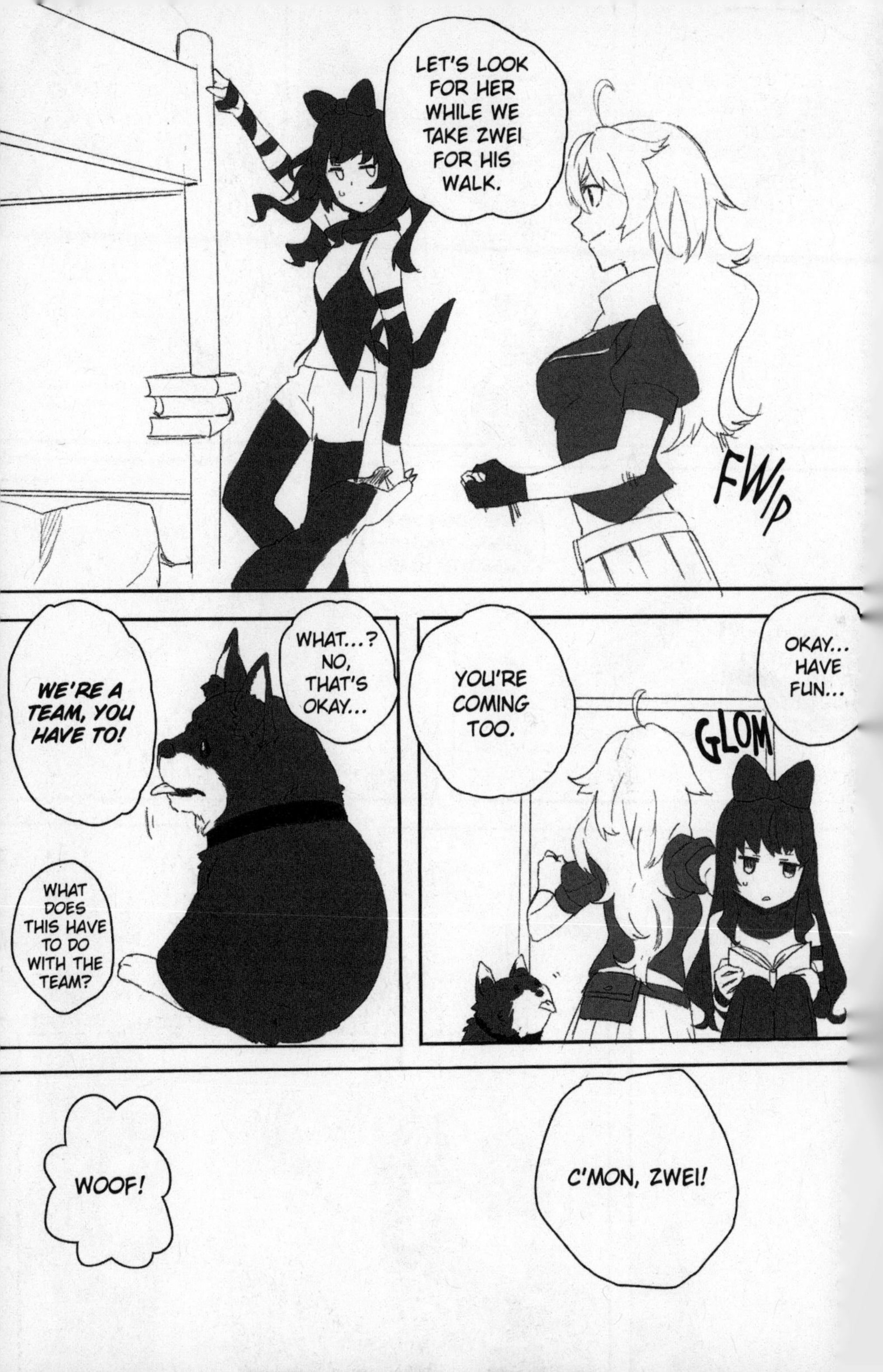

LET'S LOOK FOR HER WHILE WE TAKE ZWEI FOR HIS WALK.
FWIP
OKAY... HAVE FUN...
YOU'RE COMING TOO.
GLOM
WHAT...? NO, THAT'S OKAY...
WE'RE A TEAM, YOU HAVE TO!
WHAT DOES THIS HAVE TO DO WITH THE TEAM?
C'MON, ZWEI!
WOOF!

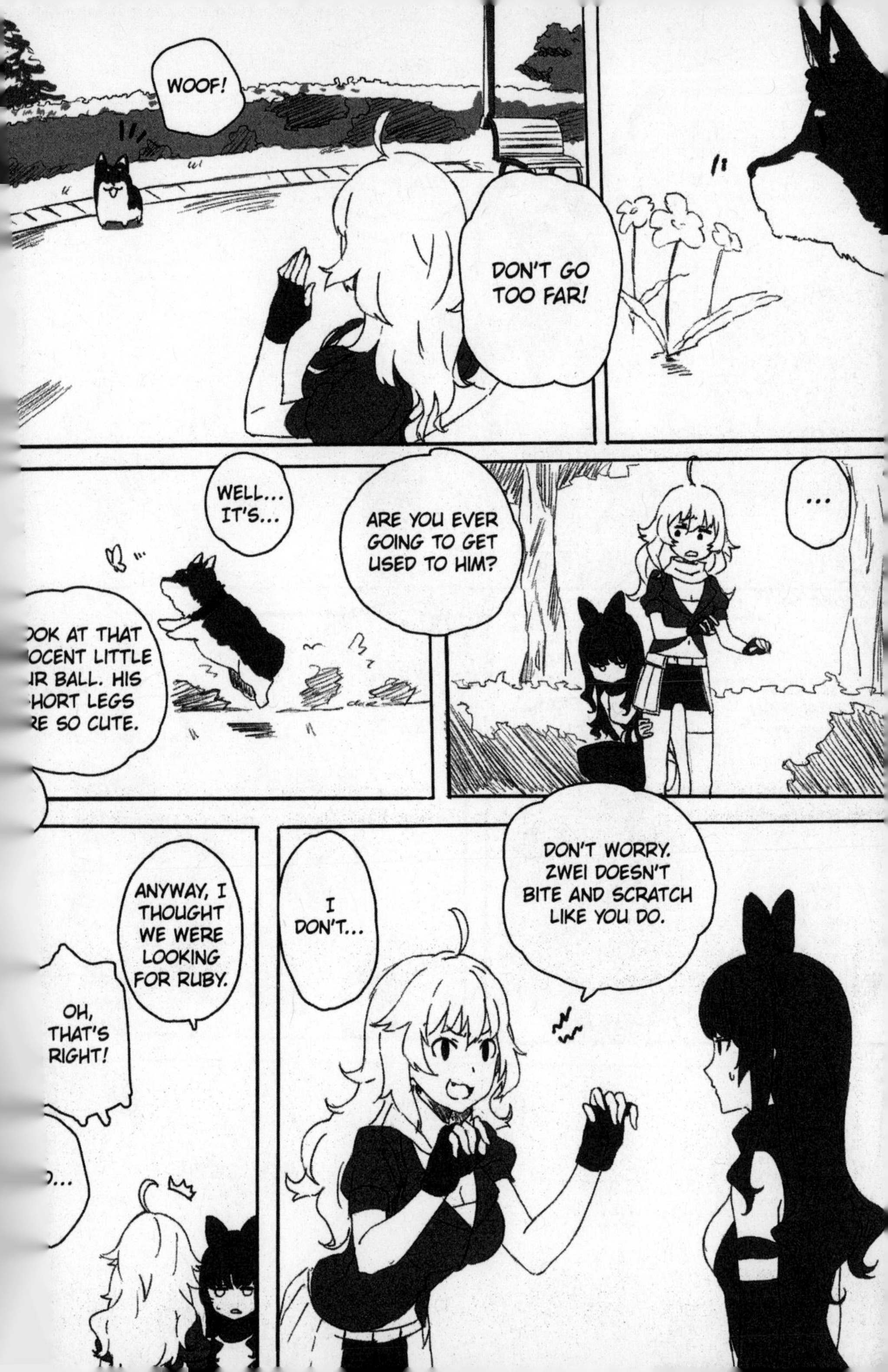
WOOF!
DON'T GO TOO FAR!
...
ARE YOU EVER GOING TO GET USED TO HIM?
WELL... IT'S...
OOK AT THAT OCENT LITTLE IR BALL. HIS HORT LEGS RE SO CUTE.
DON'T WORRY. ZWEI DOESN'T BITE AND SCRATCH LIKE YOU DO.
I DON'T...
ANYWAY, I THOUGHT WE WERE LOOKING FOR RUBY.
OH, THAT'S RIGHT!

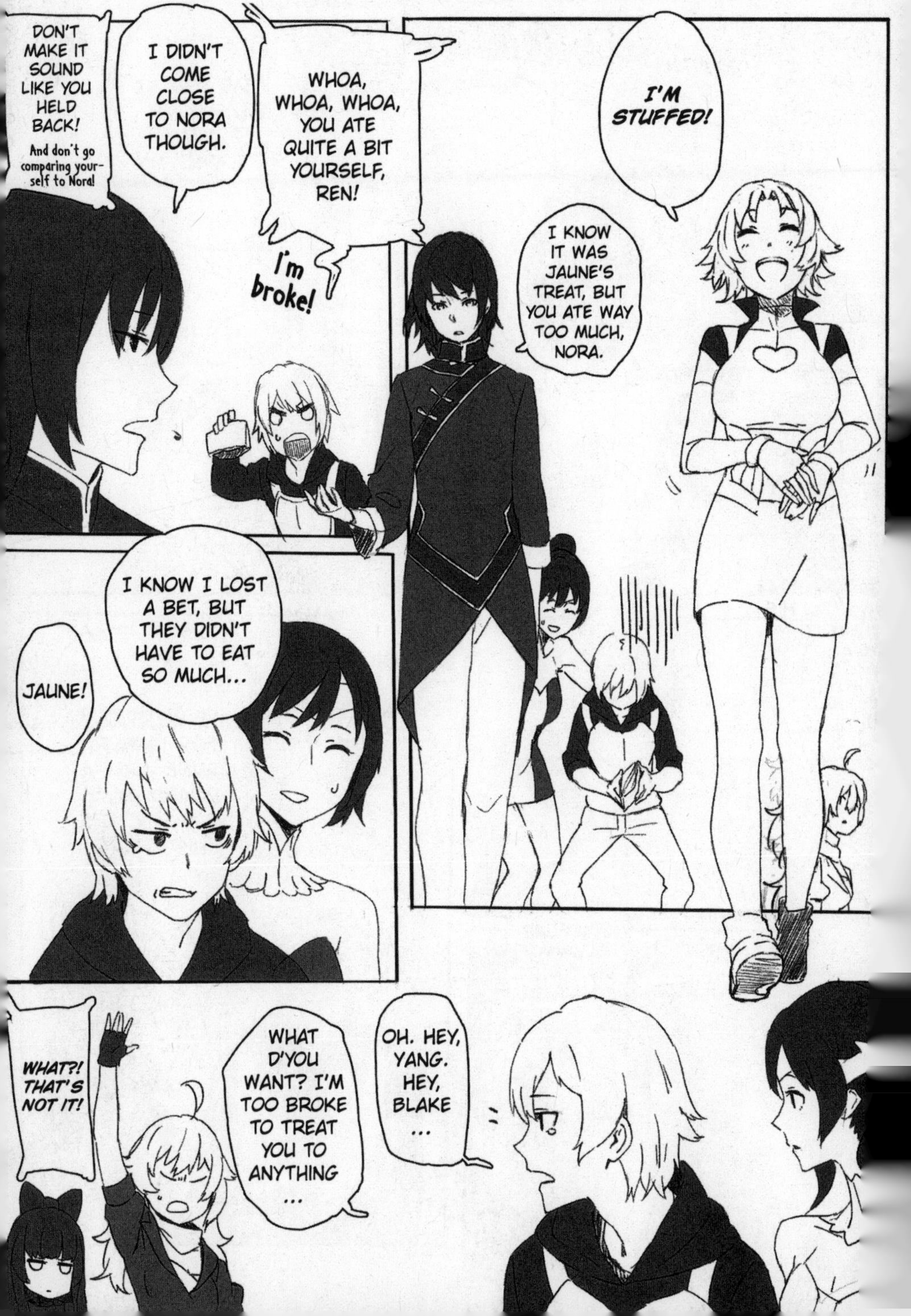
I'M STUFFED!
I KNOW IT WAS JAUNE'S TREAT, BUT YOU ATE WAY TOO MUCH, NORA.
WHOA, WHOA, WHOA, YOU ATE QUITE A BIT YOURSELF, REN!
I DIDN'T COME CLOSE TO NORA THOUGH.
DON'T MAKE IT SOUND LIKE YOU HELD BACK!
And don't go comparing your-self to Nora!
I'm broke!
I KNOW I LOST A BET, BUT THEY DIDN'T HAVE TO EAT SO MUCH...
JAUNE!
OH. HEY, YANG. HEY, BLAKE ...
WHAT D'YOU WANT? I'M TOO BROKE TO TREAT YOU TO ANYTHING ...
WHAT?! THAT'S NOT IT!

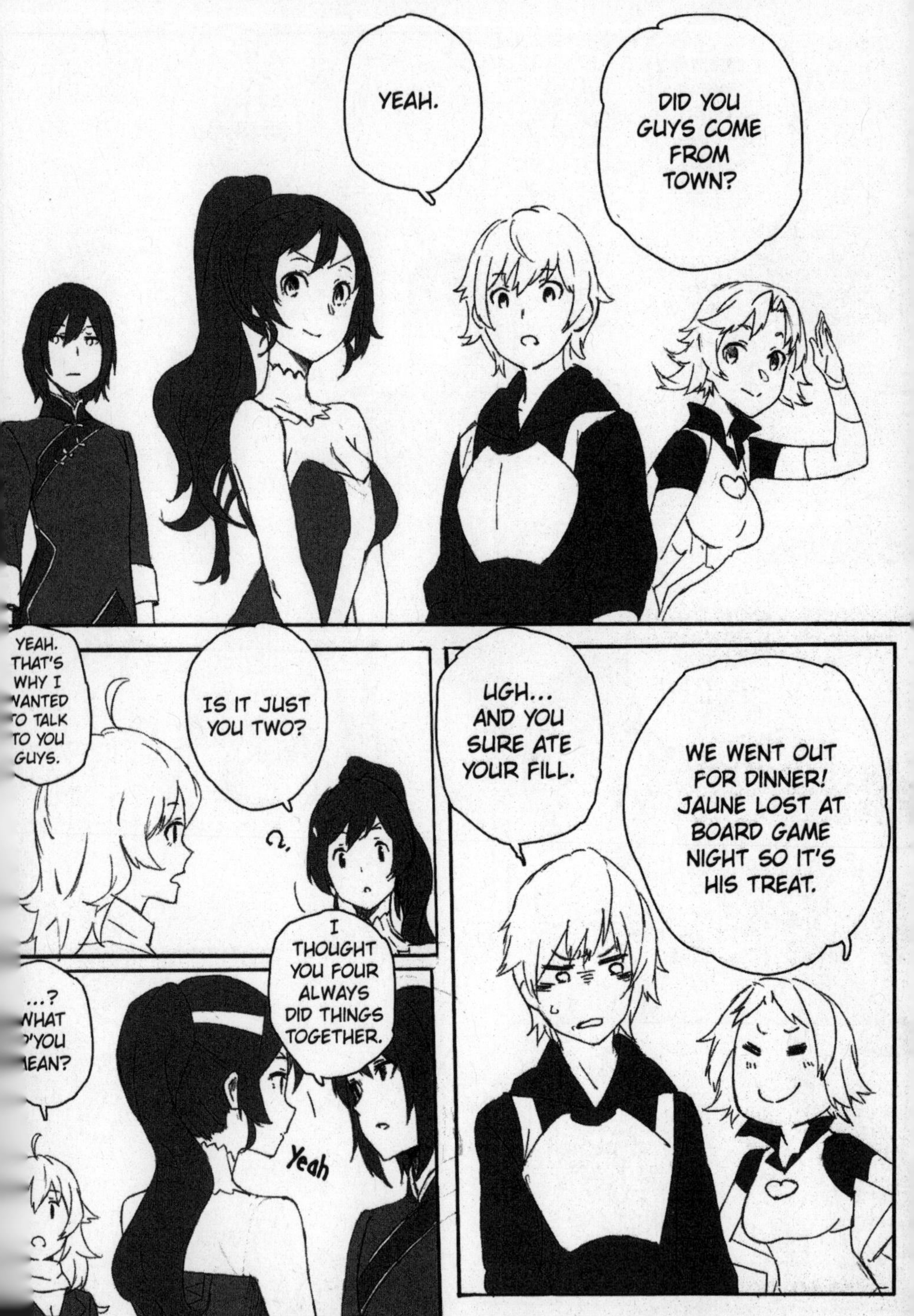
DID YOU GUYS COME FROM TOWN?
YEAH.
WE WENT OUT FOR DINNER! JAUNE LOST AT BOARD GAME NIGHT SO IT'S HIS TREAT.
UGH... AND YOU SURE ATE YOUR FILL.
IS IT JUST YOU TWO?
YEAH. THAT'S WHY I WANTED TO TALK TO YOU GUYS.
I THOUGHT YOU FOUR ALWAYS DID THINGS TOGETHER.
...? WHAT D'YOU MEAN?
Yeah

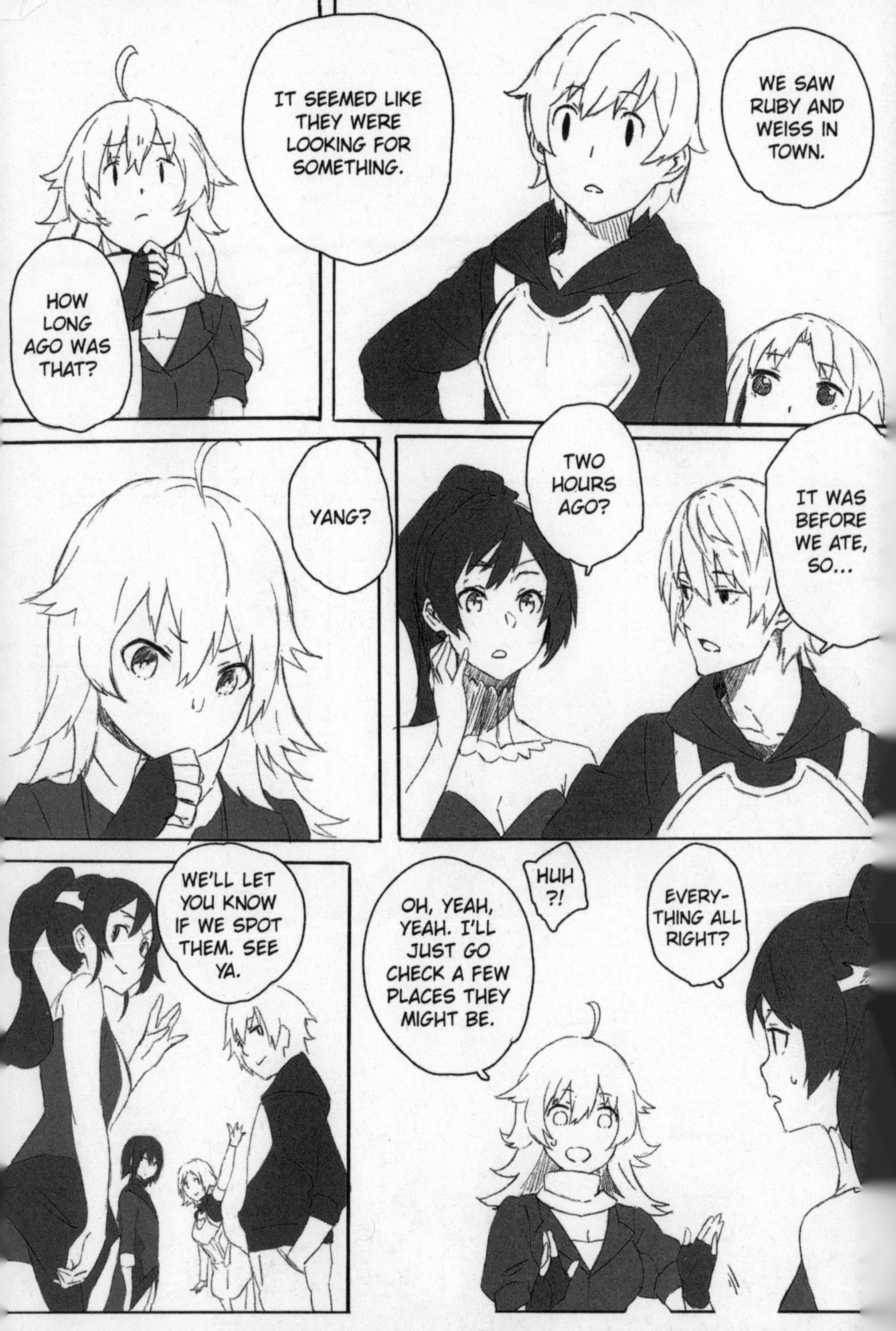
WE SAW RUBY AND WEISS IN TOWN.
IT SEEMED LIKE THEY WERE LOOKING FOR SOMETHING.
HOW LONG AGO WAS THAT?
IT WAS BEFORE WE ATE, SO...
TWO HOURS AGO?
YANG?
EVERY-THING ALL RIGHT?
HUH ?!
OH, YEAH, YEAH. I'LL JUST GO CHECK A FEW PLACES THEY MIGHT BE.
WE'LL LET YOU KNOW IF WE SPOT THEM. SEE YA.

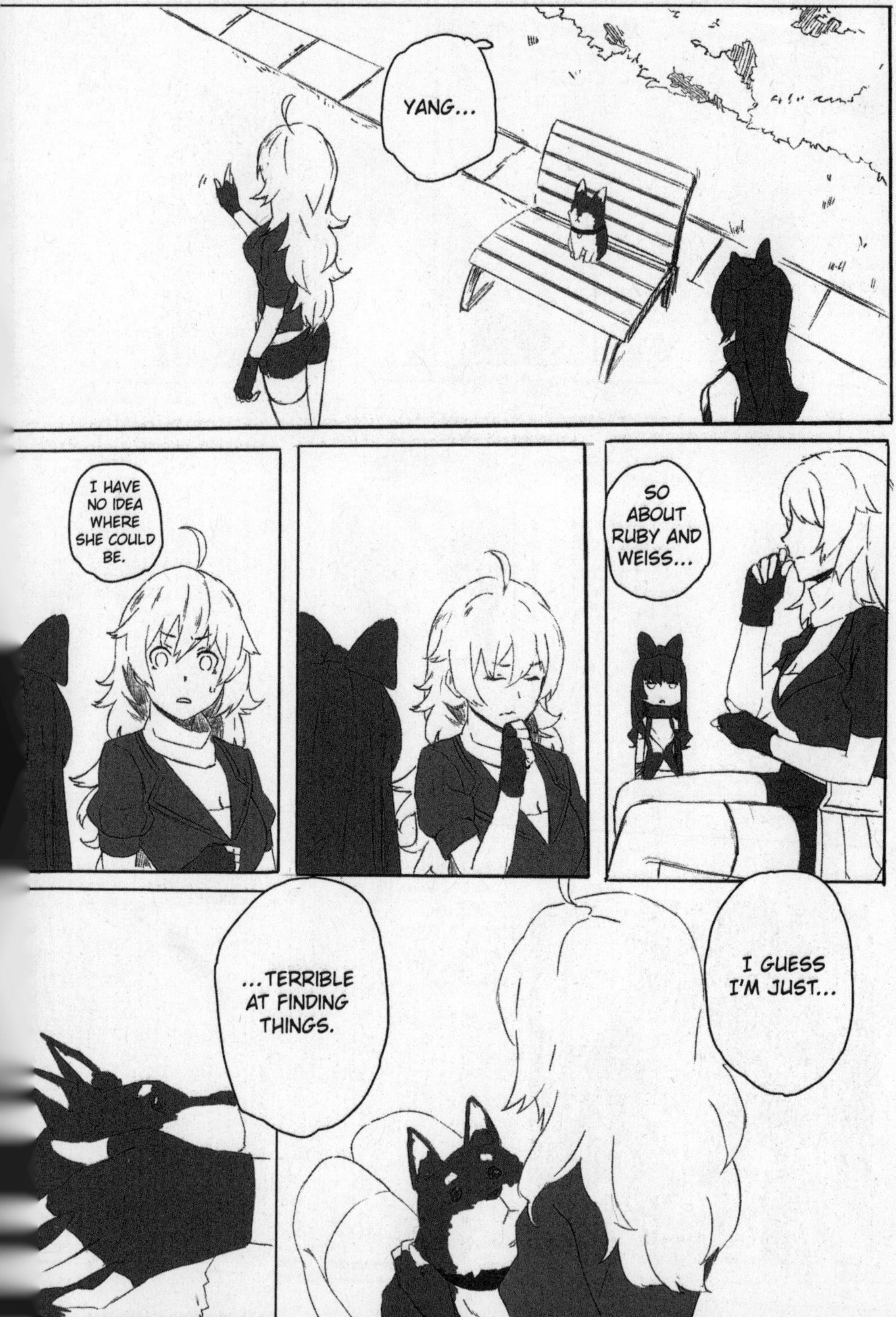
YANG...
SO ABOUT RUBY AND WEISS...
I HAVE NO IDEA WHERE SHE COULD BE.
I GUESS I'M JUST...
...TERRIBLE AT FINDING THINGS.

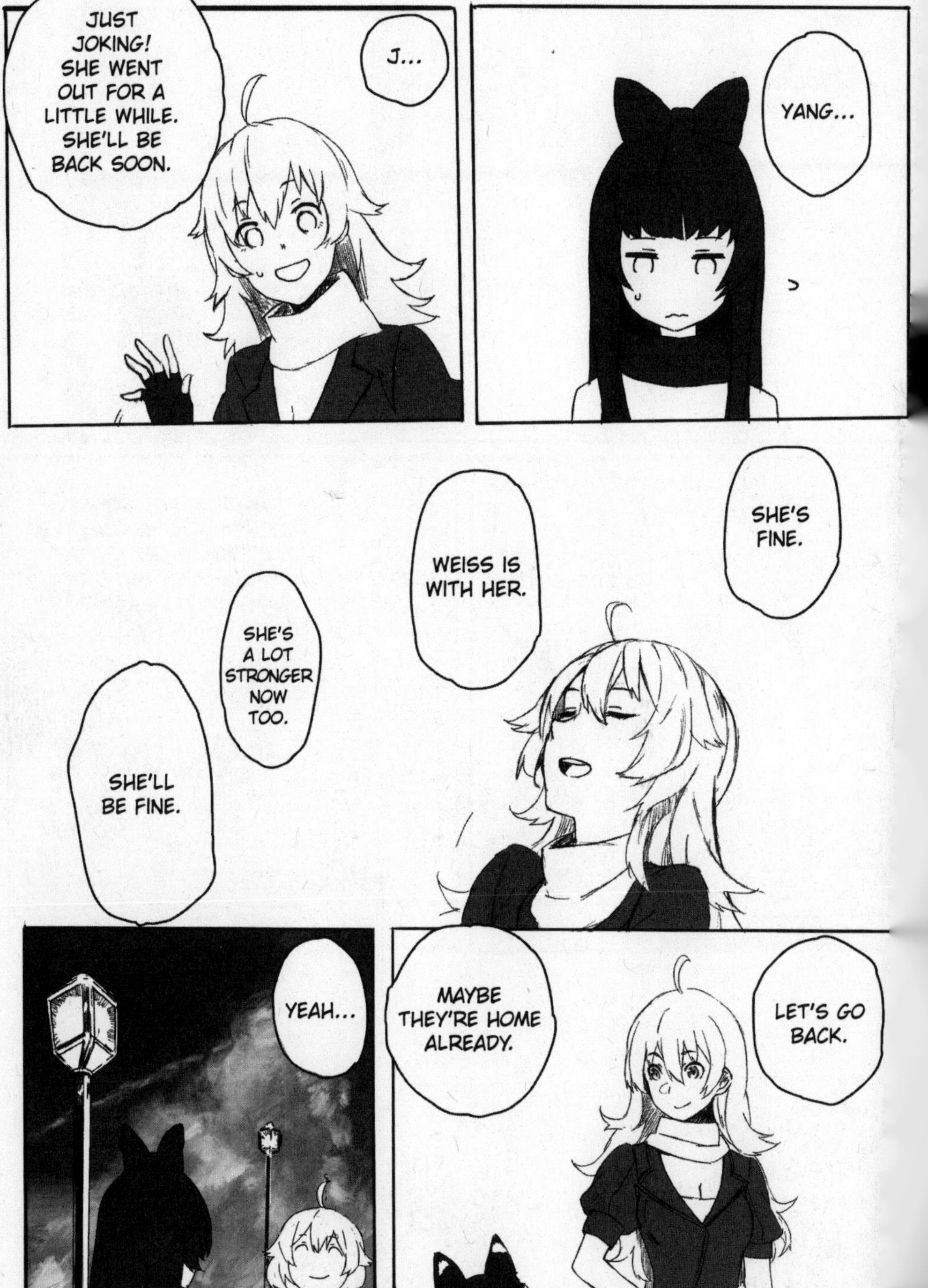
YANG...
J...
JUST JOKING! SHE WENT OUT FOR A LITTLE WHILE. SHE'LL BE BACK SOON.
SHE'S FINE.
WEISS IS WITH HER.
SHE'S A LOT STRONGER NOW TOO.
SHE'LL BE FINE.
LET'S GO BACK.
MAYBE THEY'RE HOME ALREADY.
YEAH...

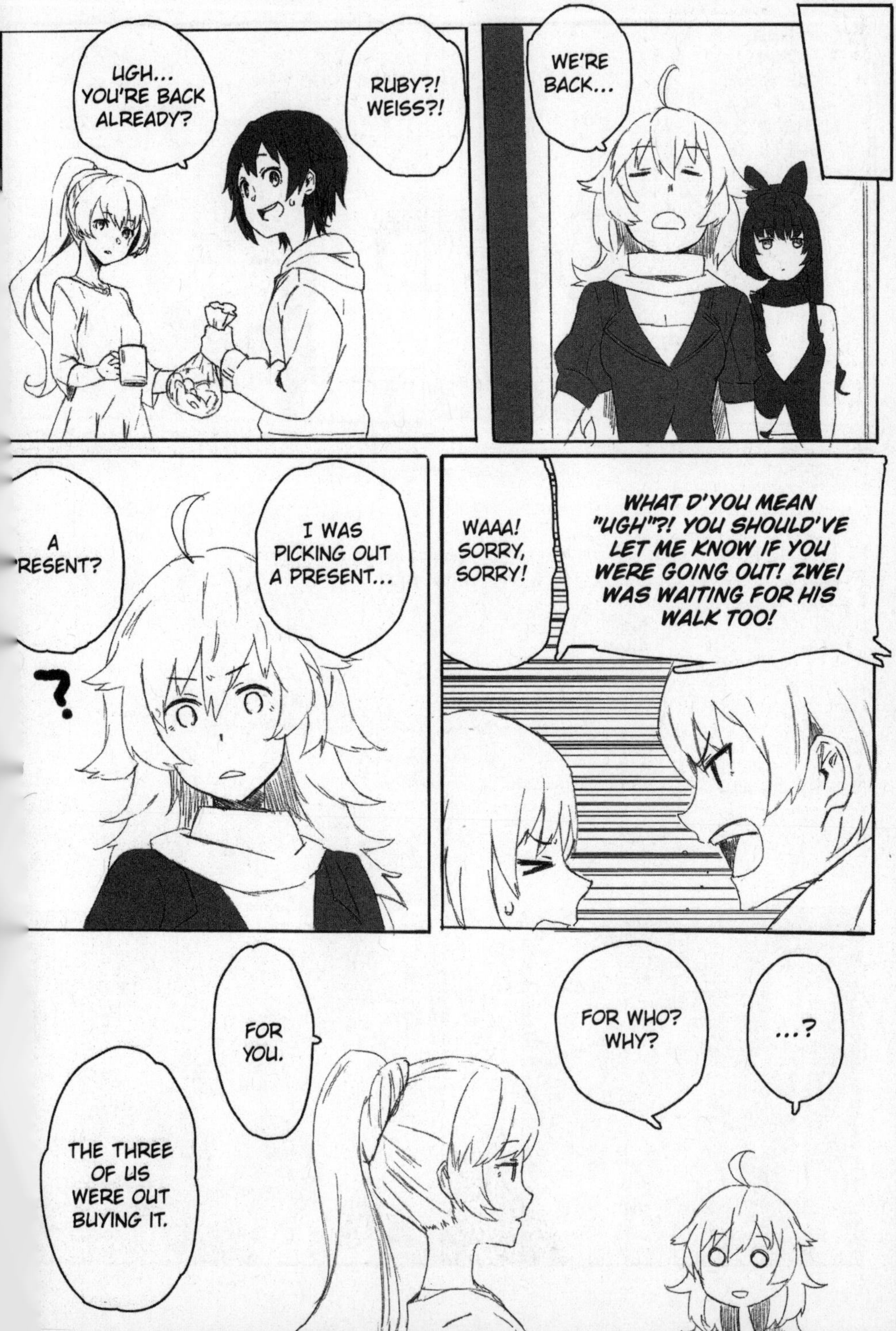
WE'RE BACK...
RUBY?! WEISS?!
UGH... YOU'RE BACK ALREADY?
WHAT D'YOU MEAN "UGH"?! YOU SHOULD'VE LET ME KNOW IF YOU WERE GOING OUT! ZWEI WAS WAITING FOR HIS WALK TOO!
WAAA! SORRY, SORRY!
I WAS PICKING OUT A PRESENT...
A PRESENT?
?
...?
FOR WHO? WHY?
FOR YOU.
THE THREE OF US WERE OUT BUYING IT.

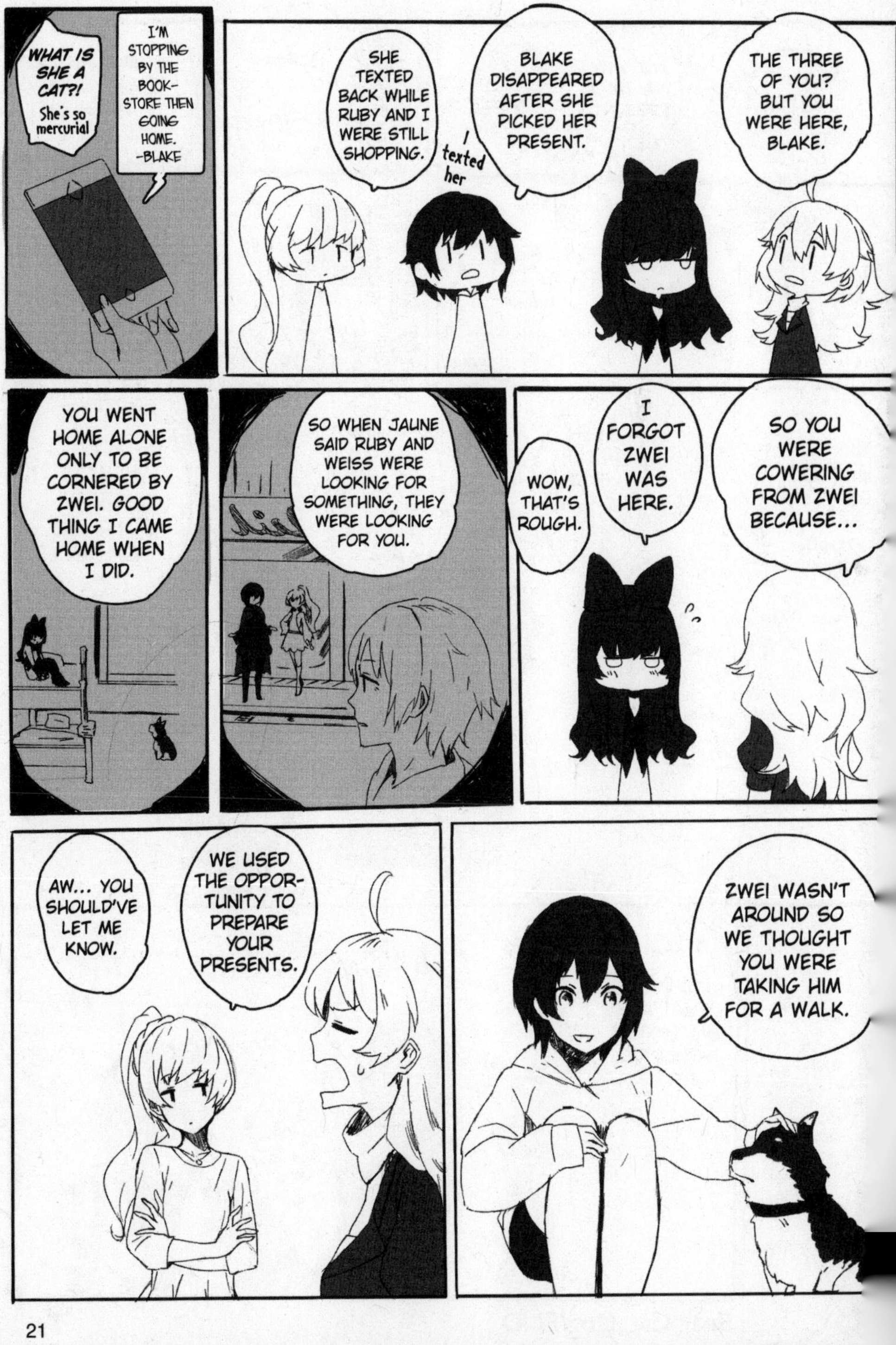
THE THREE OF YOU? BUT YOU WERE HERE, BLAKE.
BLAKE DISAPPEARED AFTER SHE PICKED HER PRESENT.
I texted her
SHE TEXTED BACK WHILE RUBY AND I WERE STILL SHOPPING.
I'M STOPPING BY THE BOOK-STORE THEN GOING HOME. -BLAKE
WHAT IS SHE A CAT?!
She's so mercurial
SO YOU WERE COWERING FROM ZWEI BECAUSE...
I FORGOT ZWEI WAS HERE.
WOW, THAT'S ROUGH.
SO WHEN JAUNE SAID RUBY AND WEISS WERE LOOKING FOR SOMETHING, THEY WERE LOOKING FOR YOU.
YOU WENT HOME ALONE ONLY TO BE CORNERED BY ZWEI. GOOD THING I CAME HOME WHEN I DID.
ZWEI WASN'T AROUND SO WE THOUGHT YOU WERE TAKING HIM FOR A WALK.
WE USED THE OPPORTUNITY TO PREPARE YOUR PRESENTS.
AW... YOU SHOULD'VE LET ME KNOW.

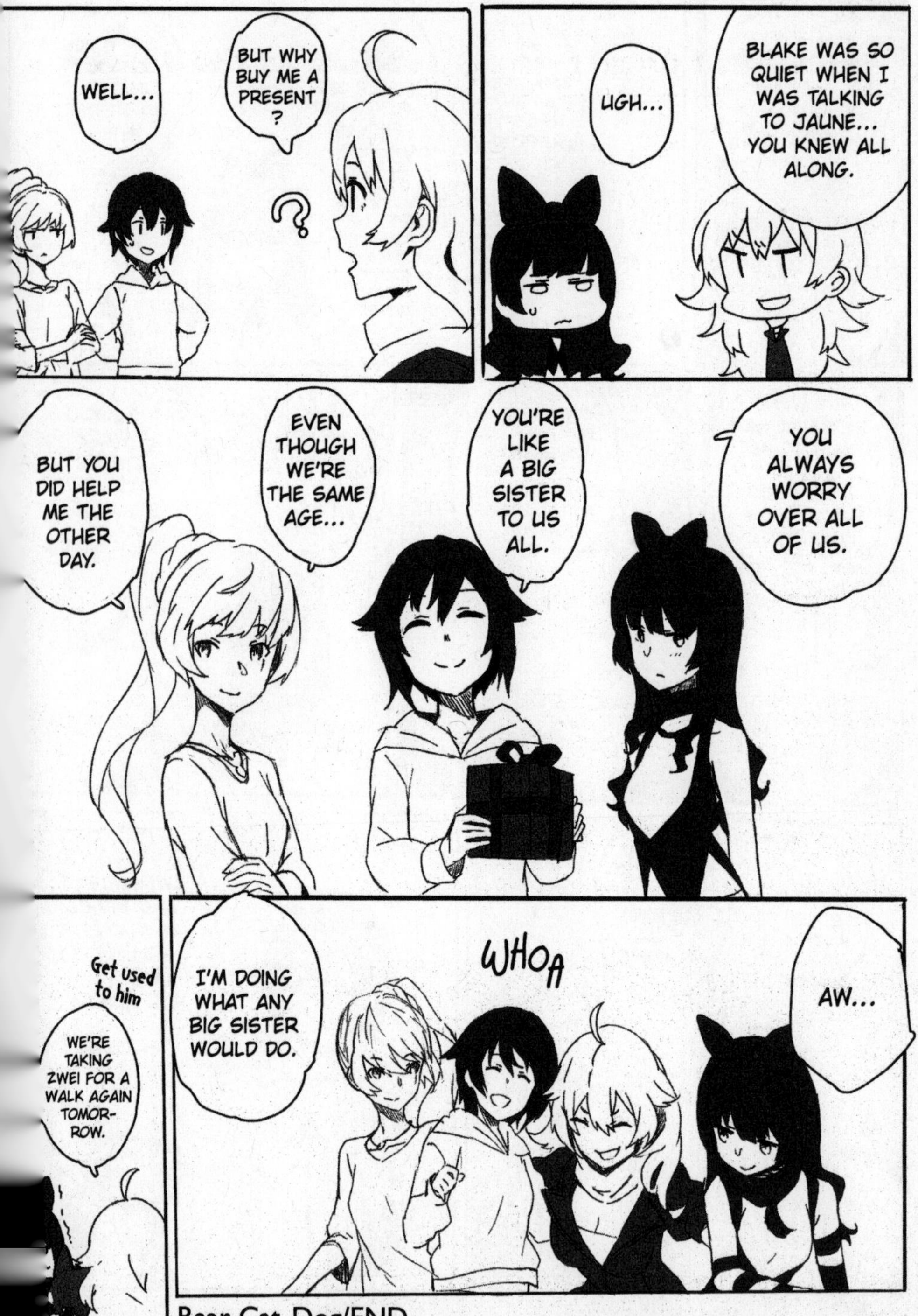
BLAKE WAS SO QUIET WHEN I WAS TALKING TO JAUNE... YOU KNEW ALL ALONG.
UGH...
BUT WHY BUY ME A PRESENT ?
WELL...
YOU ALWAYS WORRY OVER ALL OF US.
YOU'RE LIKE A BIG SISTER TO US ALL.
EVEN THOUGH WE'RE THE SAME AGE...
BUT YOU DID HELP ME THE OTHER DAY.
AW...
WHOA
I'M DOING WHAT ANY BIG SISTER WOULD DO.
Get used to him
WE'RE TAKING ZWEI FOR A WALK AGAIN TOMOR-ROW.

Bear, Cat, Dog/END

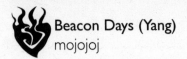

Beacon Days (Yang)

mojojoj

No. 1 on the Team

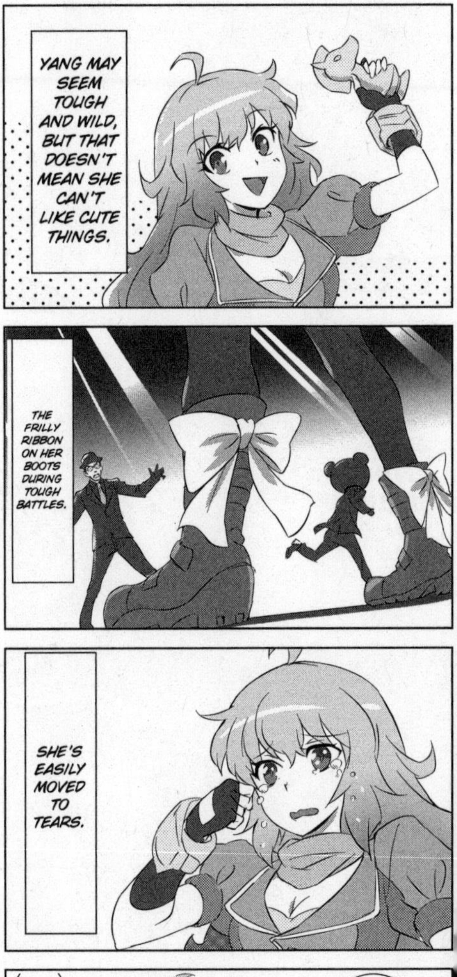
YANG MAY SEEM TOUGH AND WILD, BUT THAT DOESN'T MEAN SHE CAN'T LIKE CUTE THINGS.
THE FRILLY RIBBON ON HER BOOTS DURING TOUGH BATTLES.
SHE'S EASILY MOVED TO TEARS.
YOU'RE SO GIRLY.
WHAT?! WHAT'S WRONG WITH THAT?!

Physical Contact

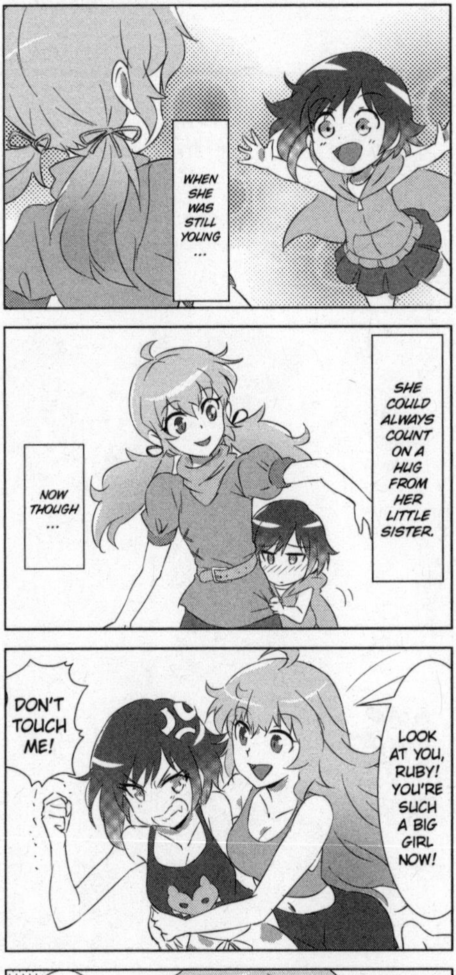
WHEN SHE WAS STILL YOUNG ...
SHE COULD ALWAYS COUNT ON A HUG FROM HER LITTLE SISTER.
NOW THOUGH ...
LOOK AT YOU, RUBY! YOU'RE SUCH A BIG GIRL NOW!
DON'T TOUCH ME!
OH, DON'T BE SHY! AGH!

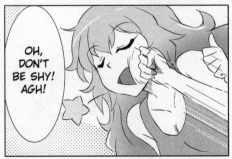

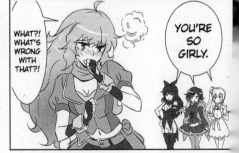

Yang Targeted

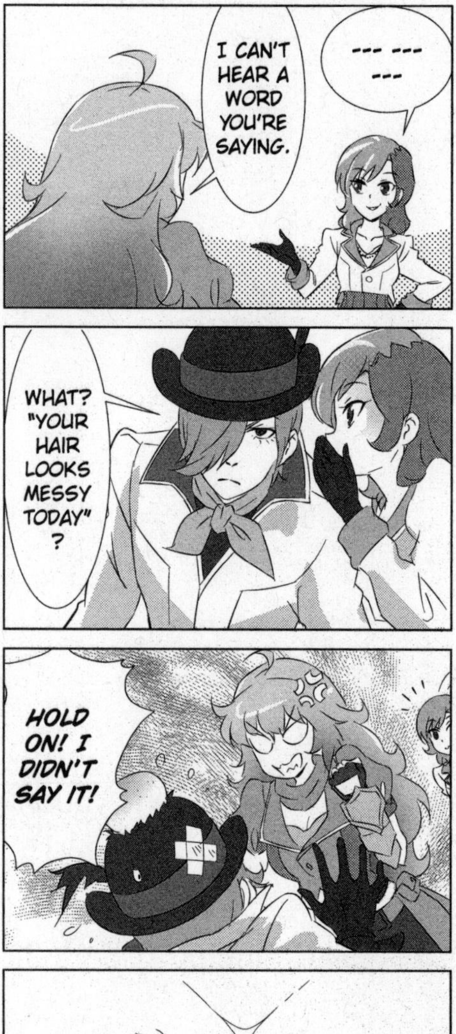
--- --- ---
I CAN'T HEAR A WORD YOU'RE SAYING.
WHAT? "YOUR HAIR LOOKS MESSY TODAY"?
HOLD ON! I DIDN'T SAY IT!

Cut Some Slack

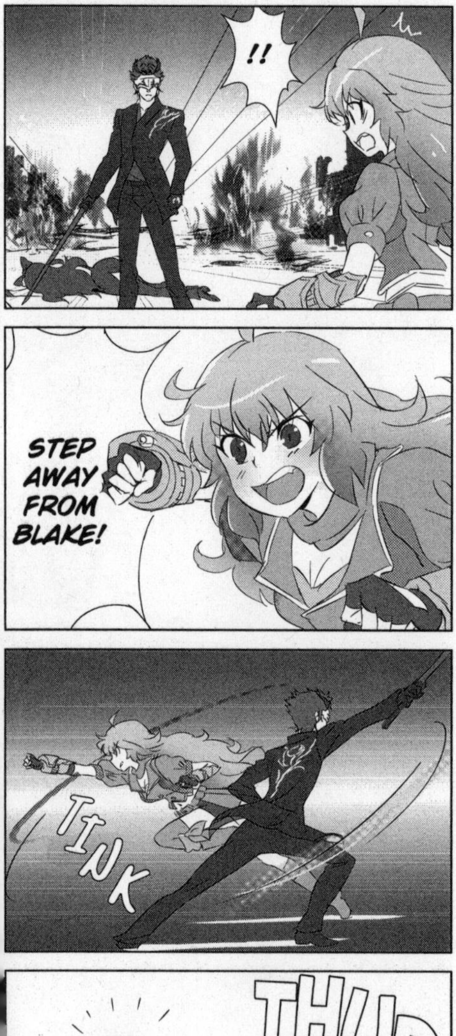
!!
STEP AWAY FROM BLAKE!
TINK
THUD

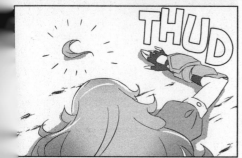

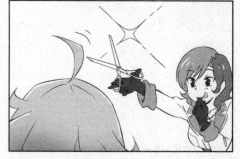

Afternoon Bumblebee

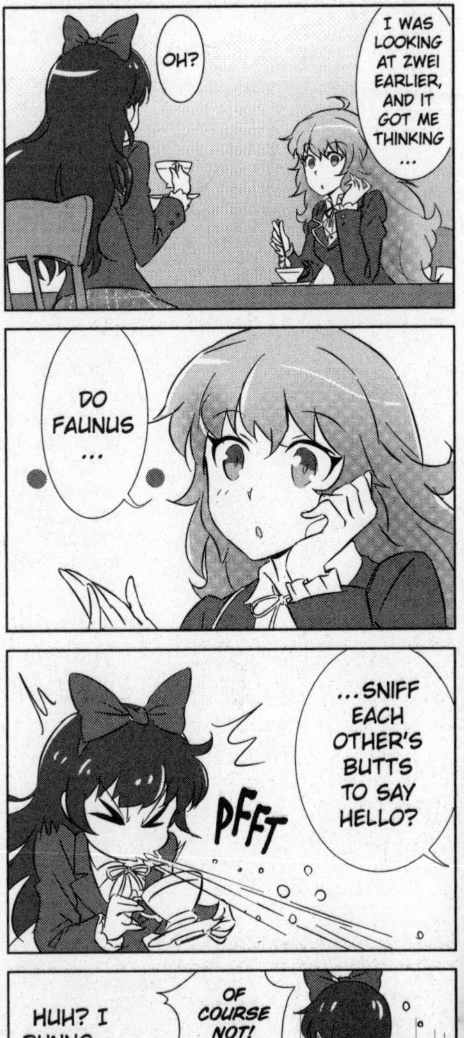
I WAS LOOKING AT ZWEI EARLIER, AND IT GOT ME THINKING ...
OH?
DO FAUNUS ...
...SNIFF EACH OTHER'S BUTTS TO SAY HELLO?
PFFT
OF COURSE NOT! WHAT DO YOU THINK WE ARE?!
HUH? I DUNNO...

Blondie

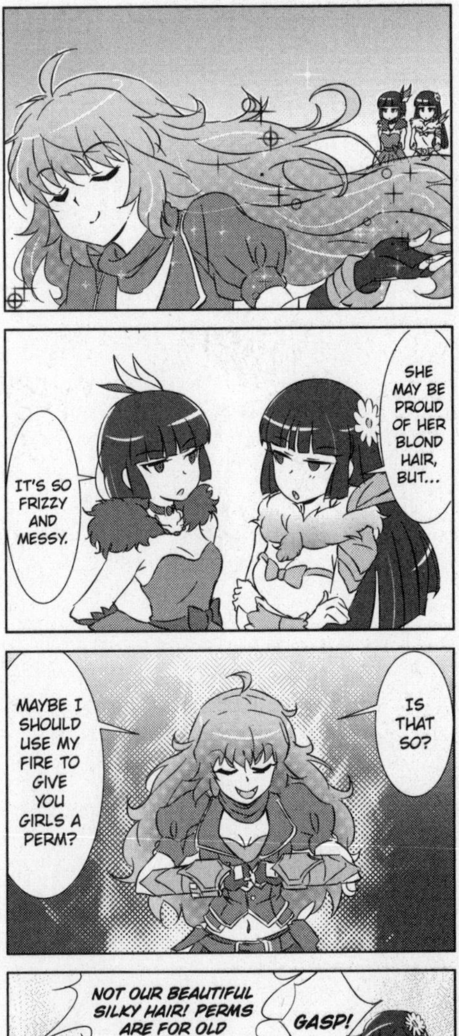
SHE MAY BE PROUD OF HER BLOND HAIR, BUT...
IT'S SO FRIZZY AND MESSY.
IS THAT SO?
MAYBE I SHOULD USE MY FIRE TO GIVE YOU GIRLS A PERM?
GASP!
NOT OUR BEAUTIFUL SILKY HAIR! PERMS ARE FOR OLD WOMEN
YOU ...

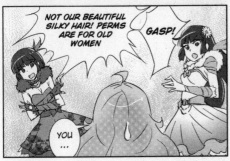

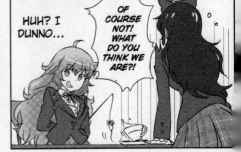

YangMer

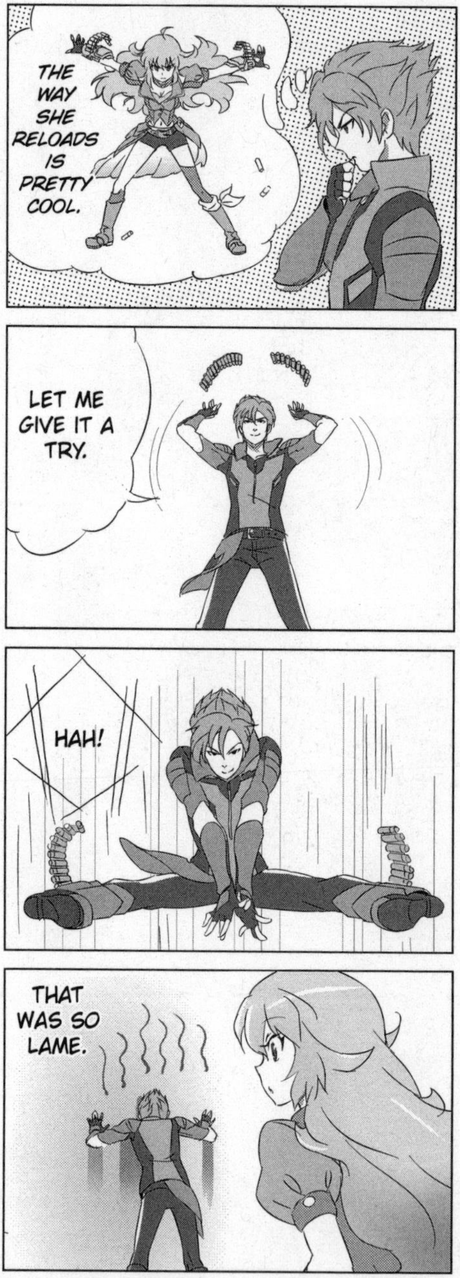
THE WAY SHE RELOADS IS PRETTY COOL.
LET ME GIVE IT A TRY.
HAH!
THAT WAS SO LAME.

Catering

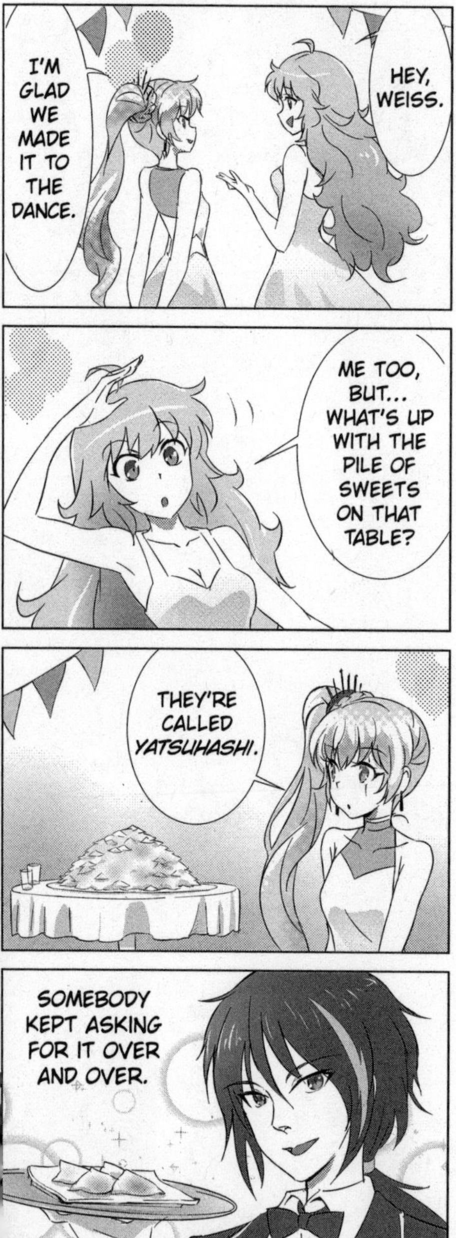
HEY, WEISS.
I'M GLAD WE MADE IT TO THE DANCE.
ME TOO, BUT... WHAT'S UP WITH THE PILE OF SWEETS ON THAT TABLE?
THEY'RE CALLED *YATSUHASHI*.
SOMEBODY KEPT ASKING FOR IT OVER AND OVER.

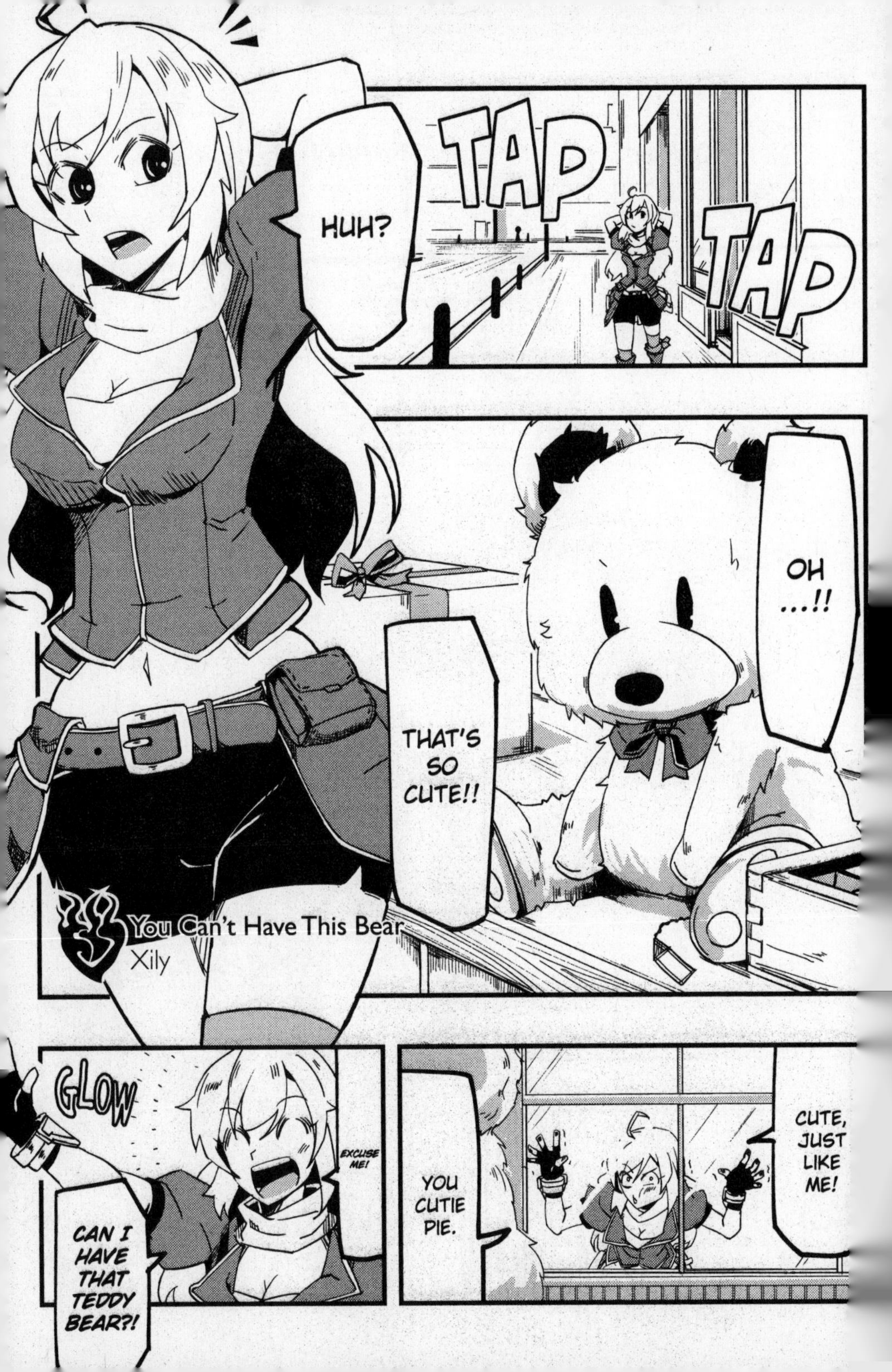
TAP
TAP
HUH?
OH ...!!
THAT'S SO CUTE!!
You Can't Have This Bear
Xily
CUTE, JUST LIKE ME!
YOU CUTIE PIE.
GLOW
EXCUSE ME!
CAN I HAVE THAT TEDDY BEAR?!

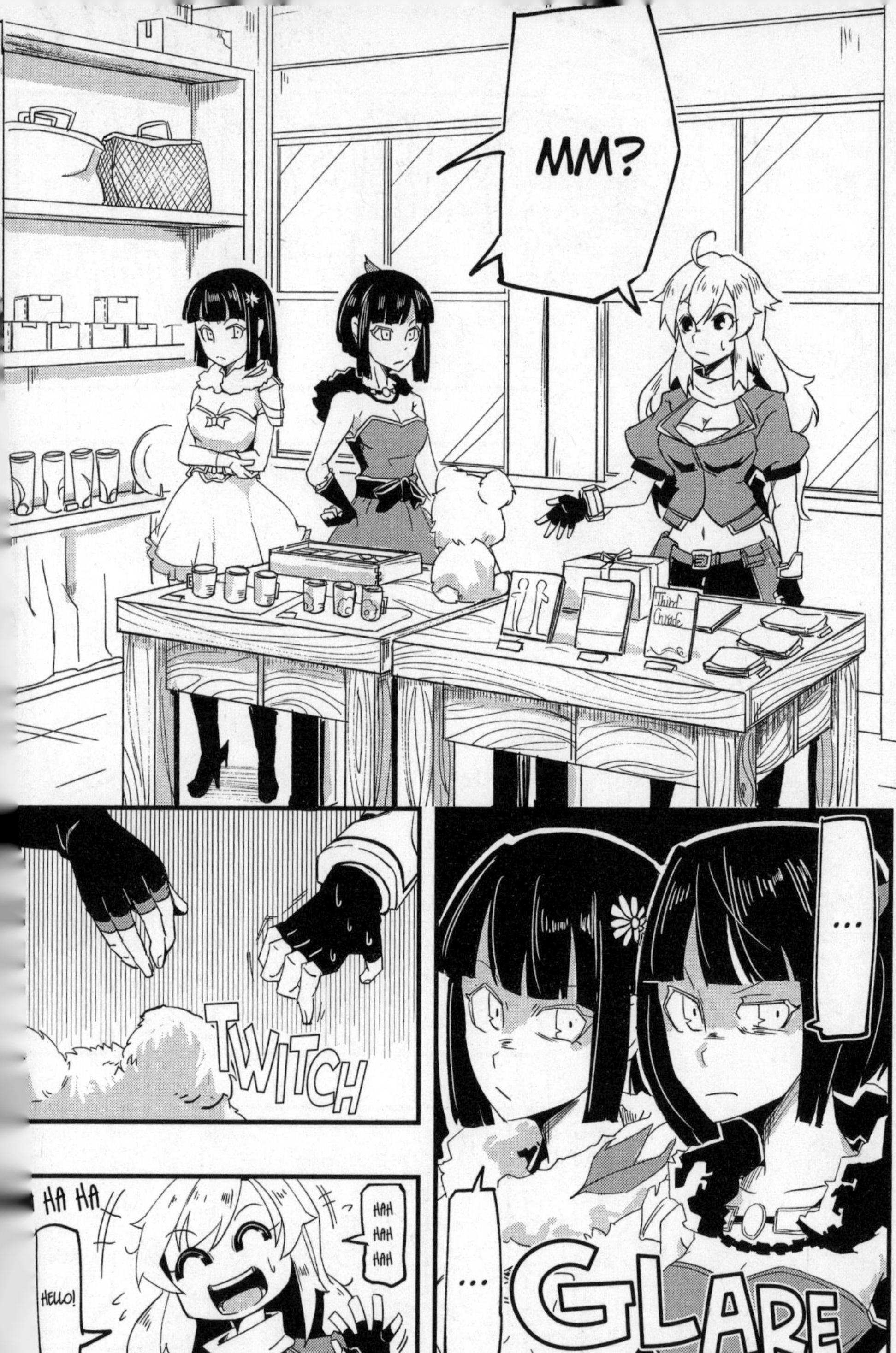
MM?
Third Charade
...
...
GLARE
TWITCH
HAH HAH HAH
HA HA
HELLO!

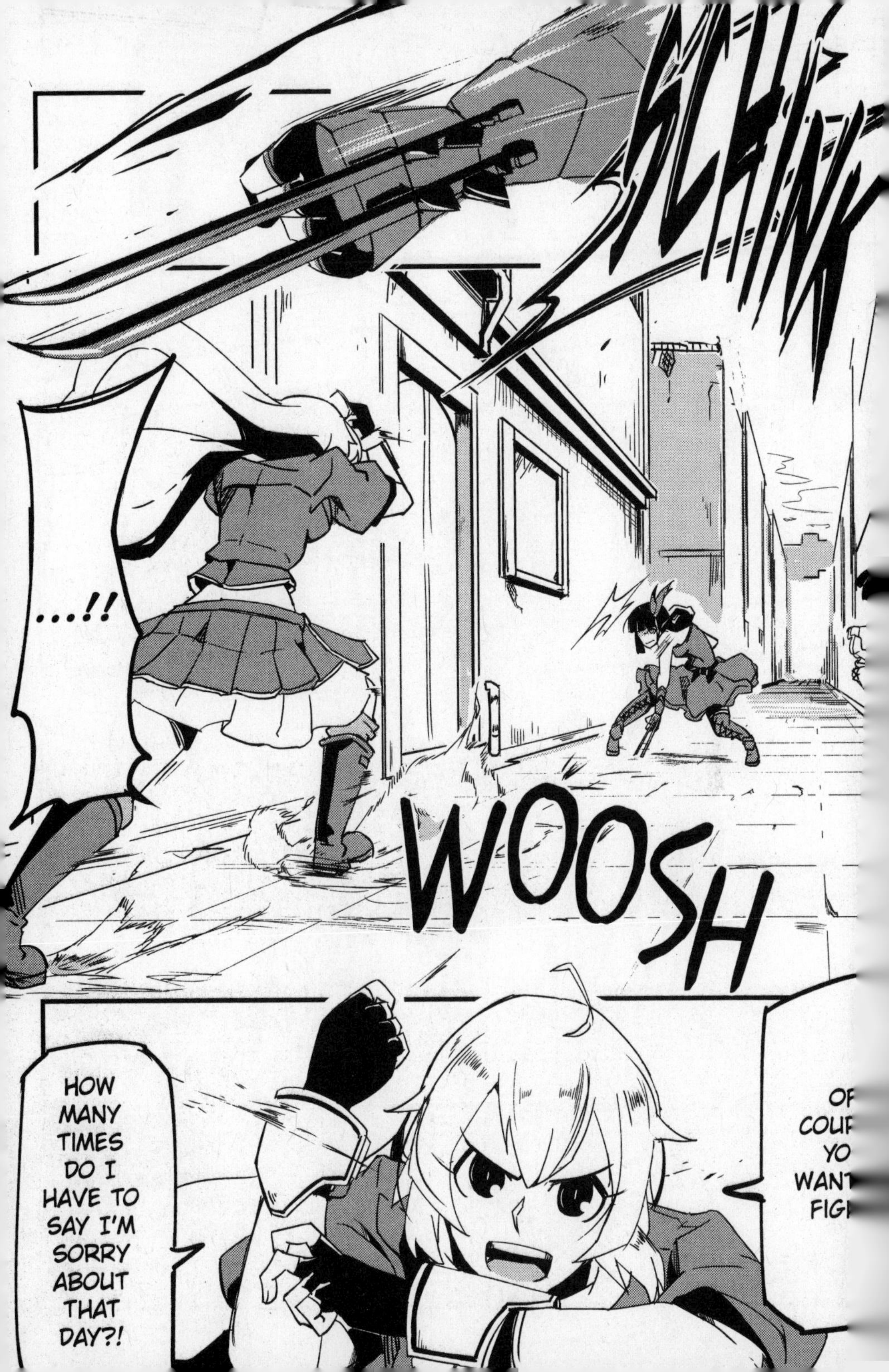

SCHING
...!!
WOOSH
OF COUR YO WANT FIG
HOW MANY TIMES DO I HAVE TO SAY I'M SORRY ABOUT THAT DAY?!

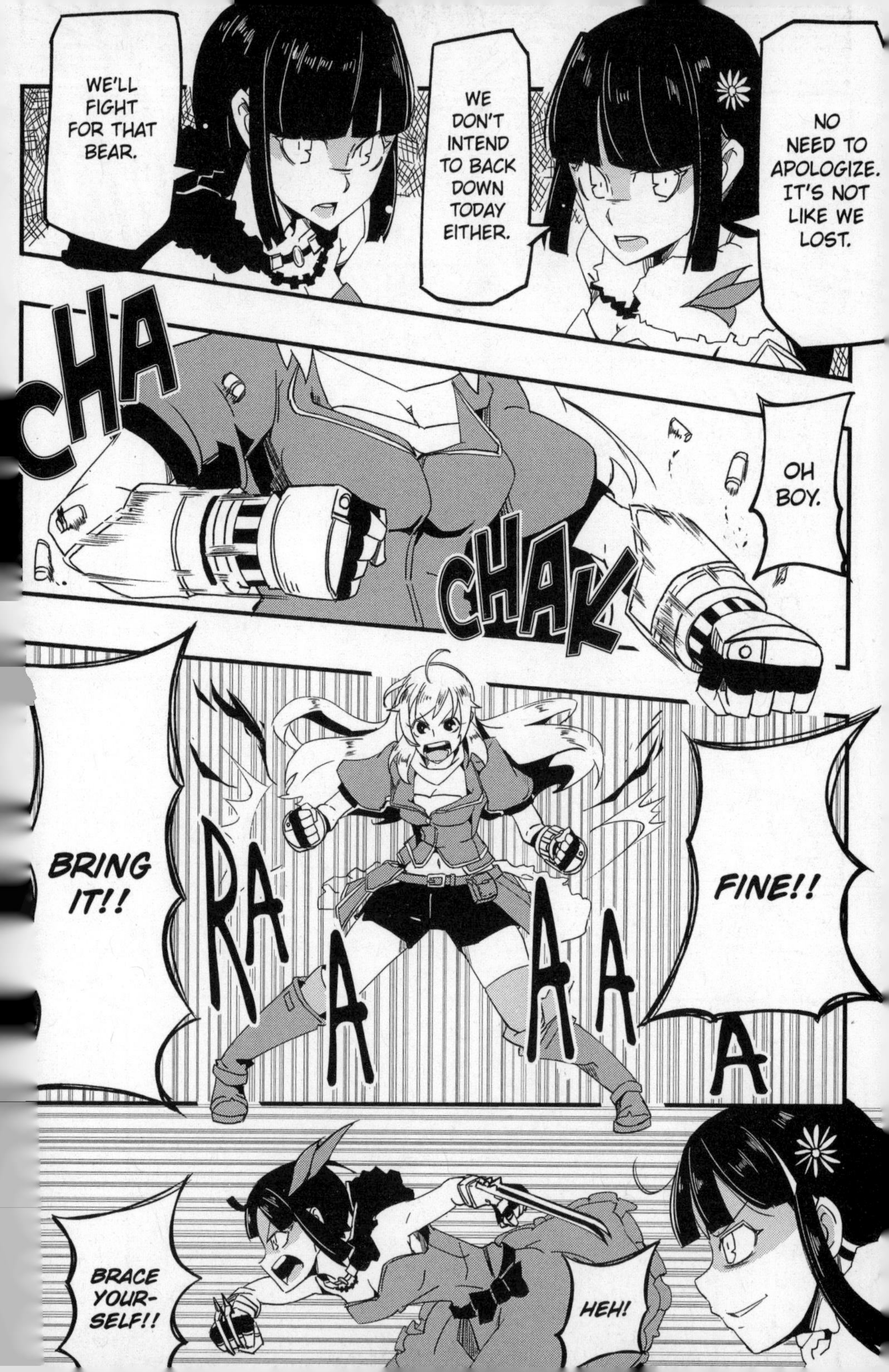
NO NEED TO APOLOGIZE. IT'S NOT LIKE WE LOST.
WE DON'T INTEND TO BACK DOWN TODAY EITHER.
WE'LL FIGHT FOR THAT BEAR.
OH BOY.
CHA
CHAK
FINE!!
RAAAAAA
BRING IT!!
HEH!
BRACE YOUR-SELF!!

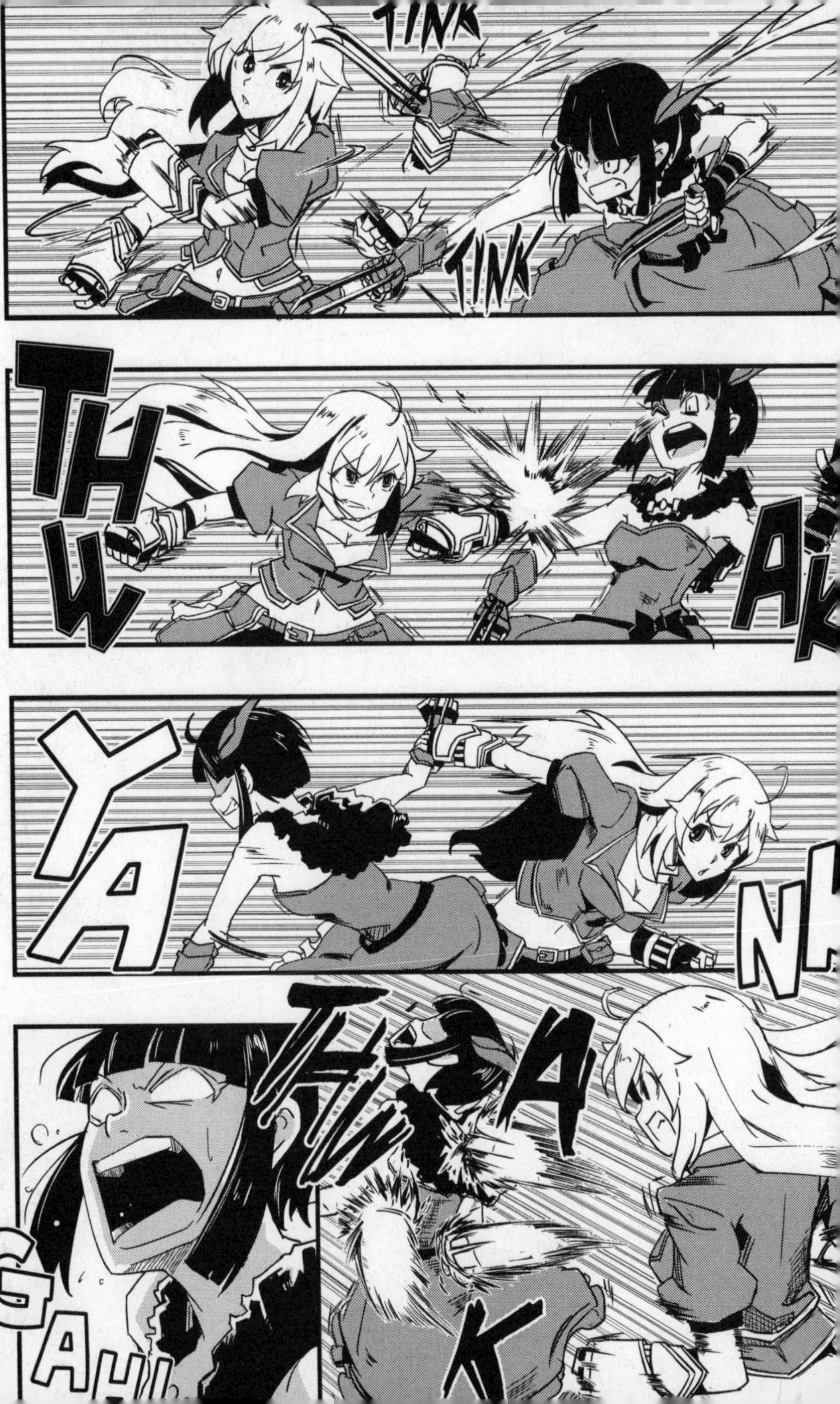
TINK
TINK
THWAK
YANK
THWAK
GAH!

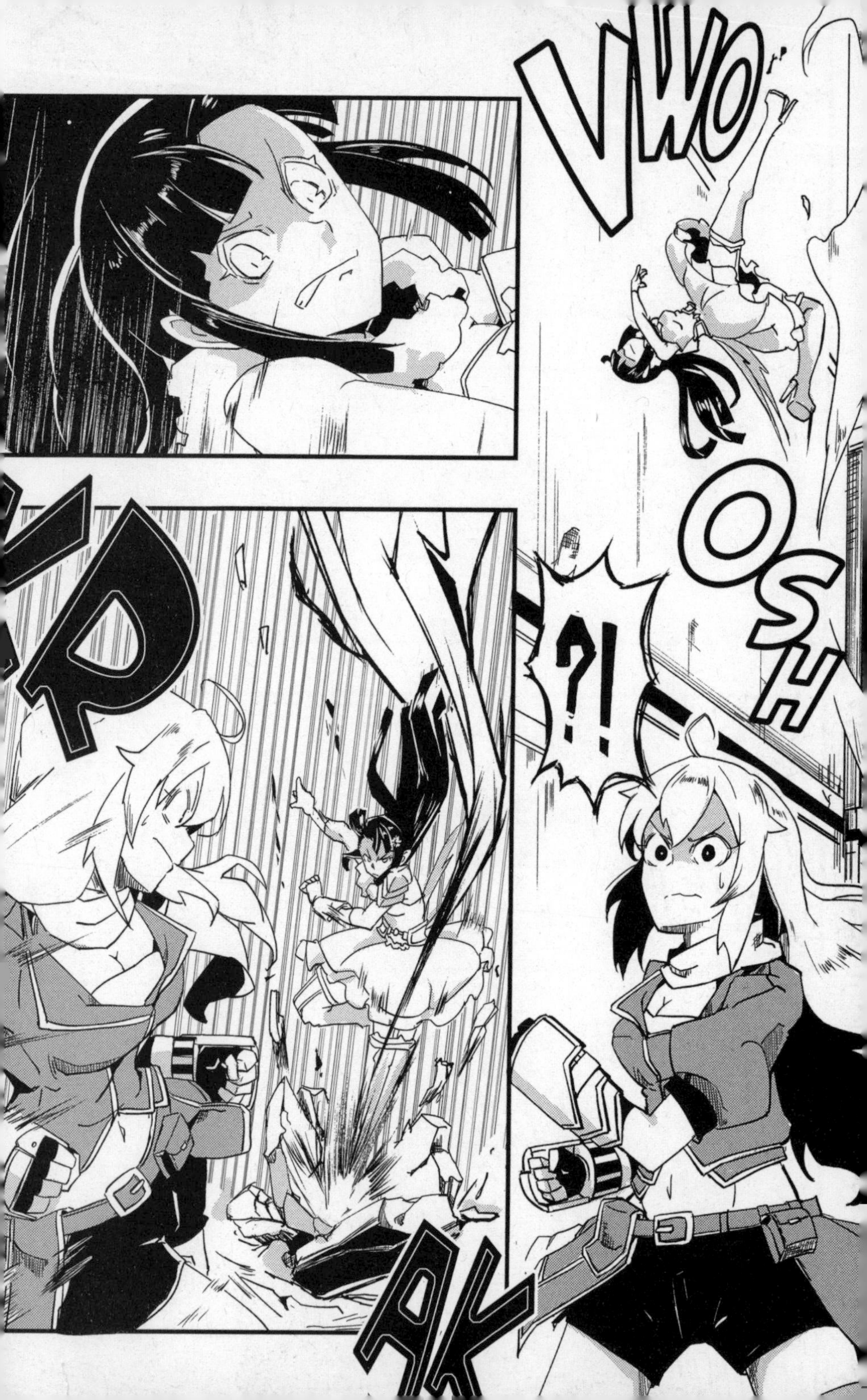
VWO
OSH
?!
P
AK

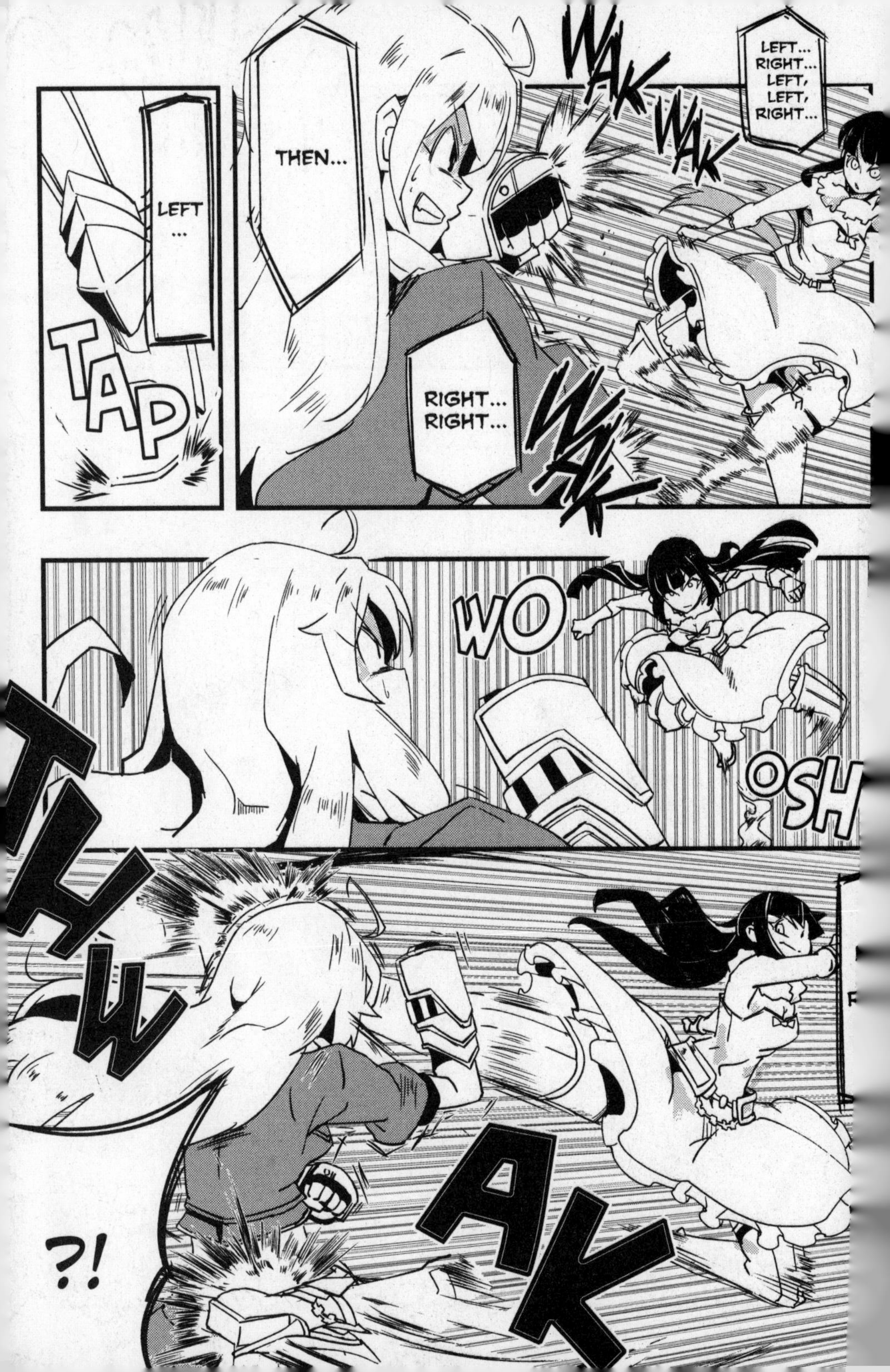
LEFT... RIGHT... LEFT, LEFT, RIGHT...
WAK WAK
THEN...
RIGHT... RIGHT...
WAK
LEFT ...
TAP
WO
OSH
THW
AK
?!

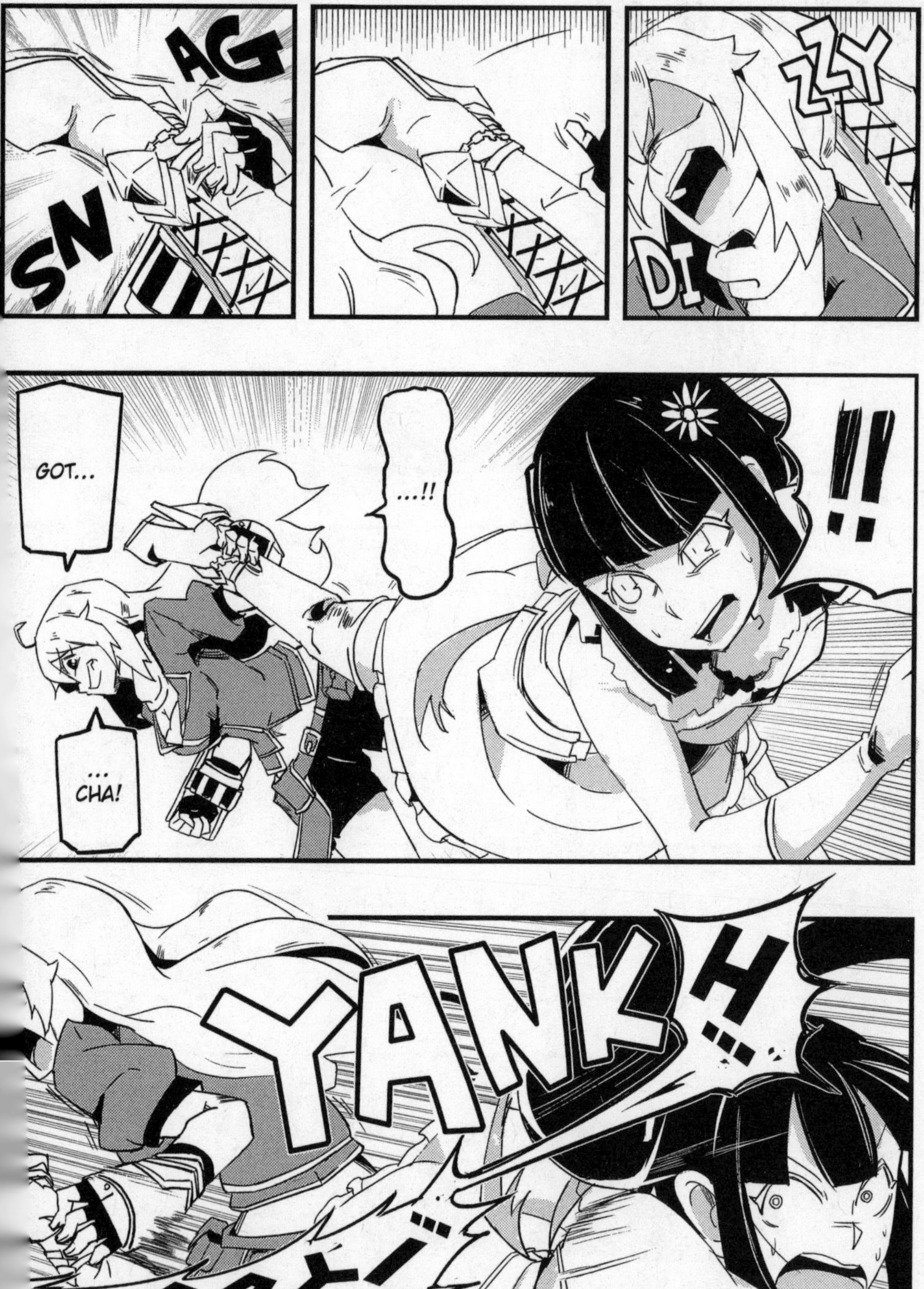
ZZY
DI
AG
SN
!!
...!!
GOT...
... CHA!
YANK
H!!
AAAAAYI!

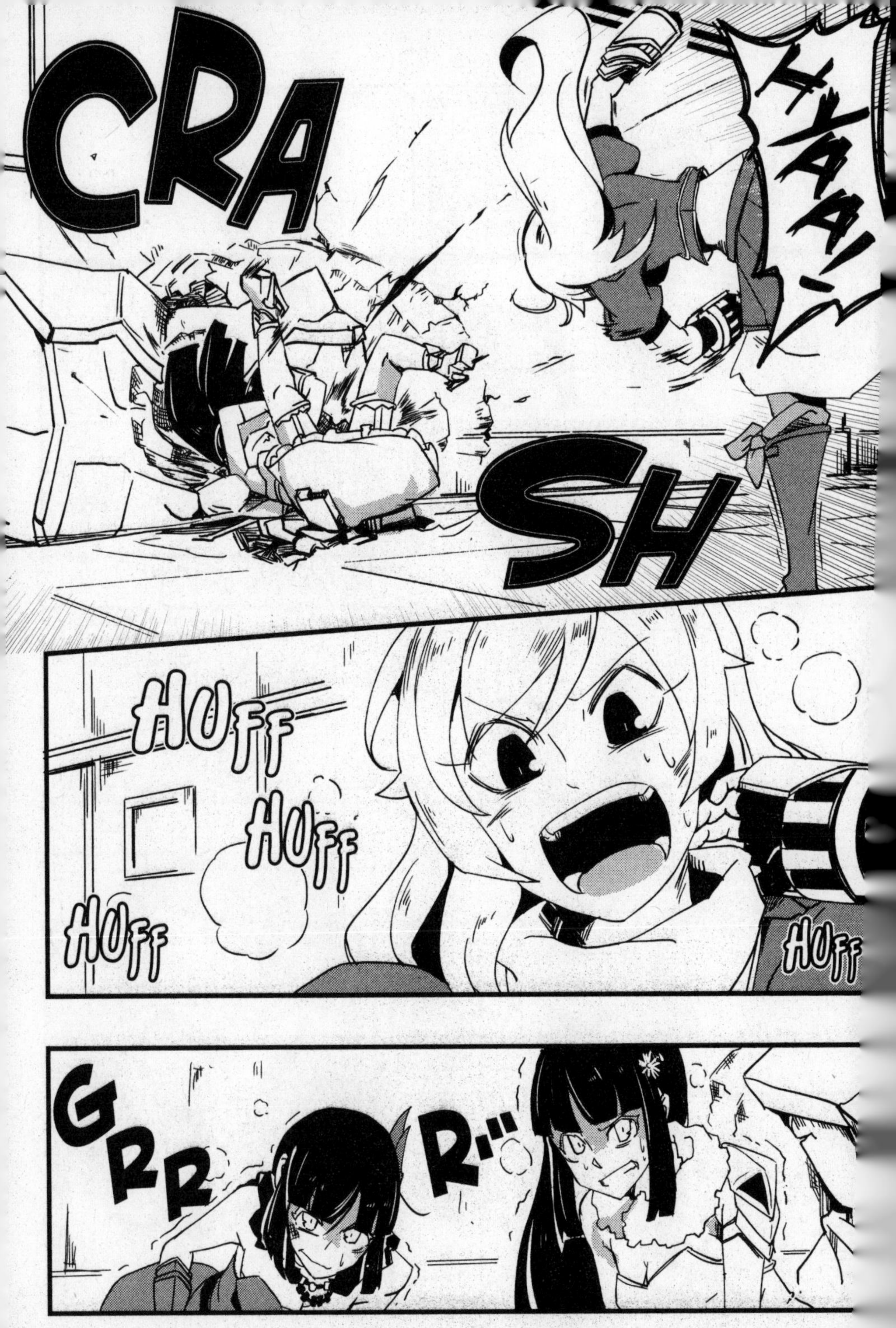
HYAA!!
CRA
SH
HUFF
HUFF
HUFF
HUFF
GRRR!!

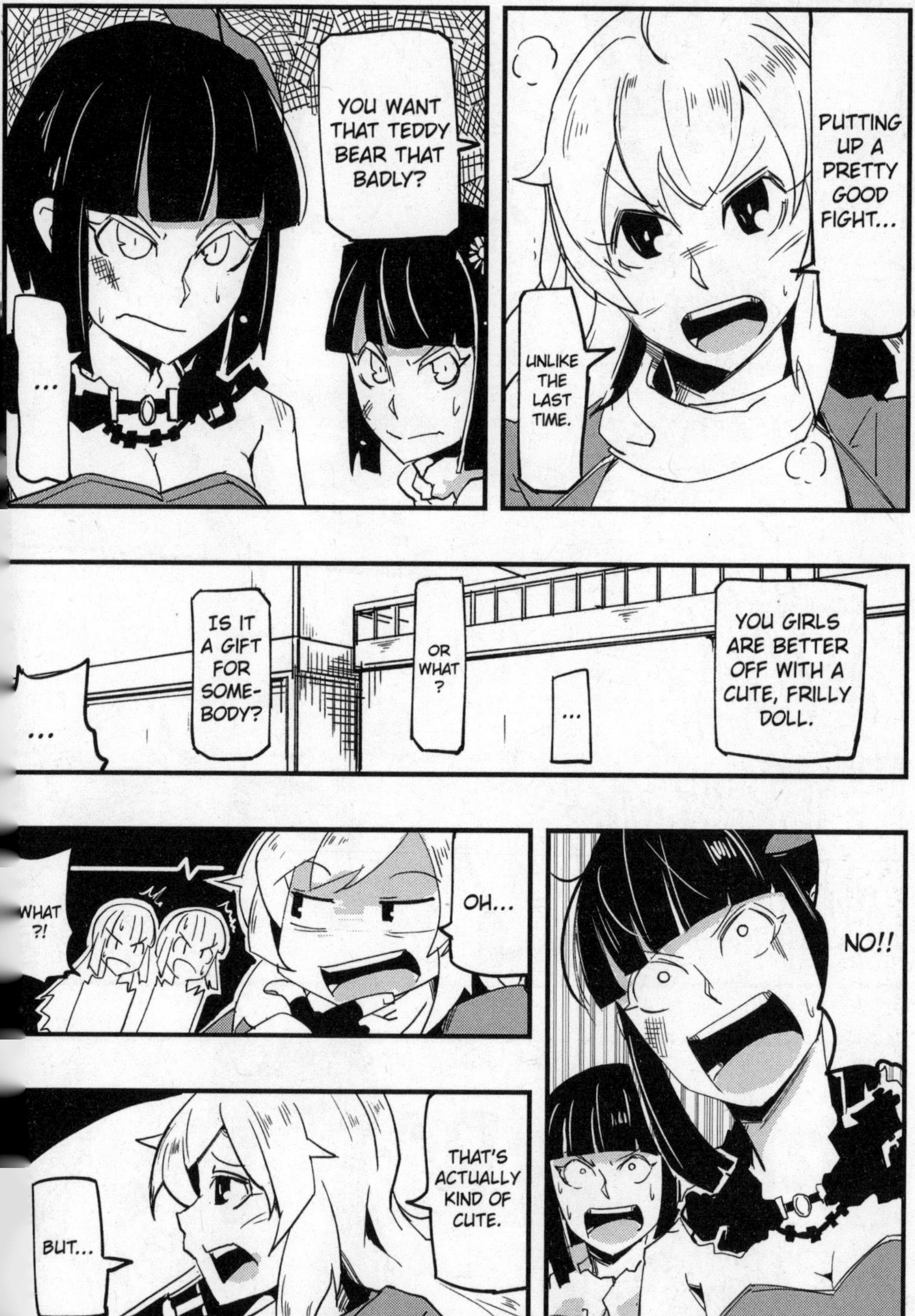
PUTTING UP A PRETTY GOOD FIGHT...
UNLIKE THE LAST TIME.
YOU WANT THAT TEDDY BEAR THAT BADLY?
...
YOU GIRLS ARE BETTER OFF WITH A CUTE, FRILLY DOLL.
...
OR WHAT?
IS IT A GIFT FOR SOMEBODY?
...
NO!!
OH...
WHAT?!
THAT'S ACTUALLY KIND OF CUTE.
BUT...

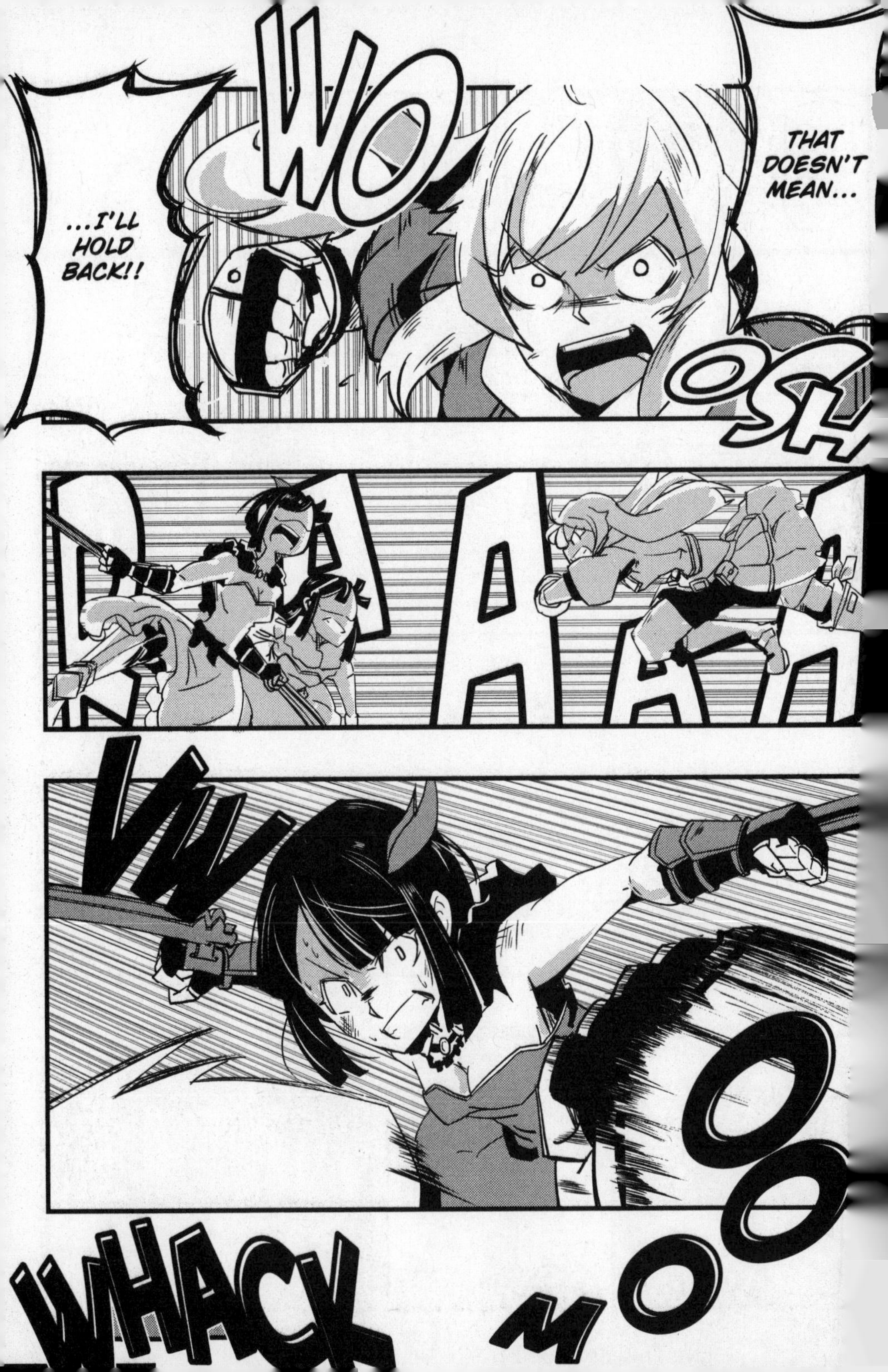
THAT DOESN'T MEAN...
...I'LL HOLD BACK!!
WO
OSH
WHACK

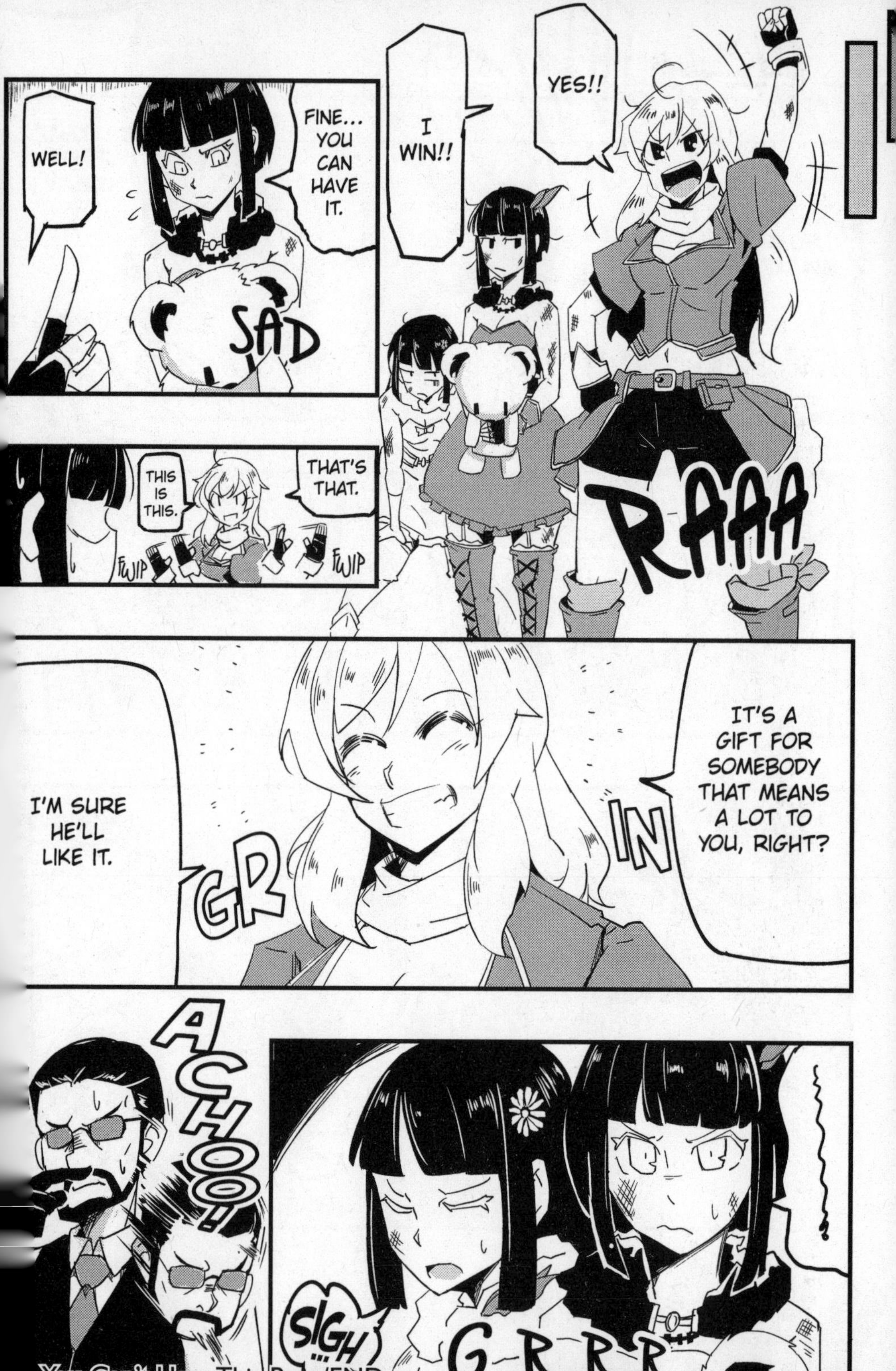
YES!!
I WIN!!
RAAA
FINE... YOU CAN HAVE IT.
WELL!
SAD
THAT'S THAT.
THIS IS THIS.
FWIP
FWIP
IT'S A GIFT FOR SOMEBODY THAT MEANS A LOT TO YOU, RIGHT?
IN
GR
I'M SURE HE'LL LIKE IT.
SIGH
GRRRR
ACHOO!

You Can't Have This Bear/END

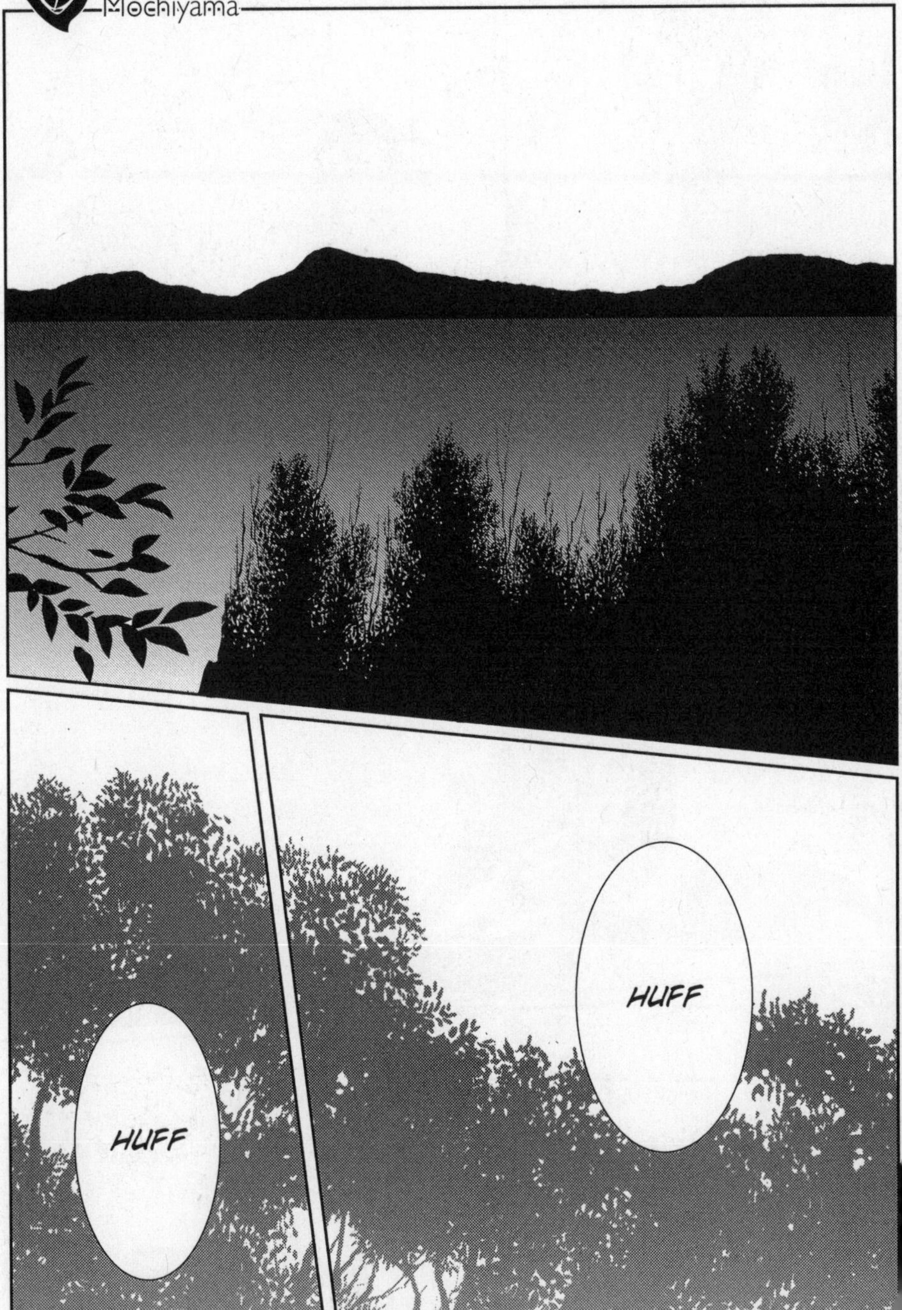
HUFF
HUFF

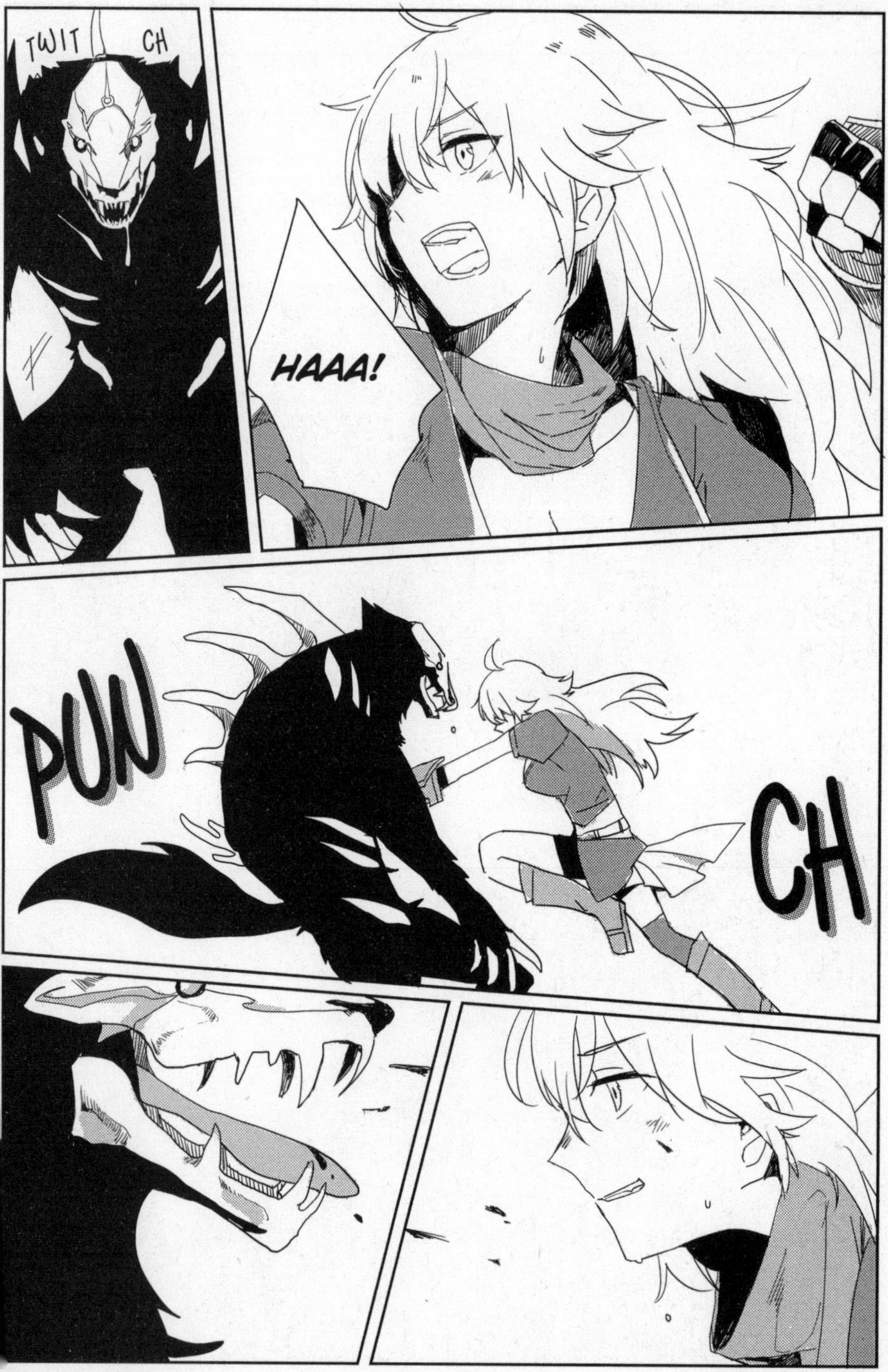
HAAA!
TWIT CH
PUN CH

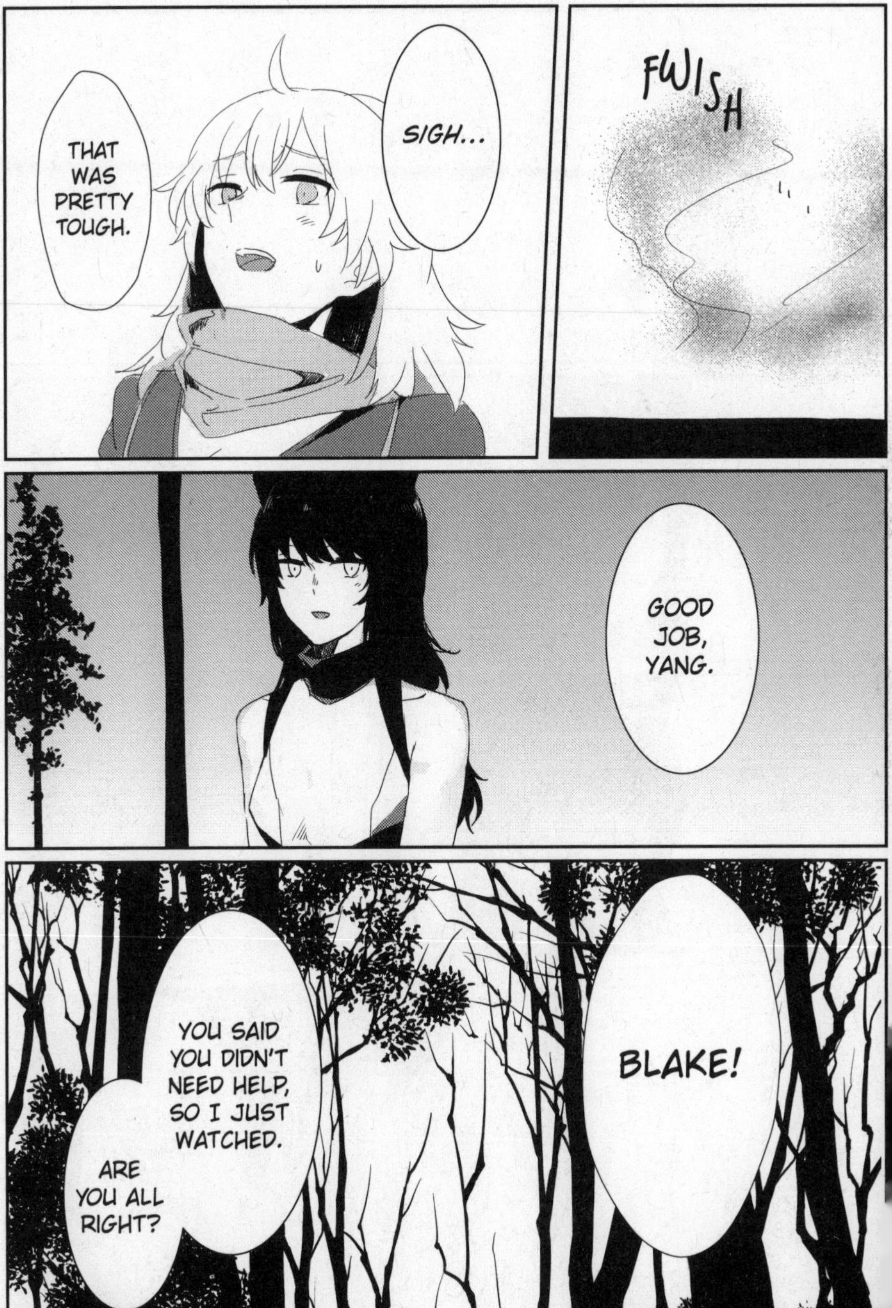
FWISH
SIGH...
THAT WAS PRETTY TOUGH.
GOOD JOB, YANG.
BLAKE!
YOU SAID YOU DIDN'T NEED HELP, SO I JUST WATCHED.
ARE YOU ALL RIGHT?

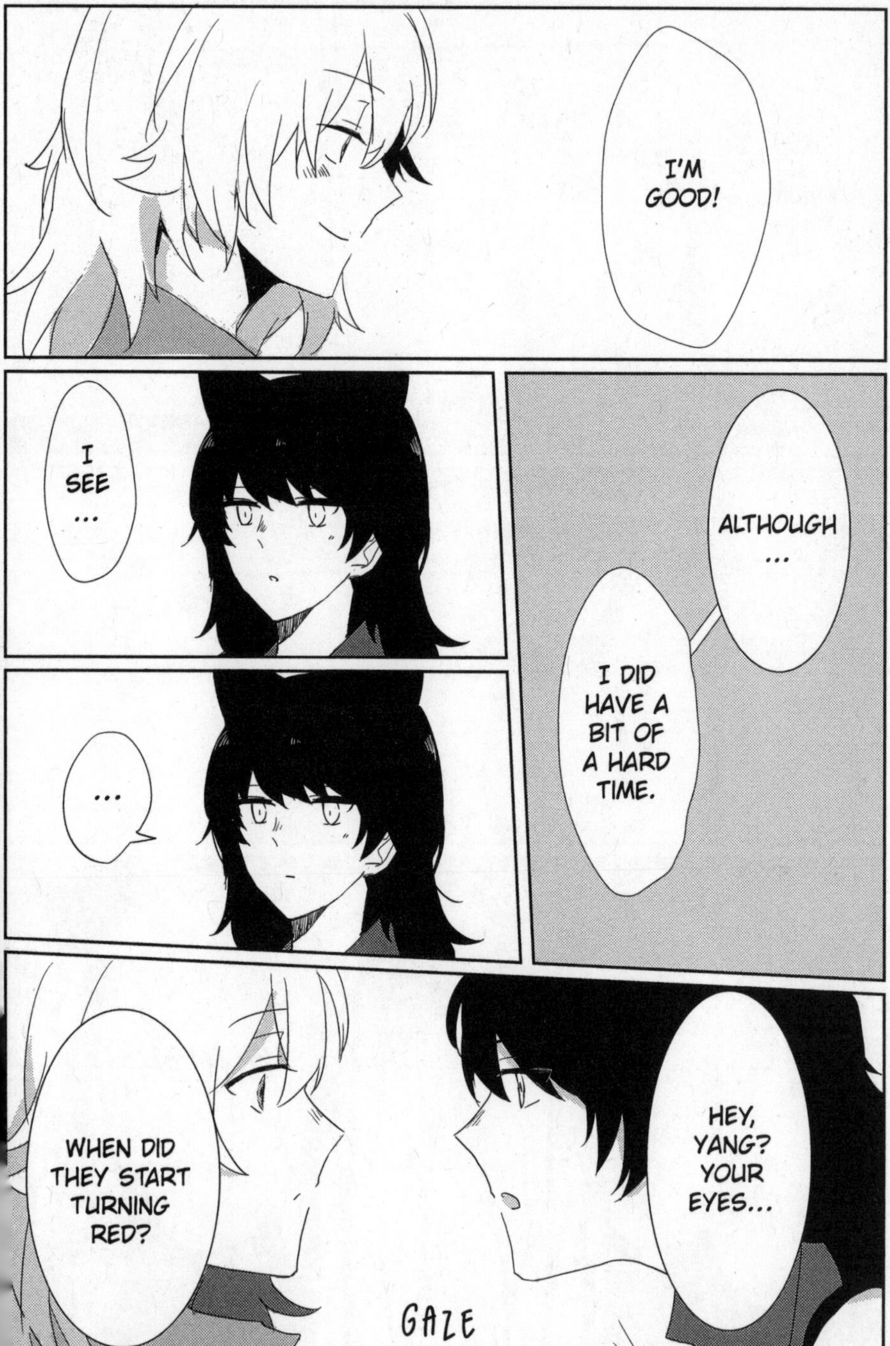
I'M GOOD!
ALTHOUGH ...
I DID HAVE A BIT OF A HARD TIME.
I SEE ...
...
HEY, YANG? YOUR EYES...
WHEN DID THEY START TURNING RED?
GAZE

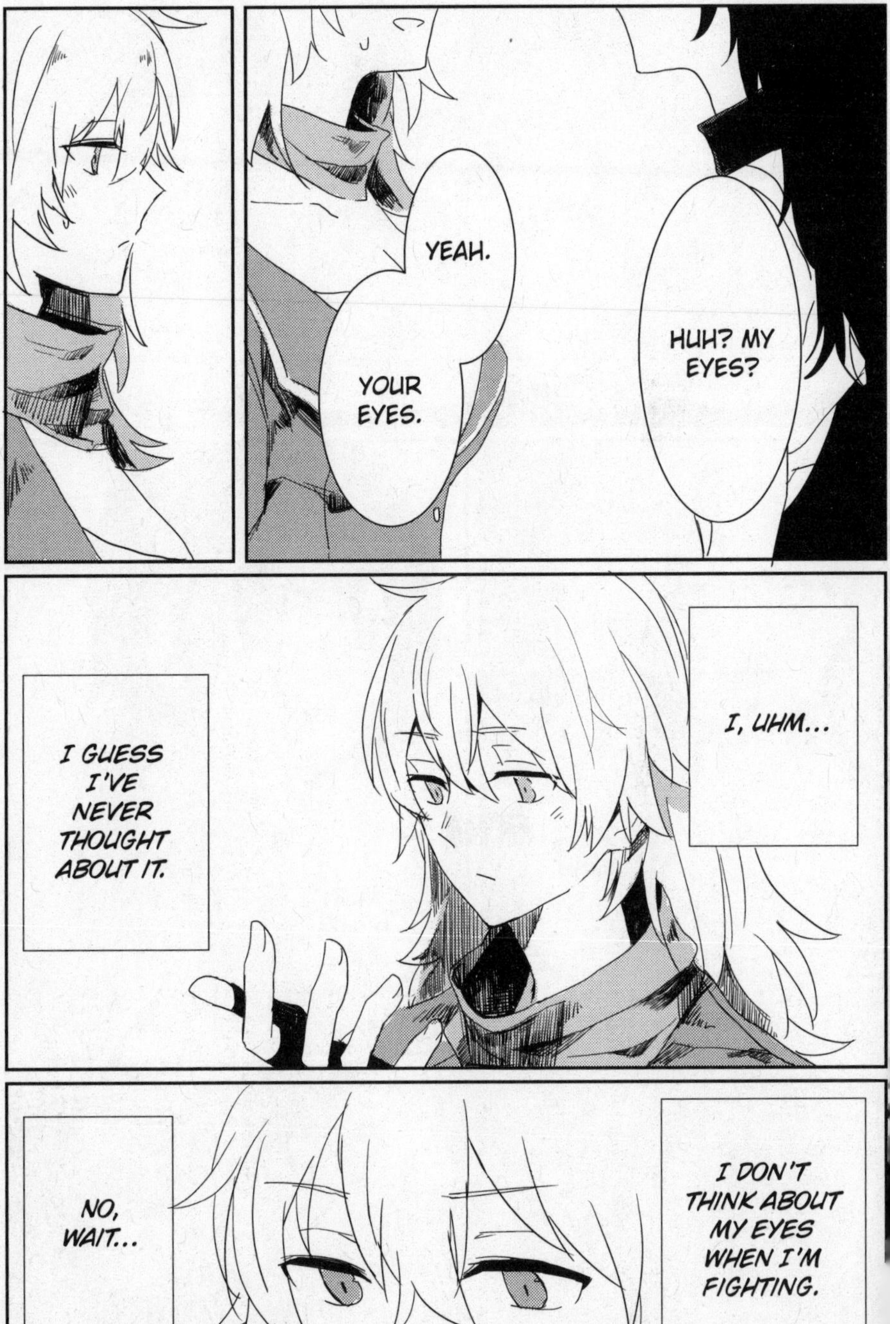
HUH? MY EYES?
YEAH.
YOUR EYES.
I, UHM...
I GUESS I'VE NEVER THOUGHT ABOUT IT.
I DON'T THINK ABOUT MY EYES WHEN I'M FIGHTING.
NO, WAIT...

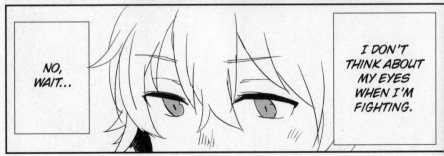

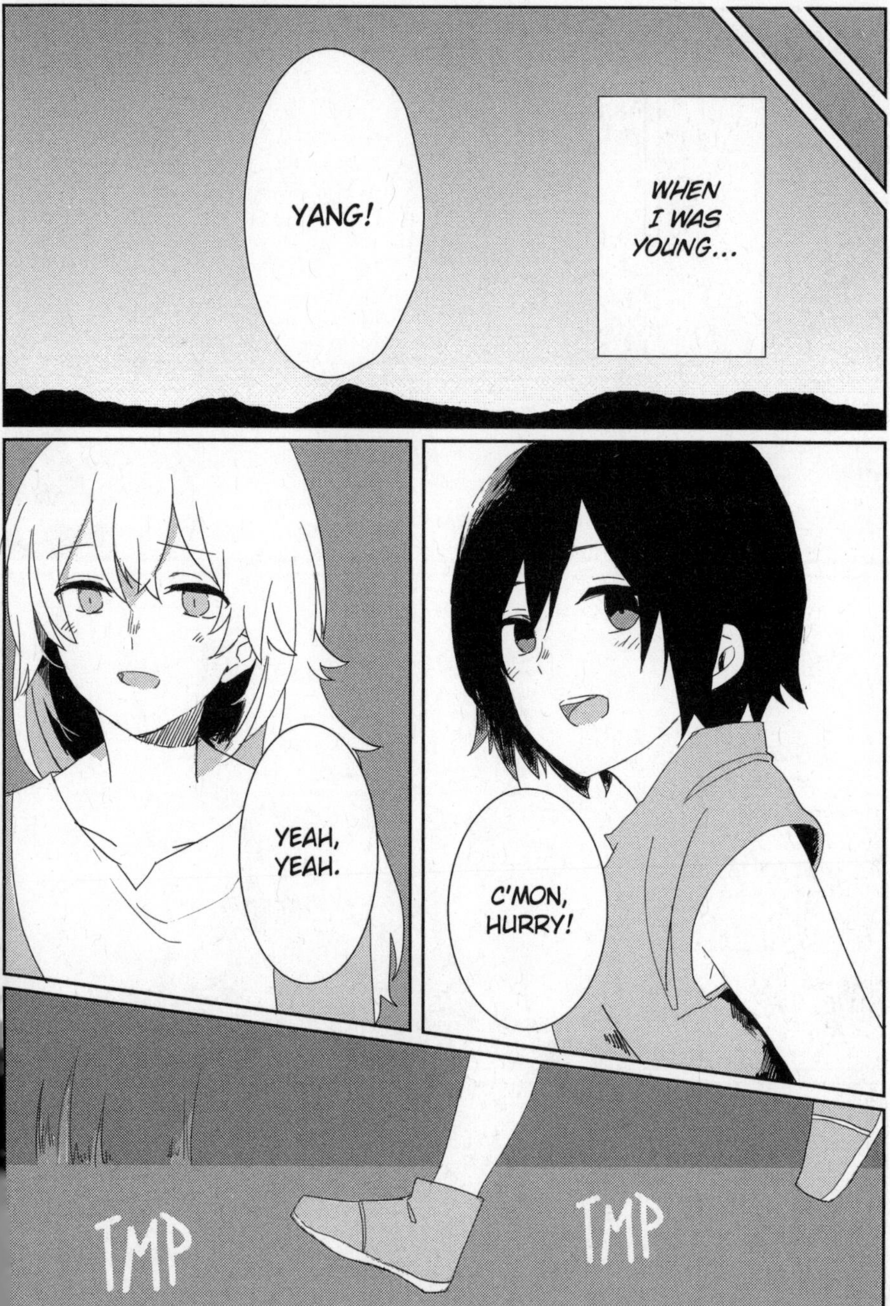
WHEN I WAS YOUNG...
YANG!
C'MON, HURRY!
YEAH, YEAH.
TMP
TMP

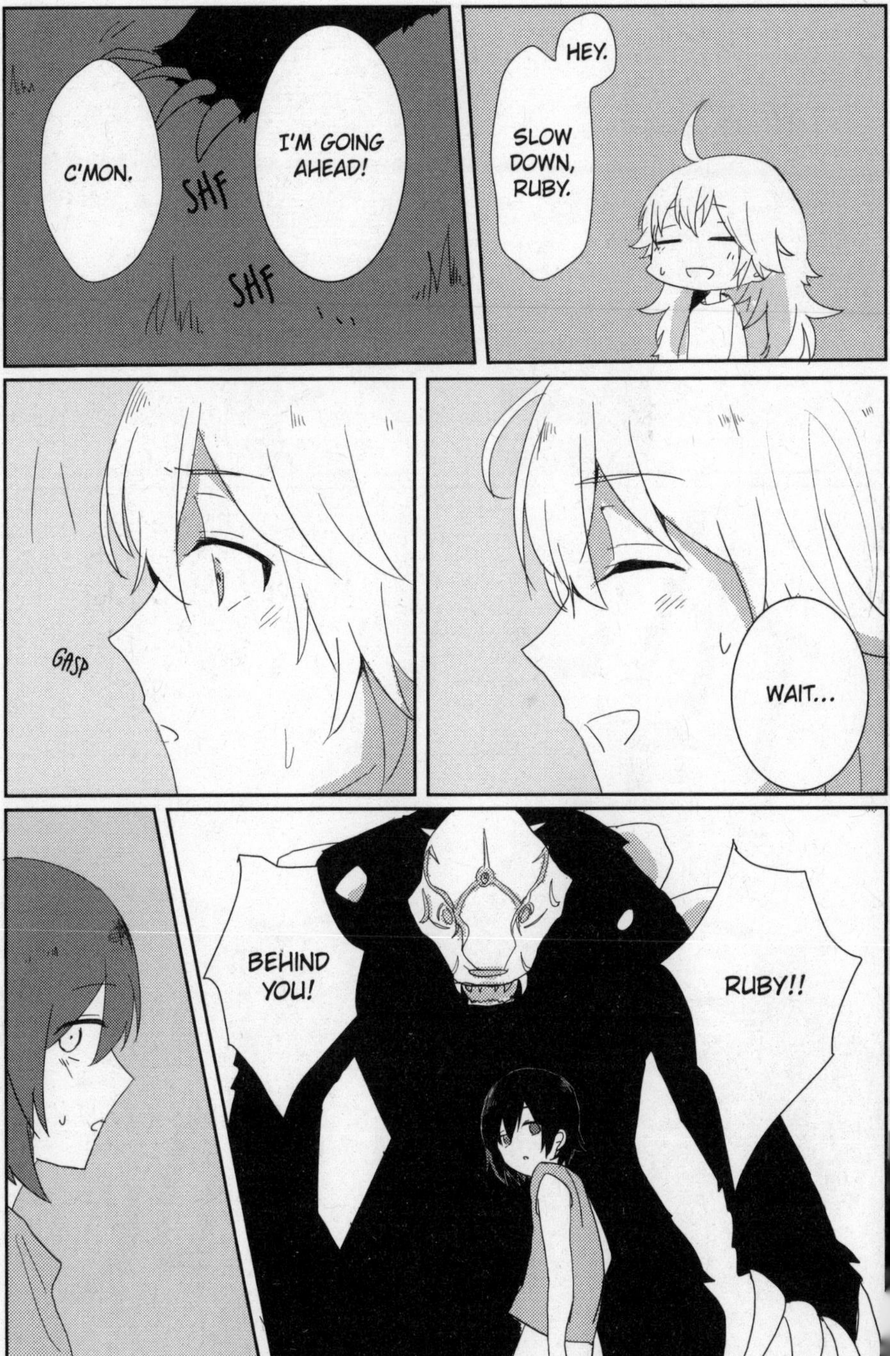
HEY.
SLOW DOWN, RUBY.
I'M GOING AHEAD!
C'MON.
SHF
SHF
WAIT...
GASP
RUBY!!
BEHIND YOU!

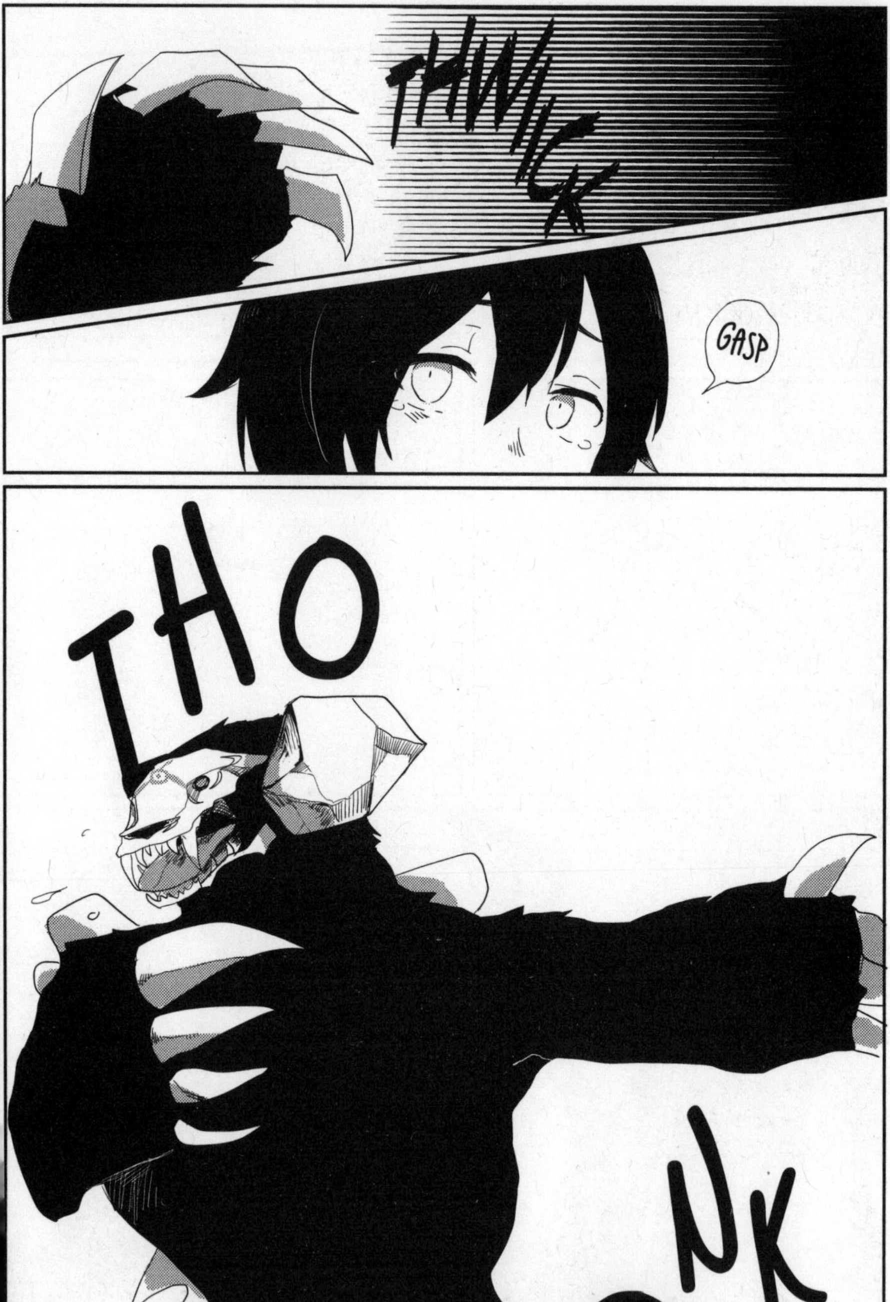
THWICK
GASP
THONK

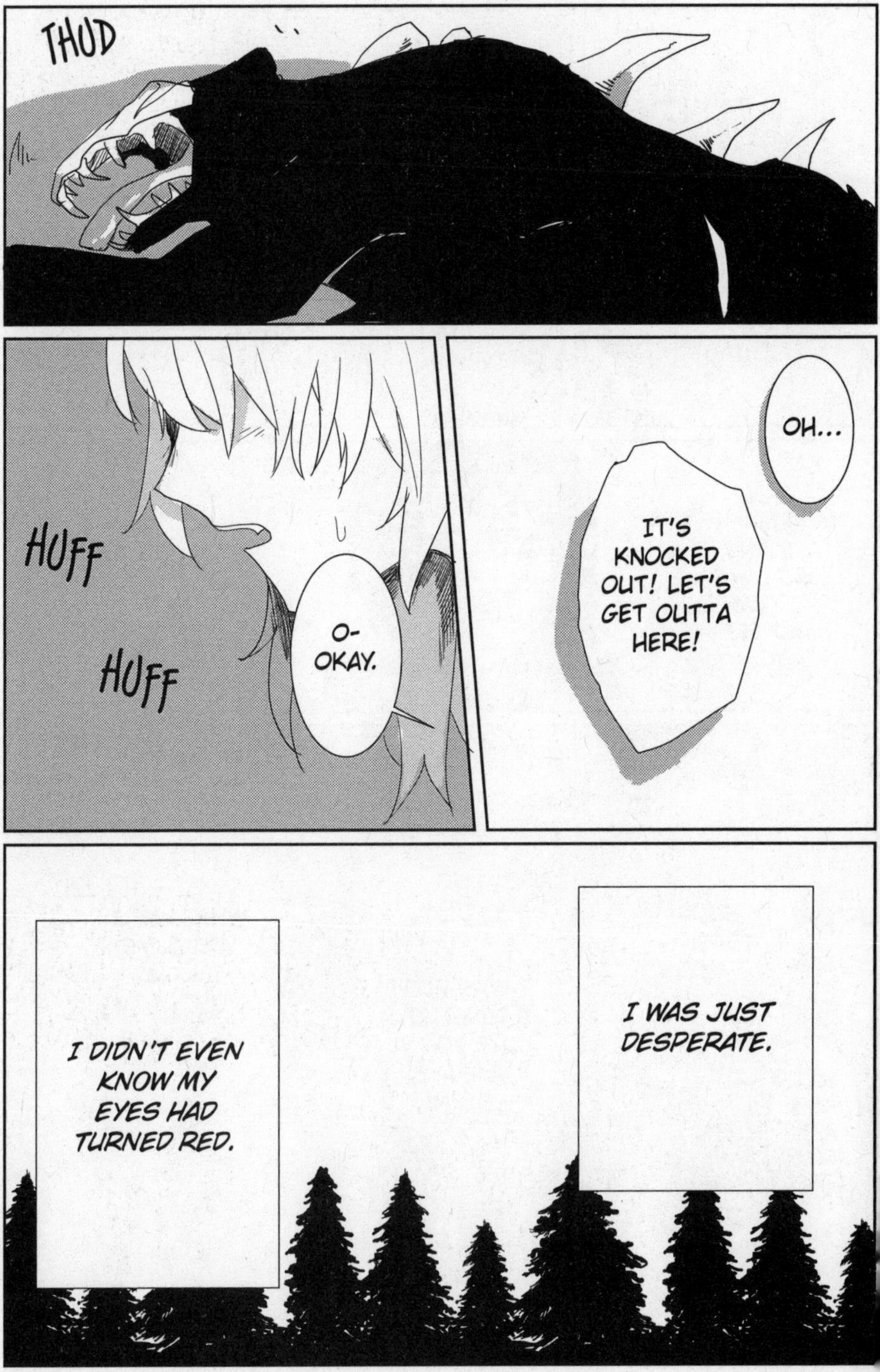
THUD
OH...
IT'S KNOCKED OUT! LET'S GET OUTTA HERE!
HUFF
HUFF
O-OKAY.
I WAS JUST DESPERATE.
I DIDN'T EVEN KNOW MY EYES HAD TURNED RED.

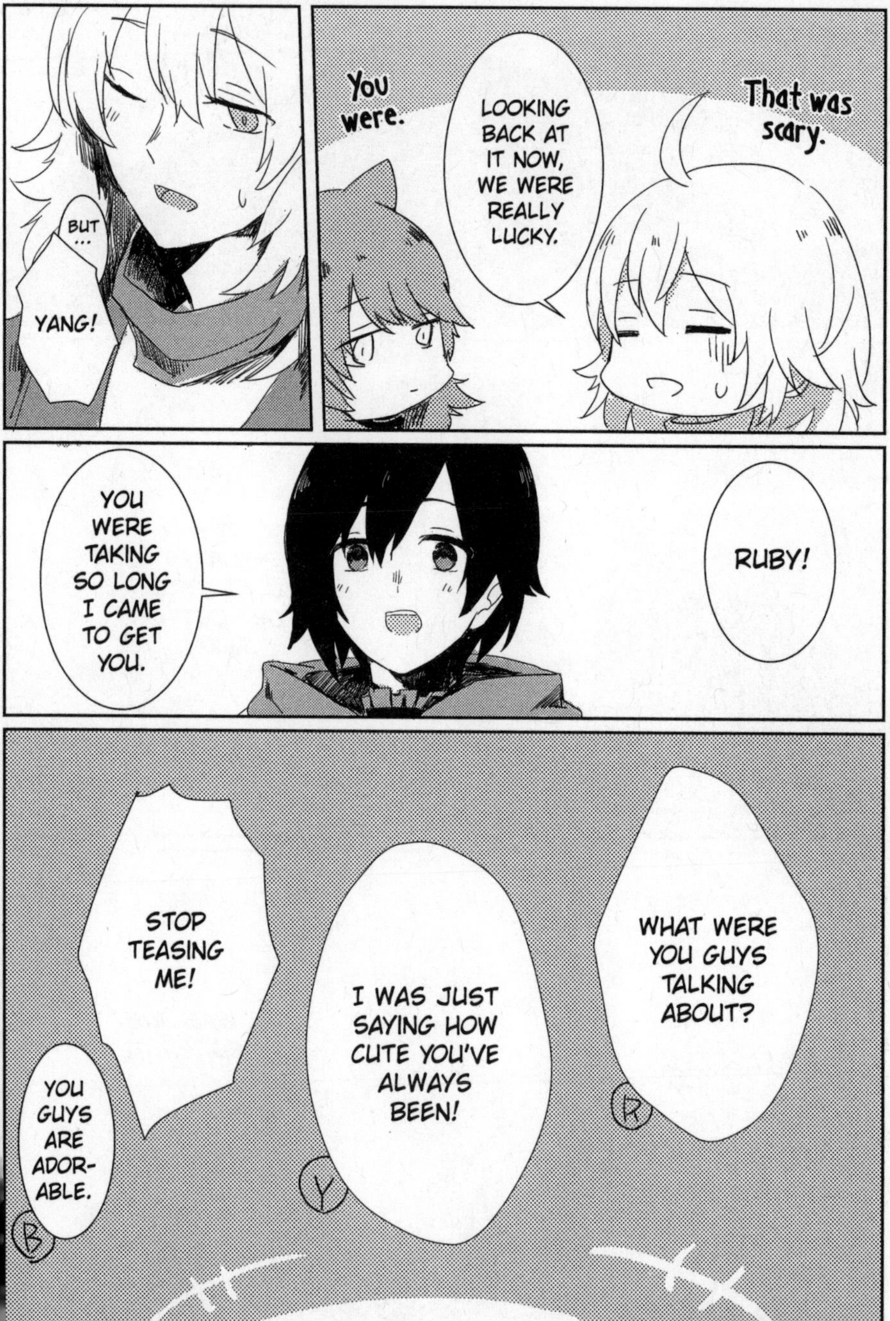
That was scary.
LOOKING BACK AT IT NOW, WE WERE REALLY LUCKY.
You were.
BUT ...
YANG!
RUBY!
YOU WERE TAKING SO LONG I CAME TO GET YOU.
WHAT WERE YOU GUYS TALKING ABOUT?
R
I WAS JUST SAYING HOW CUTE YOU'VE ALWAYS BEEN!
Y
STOP TEASING ME!
YOU GUYS ARE ADOR-ABLE.
B

Genesis/End

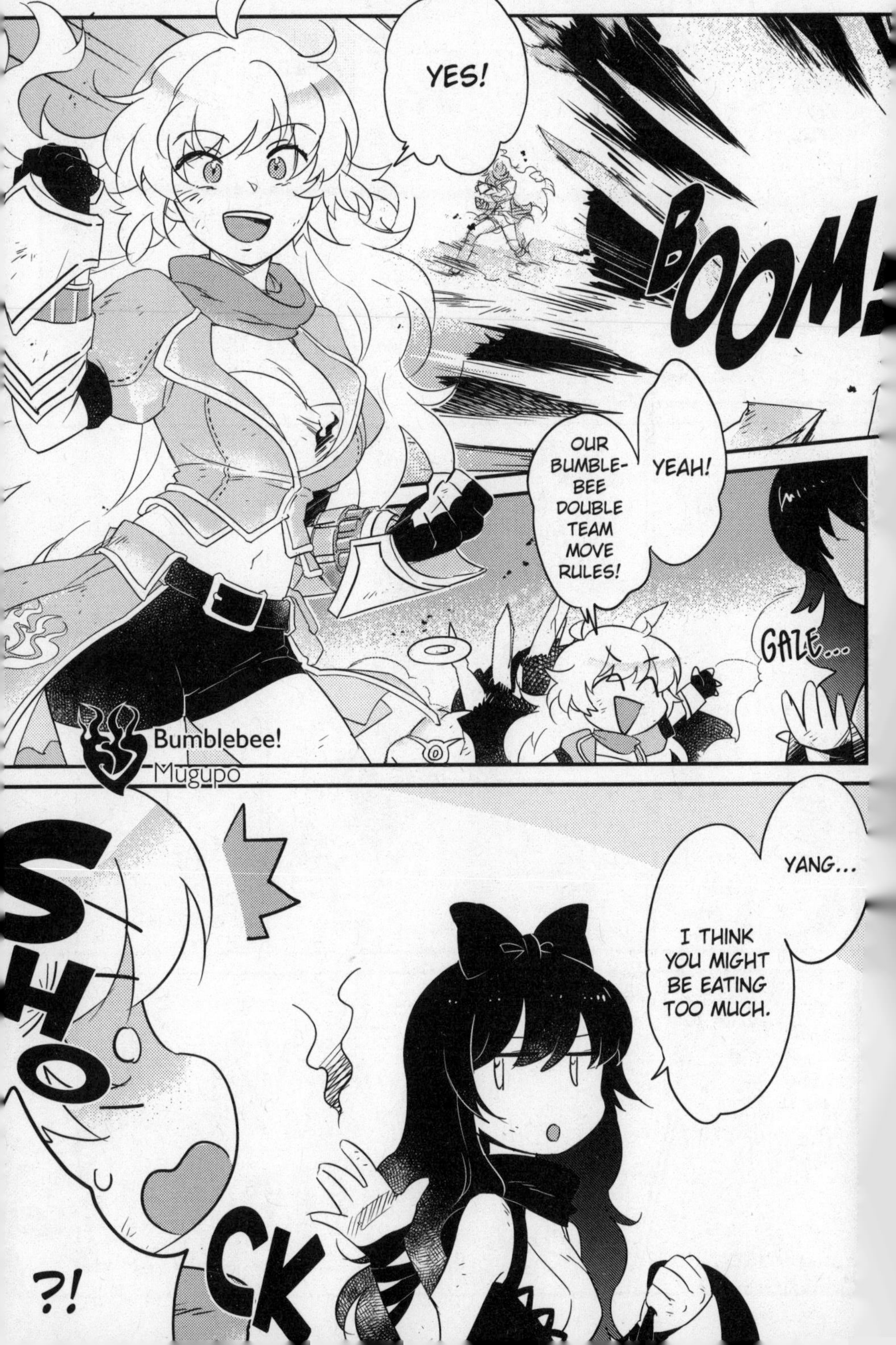
YES!
BOOM!
YEAH!
OUR BUMBLE-BEE DOUBLE TEAM MOVE RULES!
GAZE...
Bumblebee!
Mugupo
YANG...
I THINK YOU MIGHT BE EATING TOO MUCH.
SHOCK
?!

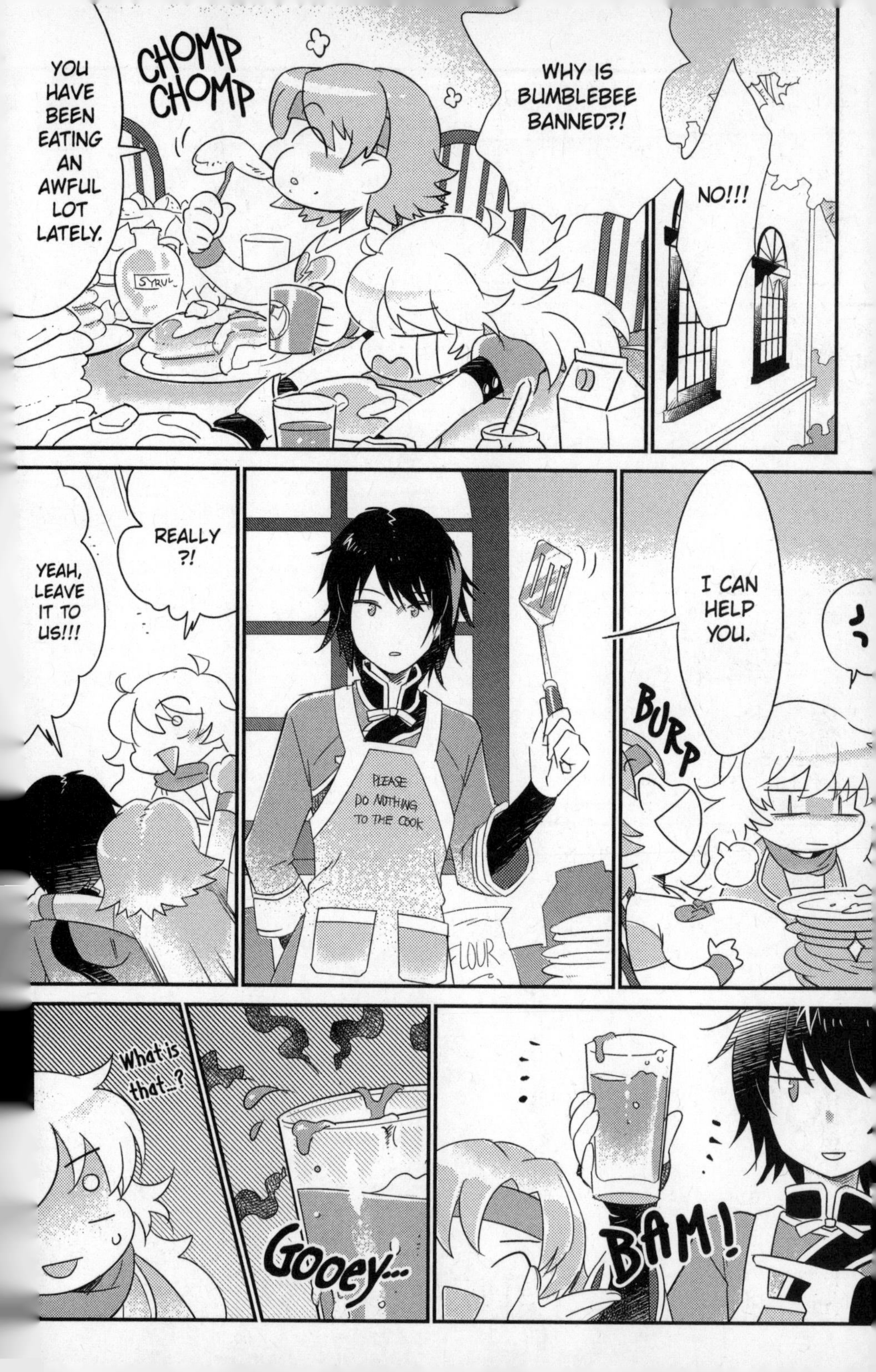
WHY IS BUMBLEBEE BANNED?!
NO!!!
CHOMP CHOMP
YOU HAVE BEEN EATING AN AWFUL LOT LATELY.
SYRUP
I CAN HELP YOU.
BURP
PLEASE DO NOTHING TO THE COOK
FLOUR
REALLY?!
YEAH, LEAVE IT TO US!!!
BAM!
What is that...?
Gooey...

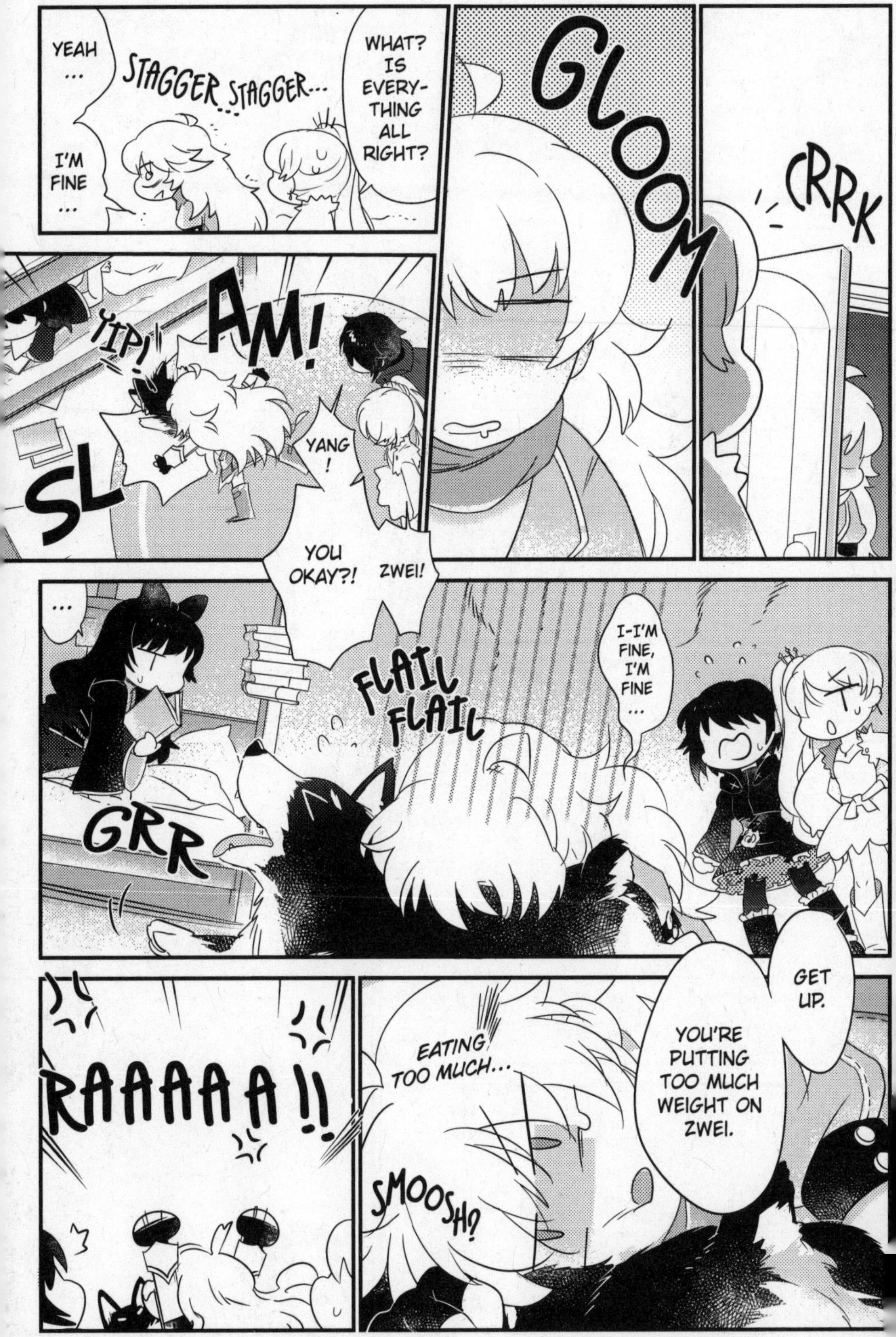
CRRK
GLOOM
WHAT? IS EVERYTHING ALL RIGHT?
STAGGER STAGGER...
YEAH ... I'M FINE ...
SL AM!
YIP!
YANG!
YOU OKAY?!
ZWEI!
I-I'M FINE, I'M FINE ...
FLAIL FLAIL
GRR
...
GET UP.
YOU'RE PUTTING TOO MUCH WEIGHT ON ZWEI.
EATING TOO MUCH...
SMOOSH?
RAAAAA!!

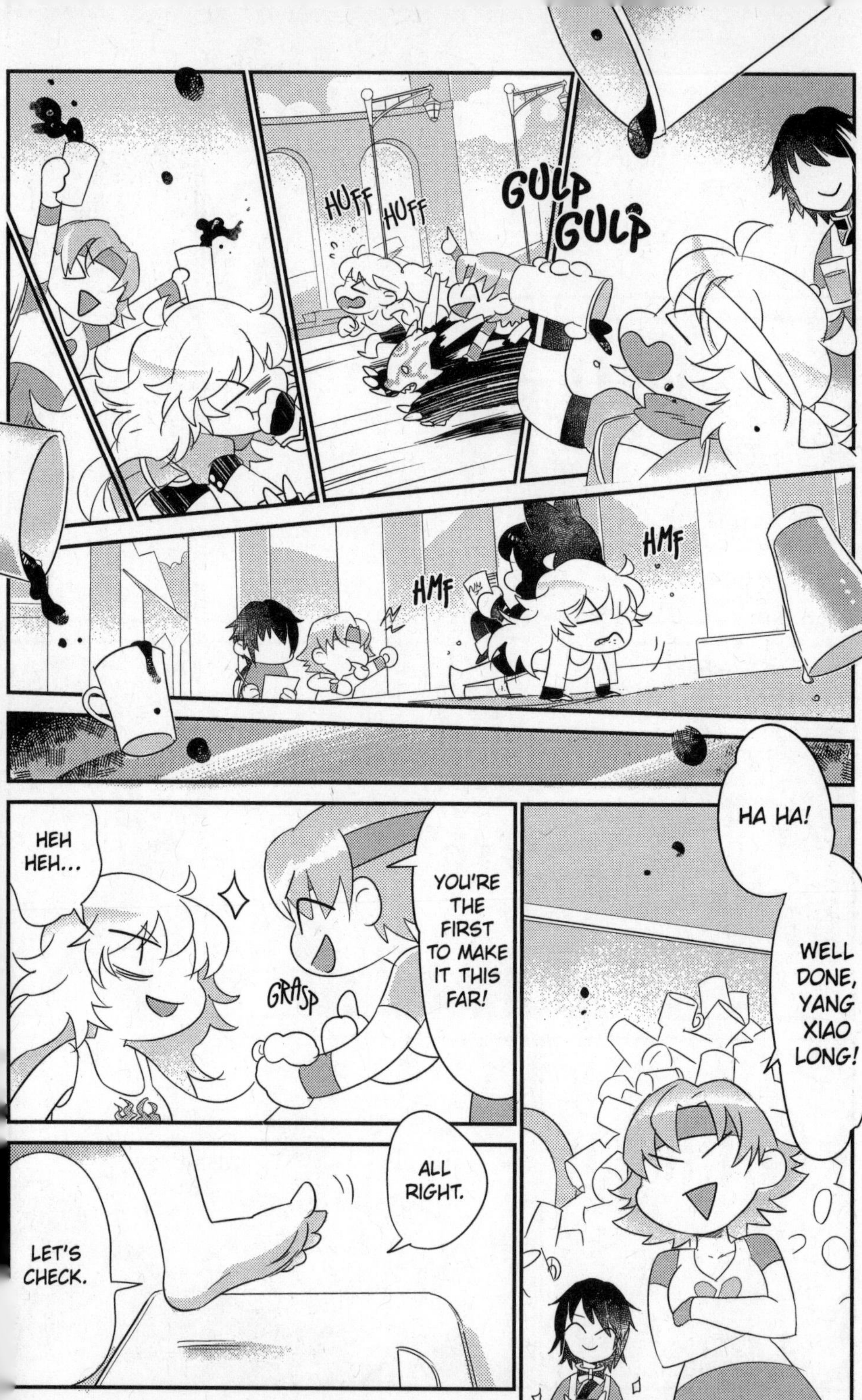
GULP
GULP
HUFF
HUFF
HMF
HMF
HA HA!
WELL DONE, YANG XIAO LONG!
YOU'RE THE FIRST TO MAKE IT THIS FAR!
GRASP
HEH HEH...
ALL RIGHT.
LET'S CHECK.

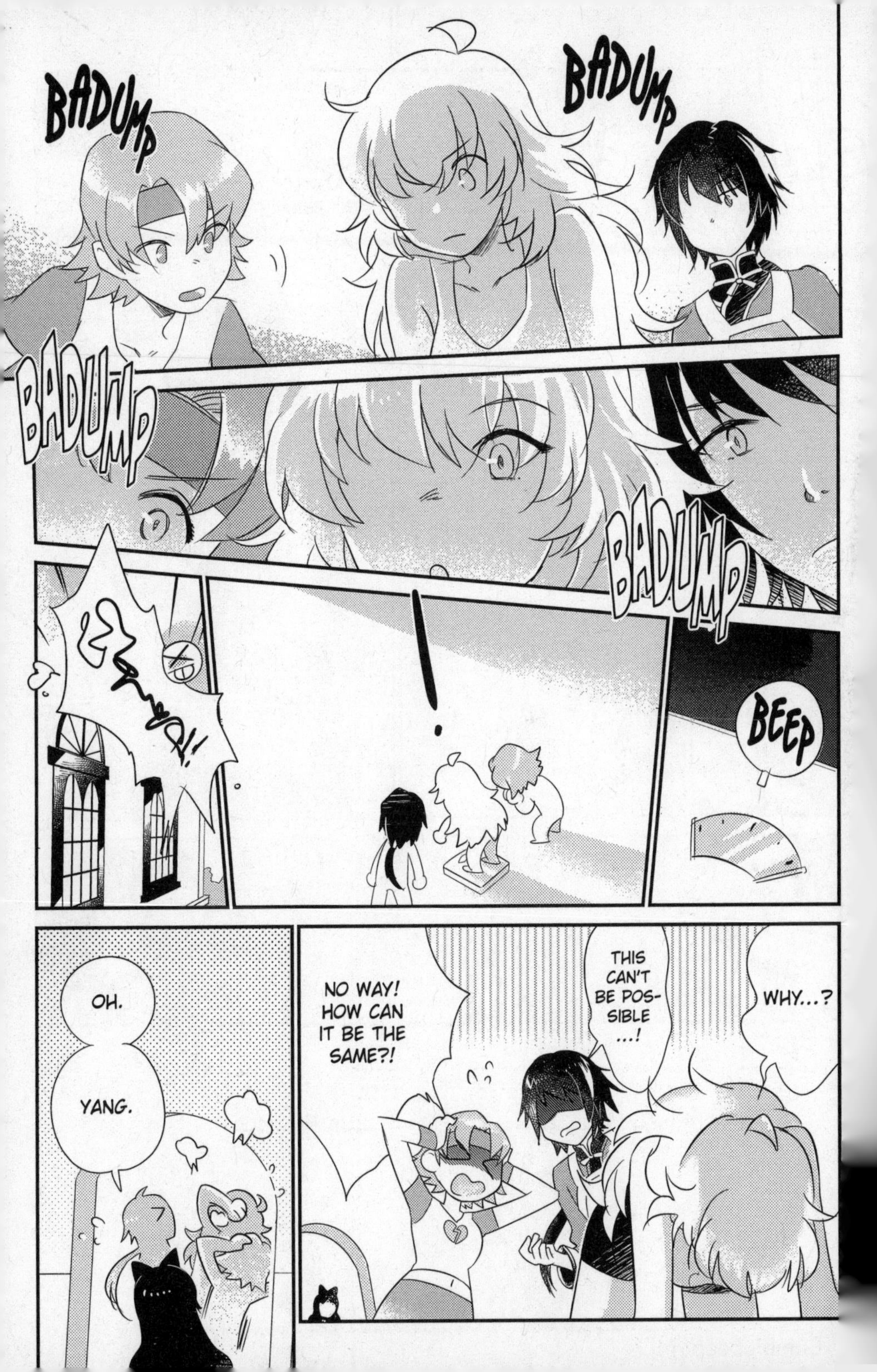
BADUMP
BADUMP
BADUMP
BADUMP
BEEP
!
WHY...?
THIS CAN'T BE POS-SIBLE ...!
NO WAY! HOW CAN IT BE THE SAME?!
OH.
YANG.

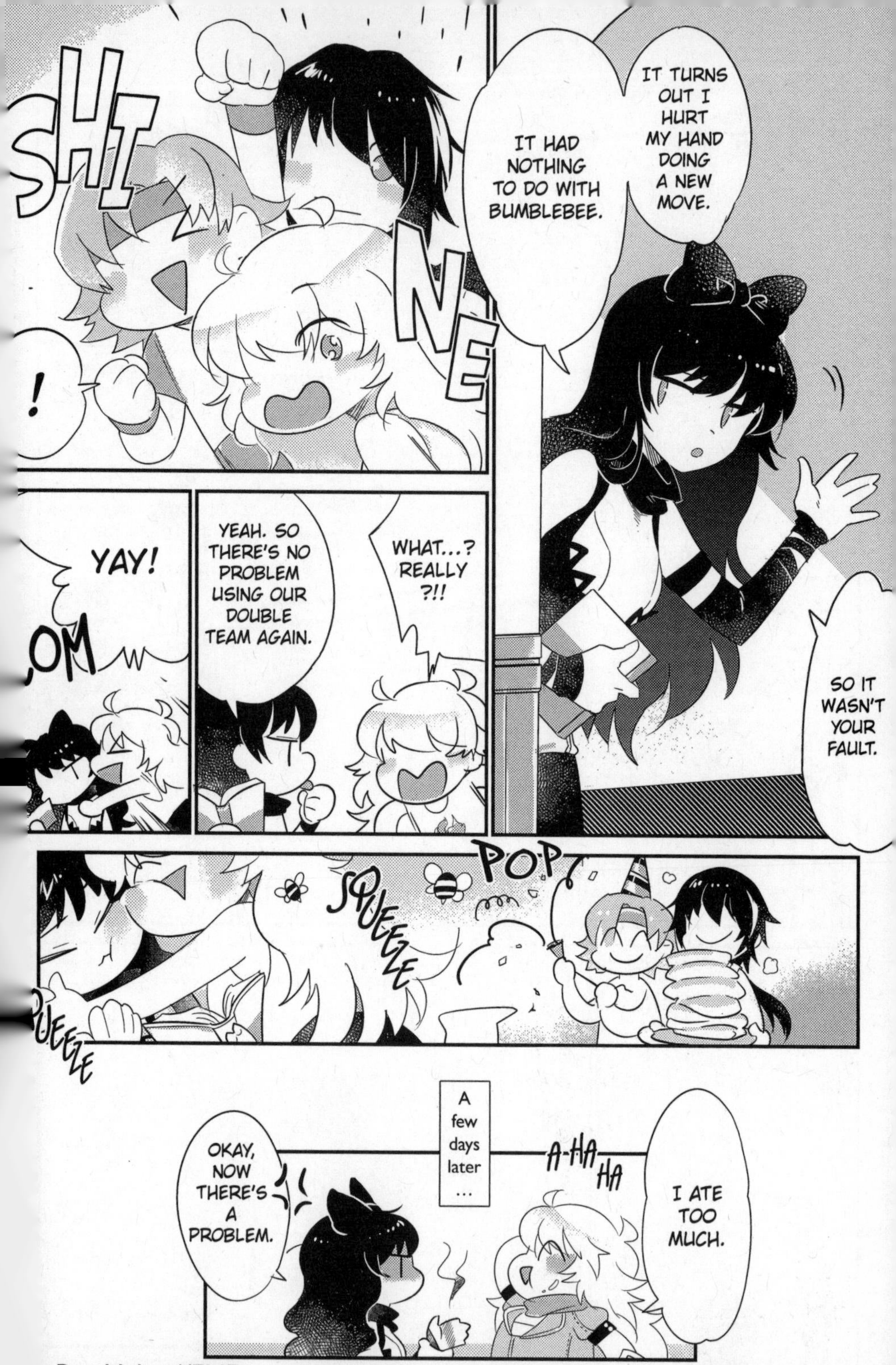
IT TURNS OUT I HURT MY HAND DOING A NEW MOVE.
IT HAD NOTHING TO DO WITH BUMBLEBEE.
SO IT WASN'T YOUR FAULT.
SHINE
!
WHAT...? REALLY ?!!
YEAH. SO THERE'S NO PROBLEM USING OUR DOUBLE TEAM AGAIN.
YAY!
OM
POP
SQUEEZE
SQUEEZE
A few days later...
I ATE TOO MUCH.
A-HA-HA
OKAY, NOW THERE'S A PROBLEM.

Bumblebee!/END

RWBY
OFFICIAL MANGA ANTHOLOGY
Volume 4

I Burn

RWBY
OFFICIAL MANGA ANTHOLOGY
Volume 4

I Burn

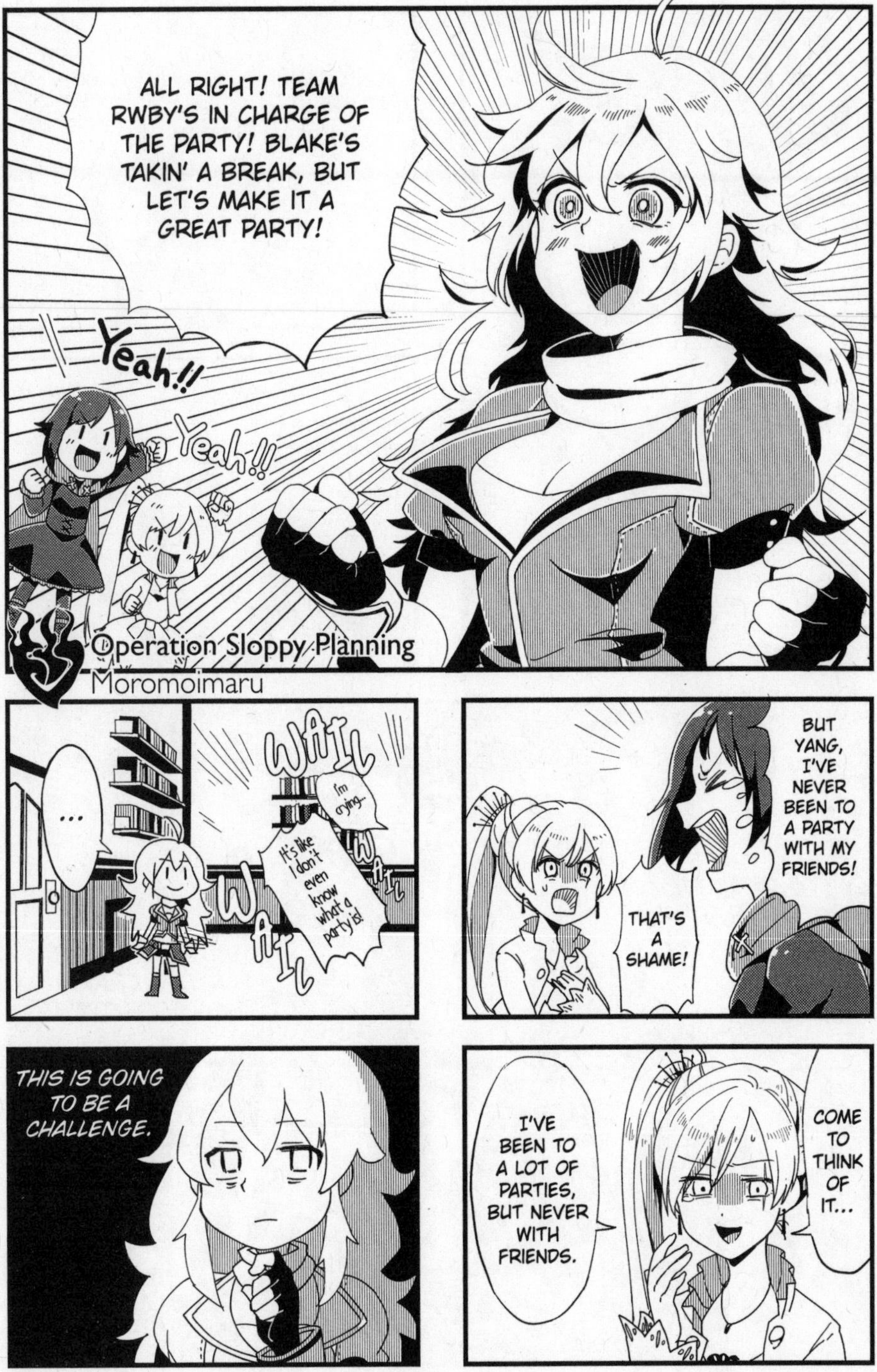
ALL RIGHT! TEAM RWBY'S IN CHARGE OF THE PARTY! BLAKE'S TAKIN' A BREAK, BUT LET'S MAKE IT A GREAT PARTY!
Yeah!!
Yeah!!
Operation Sloppy Planning
Moromoimaru
BUT YANG, I'VE NEVER BEEN TO A PARTY WITH MY FRIENDS!
THAT'S A SHAME!
WAIL
I'm crying...
It's like I don't even know what a party is!
WAIL
WAIL
...
COME TO THINK OF IT...
I'VE BEEN TO A LOT OF PARTIES, BUT NEVER WITH FRIENDS.
THIS IS GOING TO BE A CHALLENGE.

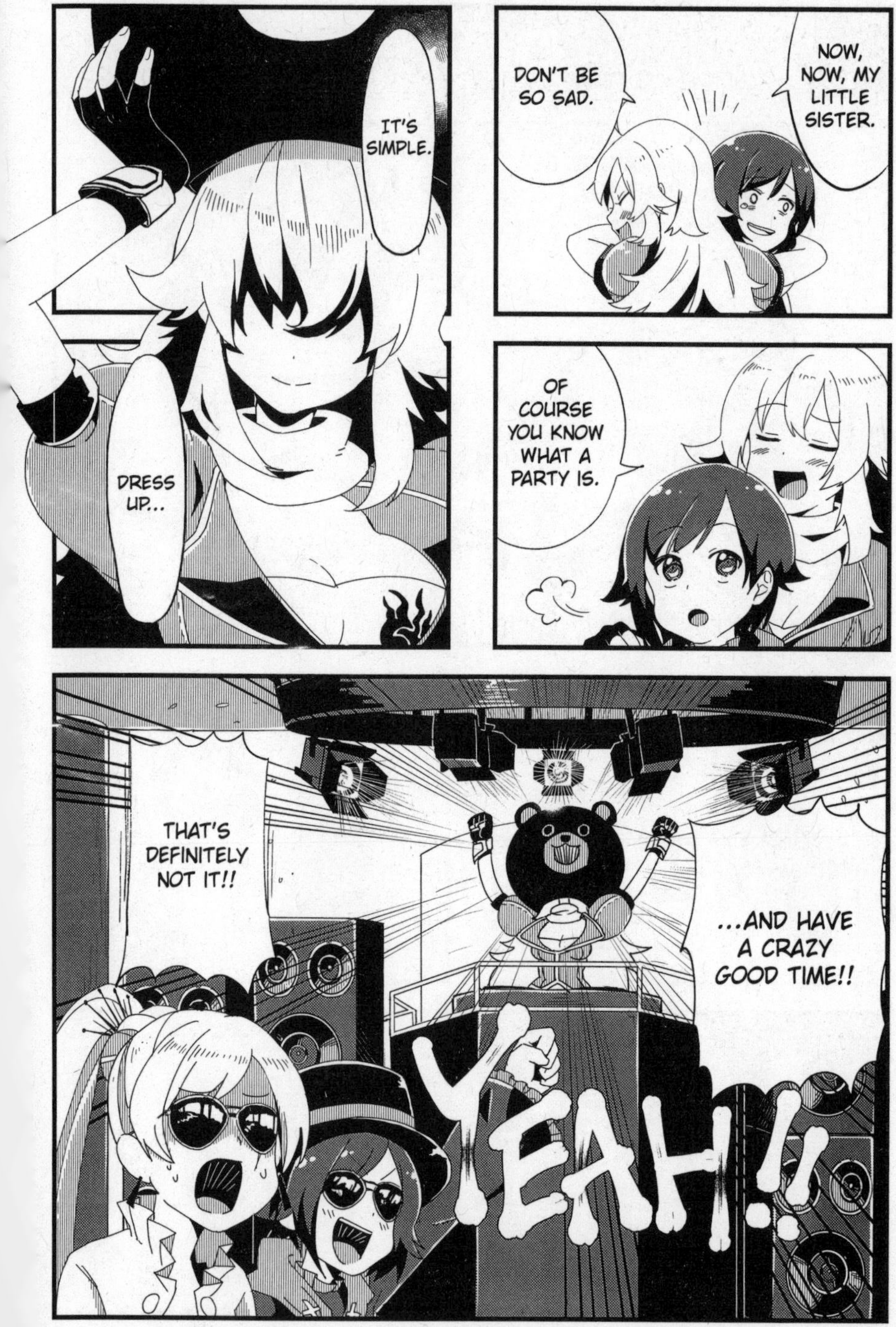
NOW, NOW, MY LITTLE SISTER.
DON'T BE SO SAD.
OF COURSE YOU KNOW WHAT A PARTY IS.
IT'S SIMPLE.
DRESS UP...
...AND HAVE A CRAZY GOOD TIME!!
YEAH!!
THAT'S DEFINITELY NOT IT!!

Duel

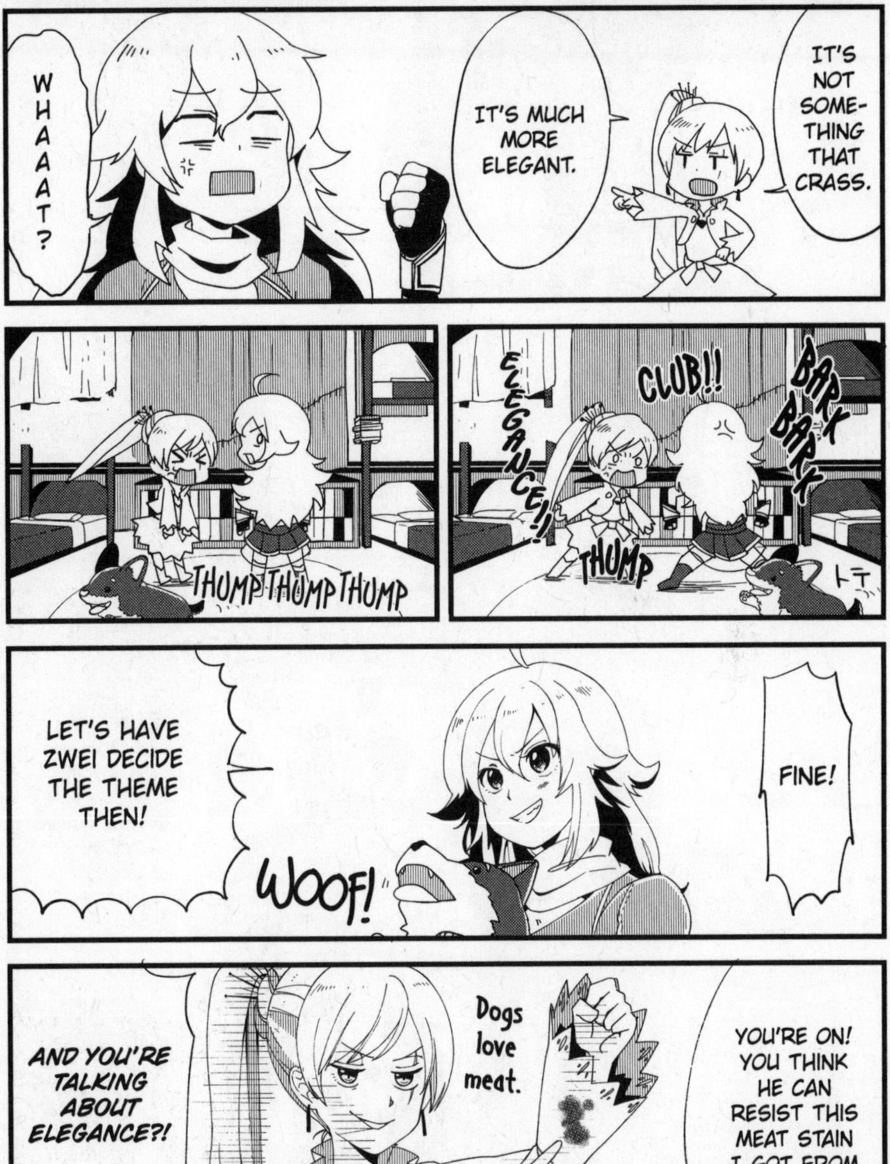
IT'S NOT SOME-THING THAT CRASS.
IT'S MUCH MORE ELEGANT.
WHAAAAT?
BARK BARK
CLUB!!
ELEGANCE!!
THUMP
トテ
THUMP THUMP THUMP
FINE!
LET'S HAVE ZWEI DECIDE THE THEME THEN!
WOOF!
YOU'RE ON! YOU THINK HE CAN RESIST THIS MEAT STAIN I GOT FROM BREAKFAST?
Dogs love meat.
AND YOU'RE TALKING ABOUT ELEGANCE?!

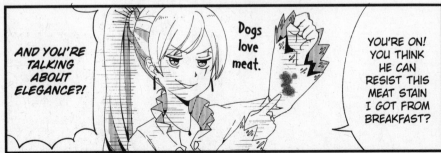

When in a Jam

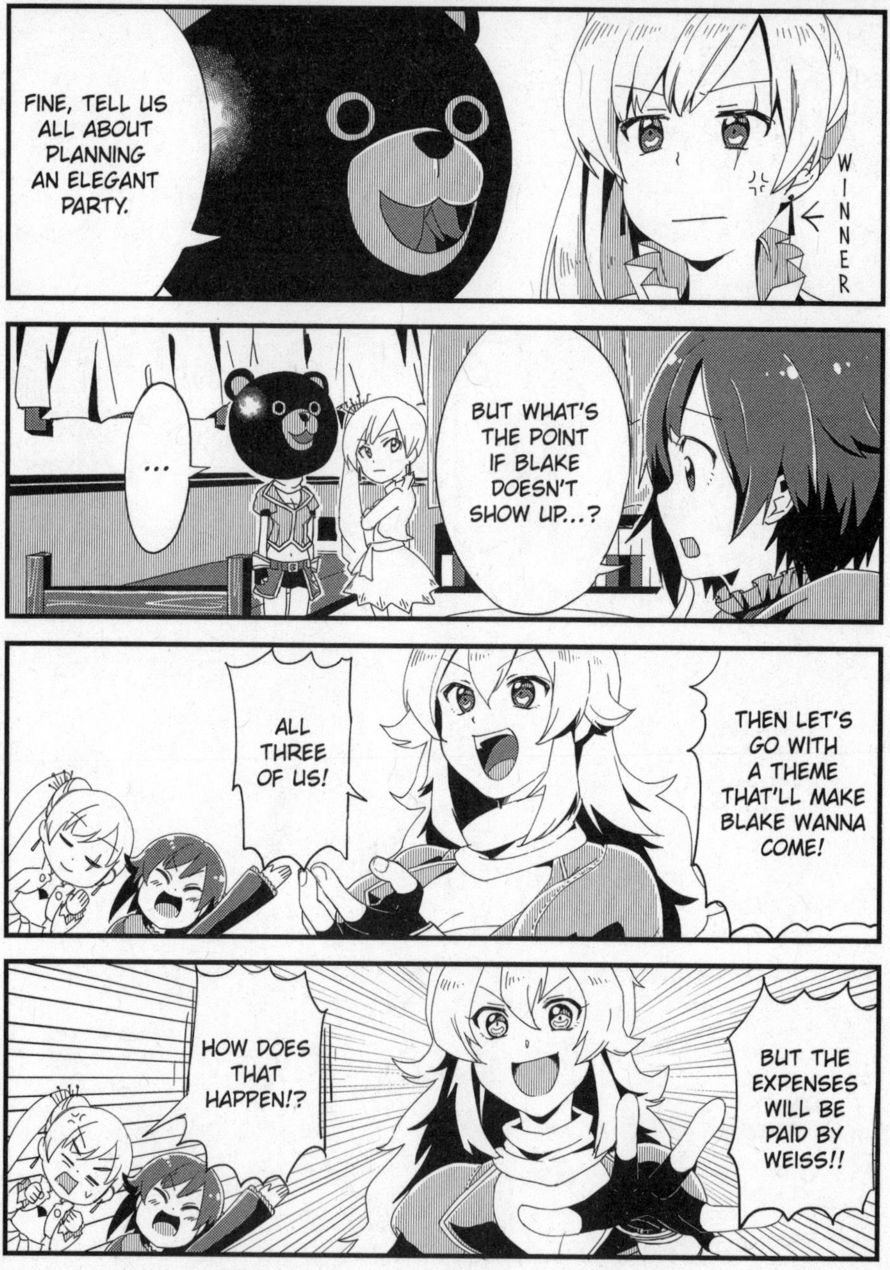
WINNER
FINE, TELL US ALL ABOUT PLANNING AN ELEGANT PARTY.
BUT WHAT'S THE POINT IF BLAKE DOESN'T SHOW UP...?
...
THEN LET'S GO WITH A THEME THAT'LL MAKE BLAKE WANNA COME!
ALL THREE OF US!
BUT THE EXPENSES WILL BE PAID BY WEISS!!
HOW DOES THAT HAPPEN!?

Planning

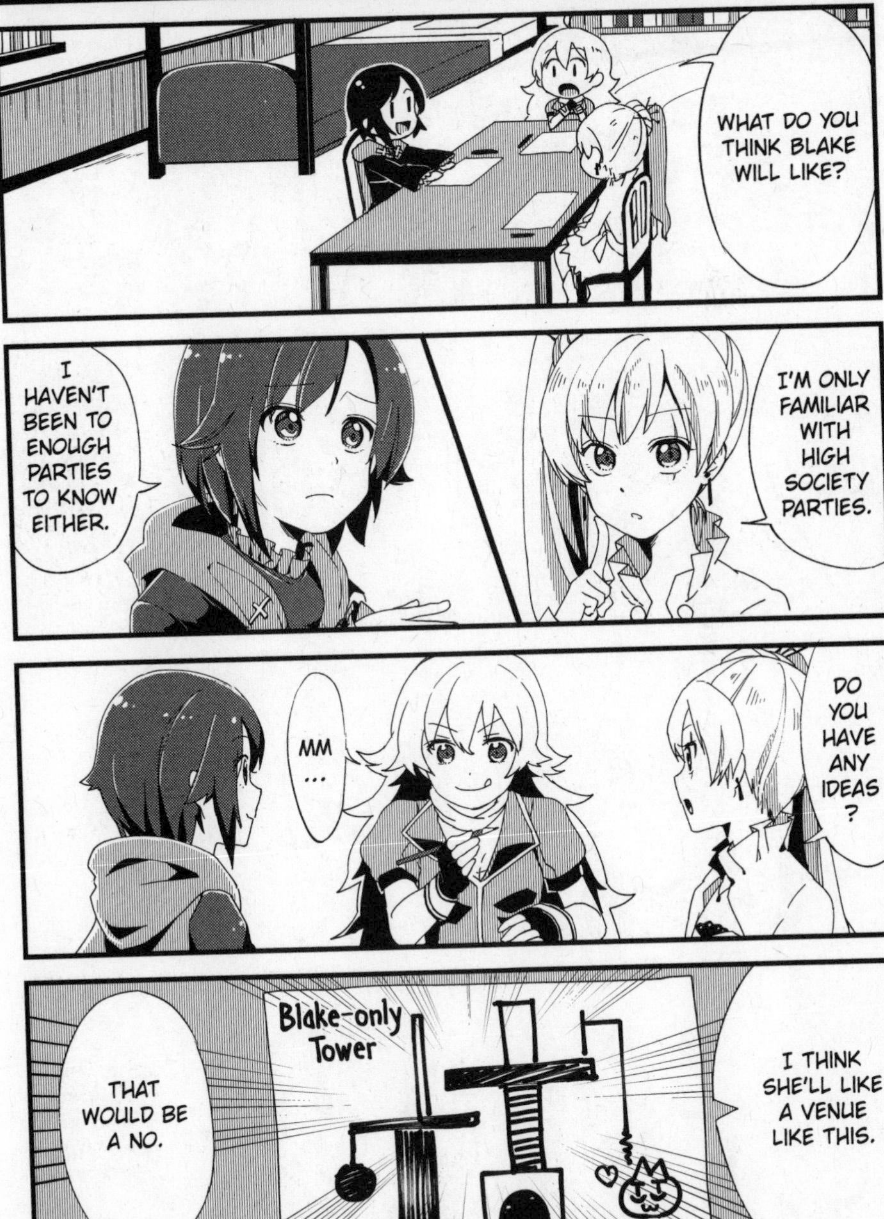
WHAT DO YOU THINK BLAKE WILL LIKE?
I'M ONLY FAMILIAR WITH HIGH SOCIETY PARTIES.
I HAVEN'T BEEN TO ENOUGH PARTIES TO KNOW EITHER.
DO YOU HAVE ANY IDEAS?
MM...
I THINK SHE'LL LIKE A VENUE LIKE THIS.
Blake-only Tower
THAT WOULD BE A NO.

Shopping

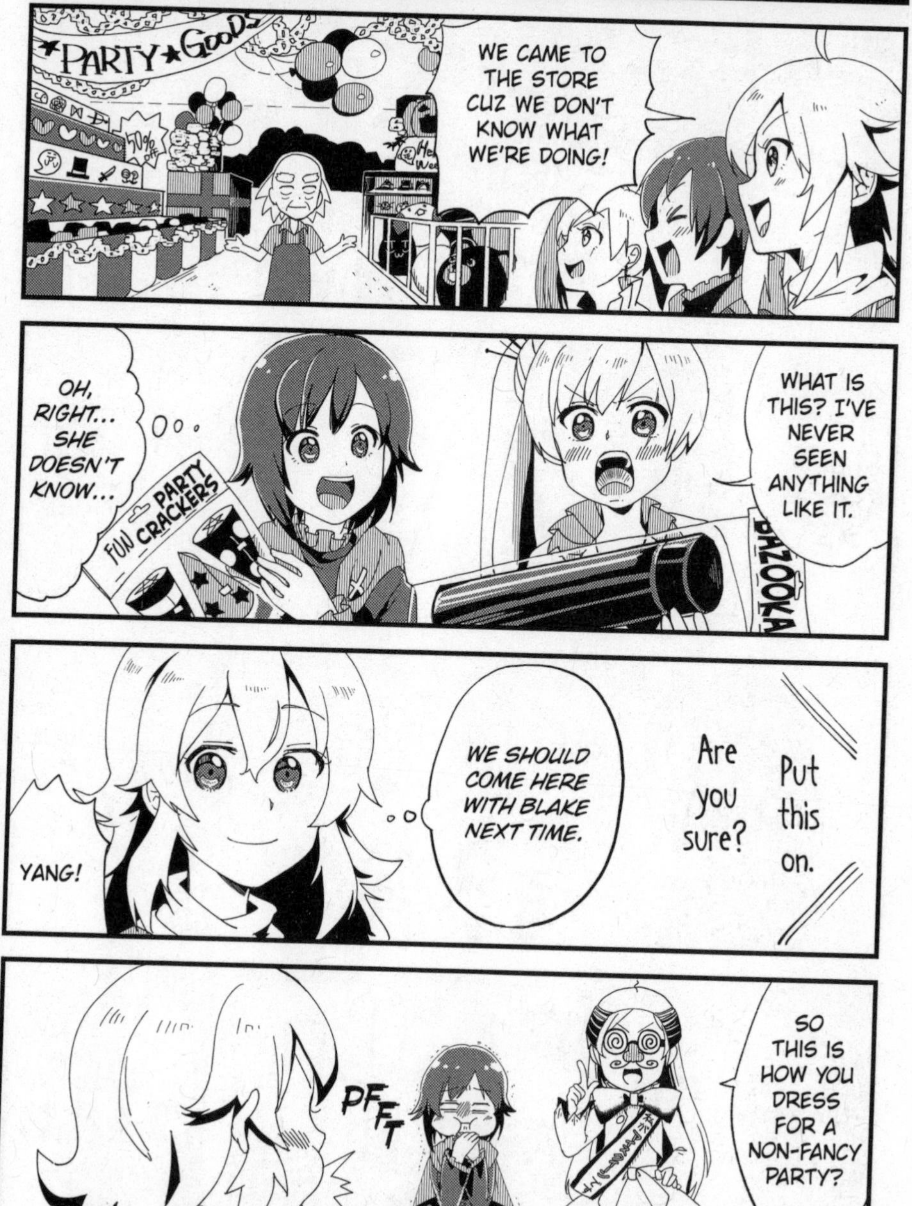

WE CAME TO THE STORE CUZ WE DON'T KNOW WHAT WE'RE DOING!
★PARTY★GOODS
50% OFF
WHAT IS THIS? I'VE NEVER SEEN ANYTHING LIKE IT.
BAZOOKA
FUN PARTY CRACKERS
OH, RIGHT... SHE DOESN'T KNOW...
Put this on.
Are you sure?
WE SHOULD COME HERE WITH BLAKE NEXT TIME.
YANG!
SO THIS IS HOW YOU DRESS FOR A NON-FANCY PARTY?
PFFT

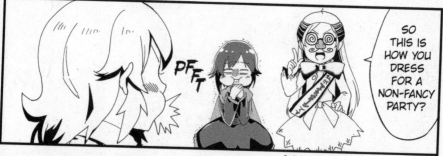

Sash: I am the Ice Queen

Heavy, Heavy

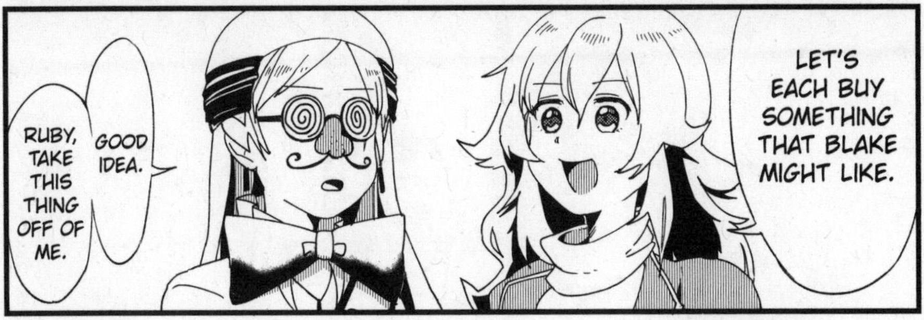
LET'S EACH BUY SOMETHING THAT BLAKE MIGHT LIKE.
GOOD IDEA.
RUBY, TAKE THIS THING OFF OF ME.

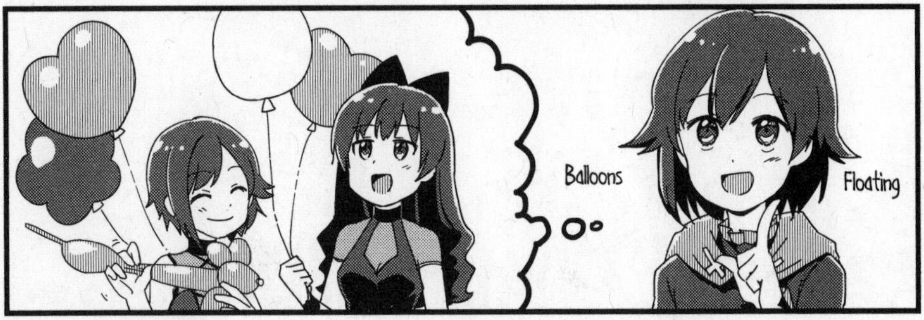
Floating
Balloons

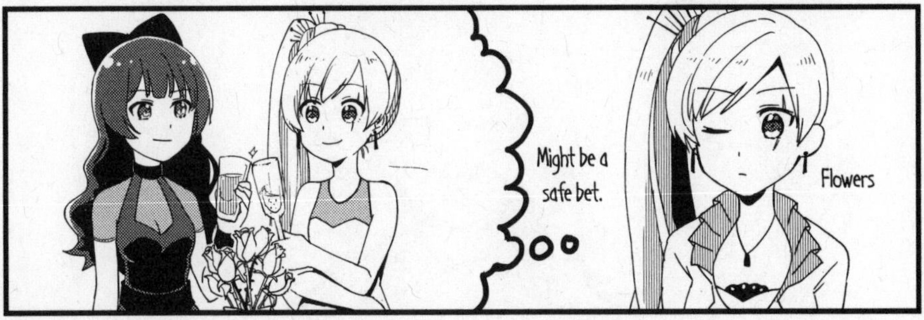
Flowers
Might be a safe bet.

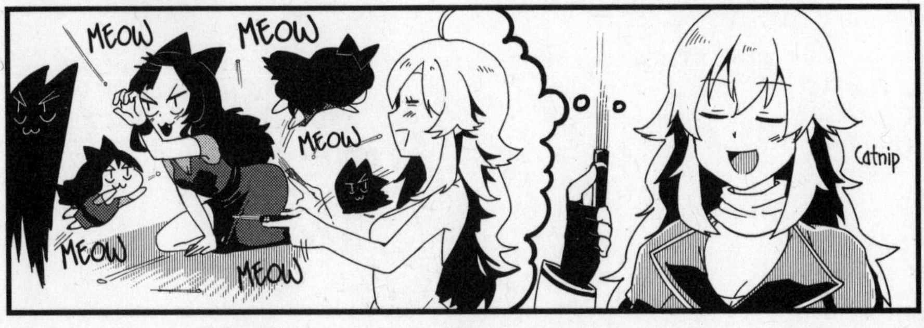
Catnip
MEOW
MEOW
MEOW
MEOW
MEOW

Coincidence

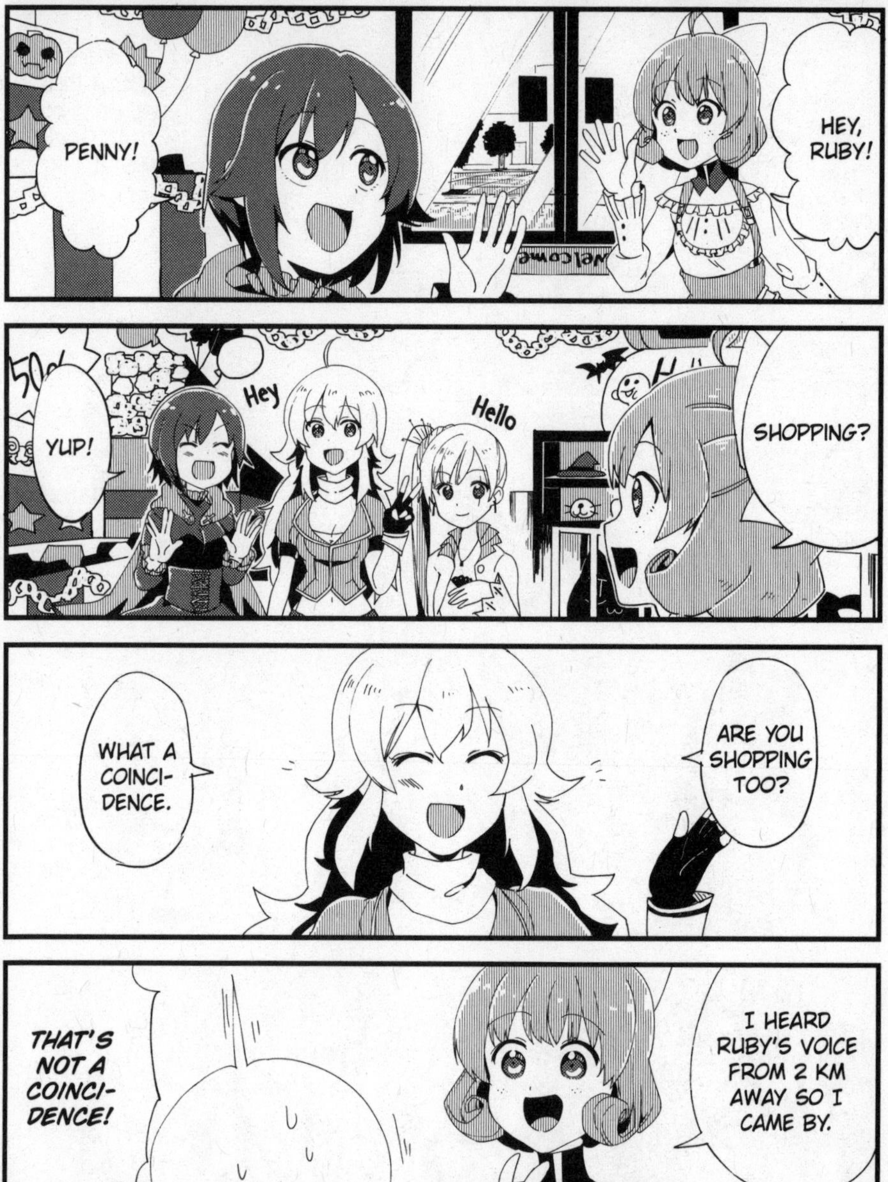
HEY, RUBY!
PENNY!
SHOPPING?
Hello
Hey
YUP!
ARE YOU SHOPPING TOO?
WHAT A COINCIDENCE.
I HEARD RUBY'S VOICE FROM 2 KM AWAY SO I CAME BY.
THAT'S NOT A COINCIDENCE!

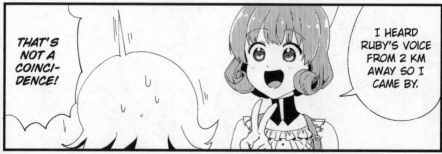

Me Too

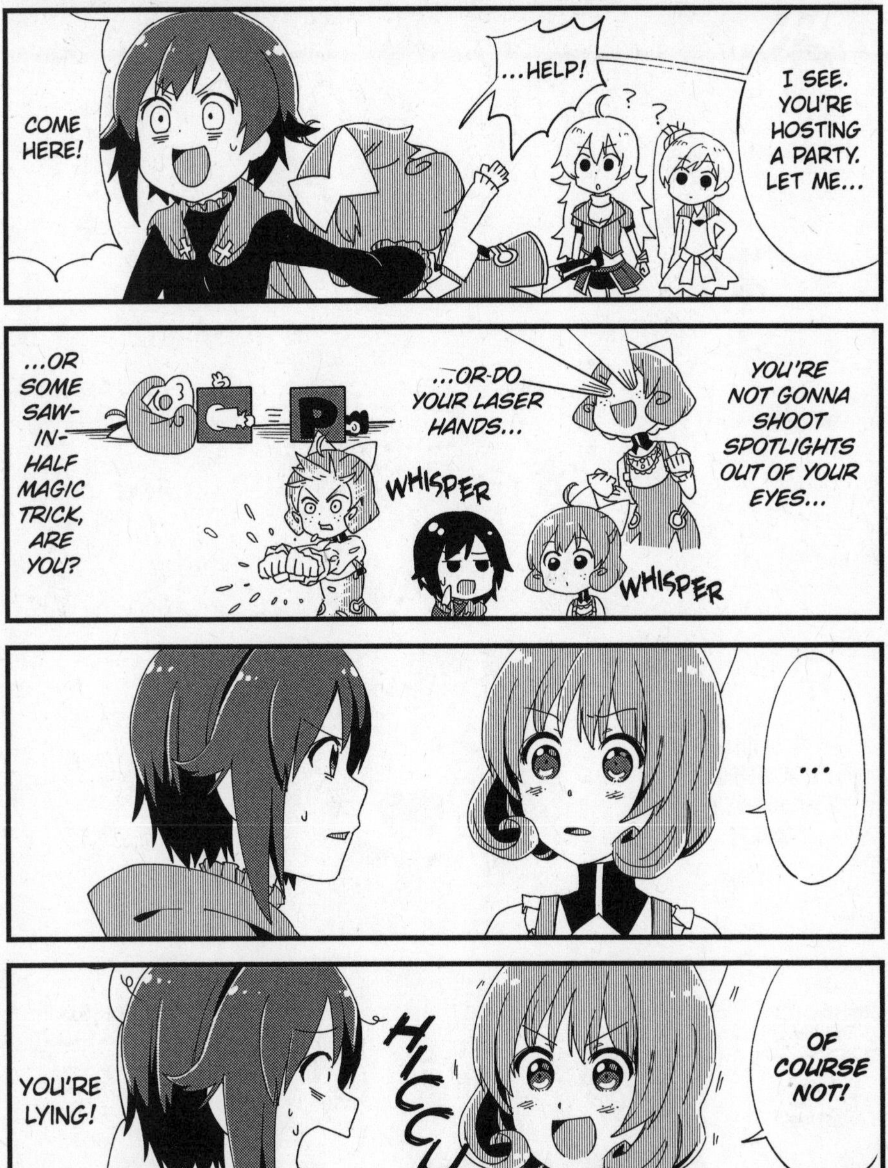
I SEE. YOU'RE HOSTING A PARTY. LET ME...
...HELP!
COME HERE!
YOU'RE NOT GONNA SHOOT SPOTLIGHTS OUT OF YOUR EYES...
...OR DO YOUR LASER HANDS...
WHISPER
WHISPER
...OR SOME SAW-IN-HALF MAGIC TRICK, ARE YOU?
...
OF COURSE NOT!
HICCUP
YOU'RE LYING!

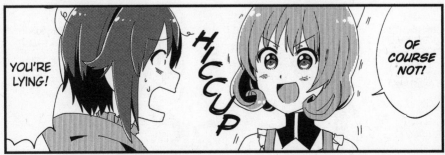

Invitation

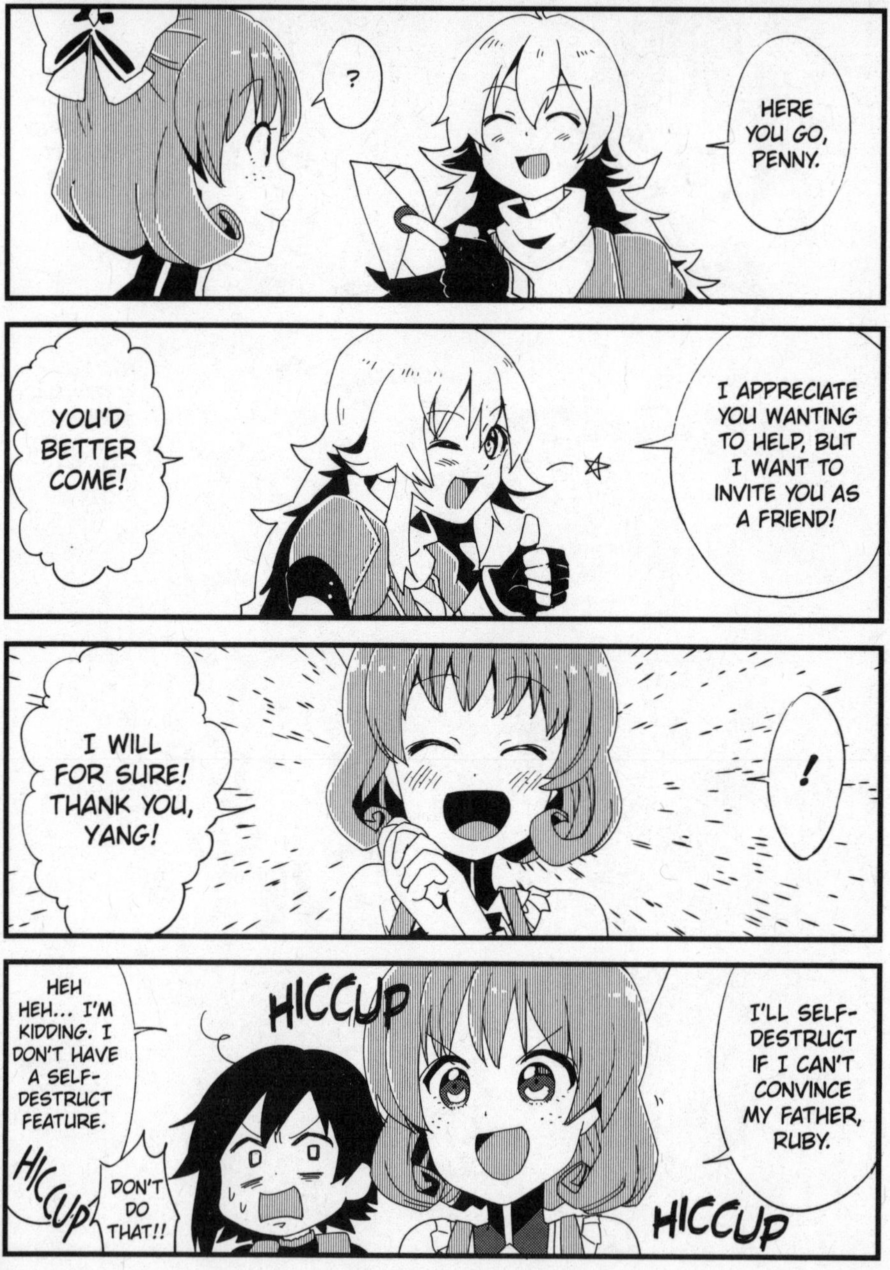
HERE YOU GO, PENNY.
?
I APPRECIATE YOU WANTING TO HELP, BUT I WANT TO INVITE YOU AS A FRIEND!
YOU'D BETTER COME!
!
I WILL FOR SURE! THANK YOU, YANG!
I'LL SELF-DESTRUCT IF I CAN'T CONVINCE MY FATHER, RUBY.
HICCUP
HEH HEH... I'M KIDDING. I DON'T HAVE A SELF-DESTRUCT FEATURE.
HICCUP
DON'T DO THAT!!
HICCUP

Preparation

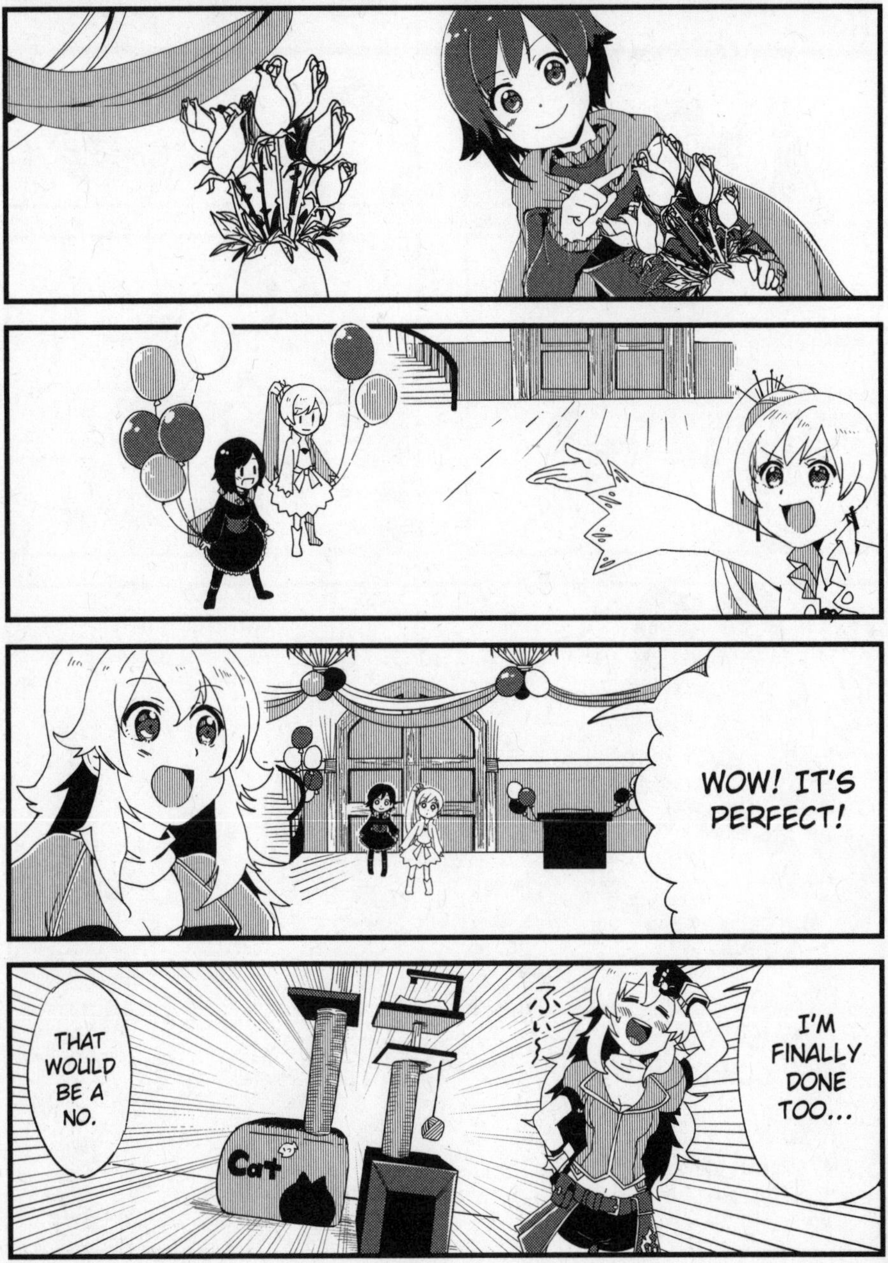
WOW! IT'S PERFECT!
I'M FINALLY DONE TOO...
ふぃ～
THAT WOULD BE A NO.

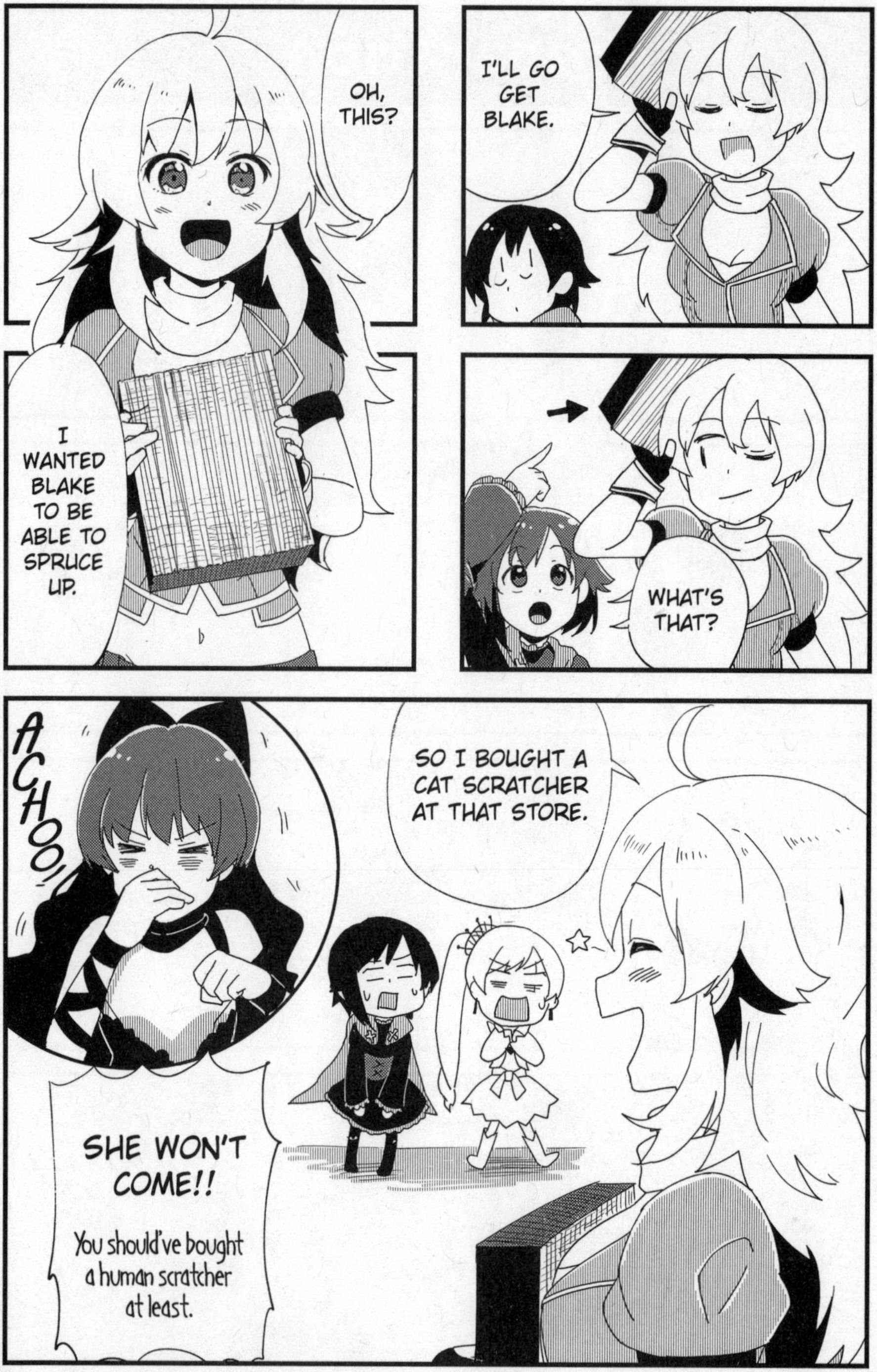
I'LL GO GET BLAKE.
WHAT'S THAT?
OH, THIS?
I WANTED BLAKE TO BE ABLE TO SPRUCE UP.
SO I BOUGHT A CAT SCRATCHER AT THAT STORE.
ACHOO!!
SHE WON'T COME!!
You should've bought a human scratcher at least.

Operation Sloppy Planning/END

Sister
Mikanuji

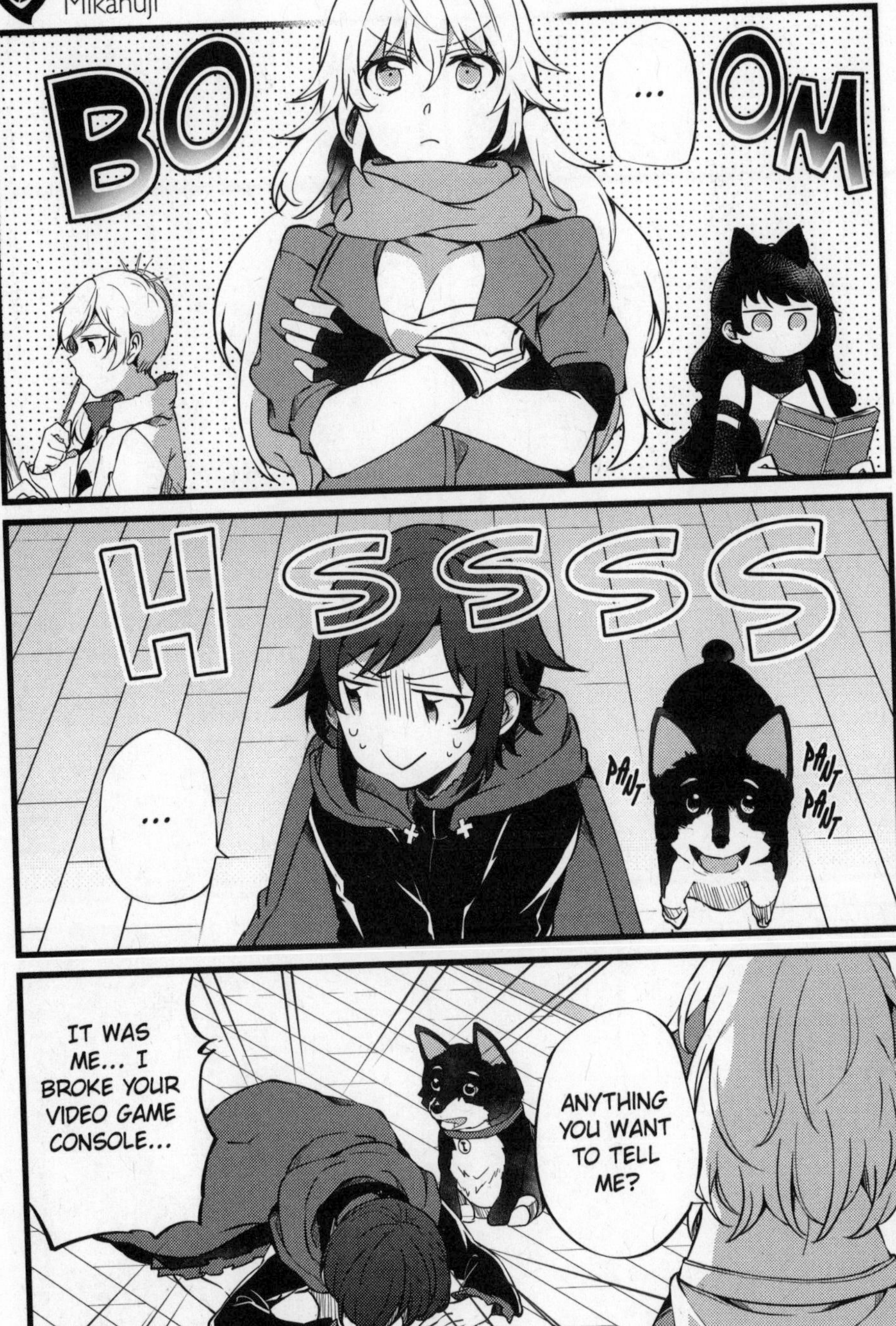
BO
OM
...
H SSSS
PANT
PANT PANT
...
ANYTHING YOU WANT TO TELL ME?
IT WAS ME... I BROKE YOUR VIDEO GAME CONSOLE...

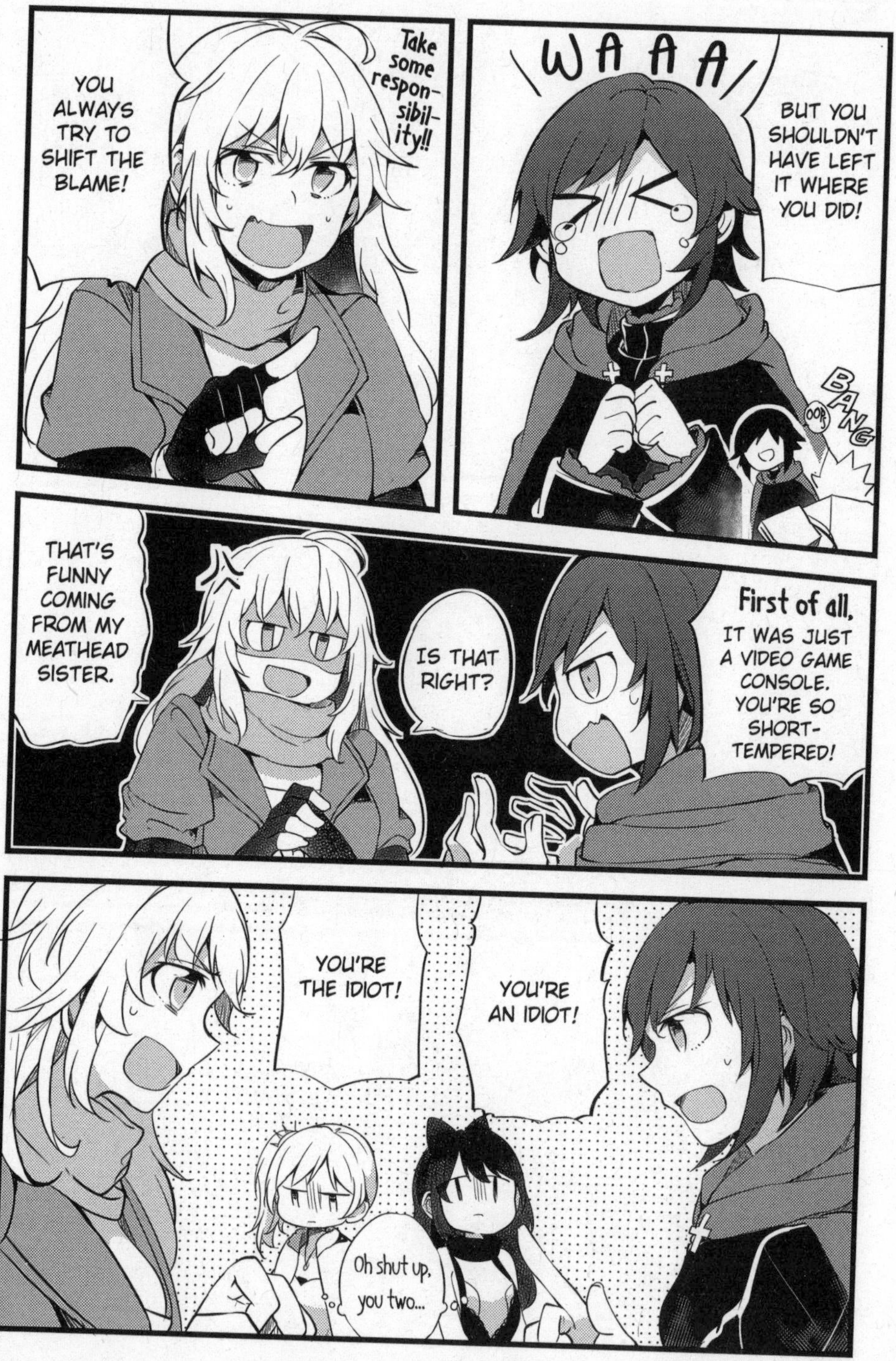
WAAA
BUT YOU SHOULDN'T HAVE LEFT IT WHERE YOU DID!
OOPS
BANG
Take some respon-sibil-ity!!
YOU ALWAYS TRY TO SHIFT THE BLAME!
First of all, IT WAS JUST A VIDEO GAME CONSOLE. YOU'RE SO SHORT-TEMPERED!
IS THAT RIGHT?
THAT'S FUNNY COMING FROM MY MEATHEAD SISTER.
YOU'RE AN IDIOT!
YOU'RE THE IDIOT!
Oh shut up, you two...

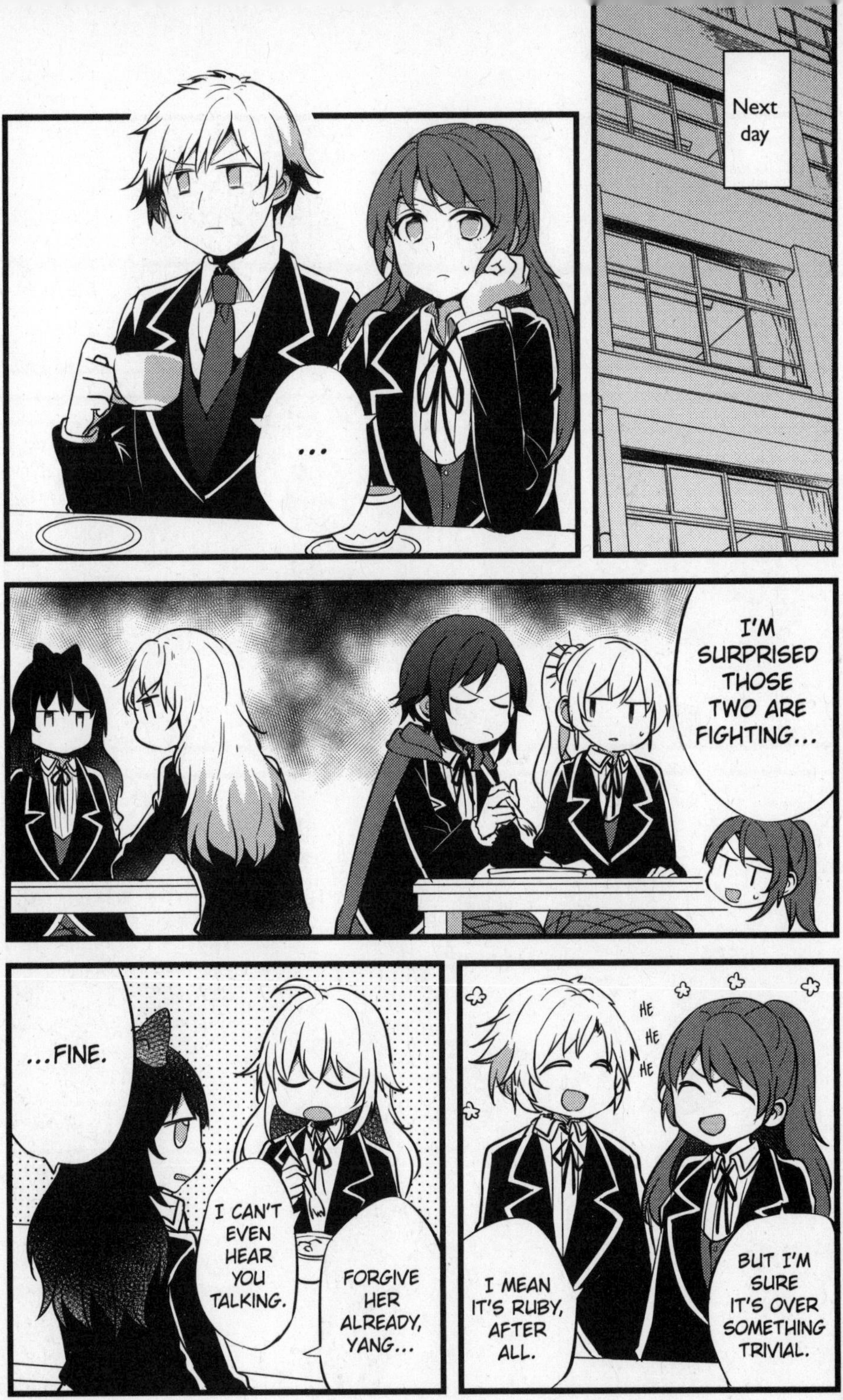
Next day
...
I'M SURPRISED THOSE TWO ARE FIGHTING...
HE HE HE
BUT I'M SURE IT'S OVER SOMETHING TRIVIAL.
I MEAN IT'S RUBY, AFTER ALL.
FORGIVE HER ALREADY, YANG...
I CAN'T EVEN HEAR YOU TALKING.
...FINE.

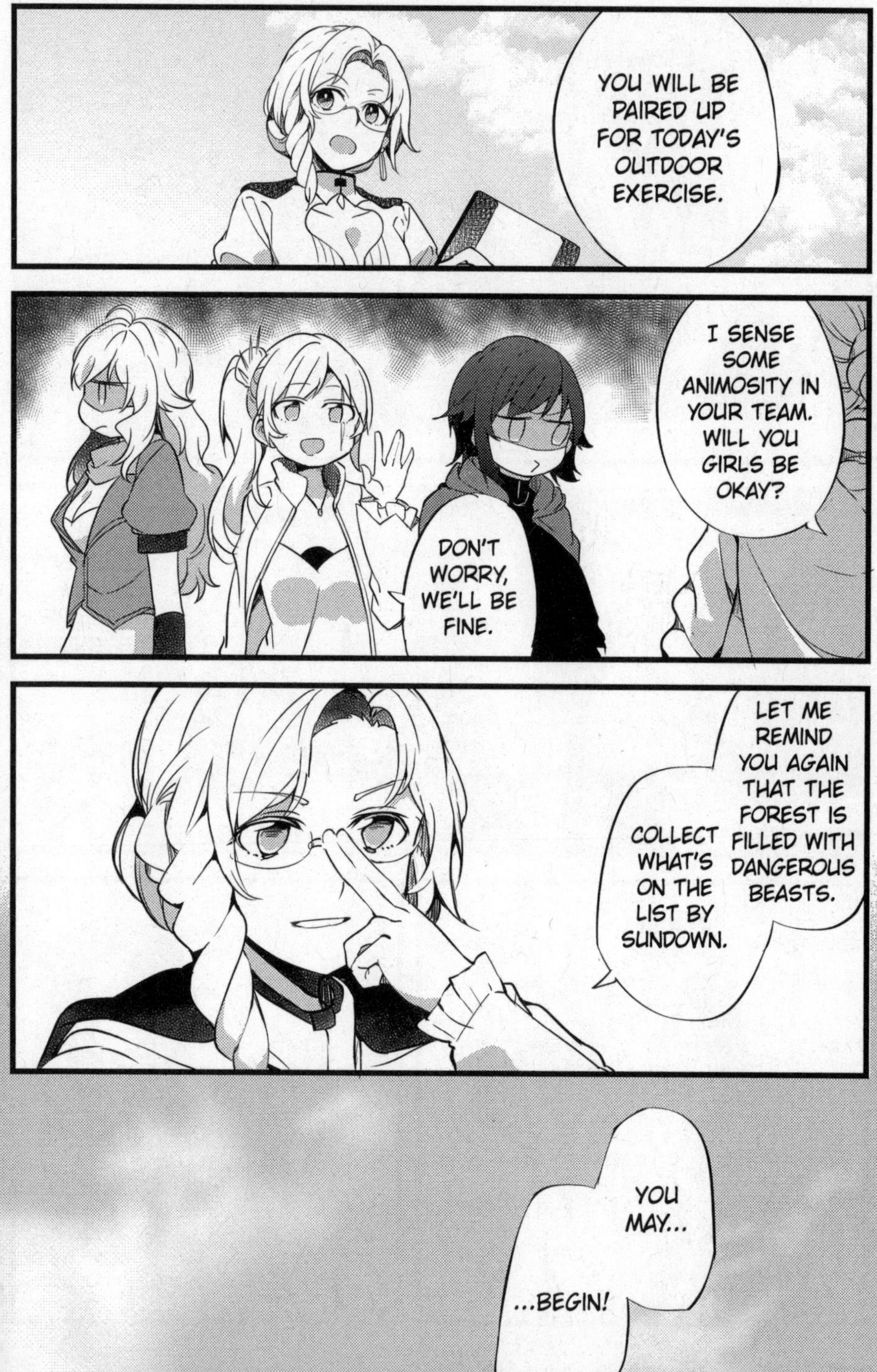
YOU WILL BE PAIRED UP FOR TODAY'S OUTDOOR EXERCISE.
I SENSE SOME ANIMOSITY IN YOUR TEAM. WILL YOU GIRLS BE OKAY?
DON'T WORRY, WE'LL BE FINE.
LET ME REMIND YOU AGAIN THAT THE FOREST IS FILLED WITH DANGEROUS BEASTS.
COLLECT WHAT'S ON THE LIST BY SUNDOWN.
YOU MAY...
...BEGIN!

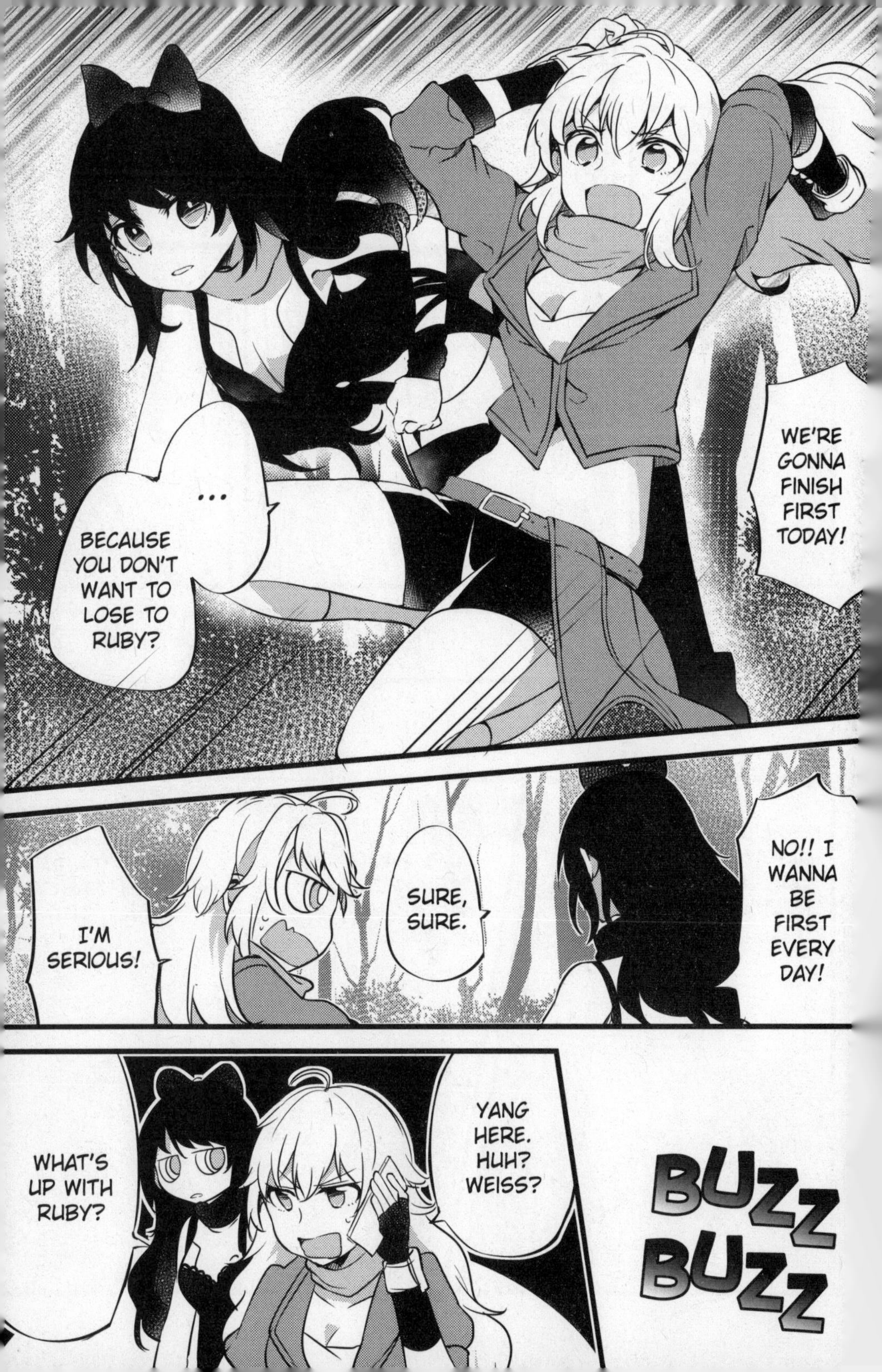
WE'RE GONNA FINISH FIRST TODAY!
...
BECAUSE YOU DON'T WANT TO LOSE TO RUBY?
NO!! I WANNA BE FIRST EVERY DAY!
SURE, SURE.
I'M SERIOUS!
BUZZ BUZZ
YANG HERE. HUH? WEISS?
WHAT'S UP WITH RUBY?

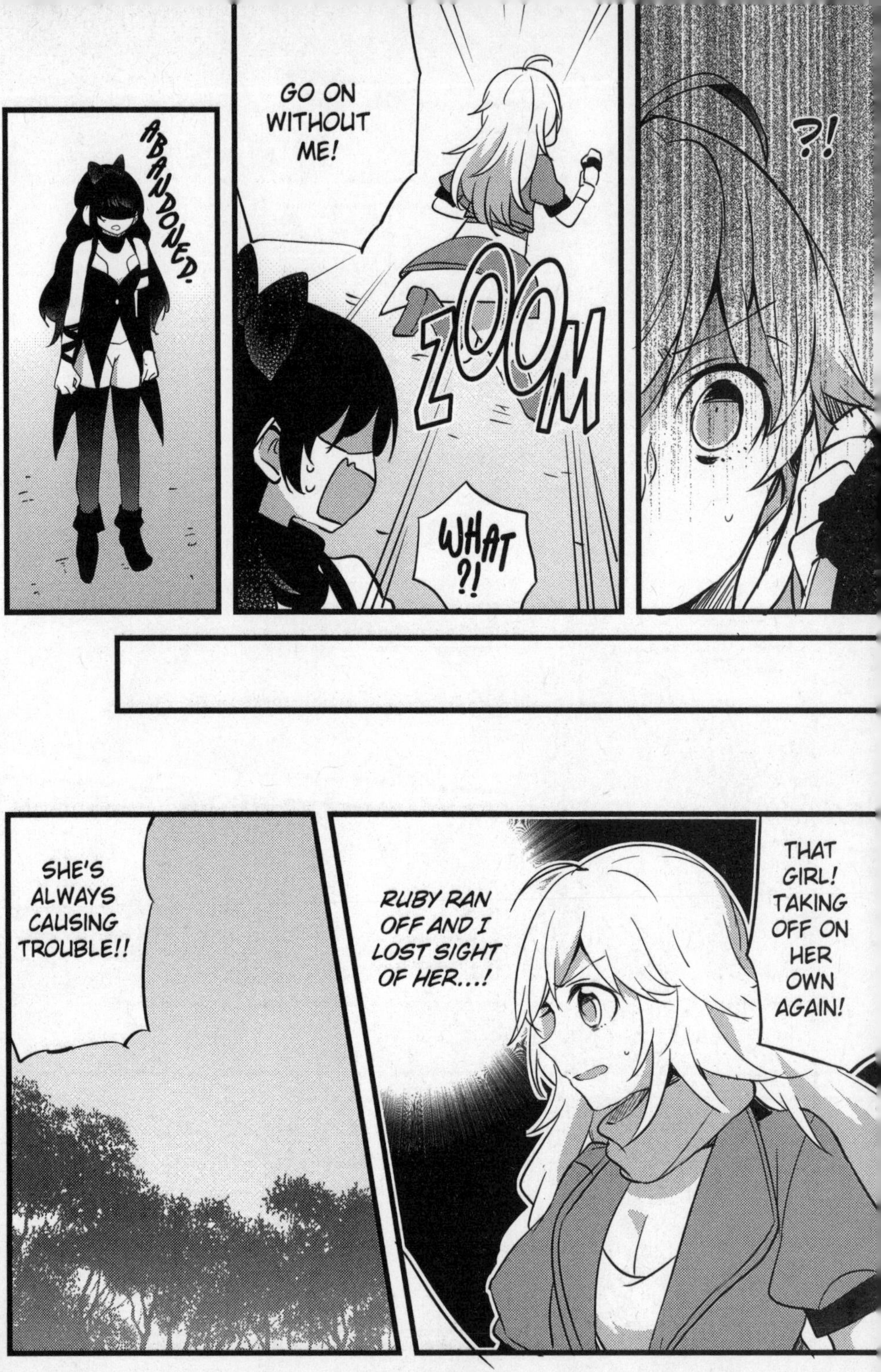
?!
GO ON WITHOUT ME!
ZOOM
WHAT ?!
ABANDONED.
THAT GIRL! TAKING OFF ON HER OWN AGAIN!
RUBY RAN OFF AND I LOST SIGHT OF HER...!
SHE'S ALWAYS CAUSING TROUBLE!!

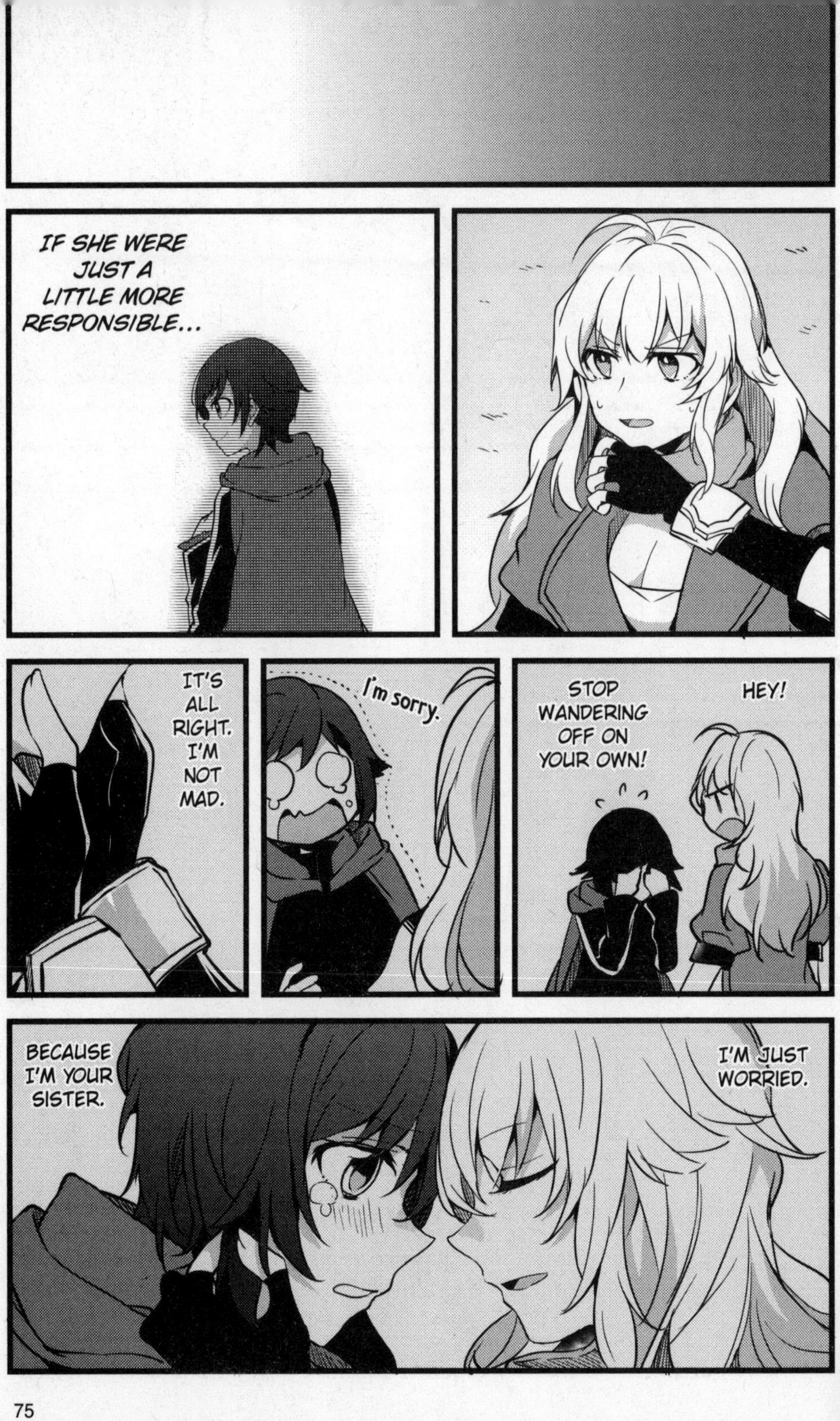
IF SHE WERE JUST A LITTLE MORE RESPONSIBLE...
HEY!
STOP WANDERING OFF ON YOUR OWN!
I'm sorry.
IT'S ALL RIGHT. I'M NOT MAD.
I'M JUST WORRIED.
BECAUSE I'M YOUR SISTER.

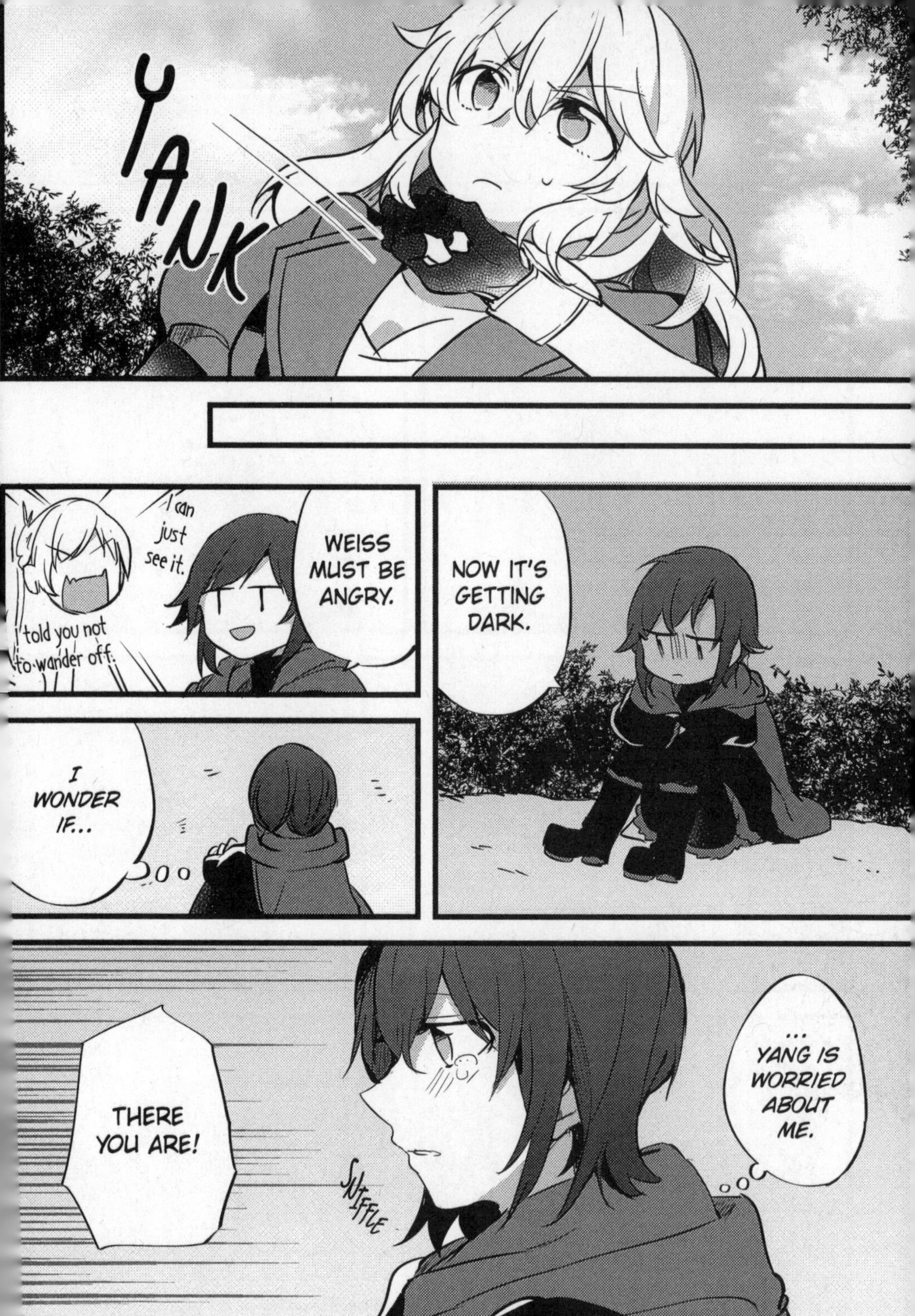
YANK
NOW IT'S GETTING DARK.
WEISS MUST BE ANGRY.
I can just see it.
I told you not to wander off.
I WONDER IF...
... YANG IS WORRIED ABOUT ME.
SNIFFLE
THERE YOU ARE!

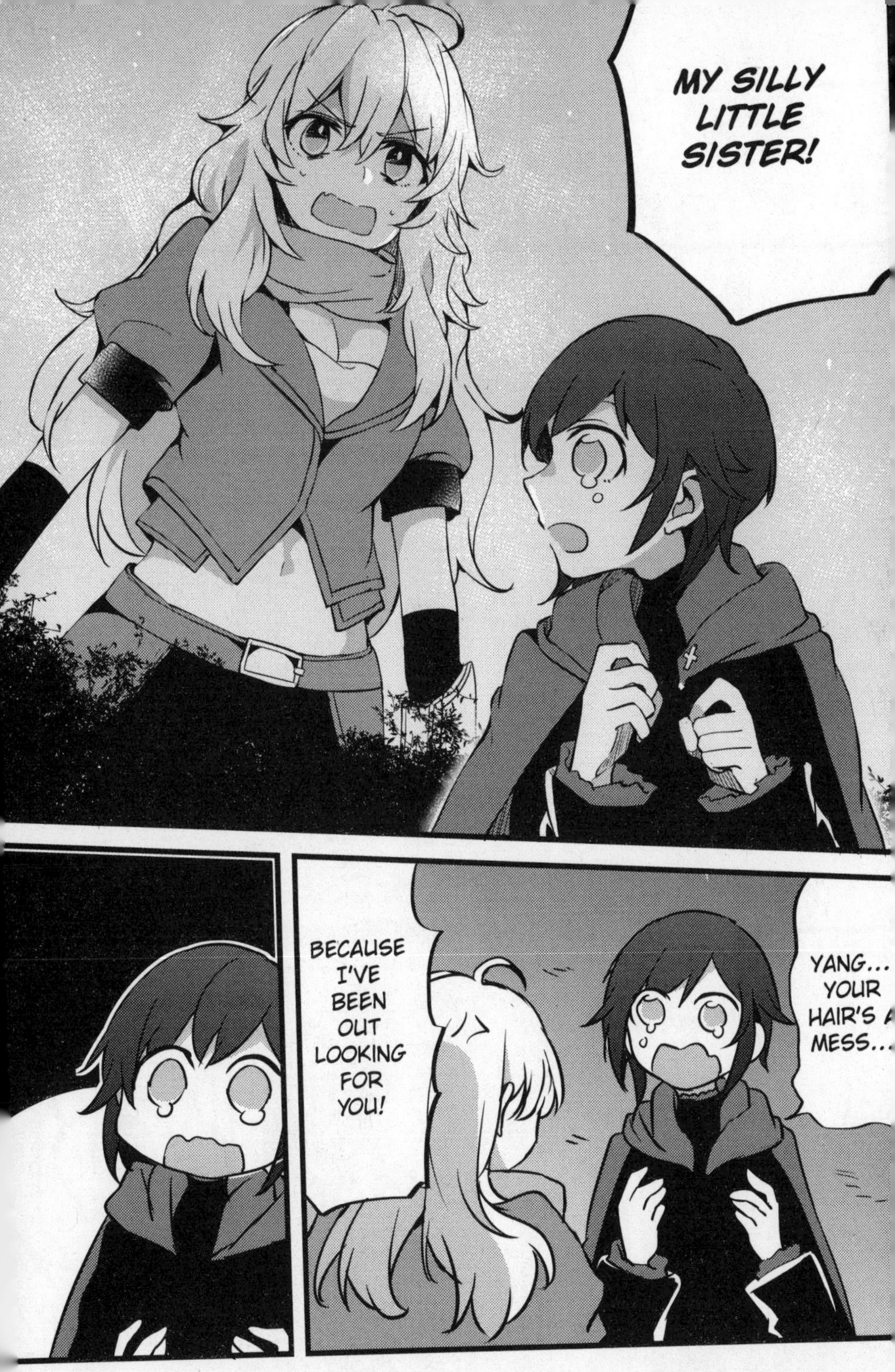
MY SILLY LITTLE SISTER!
YANG... YOUR HAIR'S A MESS...
BECAUSE I'VE BEEN OUT LOOKING FOR YOU!

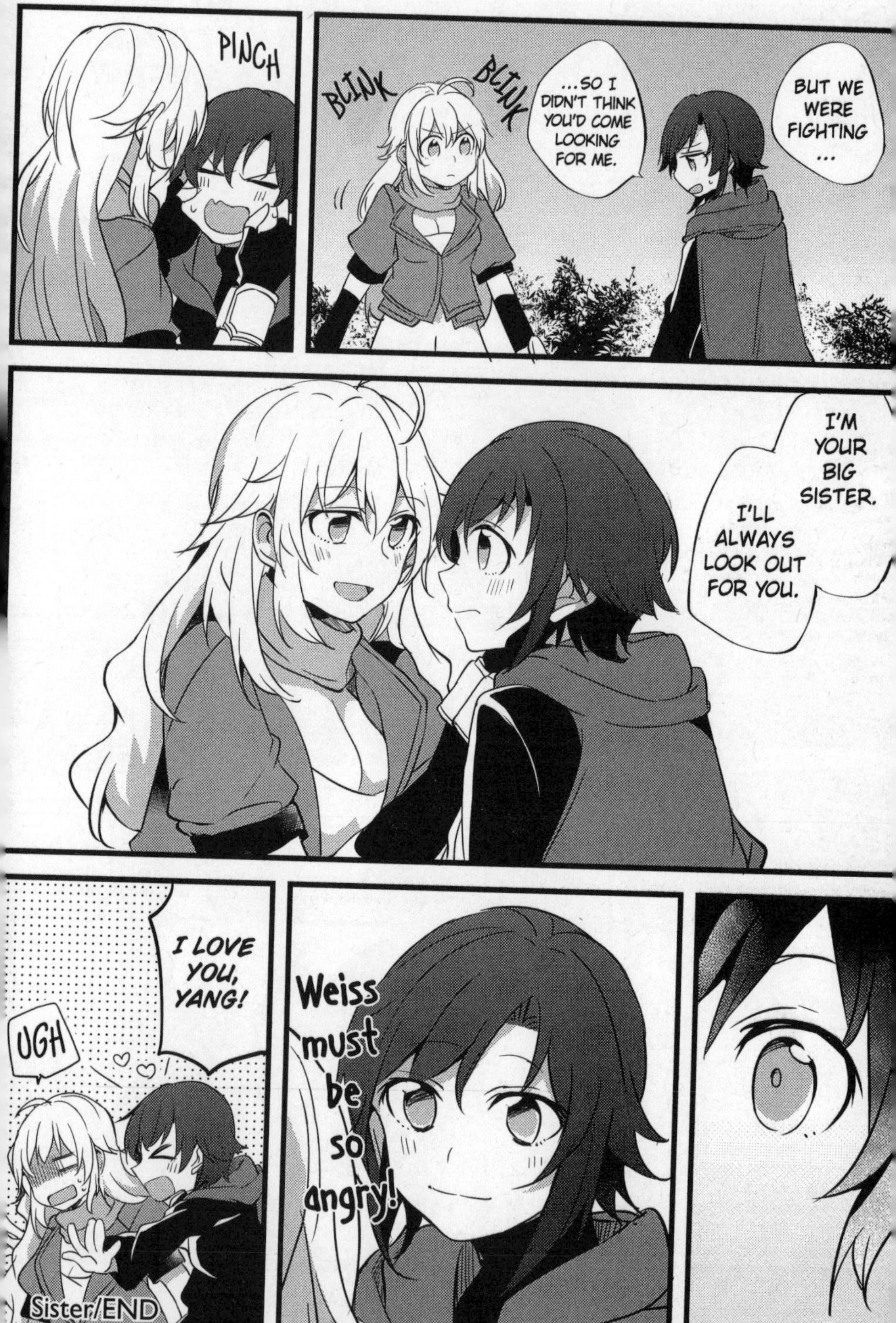
BUT WE WERE FIGHTING ...
...SO I DIDN'T THINK YOU'D COME LOOKING FOR ME.
BLINK
BLINK
PINCH
I'M YOUR BIG SISTER.
I'LL ALWAYS LOOK OUT FOR YOU.
Weiss must be so angry!
I LOVE YOU, YANG!
UGH
Sister/END

Semblance Challenge

Meteo

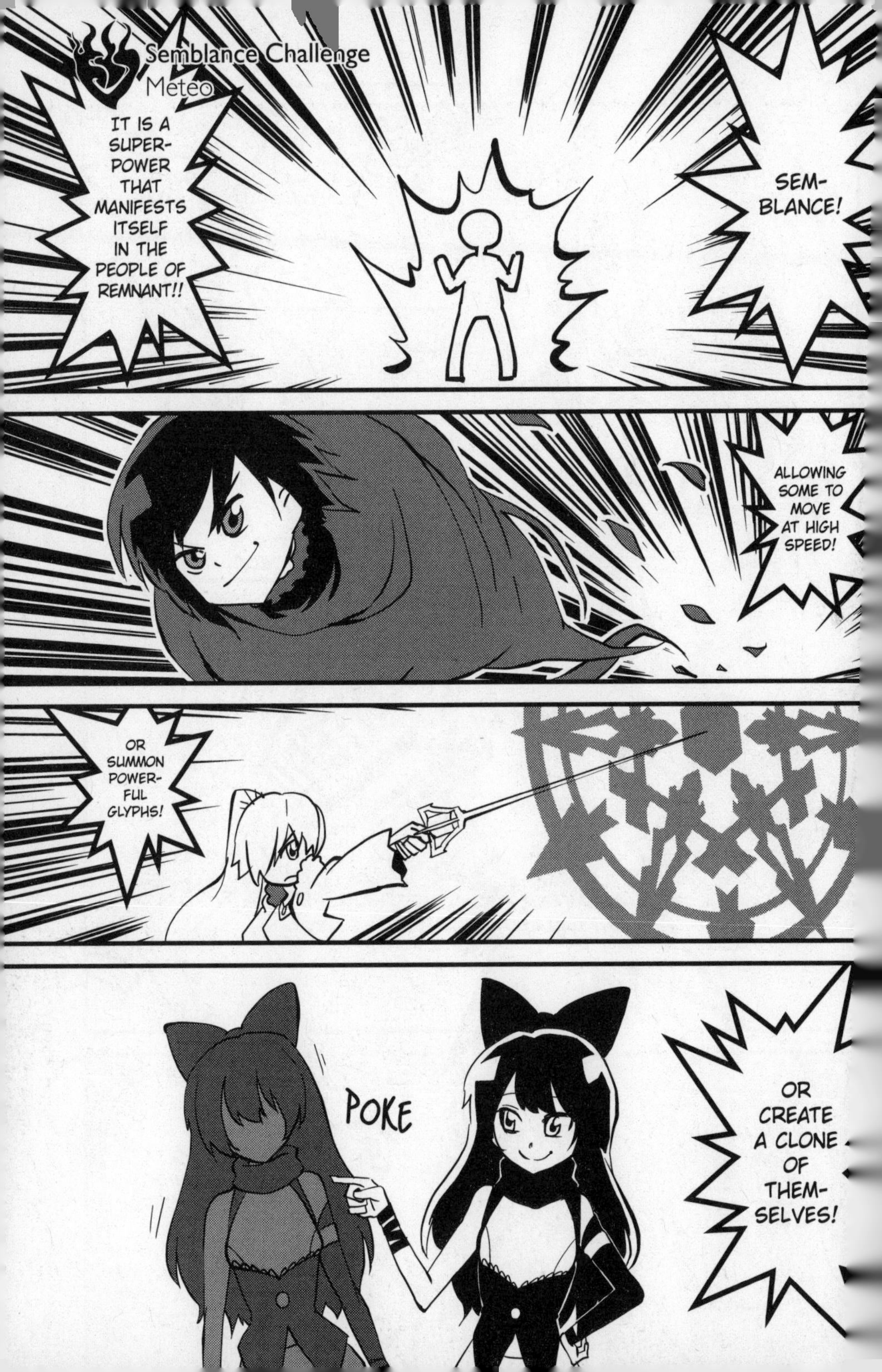

SEM-BLANCE!
IT IS A SUPER-POWER THAT MANIFESTS ITSELF IN THE PEOPLE OF REMNANT!!
ALLOWING SOME TO MOVE AT HIGH SPEED!
OR SUMMON POWER-FUL GLYPHS!
OR CREATE A CLONE OF THEM-SELVES!
POKE

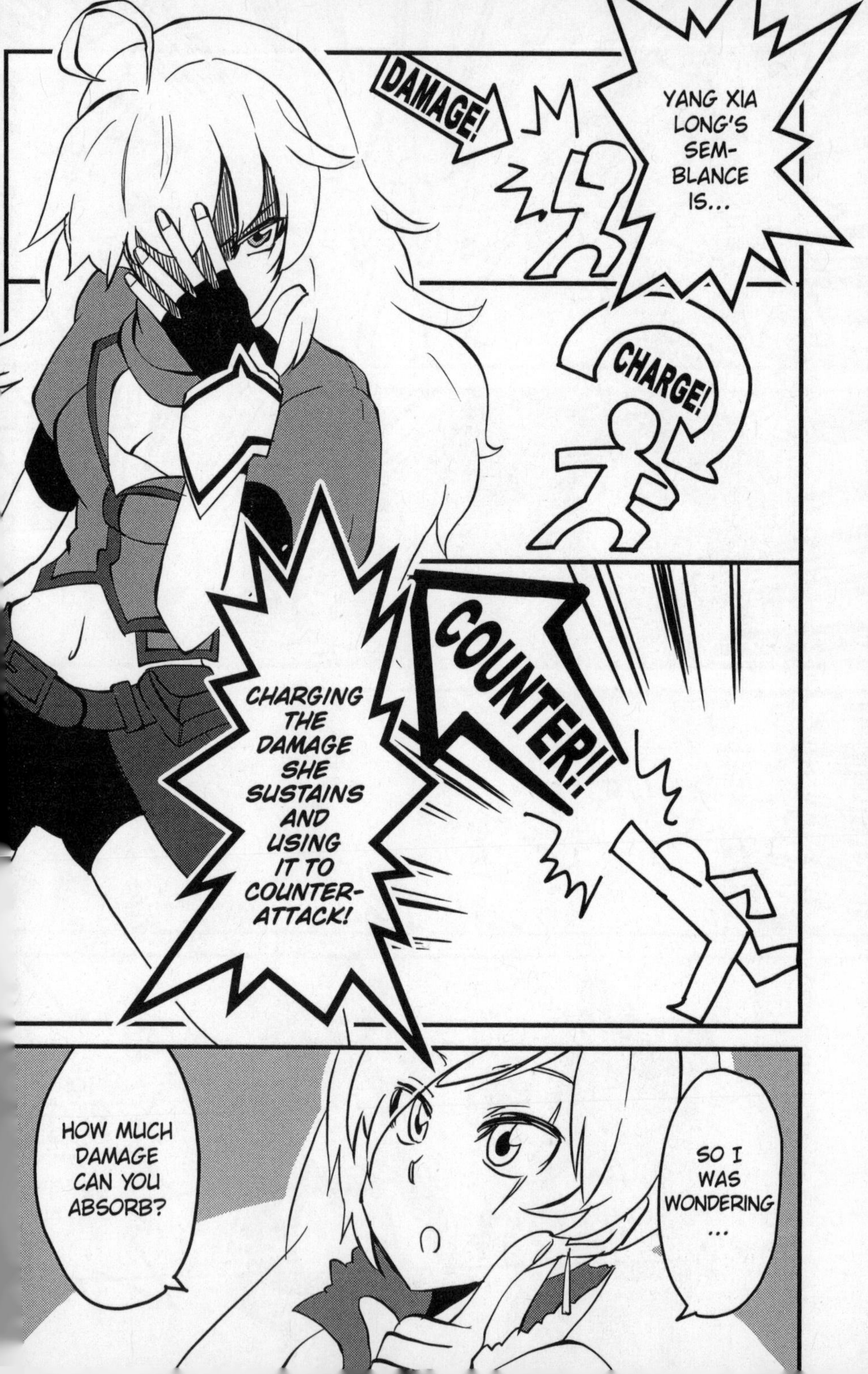
YANG XIA LONG'S SEMBLANCE IS...
DAMAGE!
CHARGE!
COUNTER!!
CHARGING THE DAMAGE SHE SUSTAINS AND USING IT TO COUNTER-ATTACK!
SO I WAS WONDERING...
HOW MUCH DAMAGE CAN YOU ABSORB?

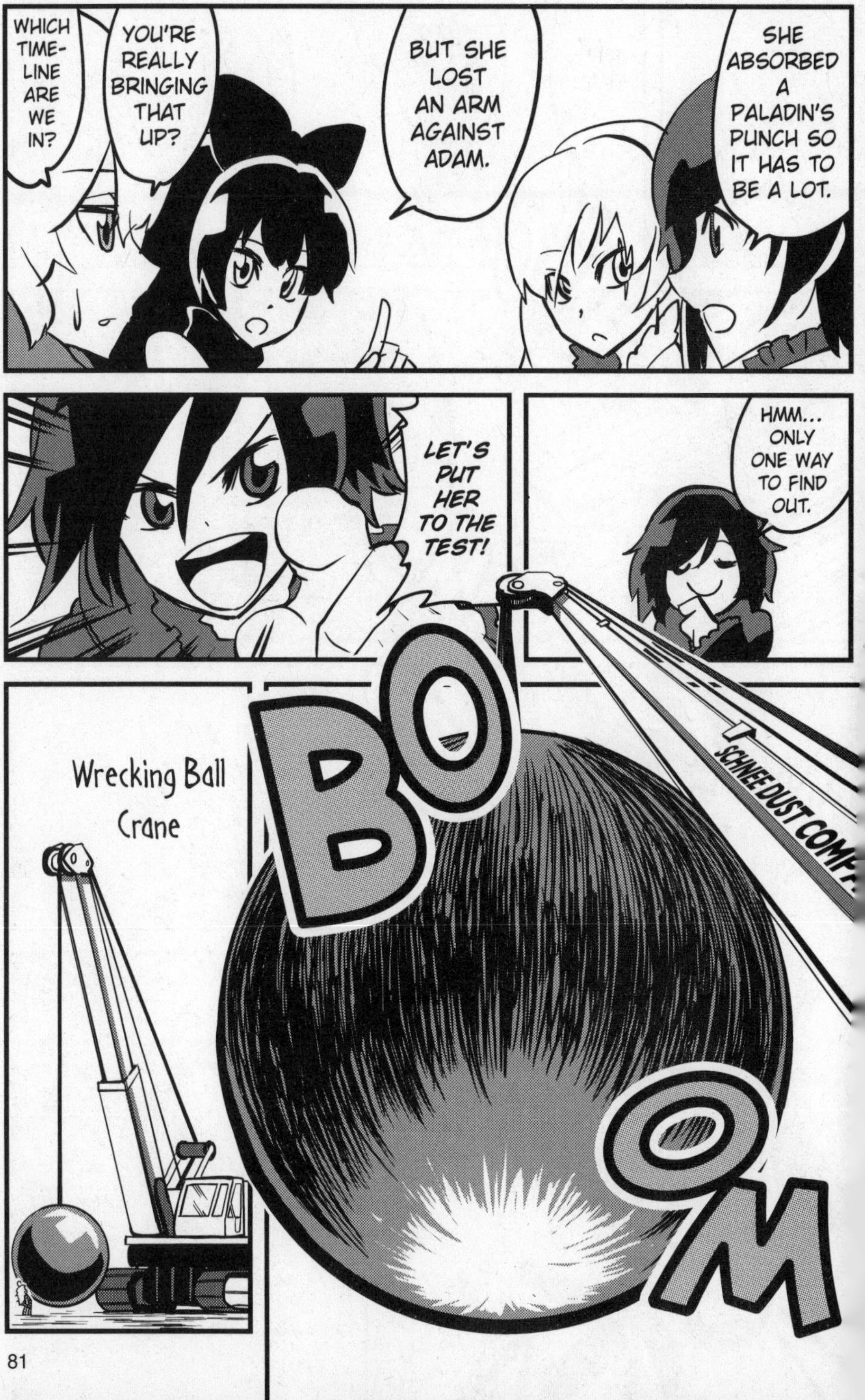
SHE ABSORBED A PALADIN'S PUNCH SO IT HAS TO BE A LOT.
BUT SHE LOST AN ARM AGAINST ADAM.
YOU'RE REALLY BRINGING THAT UP?
WHICH TIME-LINE ARE WE IN?
HMM... ONLY ONE WAY TO FIND OUT.
LET'S PUT HER TO THE TEST!
BOOM
SCHNEE DUST COMP
Wrecking Ball Crane

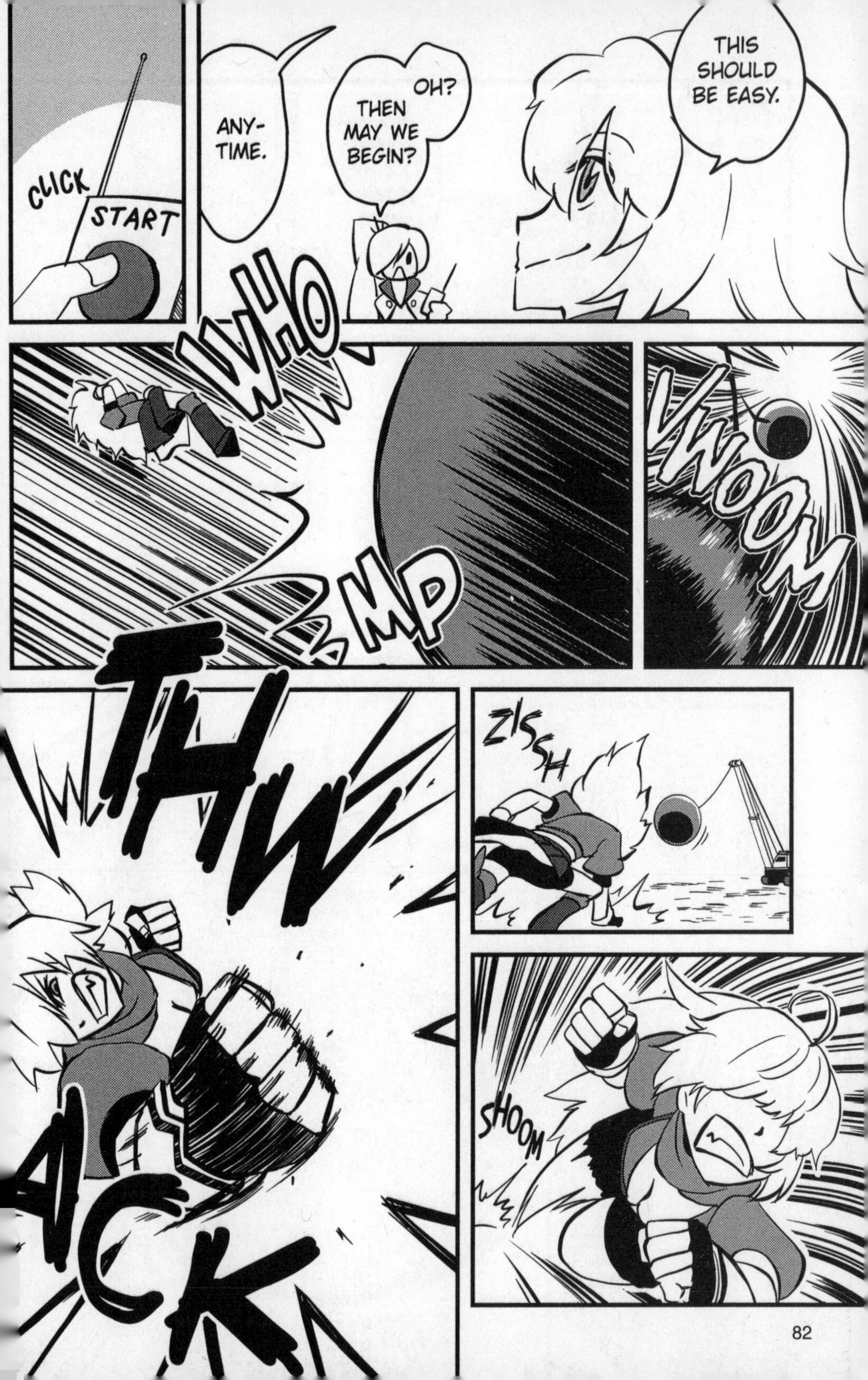
THIS SHOULD BE EASY.
OH? THEN MAY WE BEGIN?
ANY-TIME.
CLICK
START
WHO
MP
VWOOM
ZISSH
SHOOM
THWACK

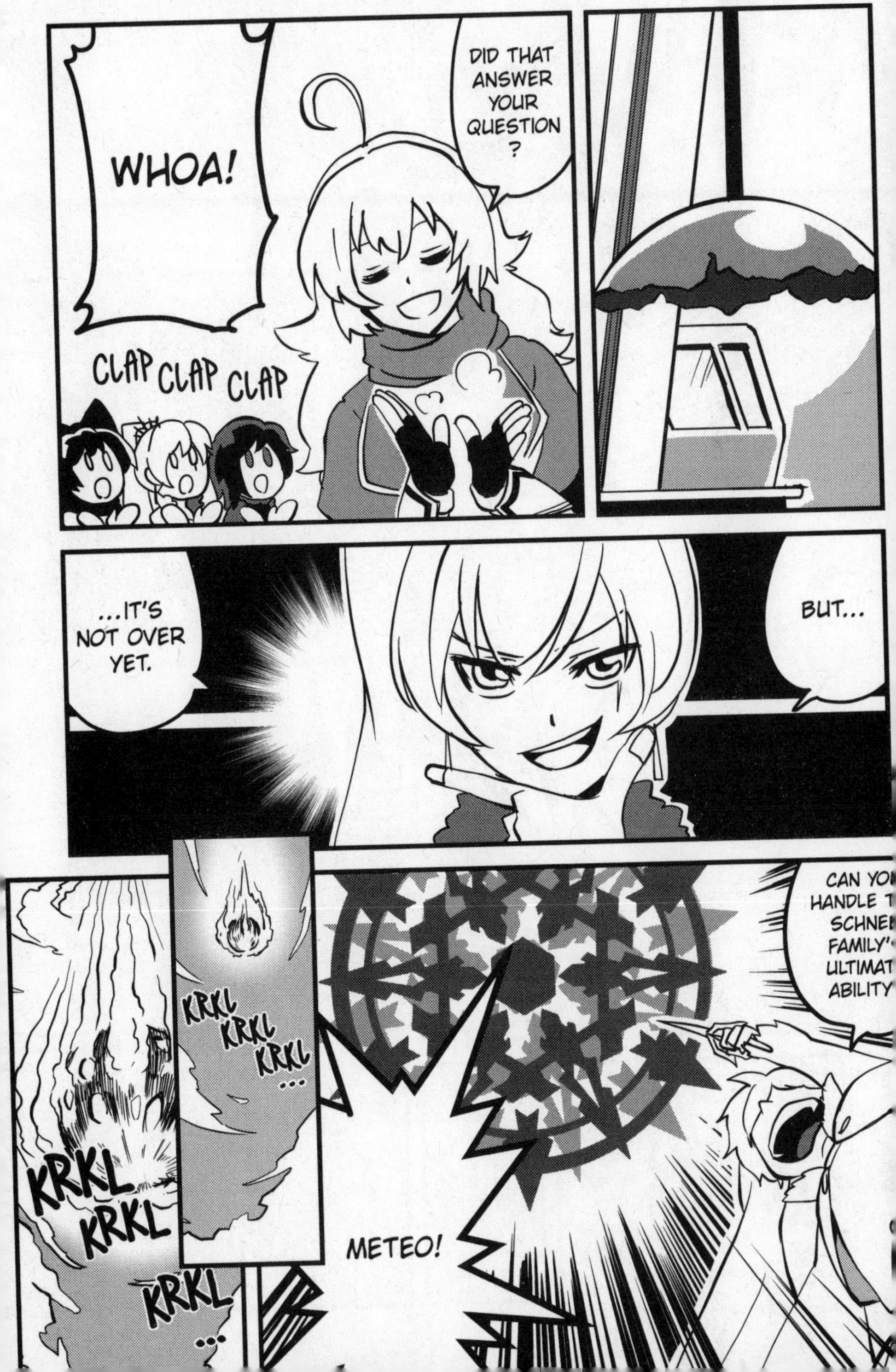
DID THAT ANSWER YOUR QUESTION ?
WHOA!
CLAP CLAP CLAP
BUT...
...IT'S NOT OVER YET.
CAN YO
HANDLE T
SCHNE
FAMILY'
ULTIMAT
ABILITY
METEO!
KRKL KRKL KRKL ...
KRKL KRKL KRKL ...

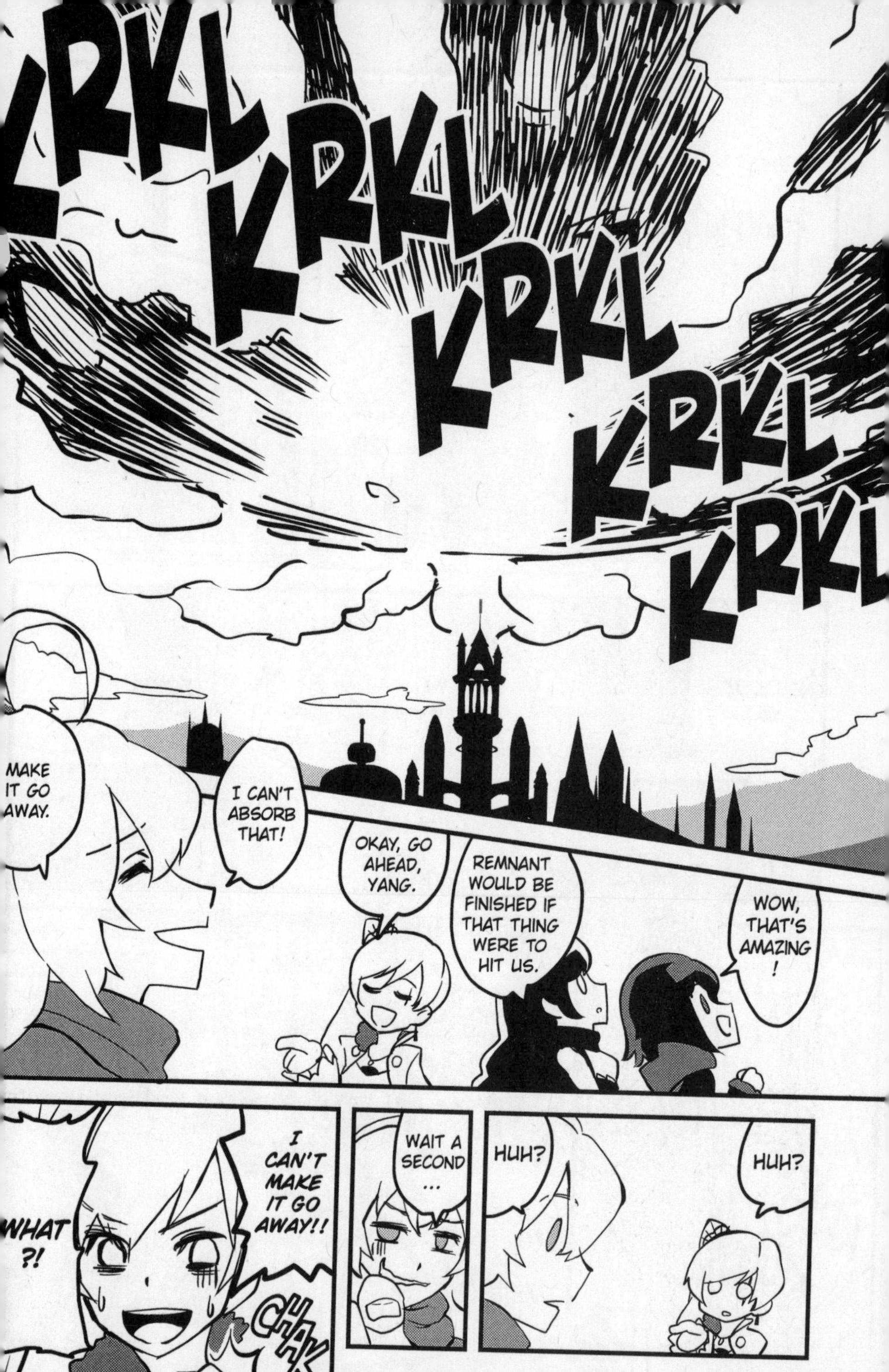
KRKL
KRKL
KRKL
KRKL
KRKL
WOW, THAT'S AMAZING!
REMNANT WOULD BE FINISHED IF THAT THING WERE TO HIT US.
OKAY, GO AHEAD, YANG.
I CAN'T ABSORB THAT!
MAKE IT GO AWAY.
HUH?
HUH?
WAIT A SECOND ...
I CAN'T MAKE IT GO AWAY!!
CHAK
WHAT?!

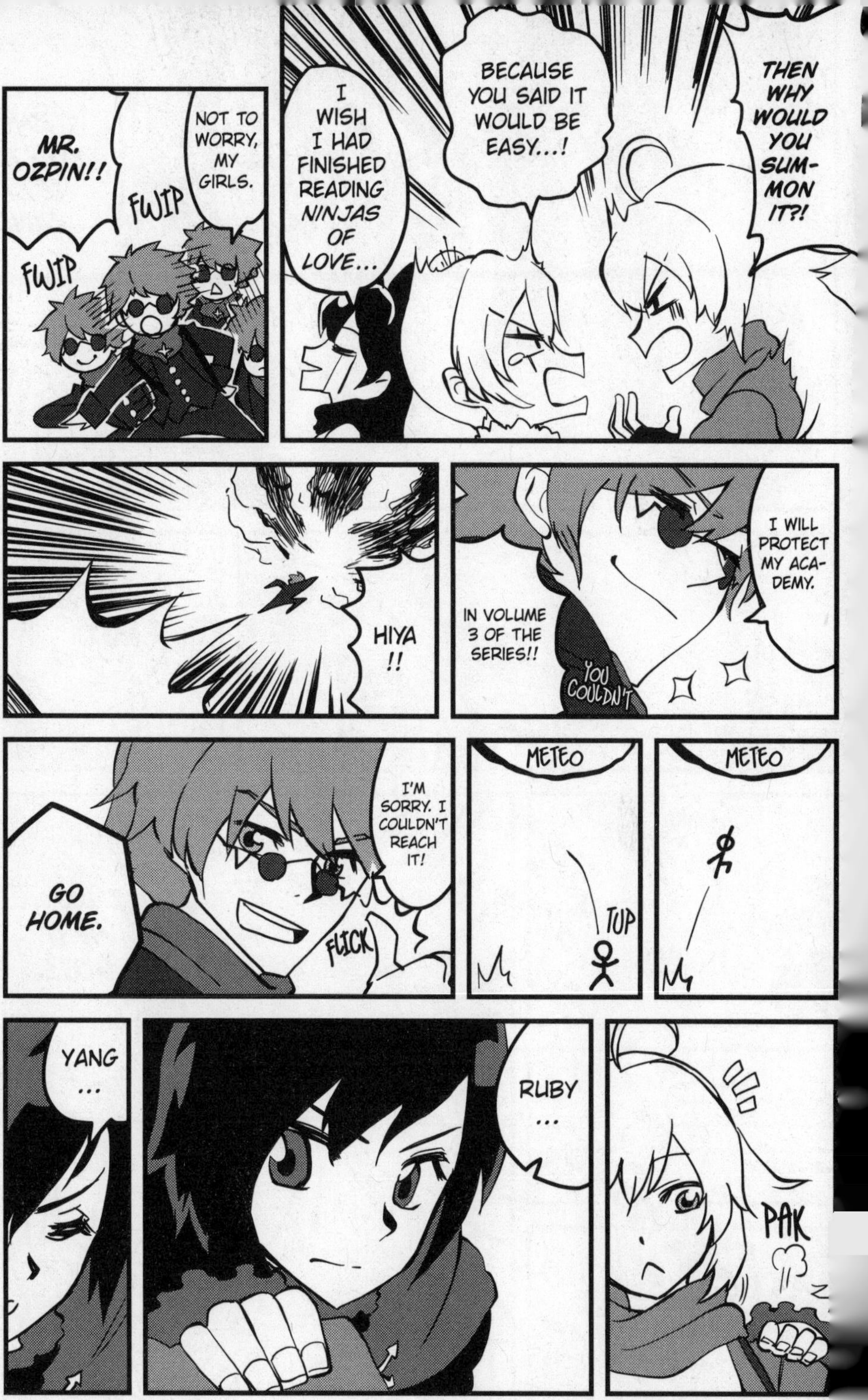
THEN WHY WOULD YOU SUMMON IT?!
BECAUSE YOU SAID IT WOULD BE EASY...!
I WISH I HAD FINISHED READING NINJAS OF LOVE...
NOT TO WORRY, MY GIRLS.
MR. OZPIN!!
FWIP
FWIP
I WILL PROTECT MY ACADEMY.
YOU COULDN'T
IN VOLUME 3 OF THE SERIES!!
HIYA!!
METEO
METEO
TUP
I'M SORRY. I COULDN'T REACH IT!
FLICK
GO HOME.
PAK
RUBY...
YANG...

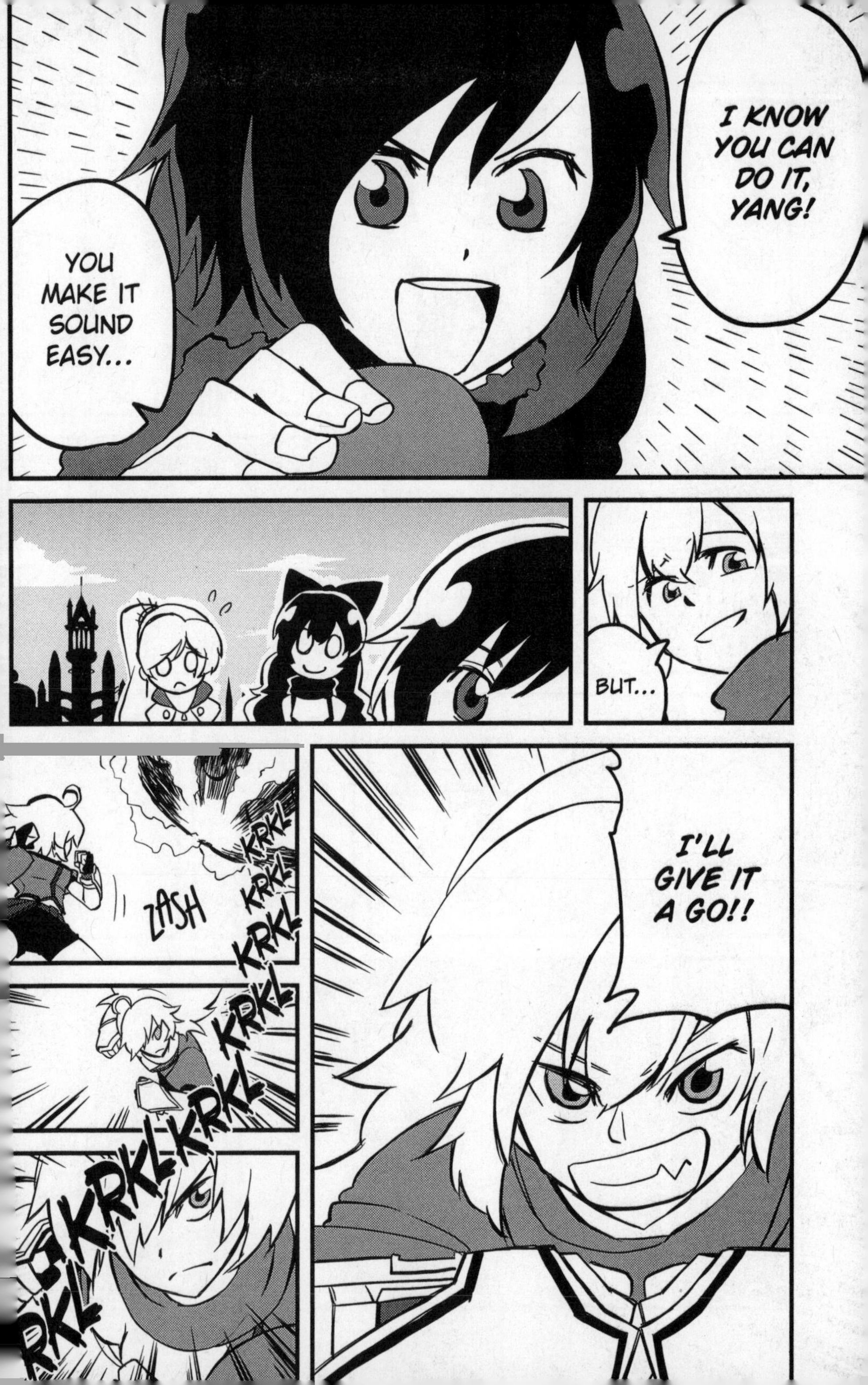
I KNOW YOU CAN DO IT, YANG!
YOU MAKE IT SOUND EASY...
BUT...
I'LL GIVE IT A GO!!
KRKL KRKL
ZASH
KRKL
KRKL
KRKL
KRKLKRKL
KRKLKRKL
KRKL

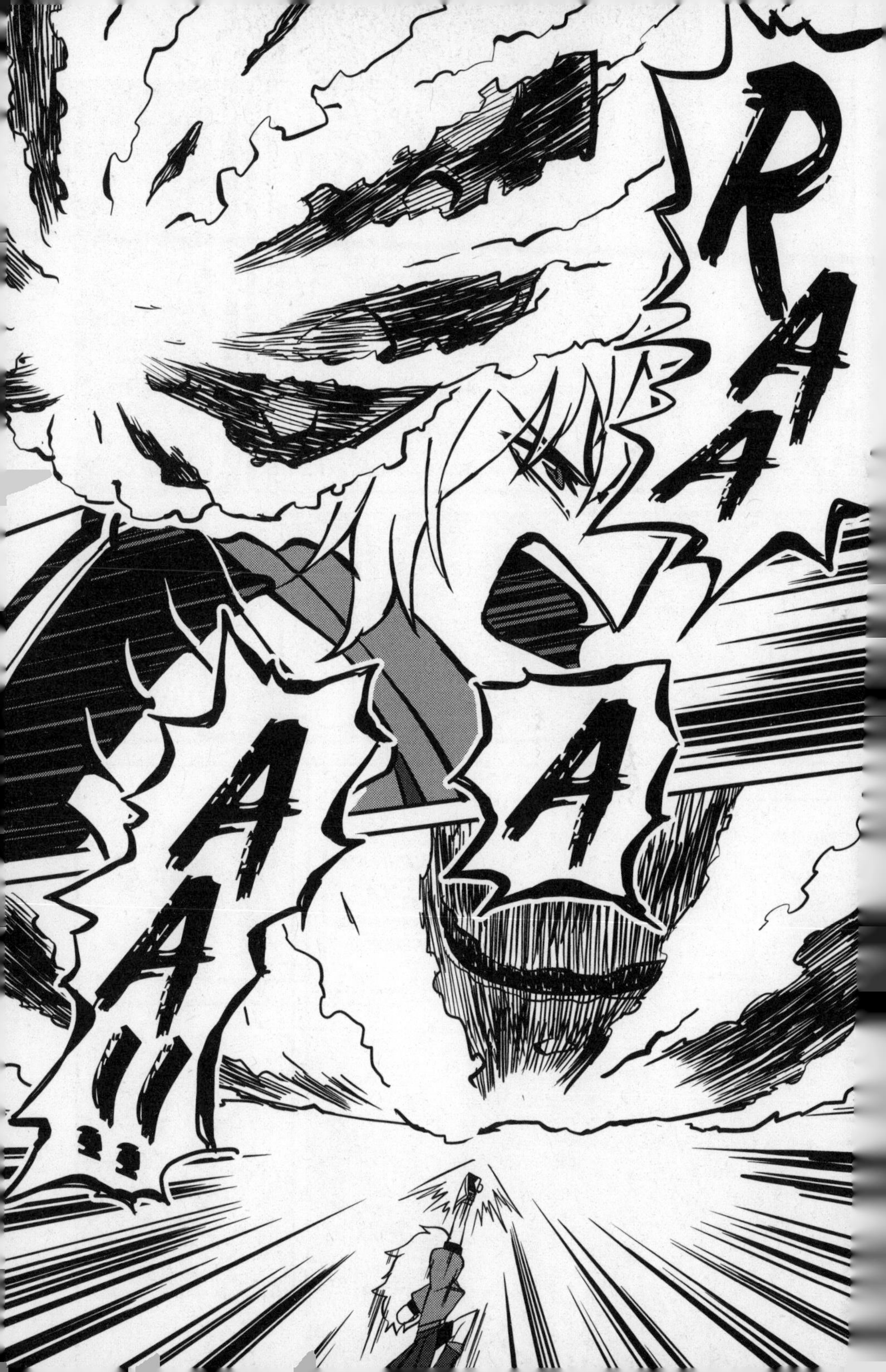
RAAAAA!!

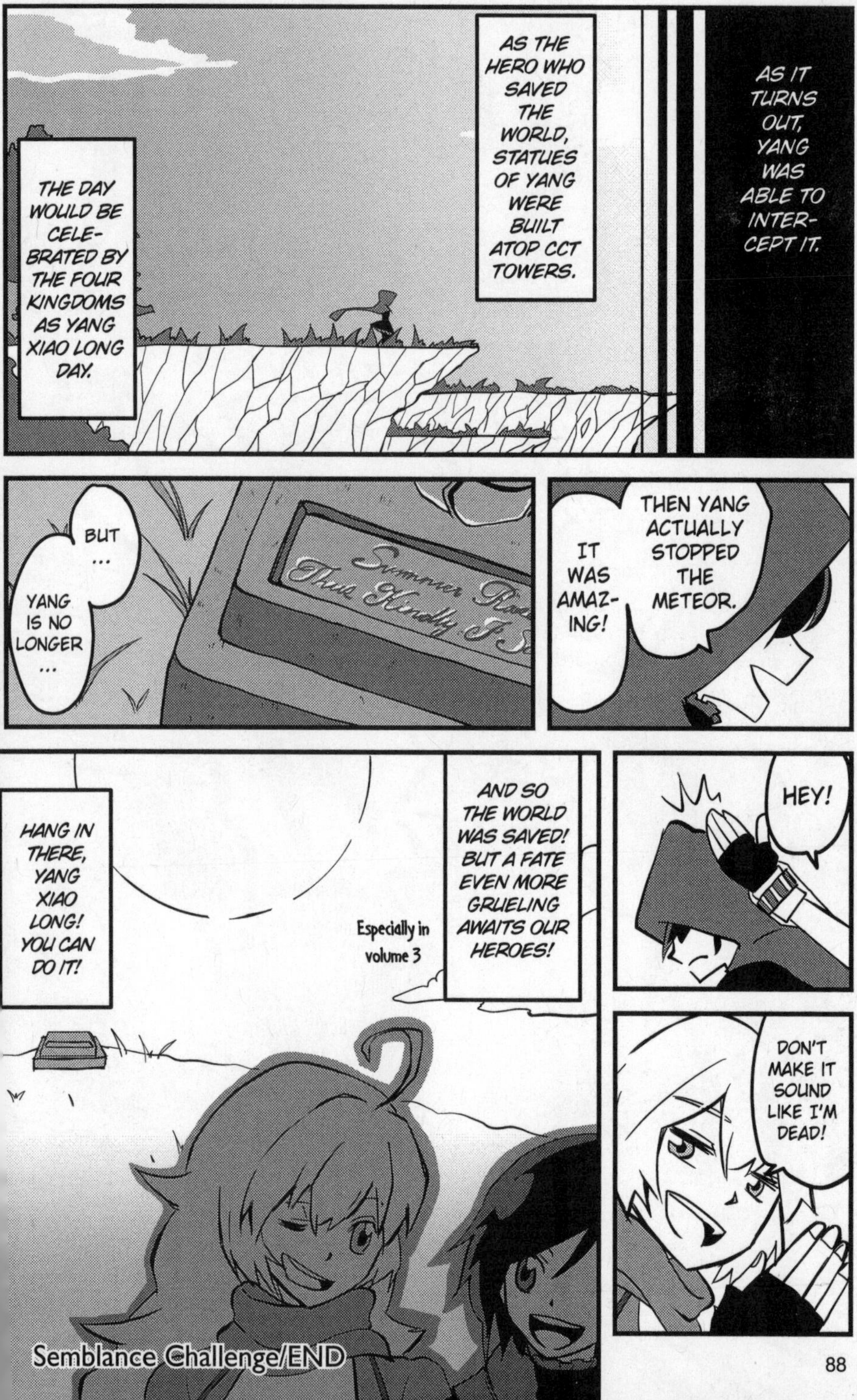

AS IT TURNS OUT, YANG WAS ABLE TO INTER-CEPT IT.
AS THE HERO WHO SAVED THE WORLD, STATUES OF YANG WERE BUILT ATOP CCT TOWERS.
THE DAY WOULD BE CELE-BRATED BY THE FOUR KINGDOMS AS YANG XIAO LONG DAY.
THEN YANG ACTUALLY STOPPED THE METEOR.
IT WAS AMAZ-ING!
BUT ...
YANG IS NO LONGER ...
HEY!
DON'T MAKE IT SOUND LIKE I'M DEAD!
AND SO THE WORLD WAS SAVED! BUT A FATE EVEN MORE GRUELING AWAITS OUR HEROES!
Especially in volume 3
HANG IN THERE, YANG XIAO LONG! YOU CAN DO IT!
Semblance Challenge/END

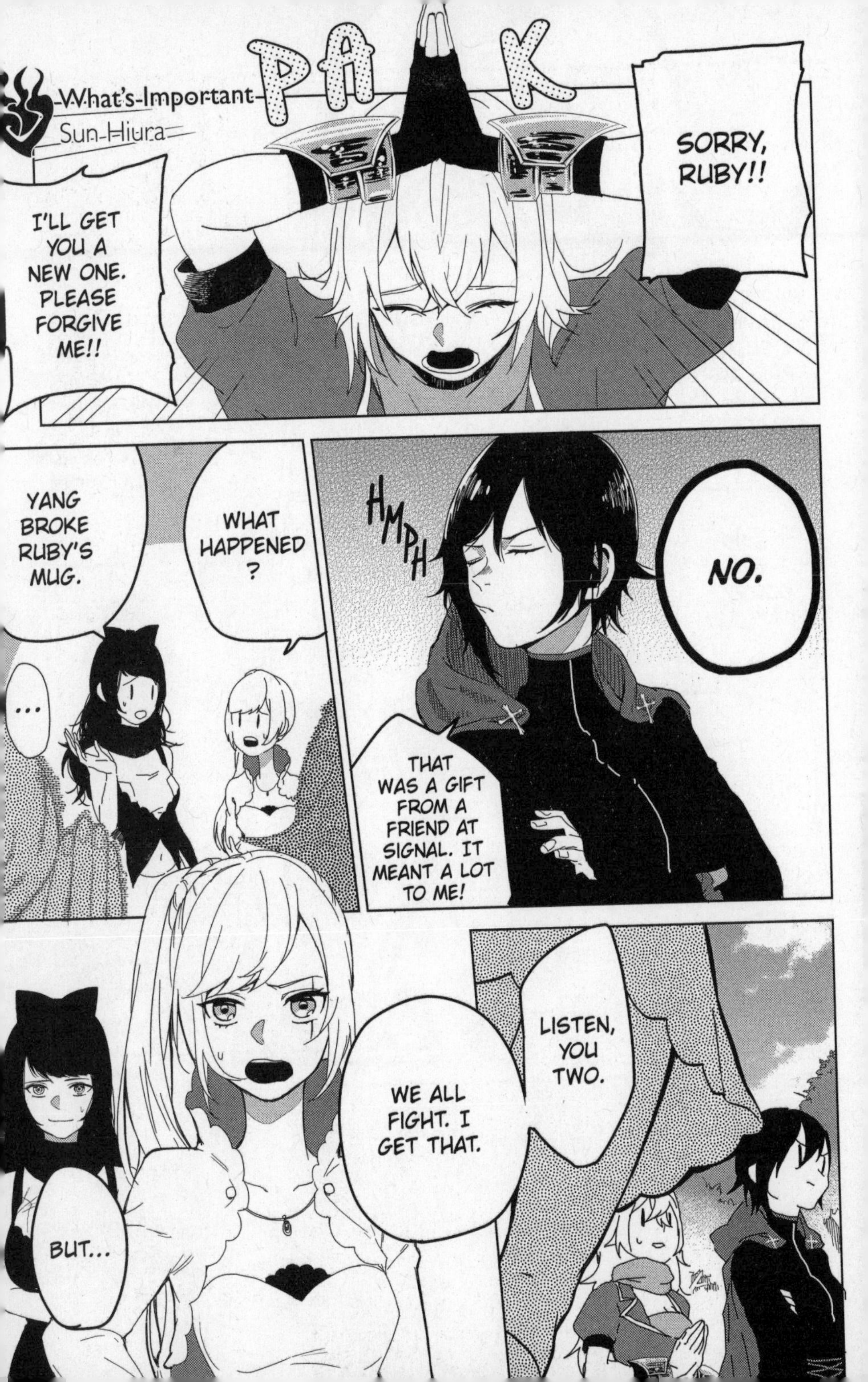
What's Important
Sun Hiura
PAK
SORRY, RUBY!!
I'LL GET YOU A NEW ONE. PLEASE FORGIVE ME!!
HMPH
NO.
THAT WAS A GIFT FROM A FRIEND AT SIGNAL. IT MEANT A LOT TO ME!
WHAT HAPPENED?
YANG BROKE RUBY'S MUG.
...
LISTEN, YOU TWO.
WE ALL FIGHT. I GET THAT.
BUT...

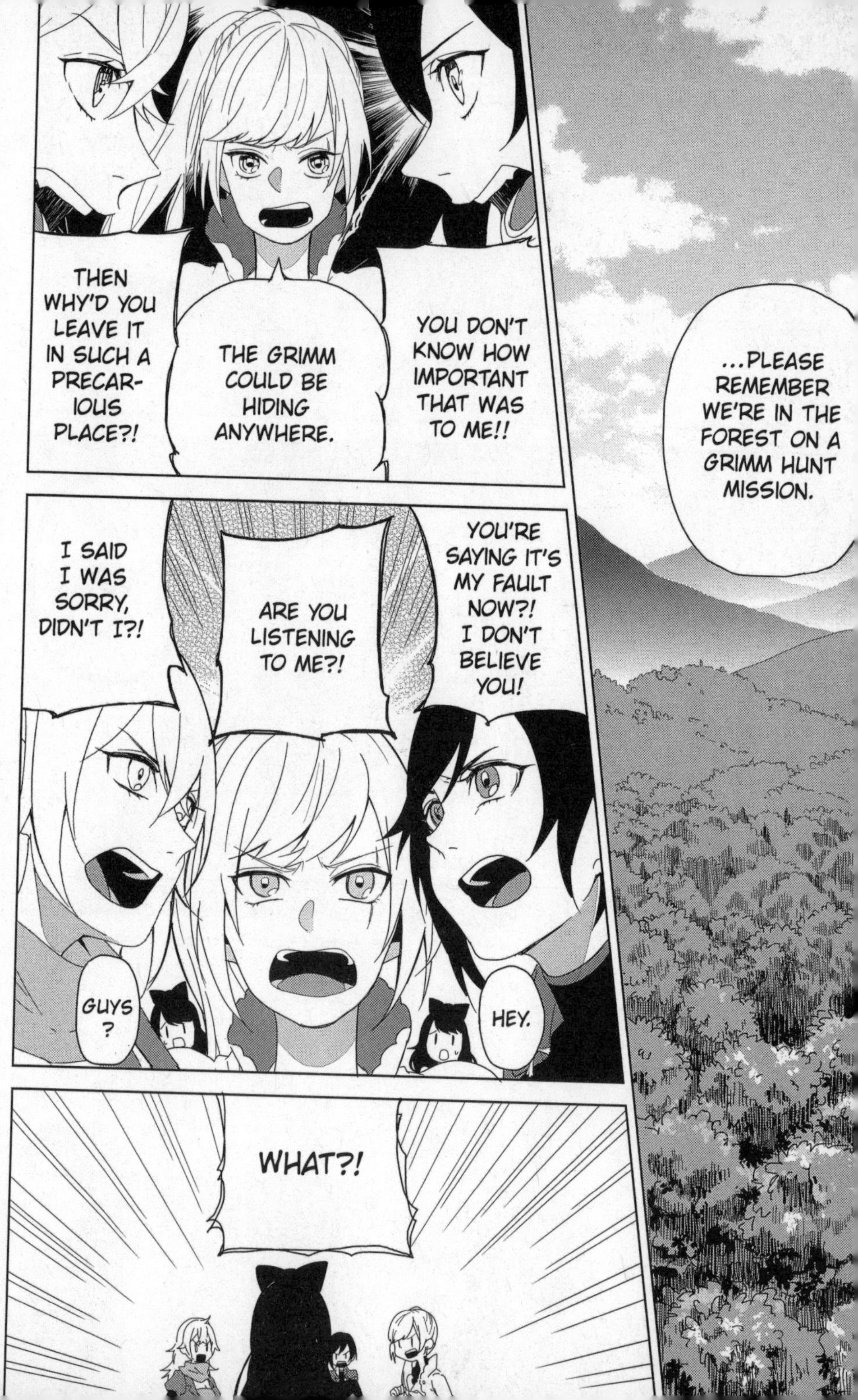
...PLEASE REMEMBER WE'RE IN THE FOREST ON A GRIMM HUNT MISSION.
YOU DON'T KNOW HOW IMPORTANT THAT WAS TO ME!!
THE GRIMM COULD BE HIDING ANYWHERE.
THEN WHY'D YOU LEAVE IT IN SUCH A PRECAR-IOUS PLACE?!
YOU'RE SAYING IT'S MY FAULT NOW?! I DON'T BELIEVE YOU!
ARE YOU LISTENING TO ME?!
I SAID I WAS SORRY, DIDN'T I?!
HEY.
GUYS?
WHAT?!

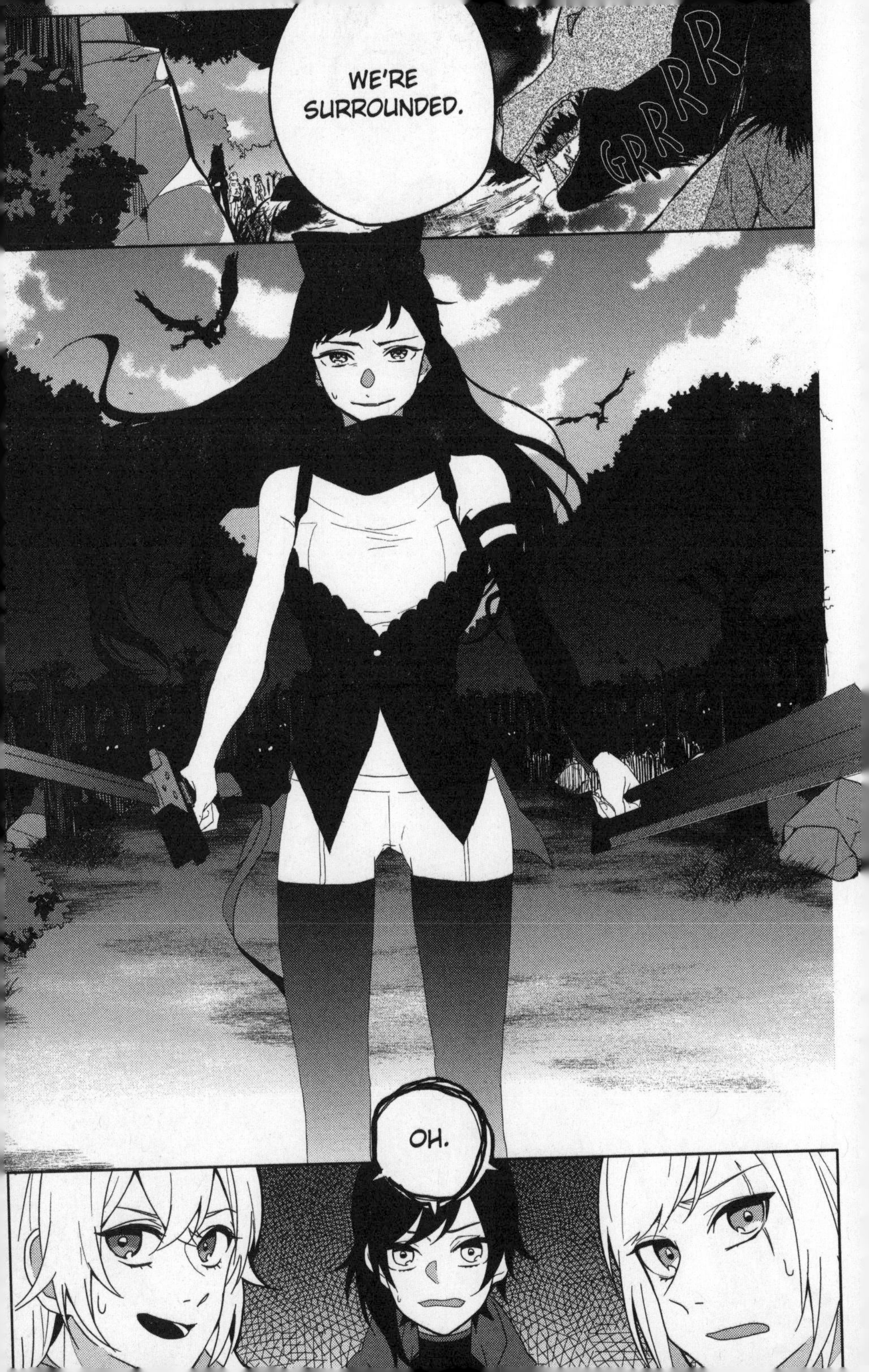
GRRRR
WE'RE SURROUNDED.
OH.

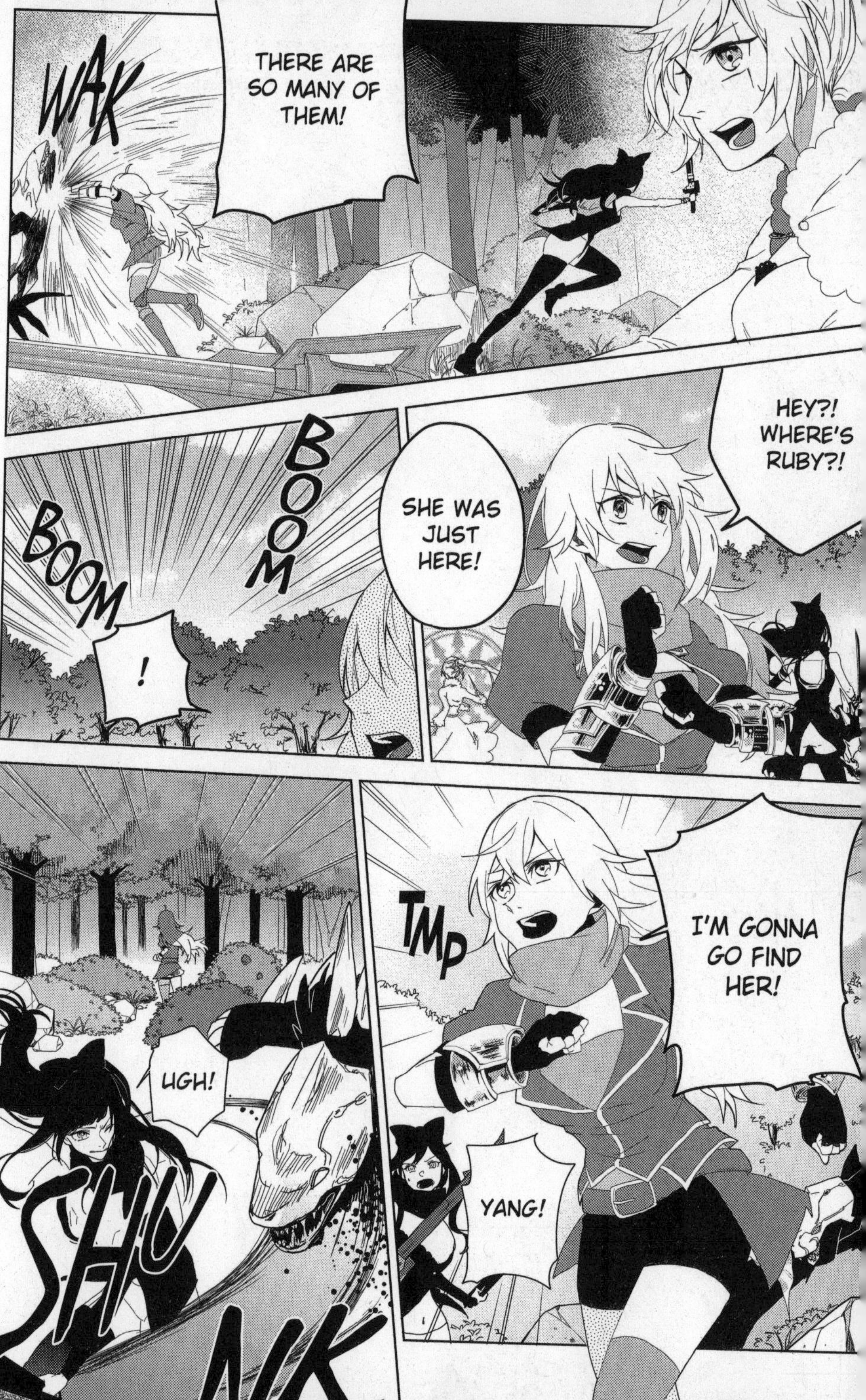
THERE ARE SO MANY OF THEM!
WAK
HEY?! WHERE'S RUBY?!
SHE WAS JUST HERE!
BOOM
BOOM
!
I'M GONNA GO FIND HER!
TMP
YANG!
UGH!
SHUNK

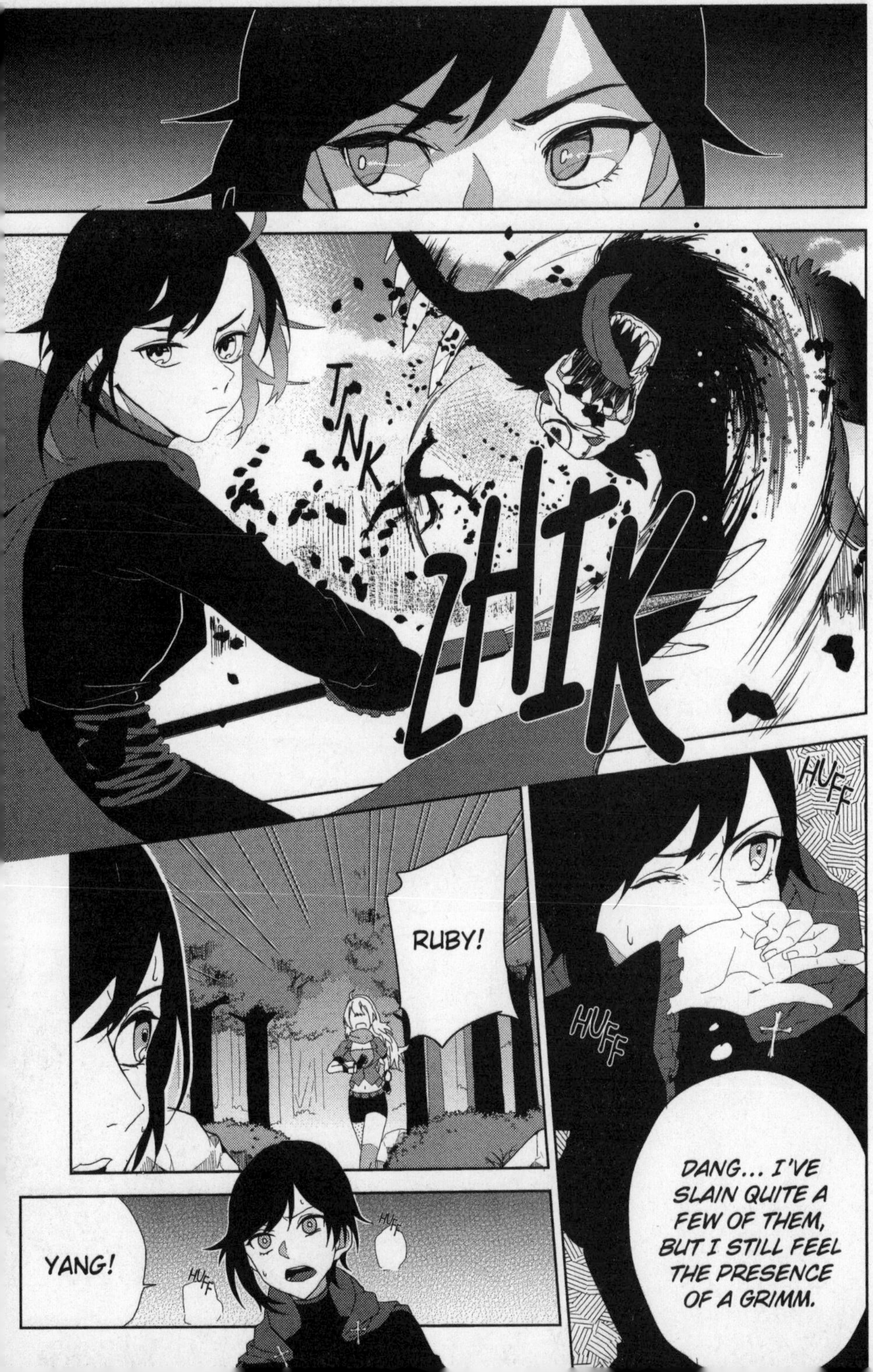
TINK
ZHIK
HUFF
HUFF
DANG... I'VE SLAIN QUITE A FEW OF THEM, BUT I STILL FEEL THE PRESENCE OF A GRIMM.
RUBY!
HUFF
HUFF
YANG!

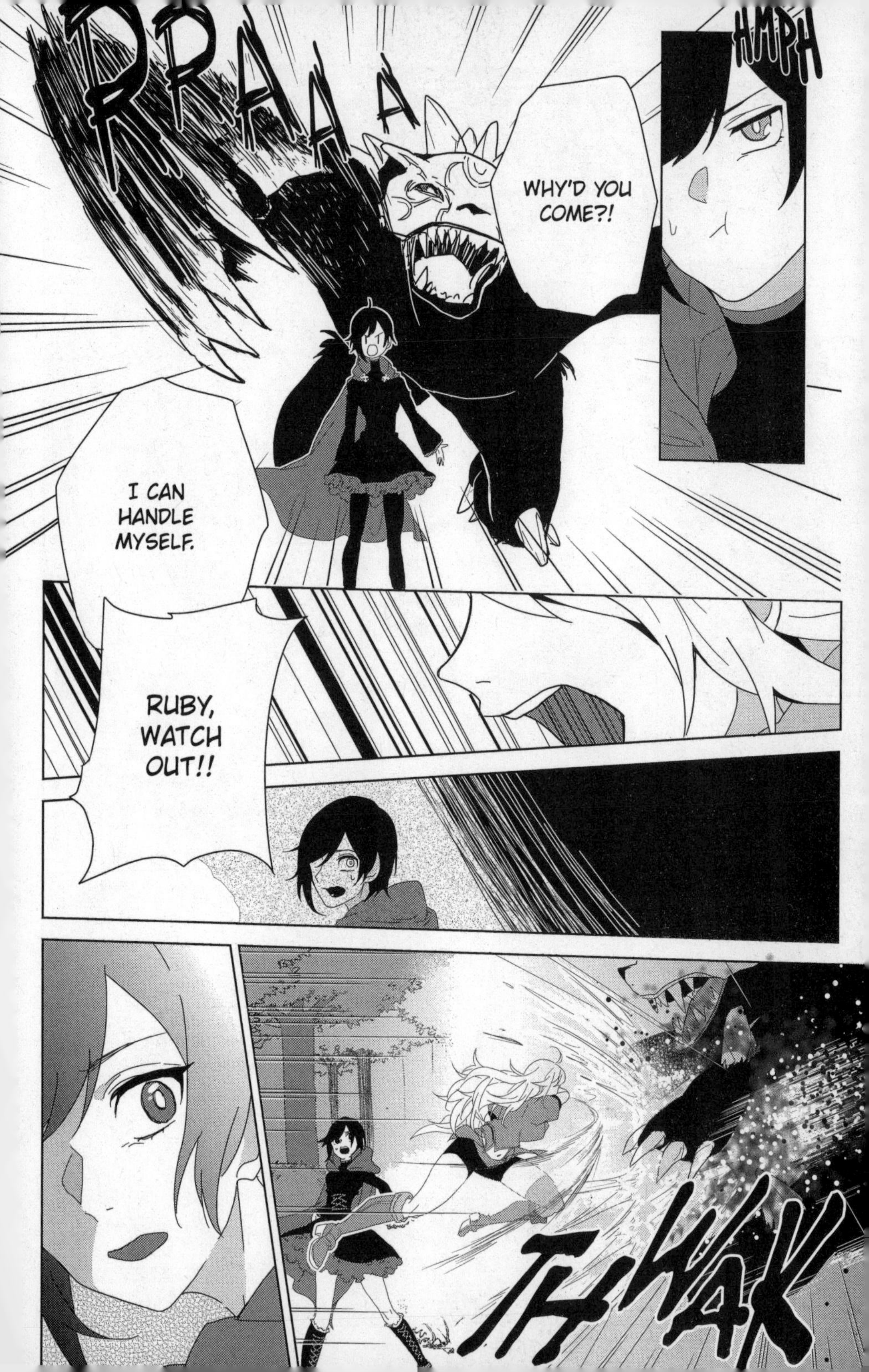
HMPH
WHY'D YOU COME?!
RRAAAA
I CAN HANDLE MYSELF.
RUBY, WATCH OUT!!
THWAK

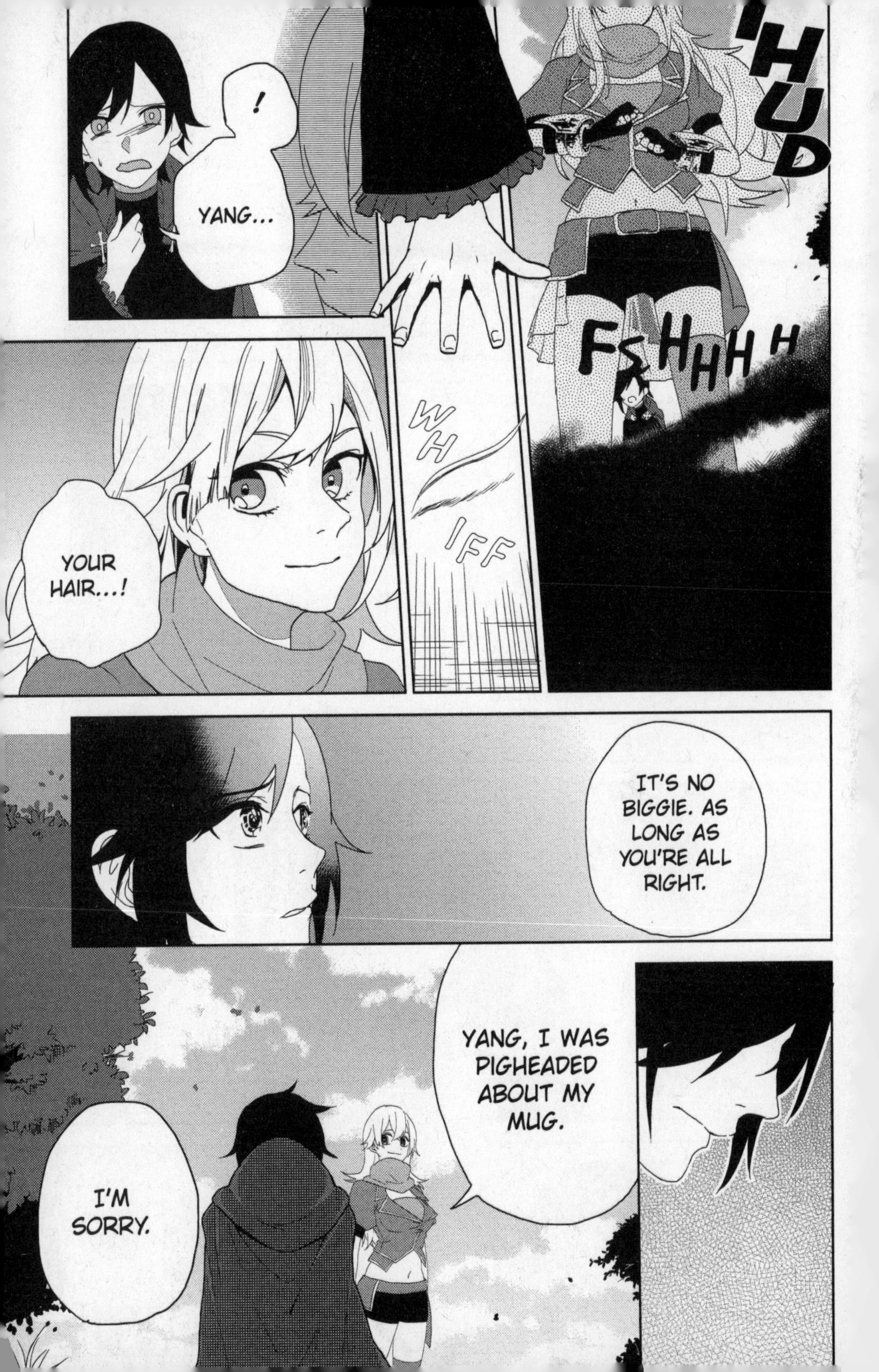
THUD
FSHHHHH
WHIFF
!
YANG...
YOUR HAIR...!
IT'S NO BIGGIE. AS LONG AS YOU'RE ALL RIGHT.
YANG, I WAS PIGHEADED ABOUT MY MUG.
I'M SORRY.

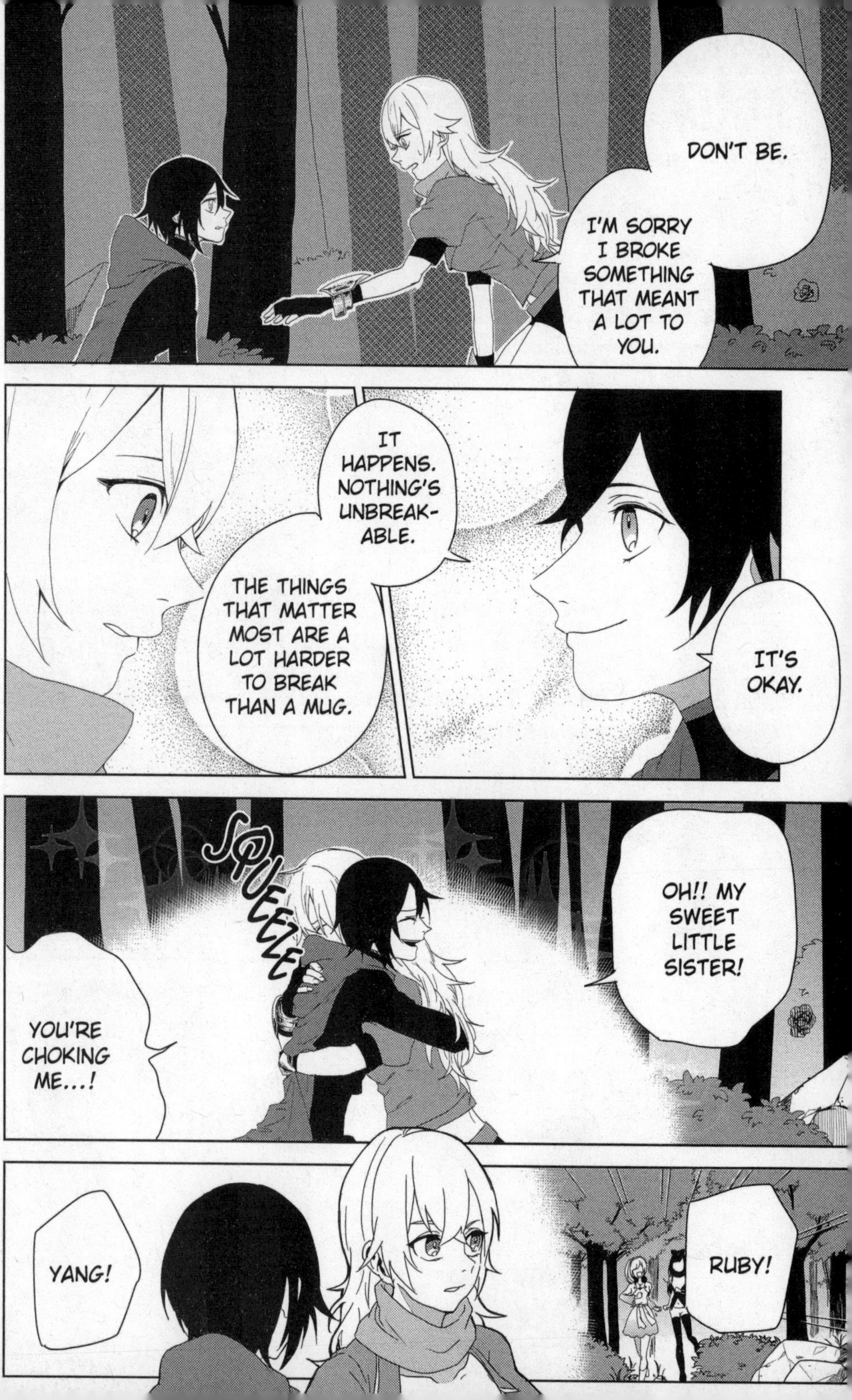
DON'T BE.
I'M SORRY I BROKE SOMETHING THAT MEANT A LOT TO YOU.
IT'S OKAY.
IT HAPPENS. NOTHING'S UNBREAK-ABLE.
THE THINGS THAT MATTER MOST ARE A LOT HARDER TO BREAK THAN A MUG.
OH!! MY SWEET LITTLE SISTER!
SQUEEZE
YOU'RE CHOKING ME...!
RUBY!
YANG!

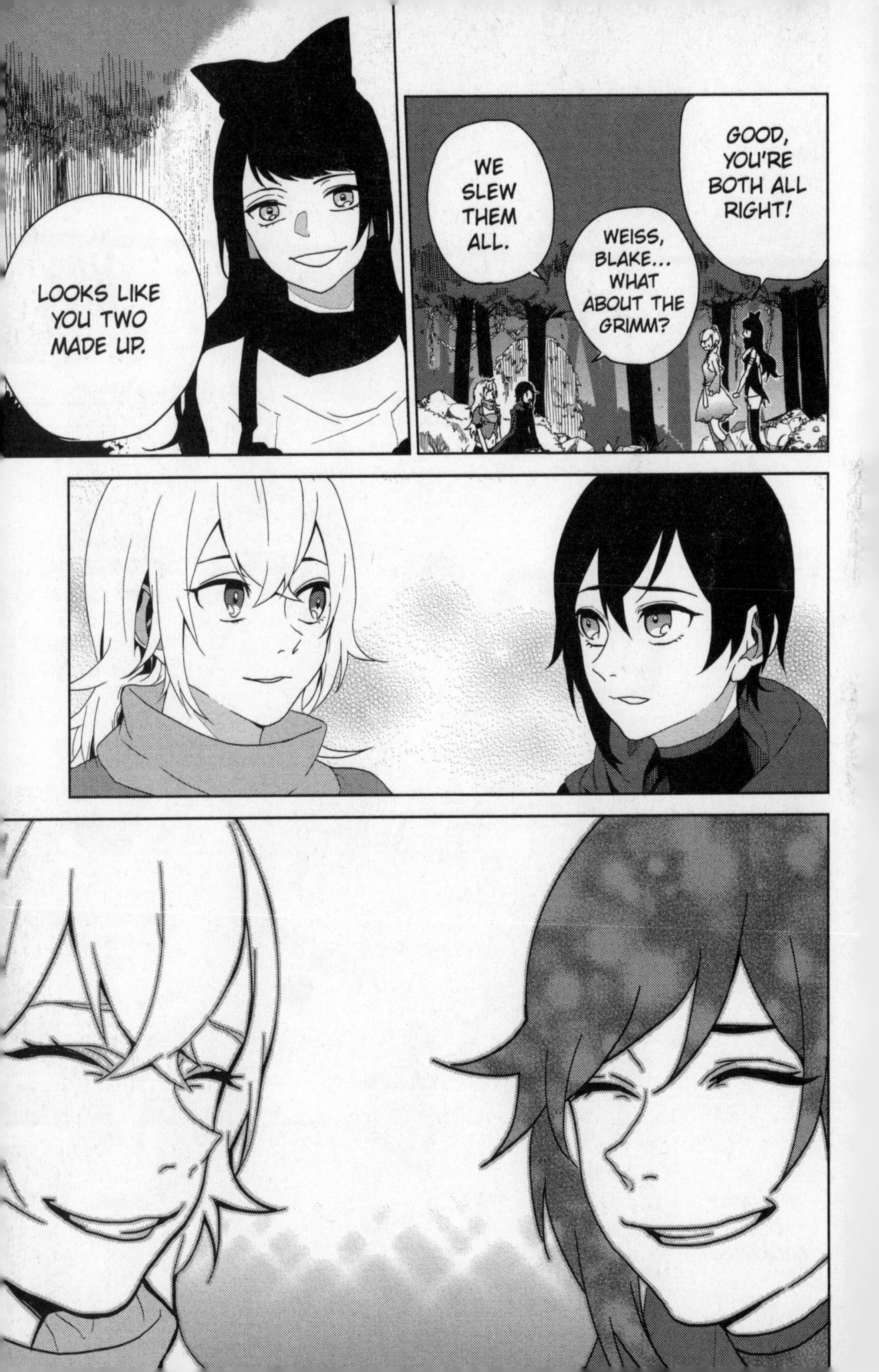
GOOD, YOU'RE BOTH ALL RIGHT!
WEISS, BLAKE... WHAT ABOUT THE GRIMM?
WE SLEW THEM ALL.
LOOKS LIKE YOU TWO MADE UP.

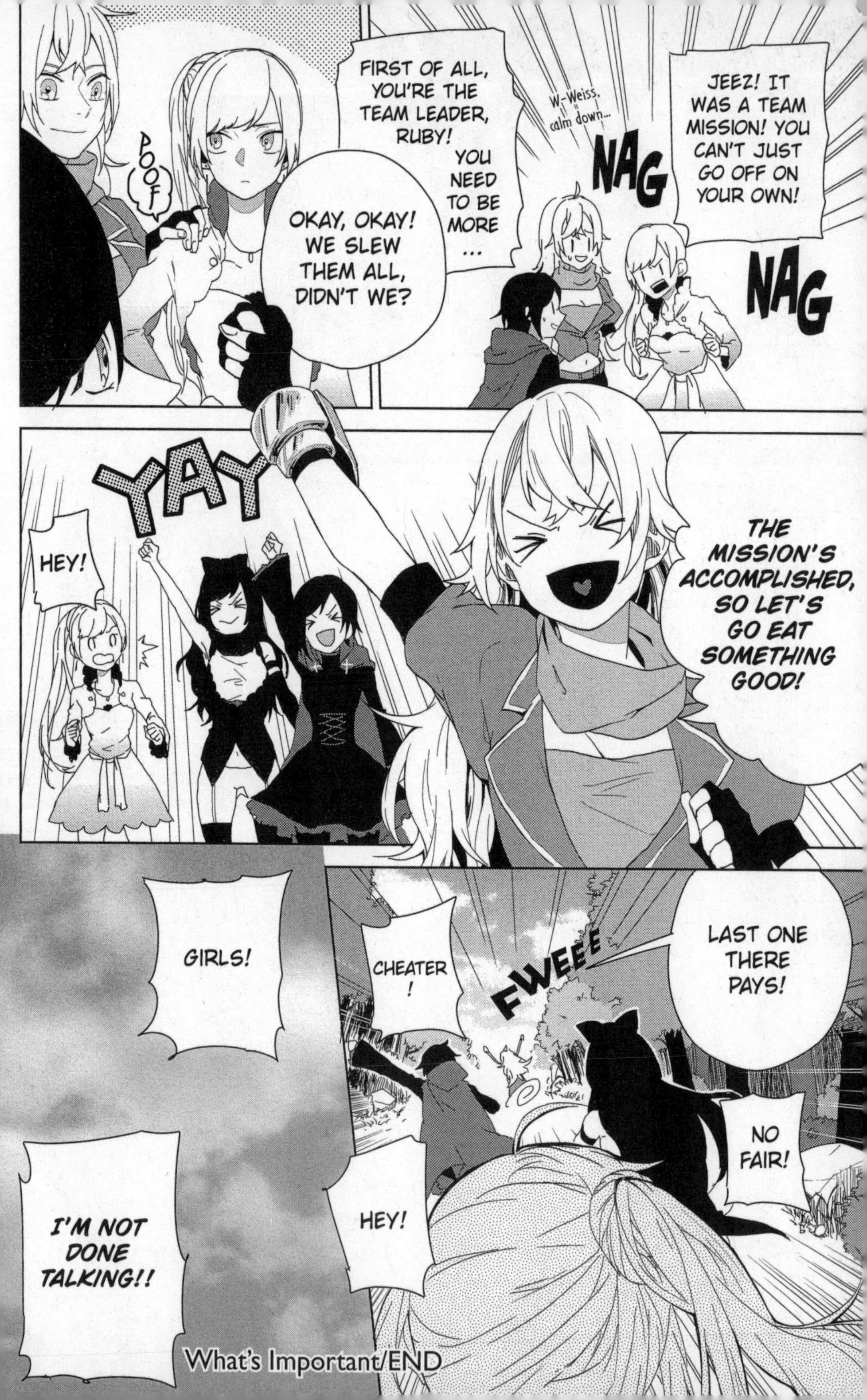
JEEZ! IT WAS A TEAM MISSION! YOU CAN'T JUST GO OFF ON YOUR OWN!
NAG
NAG
W-Weiss, calm down...
FIRST OF ALL, YOU'RE THE TEAM LEADER, RUBY!
YOU NEED TO BE MORE ...
POOF
OKAY, OKAY! WE SLEW THEM ALL, DIDN'T WE?
THE MISSION'S ACCOMPLISHED, SO LET'S GO EAT SOMETHING GOOD!
YAY
HEY!
LAST ONE THERE PAYS!
FWEEE
CHEATER!
NO FAIR!
HEY!
GIRLS!
I'M NOT DONE TALKING!!

What's Important/END

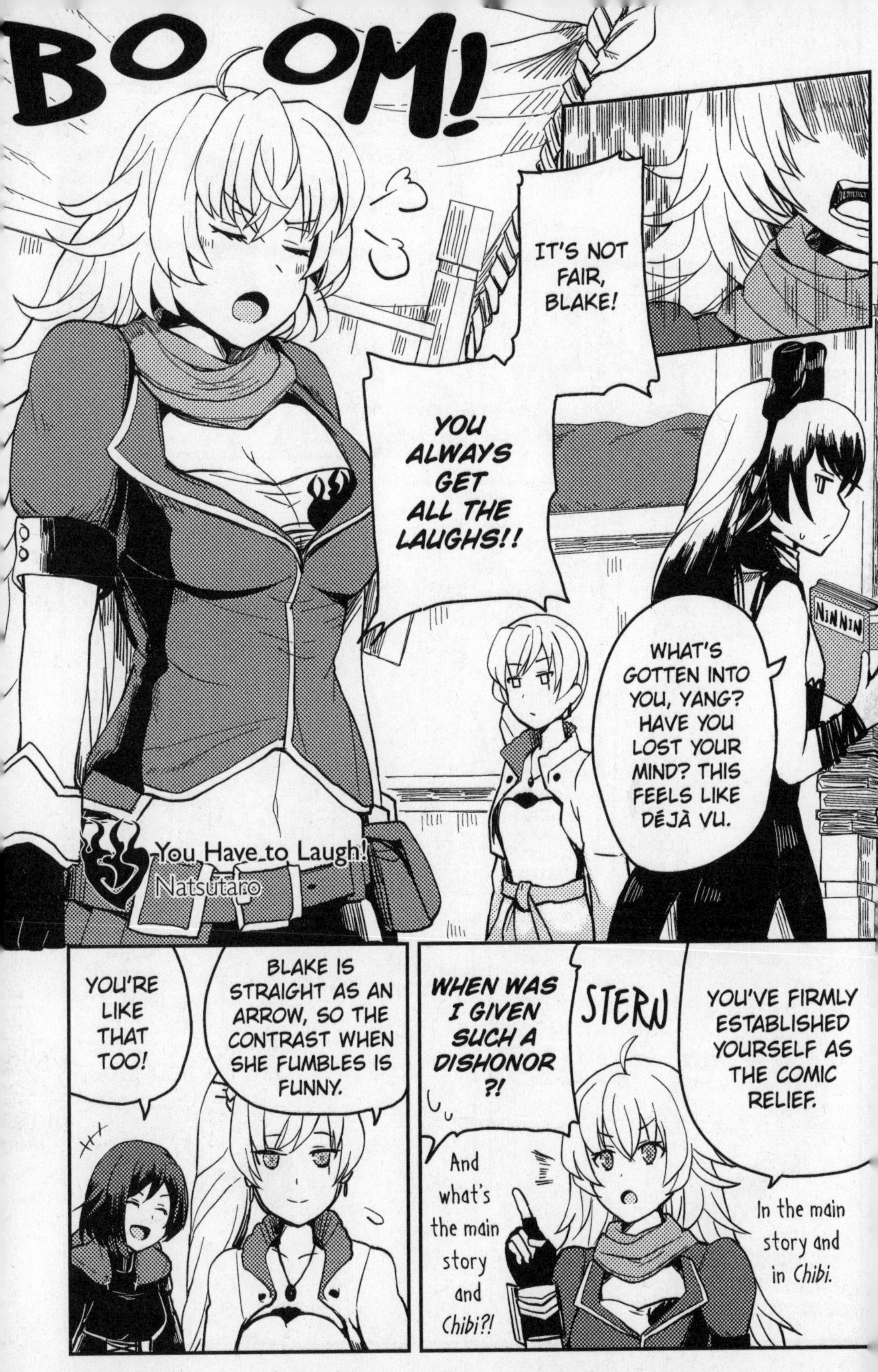
BOOM!
IT'S NOT FAIR, BLAKE!
YOU ALWAYS GET ALL THE LAUGHS!!
WHAT'S GOTTEN INTO YOU, YANG? HAVE YOU LOST YOUR MIND? THIS FEELS LIKE DÉJÀ VU.
NINNIN
You Have to Laugh!
Natsutaro
YOU'VE FIRMLY ESTABLISHED YOURSELF AS THE COMIC RELIEF.
STERN
WHEN WAS I GIVEN SUCH A DISHONOR?!
In the main story and in Chibi.
And what's the main story and Chibi?!
BLAKE IS STRAIGHT AS AN ARROW, SO THE CONTRAST WHEN SHE FUMBLES IS FUNNY.
YOU'RE LIKE THAT TOO!

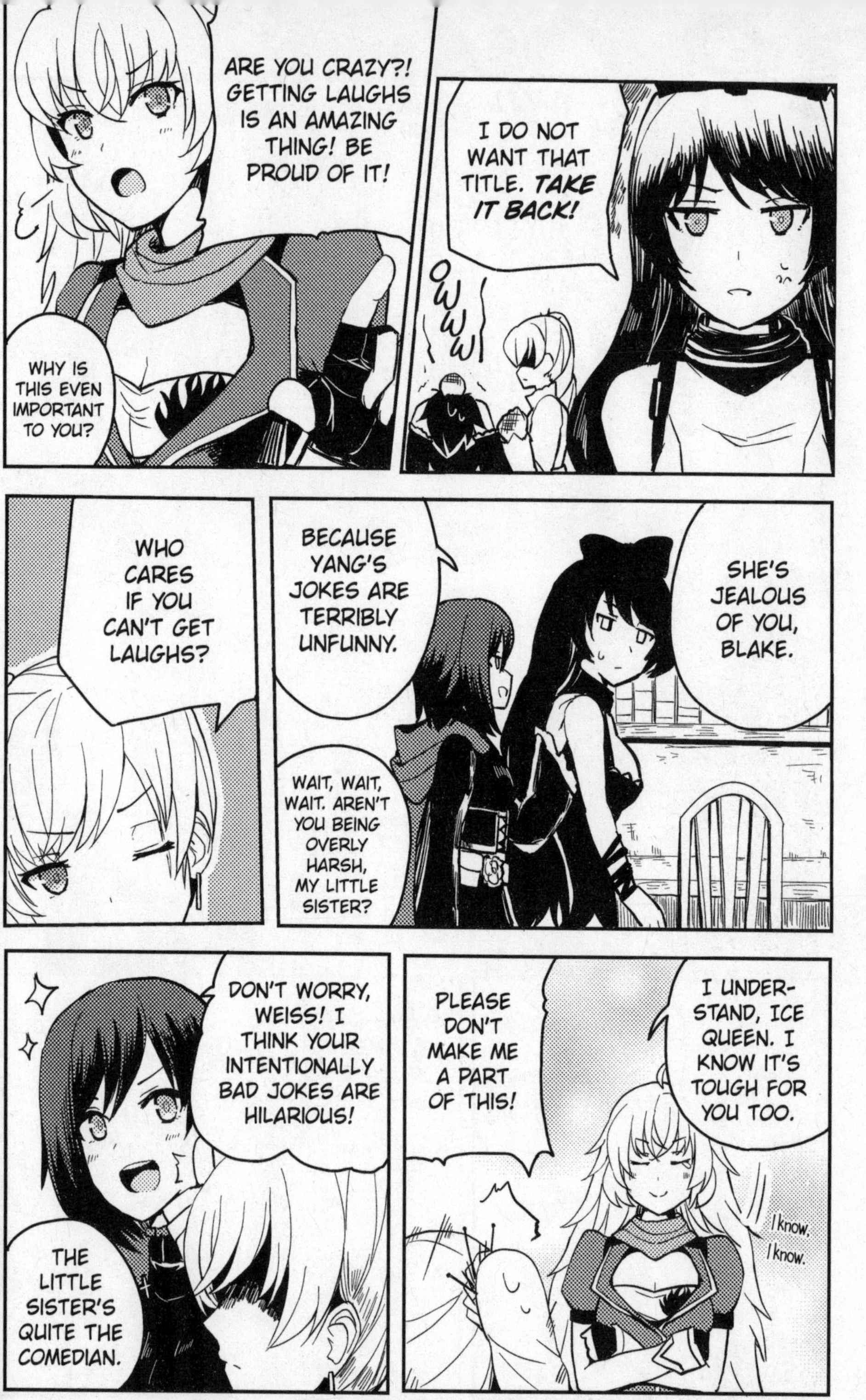
I DO NOT WANT THAT TITLE. *TAKE IT BACK!*
OWWW
ARE YOU CRAZY?! GETTING LAUGHS IS AN AMAZING THING! BE PROUD OF IT!
WHY IS THIS EVEN IMPORTANT TO YOU?
SHE'S JEALOUS OF YOU, BLAKE.
BECAUSE YANG'S JOKES ARE TERRIBLY UNFUNNY.
WAIT, WAIT, WAIT. AREN'T YOU BEING OVERLY HARSH, MY LITTLE SISTER?
WHO CARES IF YOU CAN'T GET LAUGHS?
I UNDERSTAND, ICE QUEEN. I KNOW IT'S TOUGH FOR YOU TOO.
PLEASE DON'T MAKE ME A PART OF THIS!
I know, I know.
DON'T WORRY, WEISS! I THINK YOUR INTENTIONALLY BAD JOKES ARE HILARIOUS!
THE LITTLE SISTER'S QUITE THE COMEDIAN.

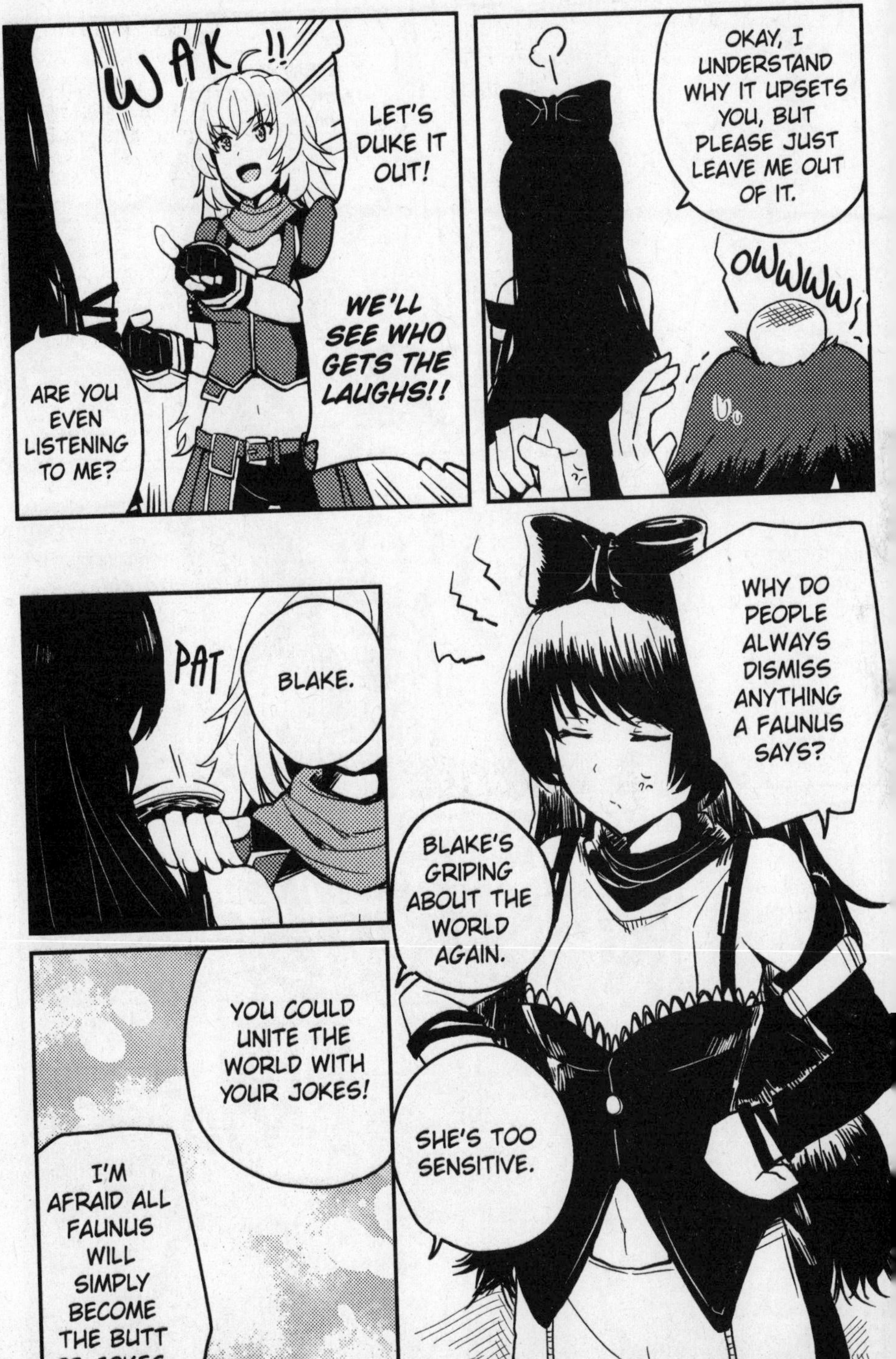
OKAY, I UNDERSTAND WHY IT UPSETS YOU, BUT PLEASE JUST LEAVE ME OUT OF IT.
OWWWW
WAK!!
LET'S DUKE IT OUT!
WE'LL SEE WHO GETS THE LAUGHS!!
ARE YOU EVEN LISTENING TO ME?
WHY DO PEOPLE ALWAYS DISMISS ANYTHING A FAUNUS SAYS?
BLAKE'S GRIPING ABOUT THE WORLD AGAIN.
SHE'S TOO SENSITIVE.
PAT
BLAKE.
YOU COULD UNITE THE WORLD WITH YOUR JOKES!
I'M AFRAID ALL FAUNUS WILL SIMPLY BECOME THE BUTT OF JOKES.

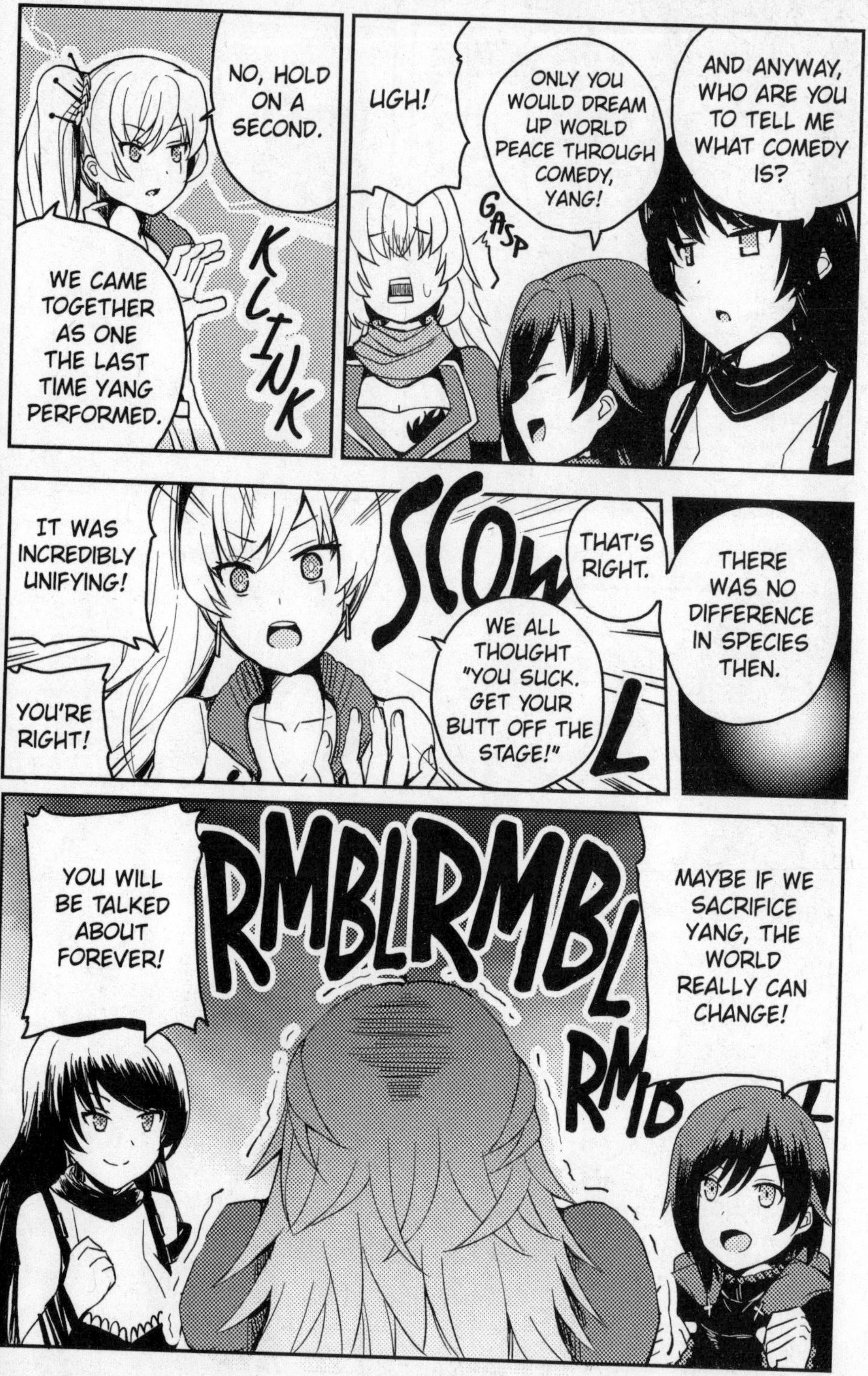
AND ANYWAY, WHO ARE YOU TO TELL ME WHAT COMEDY IS?
ONLY YOU WOULD DREAM UP WORLD PEACE THROUGH COMEDY, YANG!
GASP
UGH!
NO, HOLD ON A SECOND.
KLINK
WE CAME TOGETHER AS ONE THE LAST TIME YANG PERFORMED.
THERE WAS NO DIFFERENCE IN SPECIES THEN.
THAT'S RIGHT.
SCOWL
WE ALL THOUGHT "YOU SUCK. GET YOUR BUTT OFF THE STAGE!"
IT WAS INCREDIBLY UNIFYING!
YOU'RE RIGHT!
MAYBE IF WE SACRIFICE YANG, THE WORLD REALLY CAN CHANGE!
RMBLRMBL
RMBL
YOU WILL BE TALKED ABOUT FOREVER!

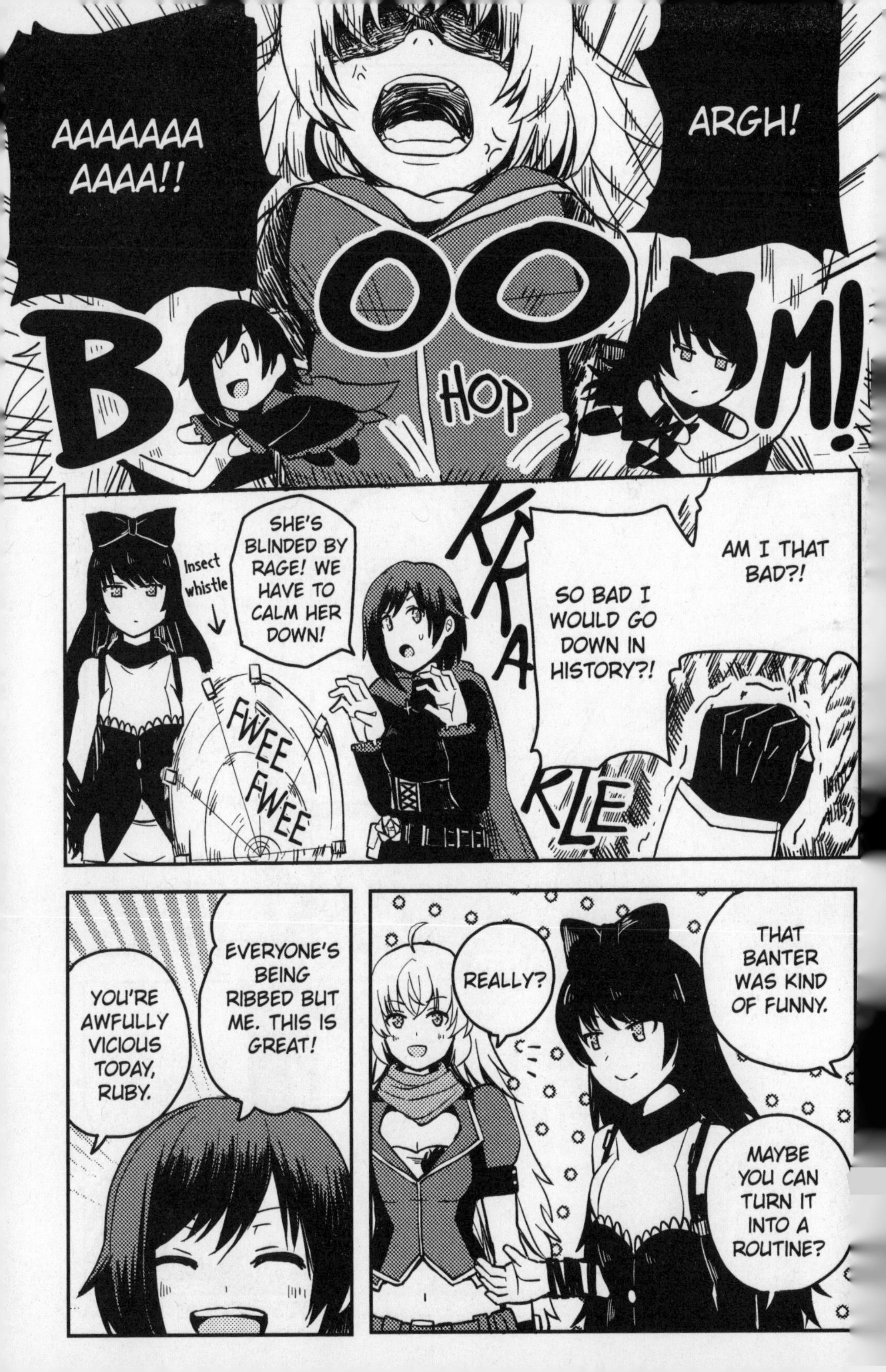
ARGH!
AAAAAAA AAAA!!
BOOM!
HOP
AM I THAT BAD?!
SO BAD I WOULD GO DOWN IN HISTORY?!
KRA
KLE
SHE'S BLINDED BY RAGE! WE HAVE TO CALM HER DOWN!
Insect whistle
FWEE FWEE
THAT BANTER WAS KIND OF FUNNY.
REALLY?
MAYBE YOU CAN TURN IT INTO A ROUTINE?
EVERYONE'S BEING RIBBED BUT ME. THIS IS GREAT!
YOU'RE AWFULLY VICIOUS TODAY, RUBY.

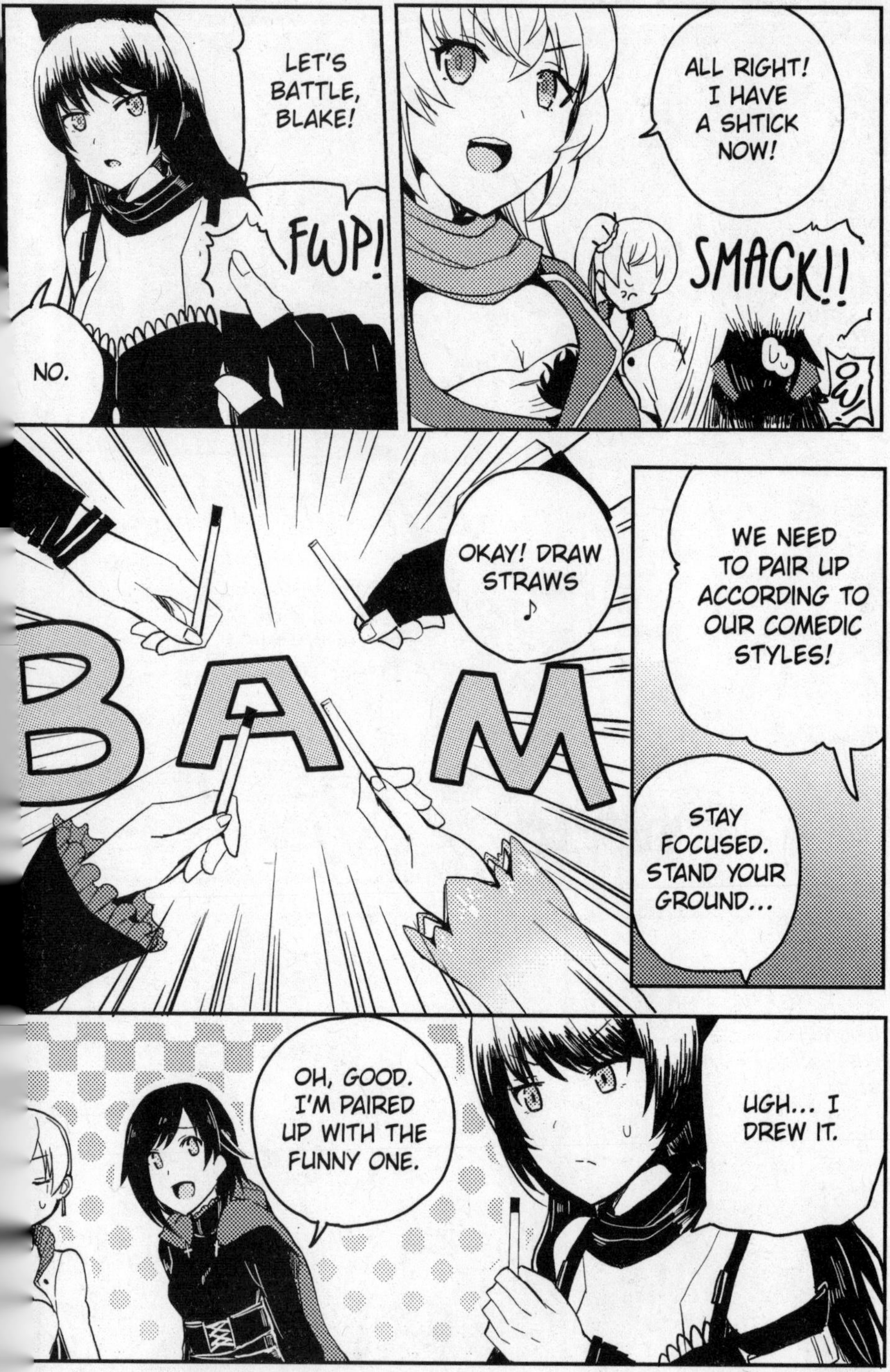
ALL RIGHT! I HAVE A SHTICK NOW!
SMACK!!
OW!
LET'S BATTLE, BLAKE!
FWP!
NO.
WE NEED TO PAIR UP ACCORDING TO OUR COMEDIC STYLES!
STAY FOCUSED. STAND YOUR GROUND...
OKAY! DRAW STRAWS ♪
BAM
UGH... I DREW IT.
OH, GOOD. I'M PAIRED UP WITH THE FUNNY ONE.

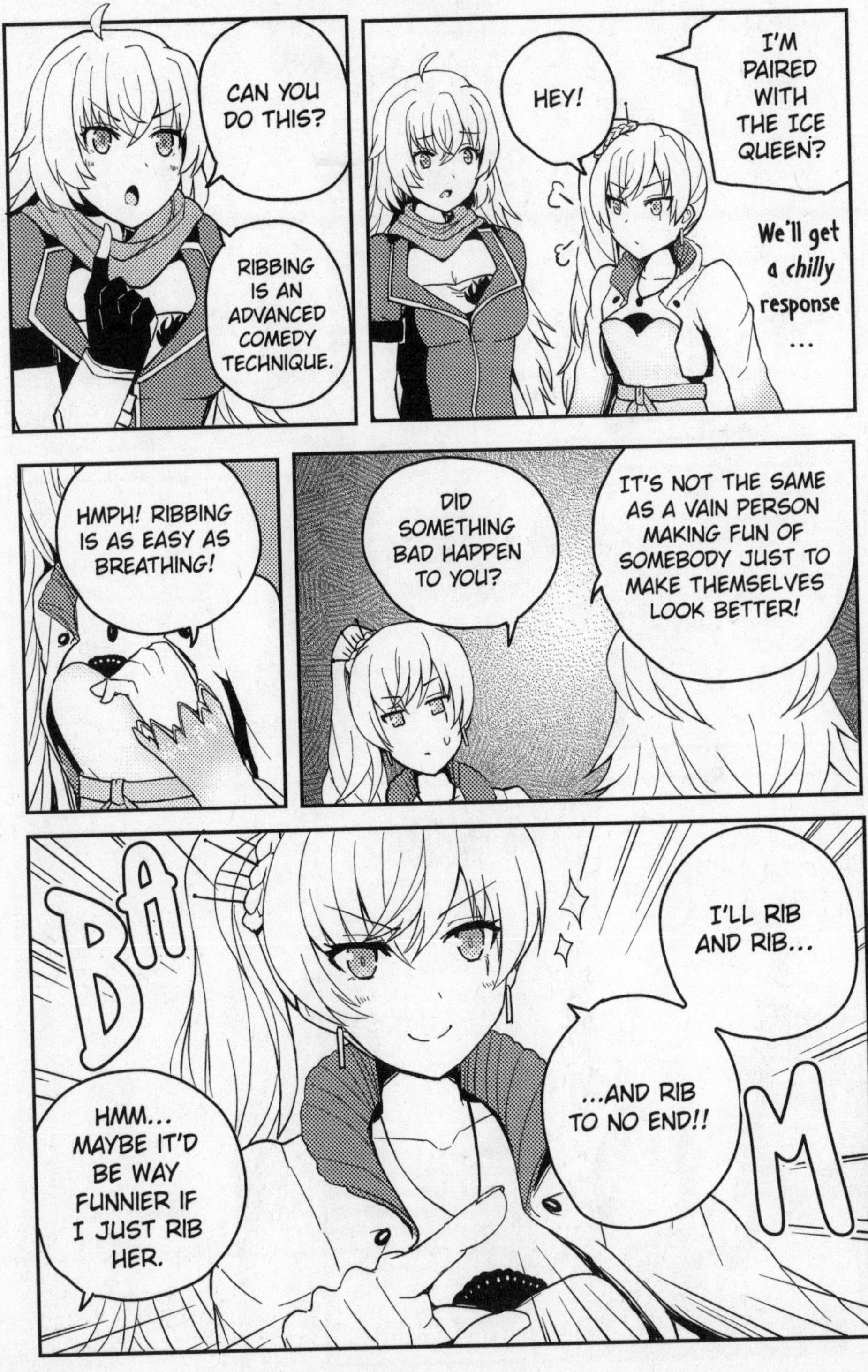
I'M PAIRED WITH THE ICE QUEEN?
HEY!
We'll get a *chilly* response ...
CAN YOU DO THIS?
RIBBING IS AN ADVANCED COMEDY TECHNIQUE.
IT'S NOT THE SAME AS A VAIN PERSON MAKING FUN OF SOMEBODY JUST TO MAKE THEMSELVES LOOK BETTER!
DID SOMETHING BAD HAPPEN TO YOU?
HMPH! RIBBING IS AS EASY AS BREATHING!
I'LL RIB AND RIB...
BA
...AND RIB TO NO END!!
M
HMM... MAYBE IT'D BE WAY FUNNIER IF I JUST RIB HER.

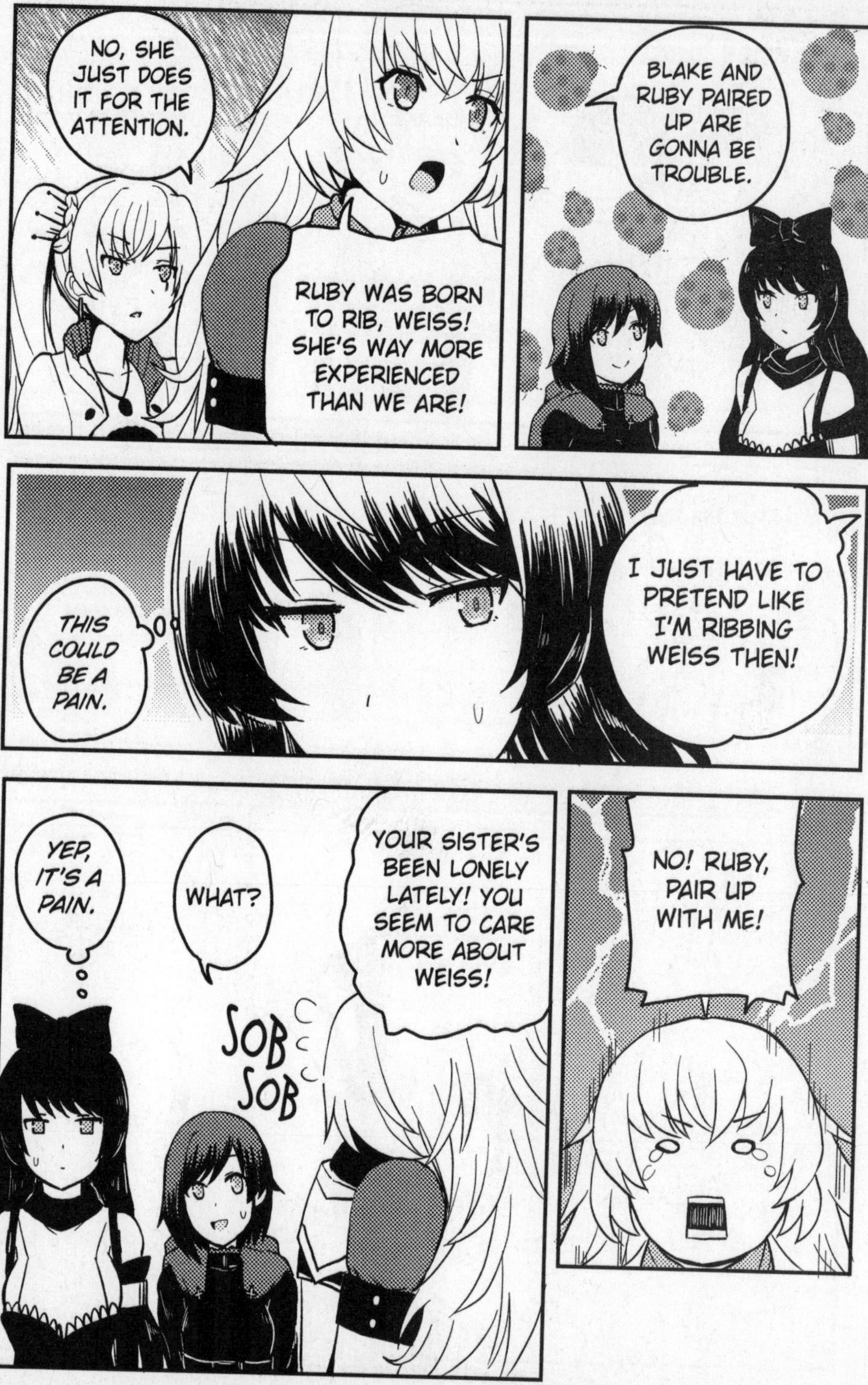
BLAKE AND RUBY PAIRED UP ARE GONNA BE TROUBLE.
RUBY WAS BORN TO RIB, WEISS! SHE'S WAY MORE EXPERIENCED THAN WE ARE!
NO, SHE JUST DOES IT FOR THE ATTENTION.
I JUST HAVE TO PRETEND LIKE I'M RIBBING WEISS THEN!
THIS COULD BE A PAIN.
NO! RUBY, PAIR UP WITH ME!
YOUR SISTER'S BEEN LONELY LATELY! YOU SEEM TO CARE MORE ABOUT WEISS!
SOB SOB
WHAT?
YEP, IT'S A PAIN.

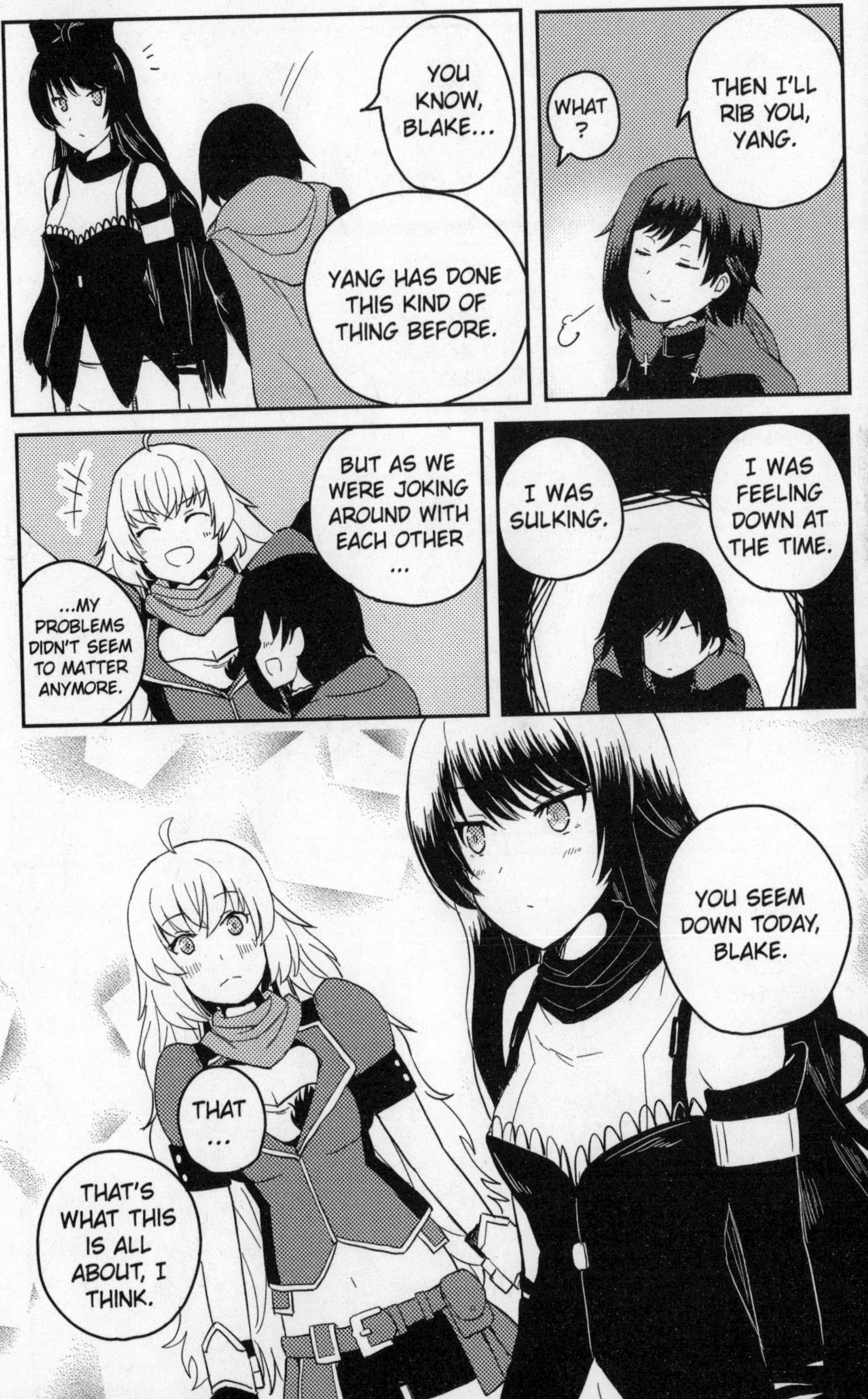
THEN I'LL RIB YOU, YANG.
WHAT ?
YOU KNOW, BLAKE...
YANG HAS DONE THIS KIND OF THING BEFORE.
I WAS FEELING DOWN AT THE TIME.
I WAS SULKING.
BUT AS WE WERE JOKING AROUND WITH EACH OTHER ...
...MY PROBLEMS DIDN'T SEEM TO MATTER ANYMORE.
YOU SEEM DOWN TODAY, BLAKE.
THAT ...
THAT'S WHAT THIS IS ALL ABOUT, I THINK.

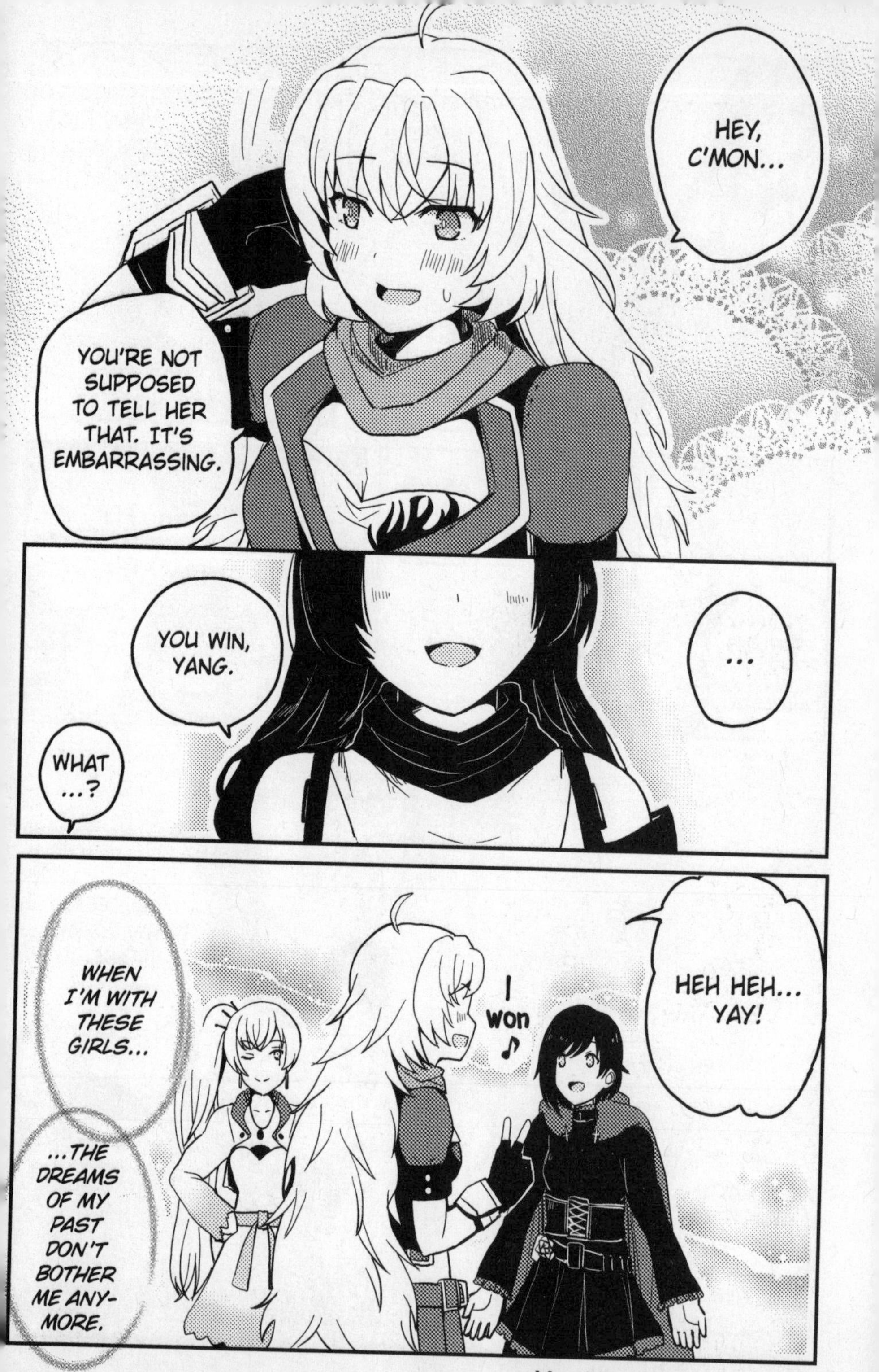
HEY, C'MON...
YOU'RE NOT SUPPOSED TO TELL HER THAT. IT'S EMBARRASSING.
...
YOU WIN, YANG.
WHAT ...?
HEH HEH... YAY!
I won ♪
WHEN I'M WITH THESE GIRLS...
...THE DREAMS OF MY PAST DON'T BOTHER ME ANY-MORE.

You Have to Laugh!/END

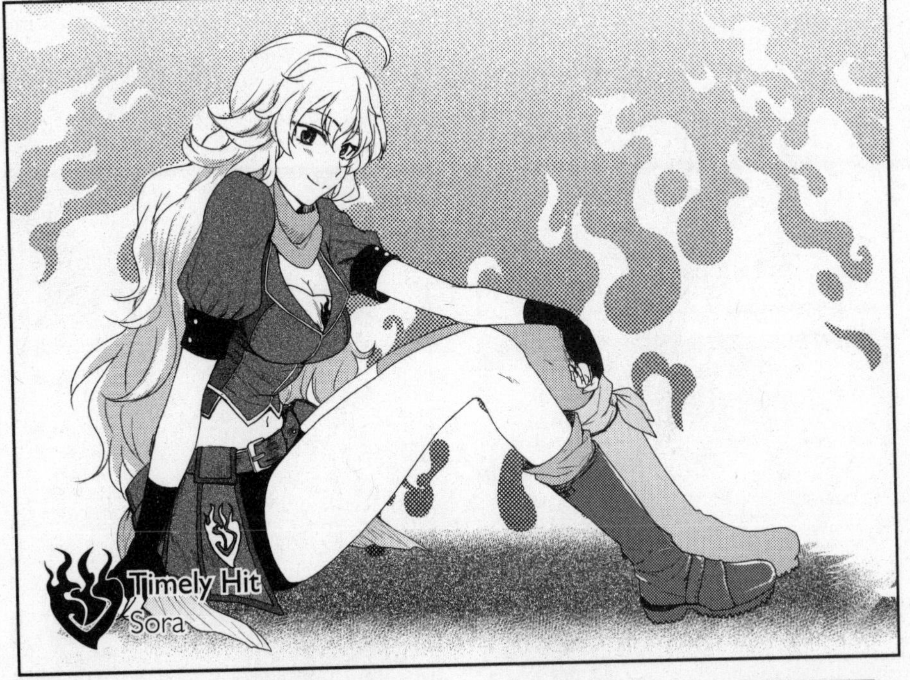
Timely Hit
Sora

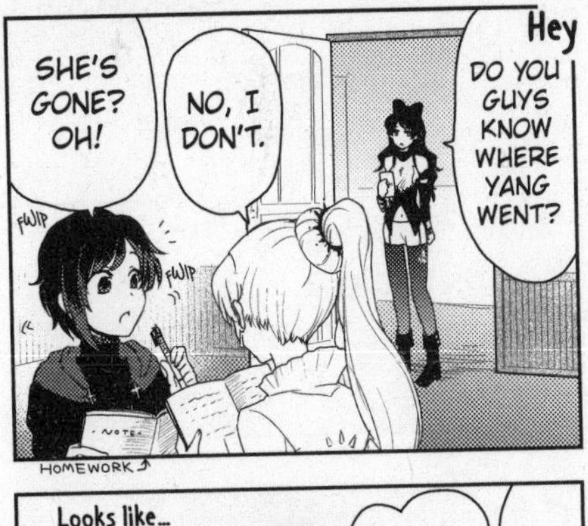
Hey
DO YOU GUYS KNOW WHERE YANG WENT?
NO, I DON'T.
SHE'S GONE? OH!
FWIP
FWIP
NOTE
HOMEWORK

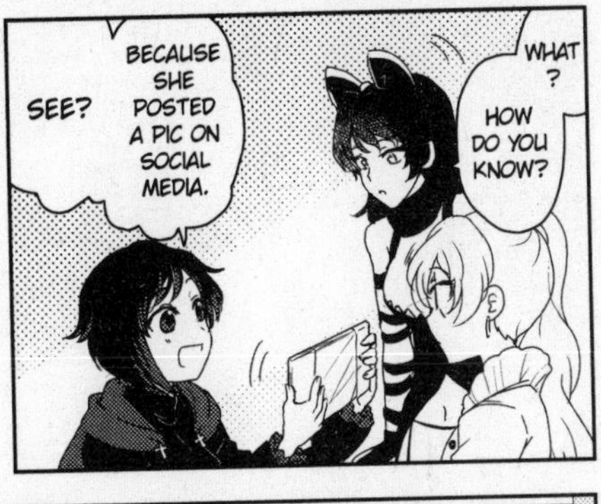
WHAT? HOW DO YOU KNOW?
BECAUSE SHE POSTED A PIC ON SOCIAL MEDIA.
SEE?

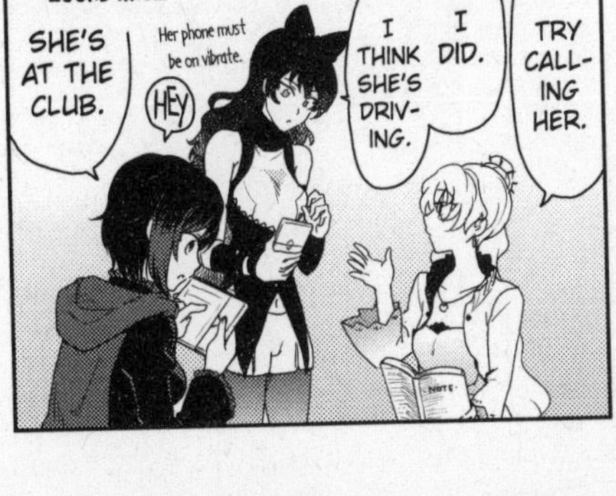
TRY CALL-ING HER.
I DID.
I THINK SHE'S DRIV-ING.
Her phone must be on vibrate.
HEY
Looks like...
SHE'S AT THE CLUB.
NOTE

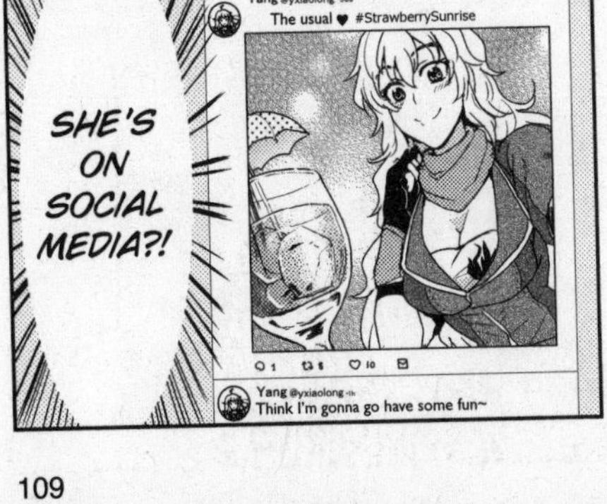
Yang @yxiaolong
The usual ♥ #StrawberrySunrise
Yang @yxiaolong
Think I'm gonna go have some fun~
SHE'S ON SOCIAL MEDIA?!

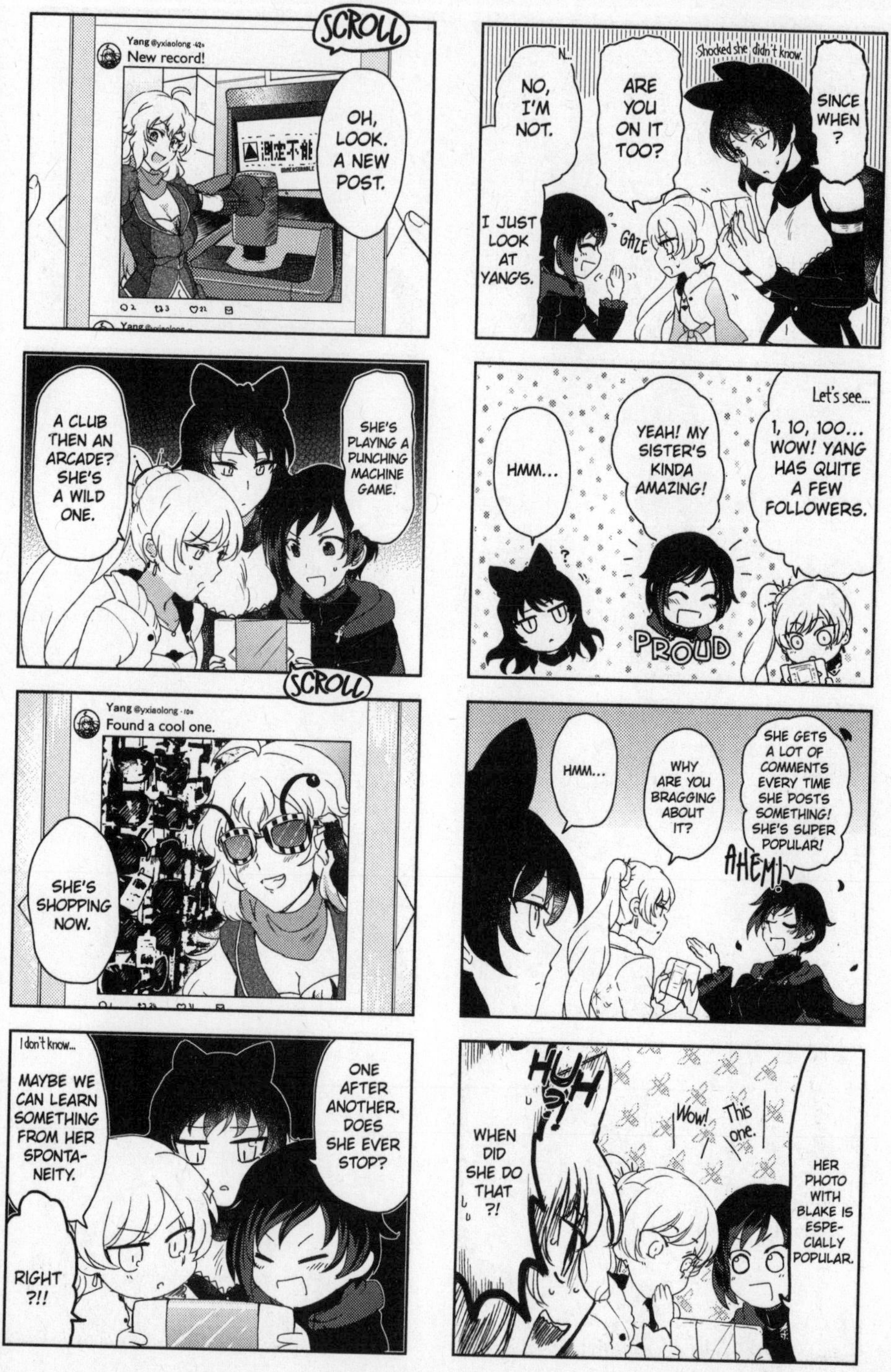
SINCE WHEN?
Shocked she didn't know.
ARE YOU ON IT TOO?
N...
NO, I'M NOT.
GAZE
I JUST LOOK AT YANG'S.
SCROLL
Yang @yxiaolong ·42s
New record!
測定不能
OH, LOOK. A NEW POST.
Let's see...
1, 10, 100... WOW! YANG HAS QUITE A FEW FOLLOWERS.
YEAH! MY SISTER'S KINDA AMAZING!
HMM...
PROUD
SHE'S PLAYING A PUNCHING MACHINE GAME.
A CLUB THEN AN ARCADE? SHE'S A WILD ONE.
SHE GETS A LOT OF COMMENTS EVERY TIME SHE POSTS SOMETHING! SHE'S SUPER POPULAR!
AHEM!
WHY ARE YOU BRAGGING ABOUT IT?
HMM...
SCROLL
Yang @yxiaolong ·10s
Found a cool one.
SHE'S SHOPPING NOW.
HER PHOTO WITH BLAKE IS ESPE-CIALLY POPULAR.
This one.
Wow!
HUH?!
WHEN DID SHE DO THAT?!
ONE AFTER ANOTHER. DOES SHE EVER STOP?
I don't know...
MAYBE WE CAN LEARN SOMETHING FROM HER SPONTA-NEITY.
RIGHT?!!

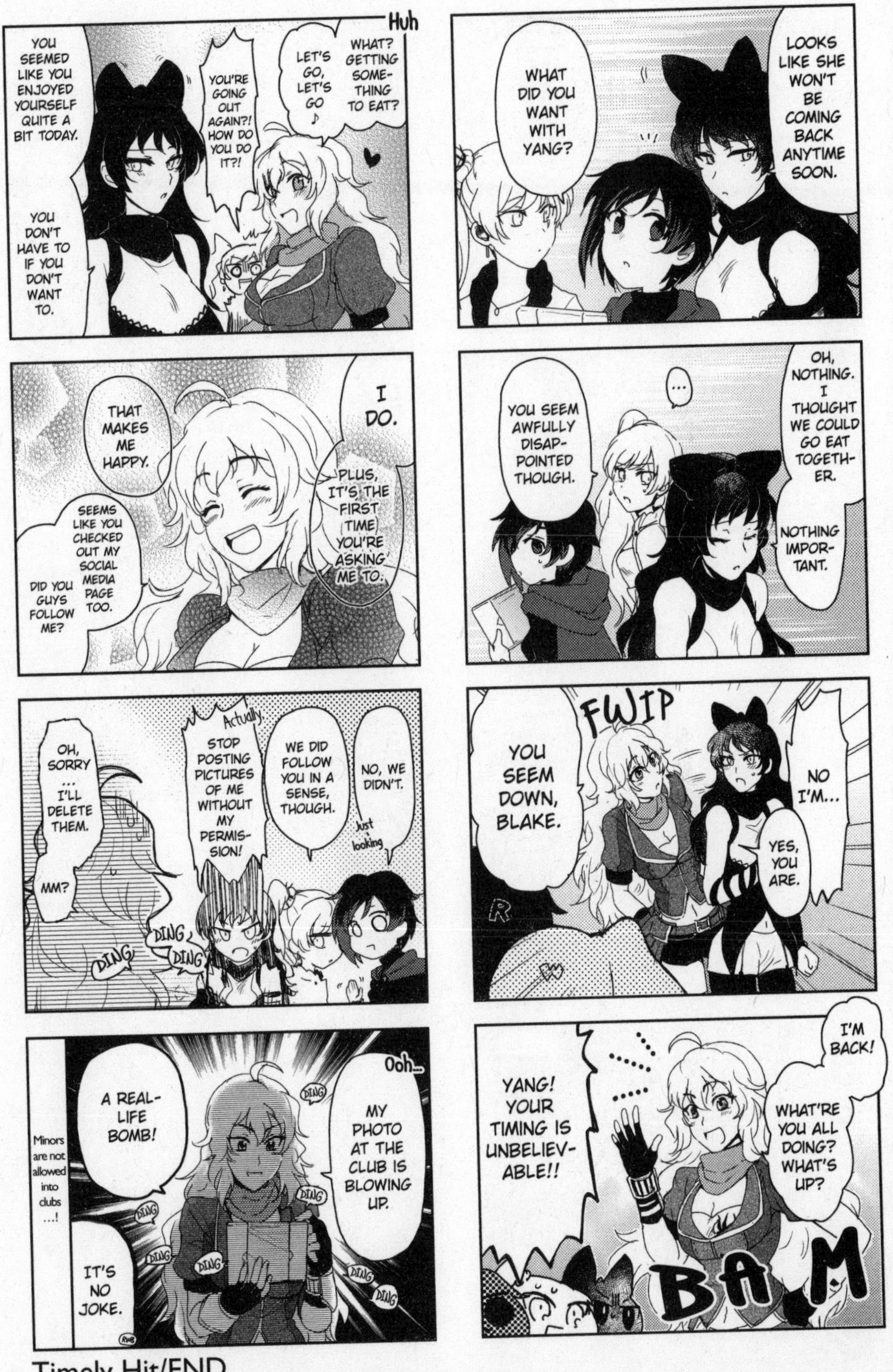
LOOKS LIKE SHE WON'T BE COMING BACK ANYTIME SOON.
WHAT DID YOU WANT WITH YANG?
OH, NOTHING. I THOUGHT WE COULD GO EAT TOGETH-ER.
NOTHING IMPOR-TANT.
...
YOU SEEM AWFULLY DISAP-POINTED THOUGH.
FWIP
NO I'M...
YES, YOU ARE.
YOU SEEM DOWN, BLAKE.
I'M BACK!
WHAT'RE YOU ALL DOING? WHAT'S UP?
......
YANG! YOUR TIMING IS UNBELIEV-ABLE!!
BAM
WHAT? GETTING SOME-THING TO EAT?
LET'S GO, LET'S GO ♪
Huh
YOU'RE GOING OUT AGAIN?! HOW DO YOU DO IT?!
YOU SEEMED LIKE YOU ENJOYED YOURSELF QUITE A BIT TODAY.
YOU DON'T HAVE TO IF YOU DON'T WANT TO.
I DO.
PLUS, IT'S THE FIRST TIME YOU'RE ASKING ME TO.
THAT MAKES ME HAPPY.
SEEMS LIKE YOU CHECKED OUT MY SOCIAL MEDIA PAGE TOO.
DID YOU GUYS FOLLOW ME?
NO, WE DIDN'T.
WE DID FOLLOW YOU IN A SENSE, THOUGH.
Just looking
Actually
STOP POSTING PICTURES OF ME WITHOUT MY PERMIS-SION!
OH, SORRY ... I'LL DELETE THEM.
MM?
DING DING DING
Ooh...
MY PHOTO AT THE CLUB IS BLOWING UP.
A REAL-LIFE BOMB!
IT'S NO JOKE.
DING DING DING DING DING DING DING
Minors are not allowed into clubs ...!

Timely Hit/END

RWBY
OFFICIAL MANGA ANTHOLOGY
Volume 4

I Burn

METEO

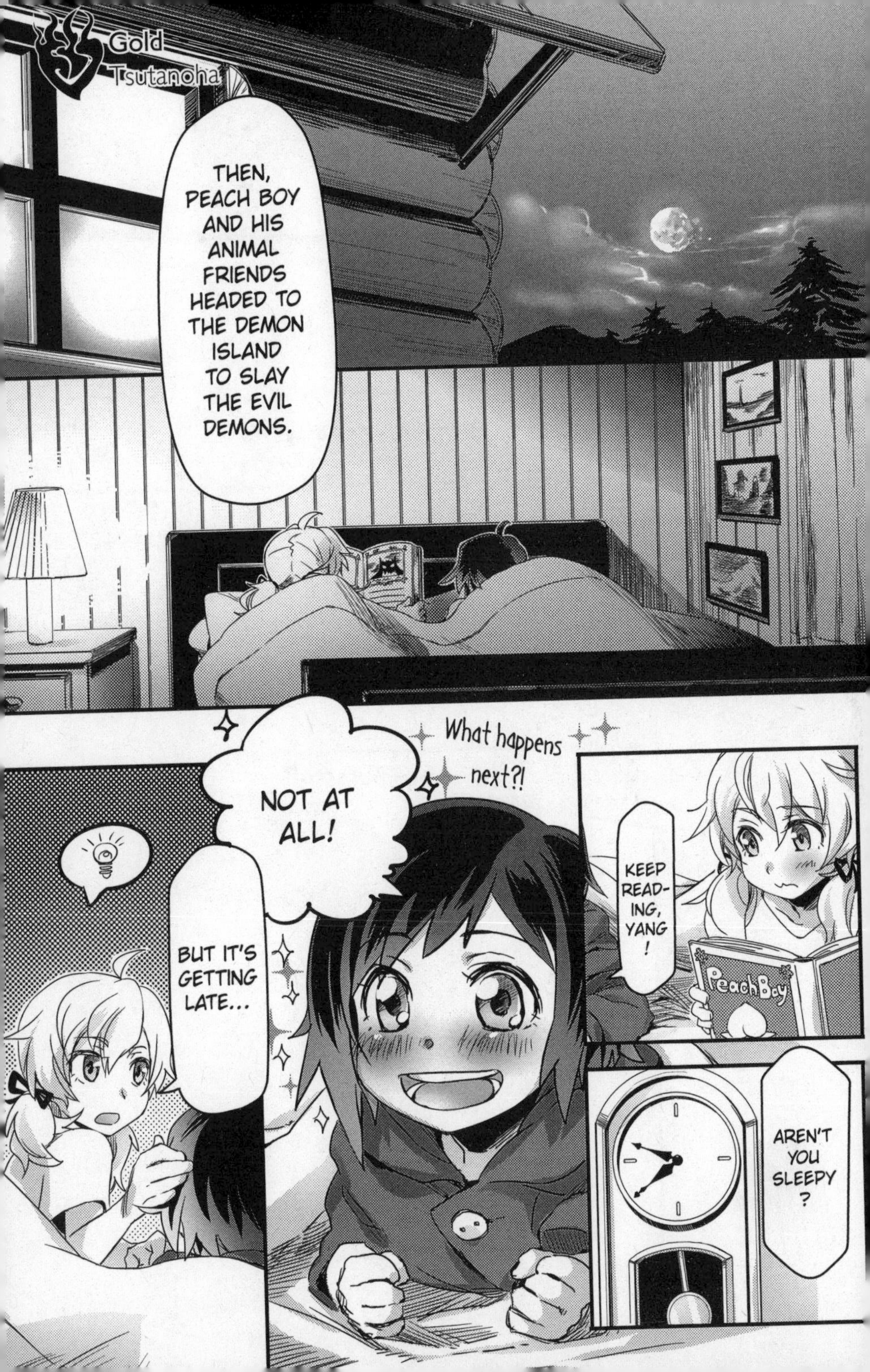
Gold Tsutanoha
THEN, PEACH BOY AND HIS ANIMAL FRIENDS HEADED TO THE DEMON ISLAND TO SLAY THE EVIL DEMONS.
KEEP READING, YANG!
PeachBoy
AREN'T YOU SLEEPY?
What happens next?!
NOT AT ALL!
BUT IT'S GETTING LATE...

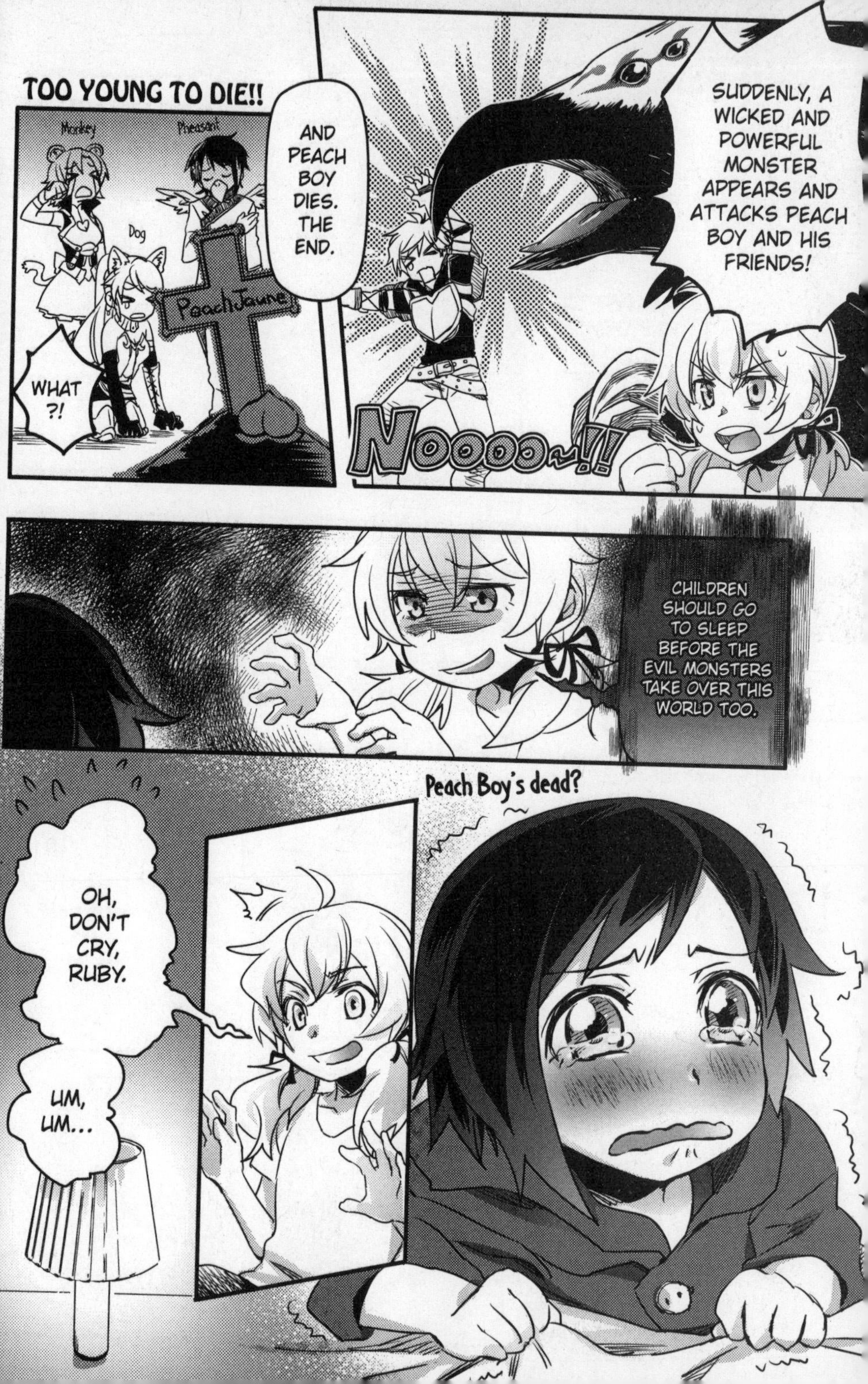
SUDDENLY, A WICKED AND POWERFUL MONSTER APPEARS AND ATTACKS PEACH BOY AND HIS FRIENDS!
NOOOOO~!!
AND PEACH BOY DIES. THE END.
TOO YOUNG TO DIE!!
Pheasant
Monkey
Dog
PeachJaune
WHAT?!
CHILDREN SHOULD GO TO SLEEP BEFORE THE EVIL MONSTERS TAKE OVER THIS WORLD TOO.
Peach Boy's dead?
OH, DON'T CRY, RUBY.
UM, UM...

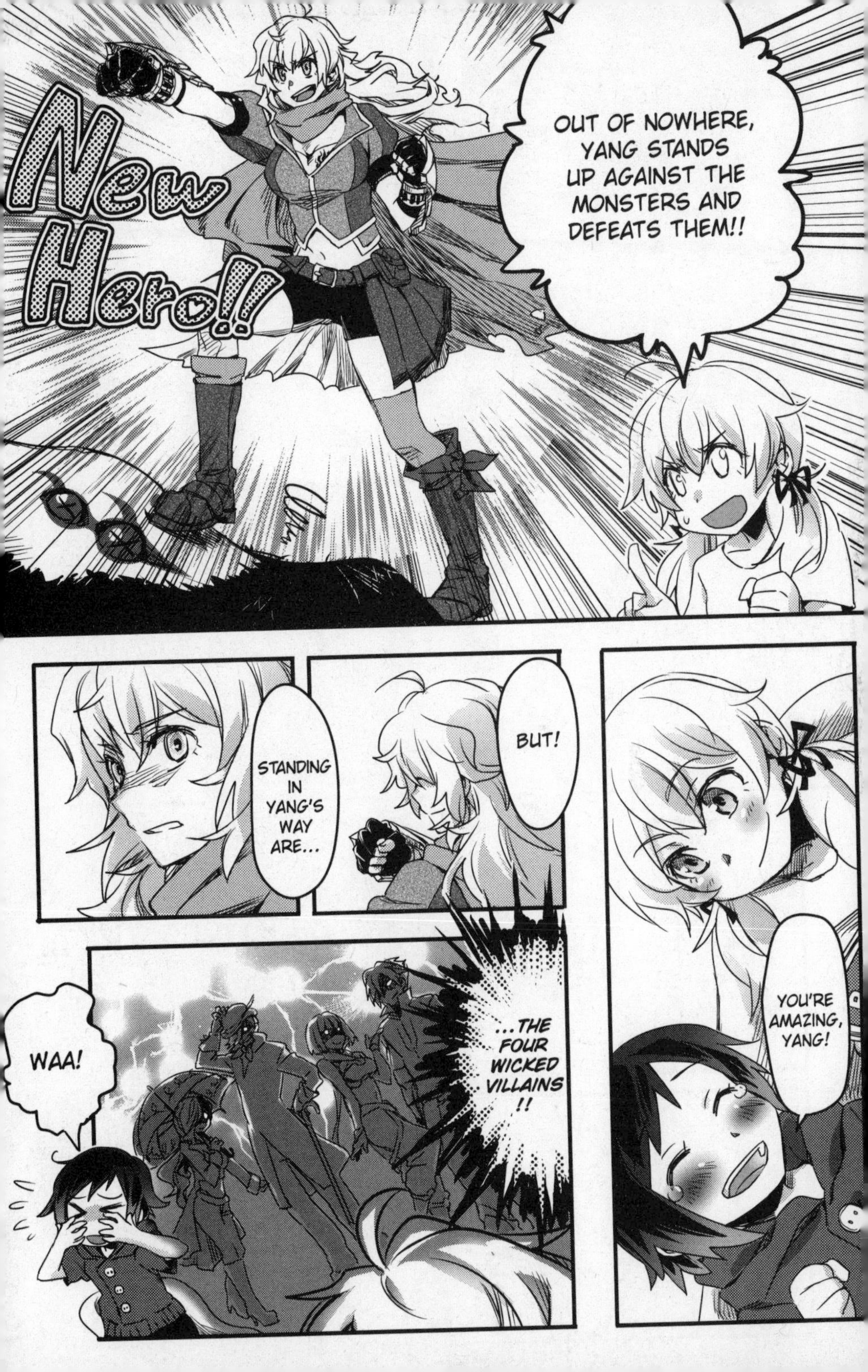
OUT OF NOWHERE, YANG STANDS UP AGAINST THE MONSTERS AND DEFEATS THEM!!
New Hero!!
YOU'RE AMAZING, YANG!
BUT!
STANDING IN YANG'S WAY ARE...
...THE FOUR WICKED VILLAINS!!
WAA!

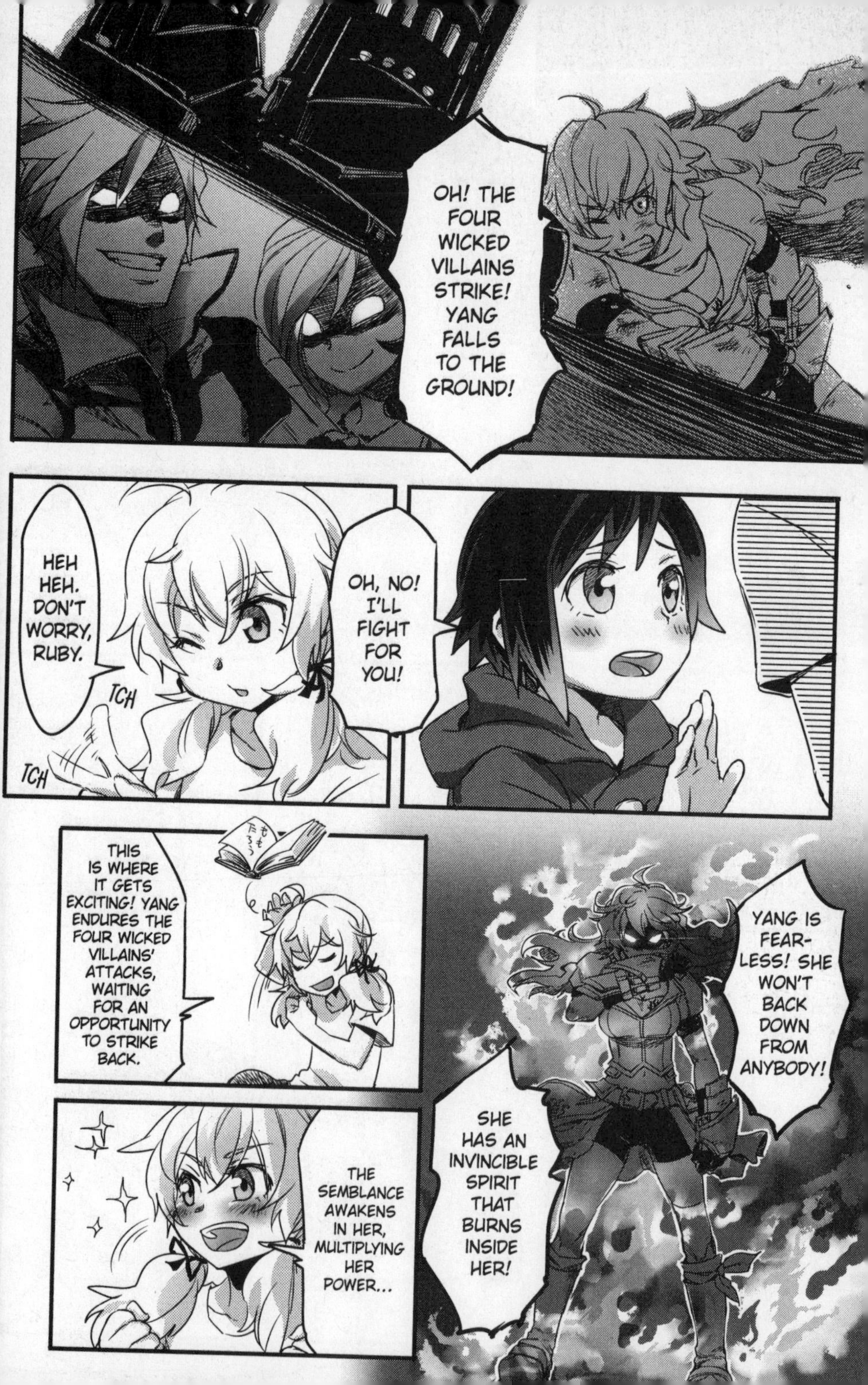
OH! THE FOUR WICKED VILLAINS STRIKE! YANG FALLS TO THE GROUND!
OH, NO! I'LL FIGHT FOR YOU!
HEH HEH. DON'T WORRY, RUBY.
TCH
TCH
YANG IS FEARLESS! SHE WON'T BACK DOWN FROM ANYBODY!
SHE HAS AN INVINCIBLE SPIRIT THAT BURNS INSIDE HER!
ももたろう
THIS IS WHERE IT GETS EXCITING! YANG ENDURES THE FOUR WICKED VILLAINS' ATTACKS, WAITING FOR AN OPPORTUNITY TO STRIKE BACK.
THE SEMBLANCE AWAKENS IN HER, MULTIPLYING HER POWER...

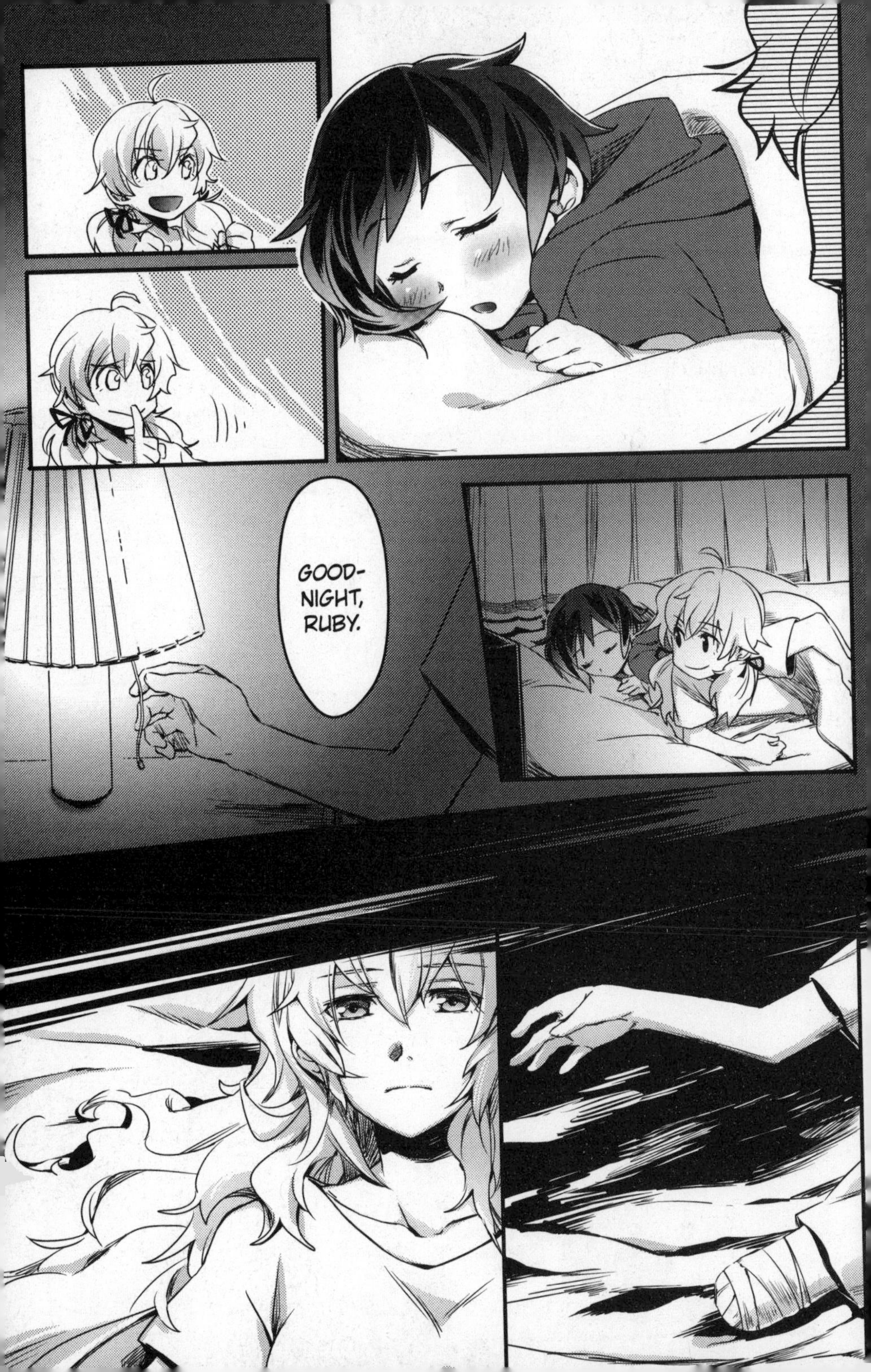
GOOD-NIGHT, RUBY.

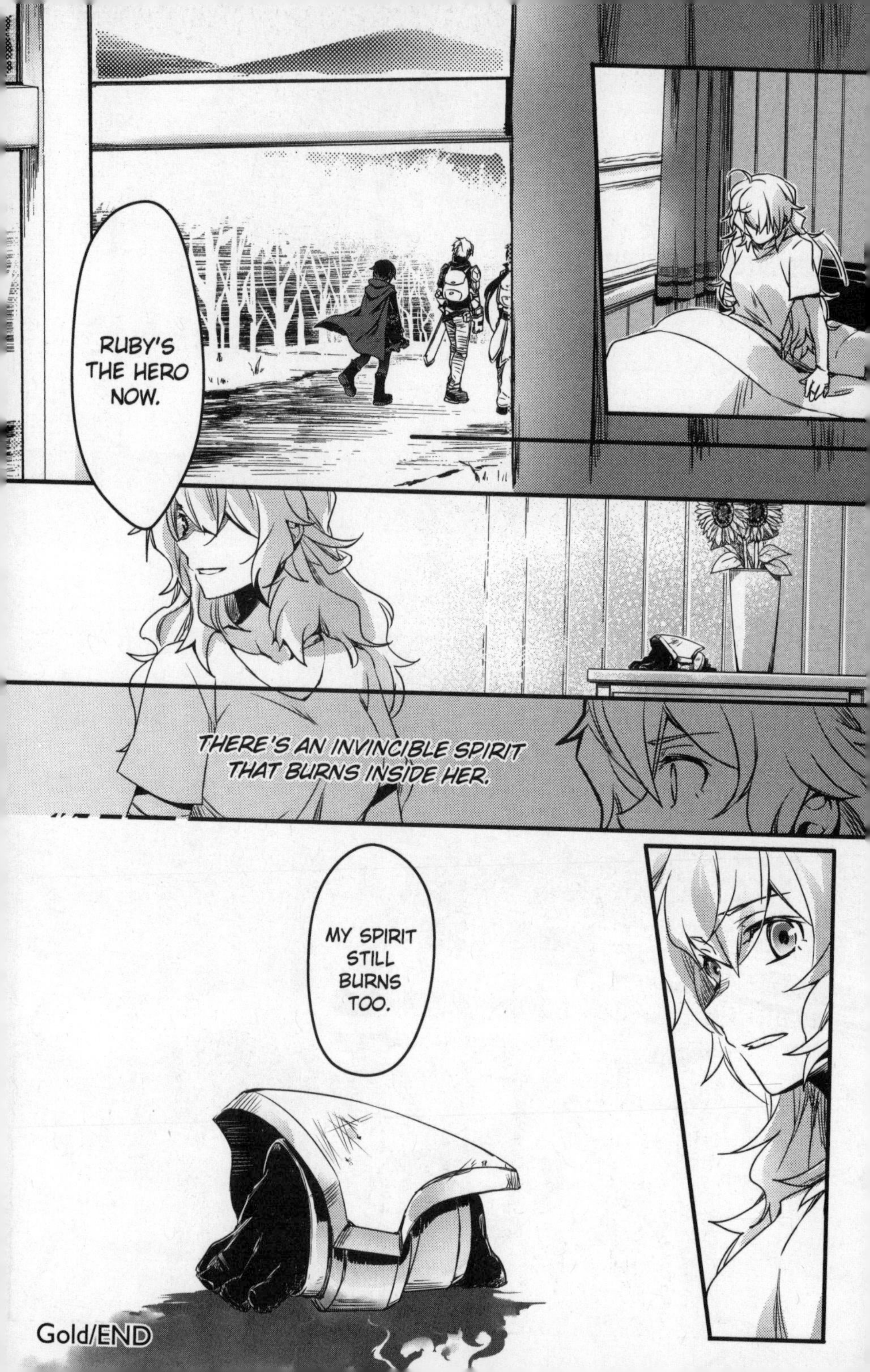
RUBY'S THE HERO NOW.
THERE'S AN INVINCIBLE SPIRIT THAT BURNS INSIDE HER.
MY SPIRIT STILL BURNS TOO.

Gold/END

The Blond Girl and Her Three Friends

Kaogeimoai

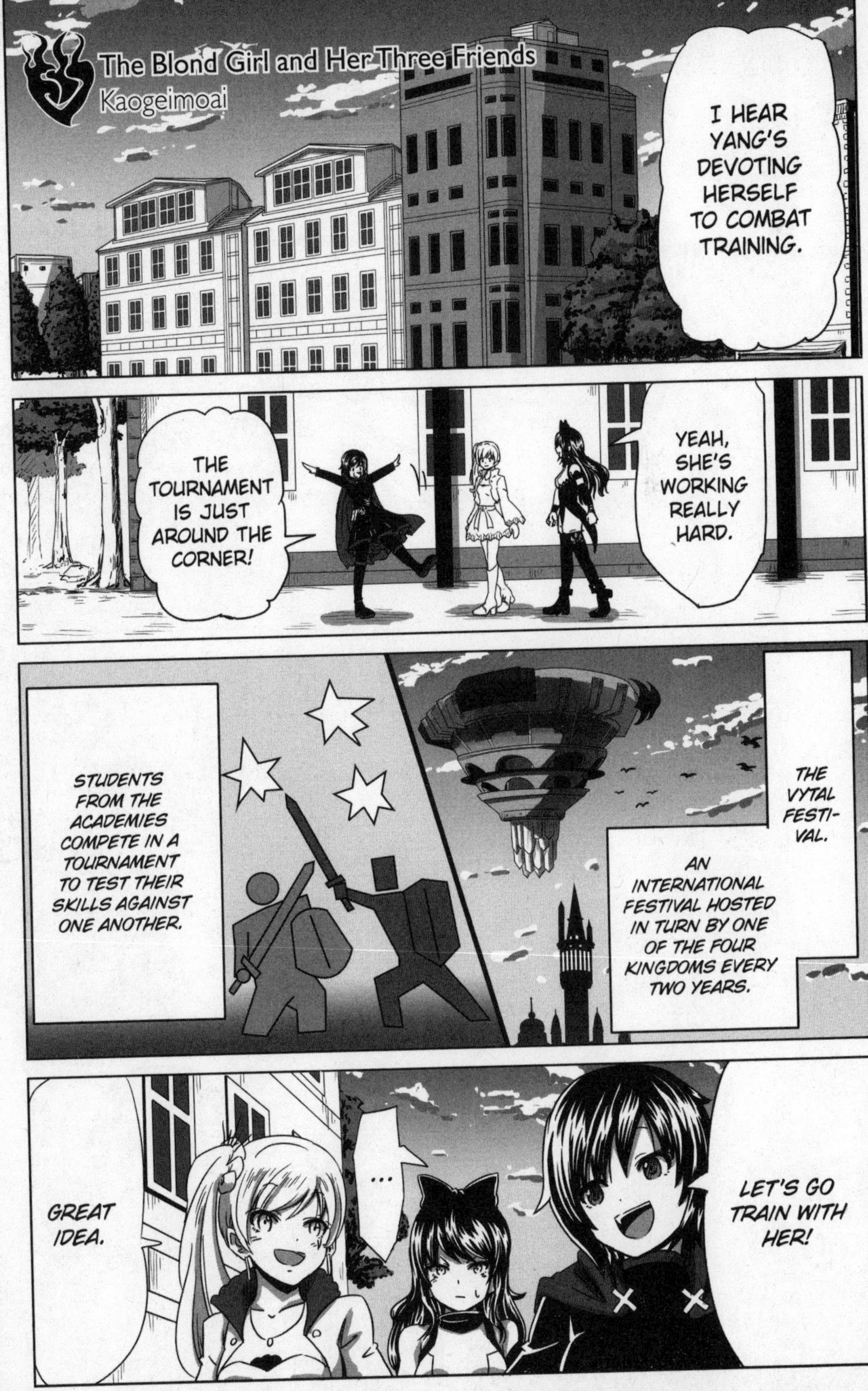
I HEAR YANG'S DEVOTING HERSELF TO COMBAT TRAINING.
YEAH, SHE'S WORKING REALLY HARD.
THE TOURNAMENT IS JUST AROUND THE CORNER!
THE VYTAL FESTI-VAL.
AN INTERNATIONAL FESTIVAL HOSTED IN TURN BY ONE OF THE FOUR KINGDOMS EVERY TWO YEARS.
STUDENTS FROM THE ACADEMIES COMPETE IN A TOURNAMENT TO TEST THEIR SKILLS AGAINST ONE ANOTHER.
LET'S GO TRAIN WITH HER!
...
GREAT IDEA.

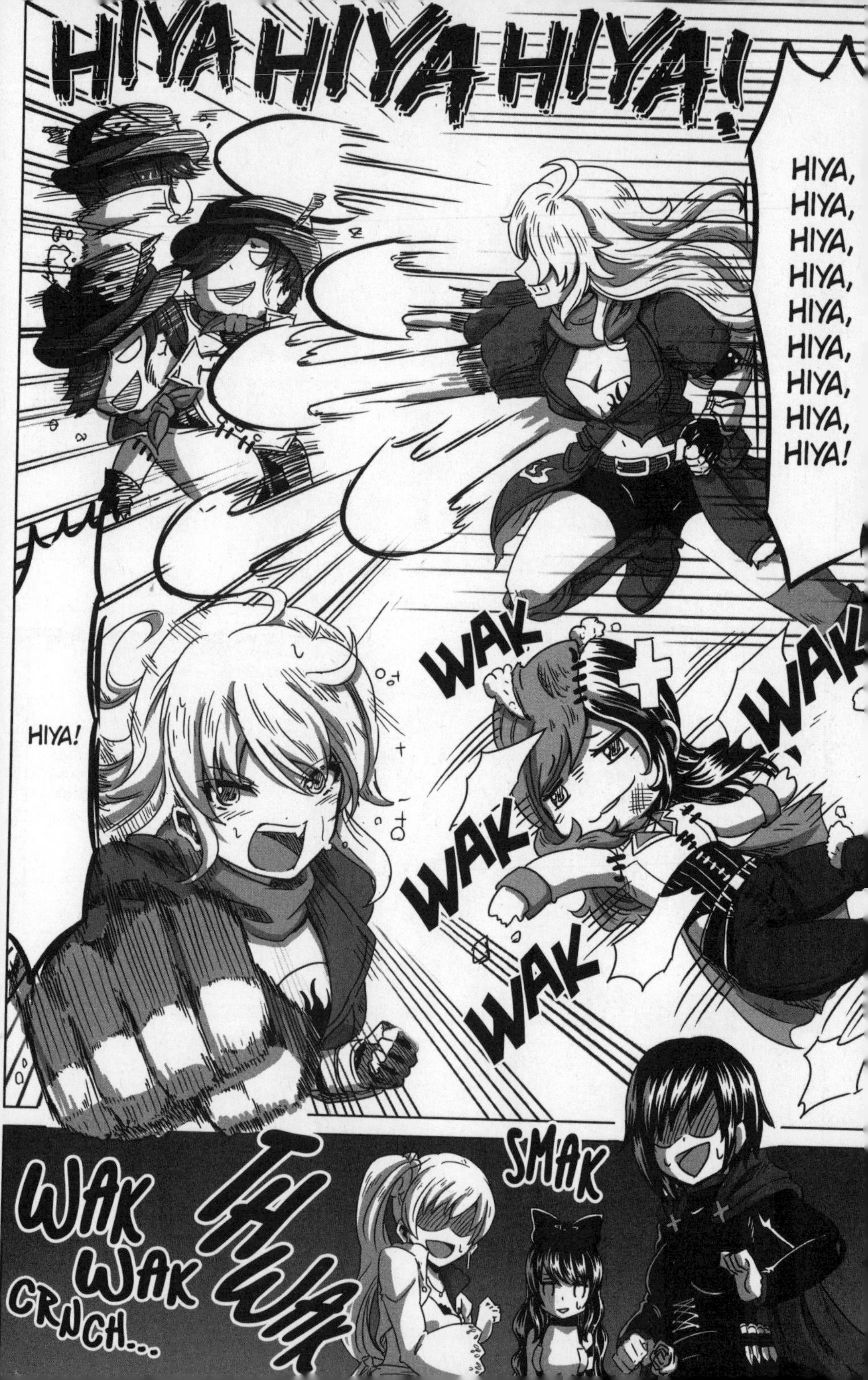
HIYA HIYA HIYA!
HIYA, HIYA, HIYA, HIYA, HIYA, HIYA, HIYA, HIYA, HIYA!
WAK
WAK
WAK
WAK
WAK
HIYA!
SMAK
THWAK
WAK WAK CRNCH...

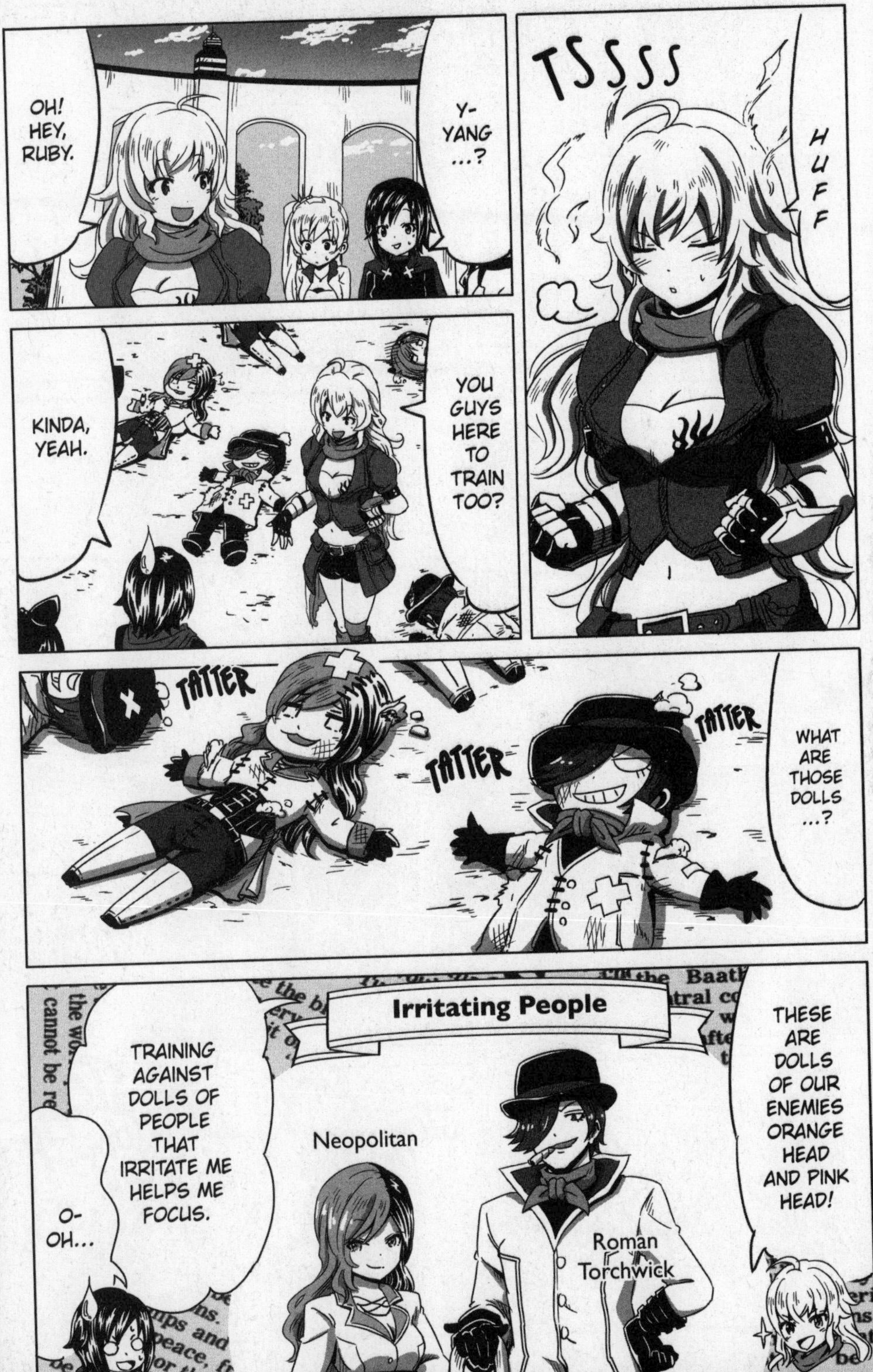
TSSSS
HUFF
Y-YANG...?
OH! HEY, RUBY.
YOU GUYS HERE TO TRAIN TOO?
KINDA, YEAH.
TATTER
TATTER
TATTER
WHAT ARE THOSE DOLLS...?
Irritating People
THESE ARE DOLLS OF OUR ENEMIES ORANGE HEAD AND PINK HEAD!
Roman Torchwick
Neopolitan
TRAINING AGAINST DOLLS OF PEOPLE THAT IRRITATE ME HELPS ME FOCUS.
O-OH...

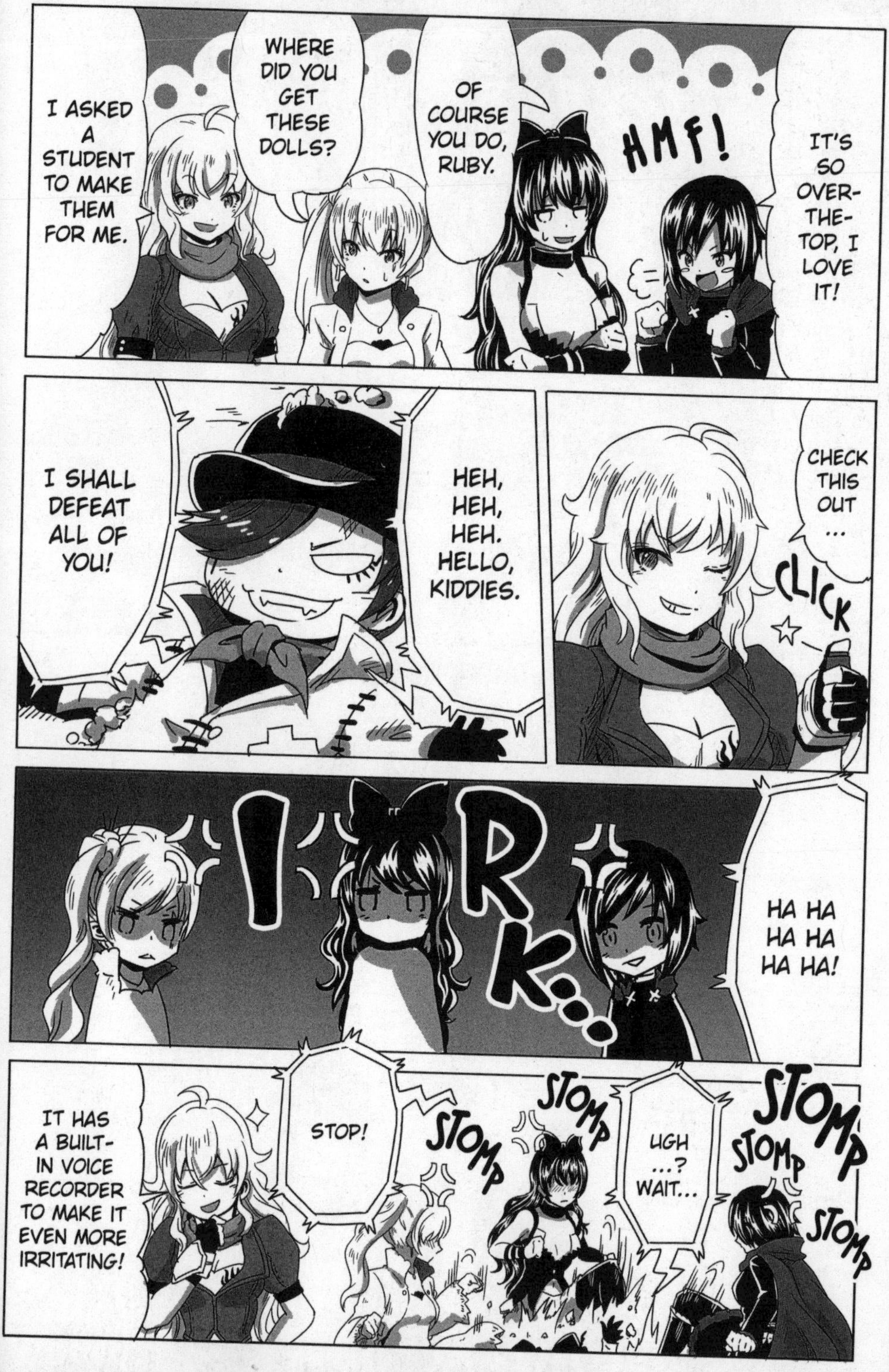
IT'S SO OVER-THE-TOP, I LOVE IT!
HMF!
OF COURSE YOU DO, RUBY.
WHERE DID YOU GET THESE DOLLS?
I ASKED A STUDENT TO MAKE THEM FOR ME.
CHECK THIS OUT ...
CLICK
HEH, HEH, HEH. HELLO, KIDDIES.
I SHALL DEFEAT ALL OF YOU!
HA HA HA HA HA HA!
IRK...
STOMP
STOMP
STOMP
UGH ...? WAIT...
STOMP
STOMP
STOP!
IT HAS A BUILT-IN VOICE RECORDER TO MAKE IT EVEN MORE IRRITATING!

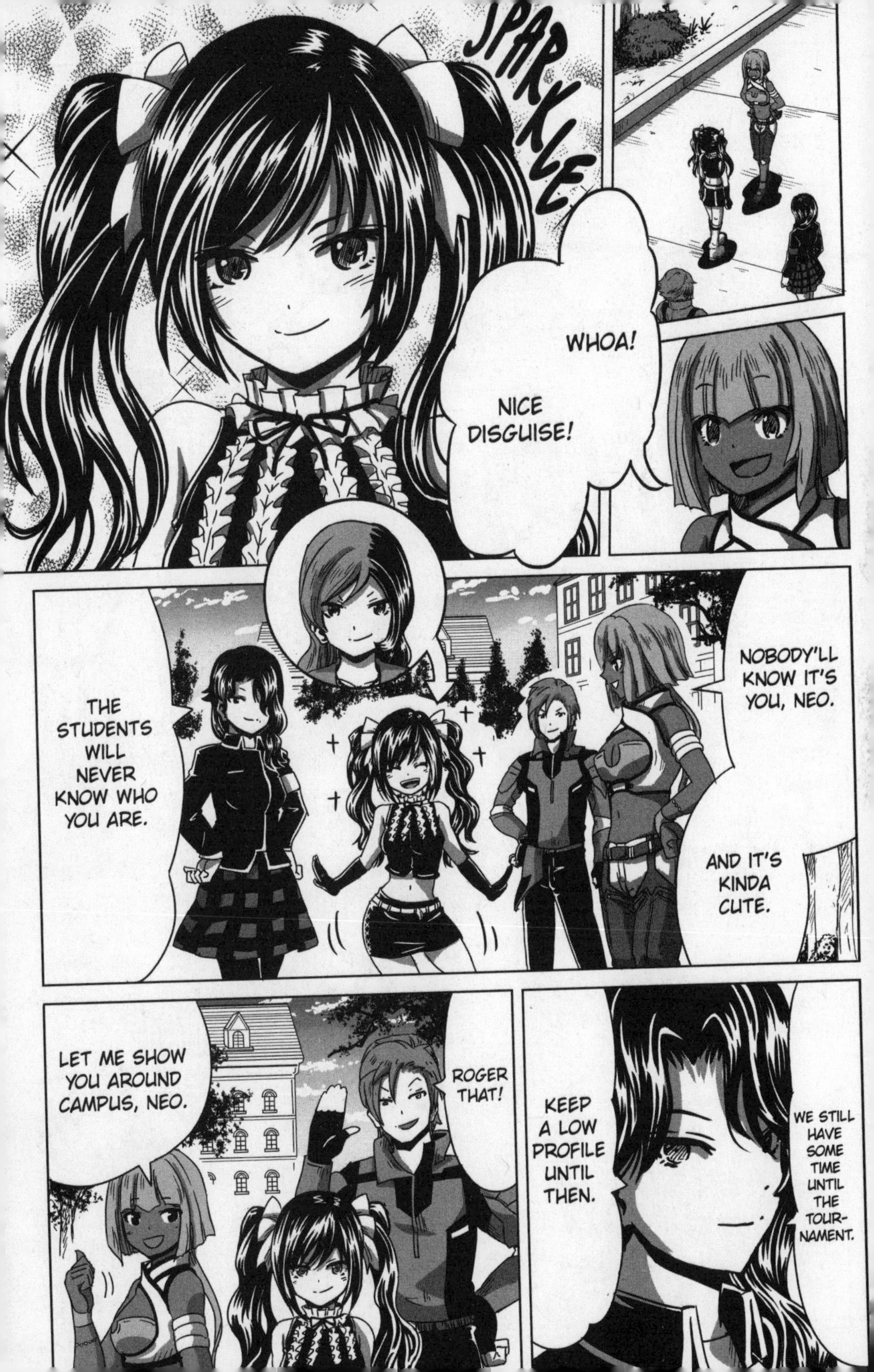
WHOA!
NICE DISGUISE!
SPARKLE
NOBODY'LL KNOW IT'S YOU, NEO.
AND IT'S KINDA CUTE.
THE STUDENTS WILL NEVER KNOW WHO YOU ARE.
WE STILL HAVE SOME TIME UNTIL THE TOUR-NAMENT.
KEEP A LOW PROFILE UNTIL THEN.
ROGER THAT!
LET ME SHOW YOU AROUND CAMPUS, NEO.

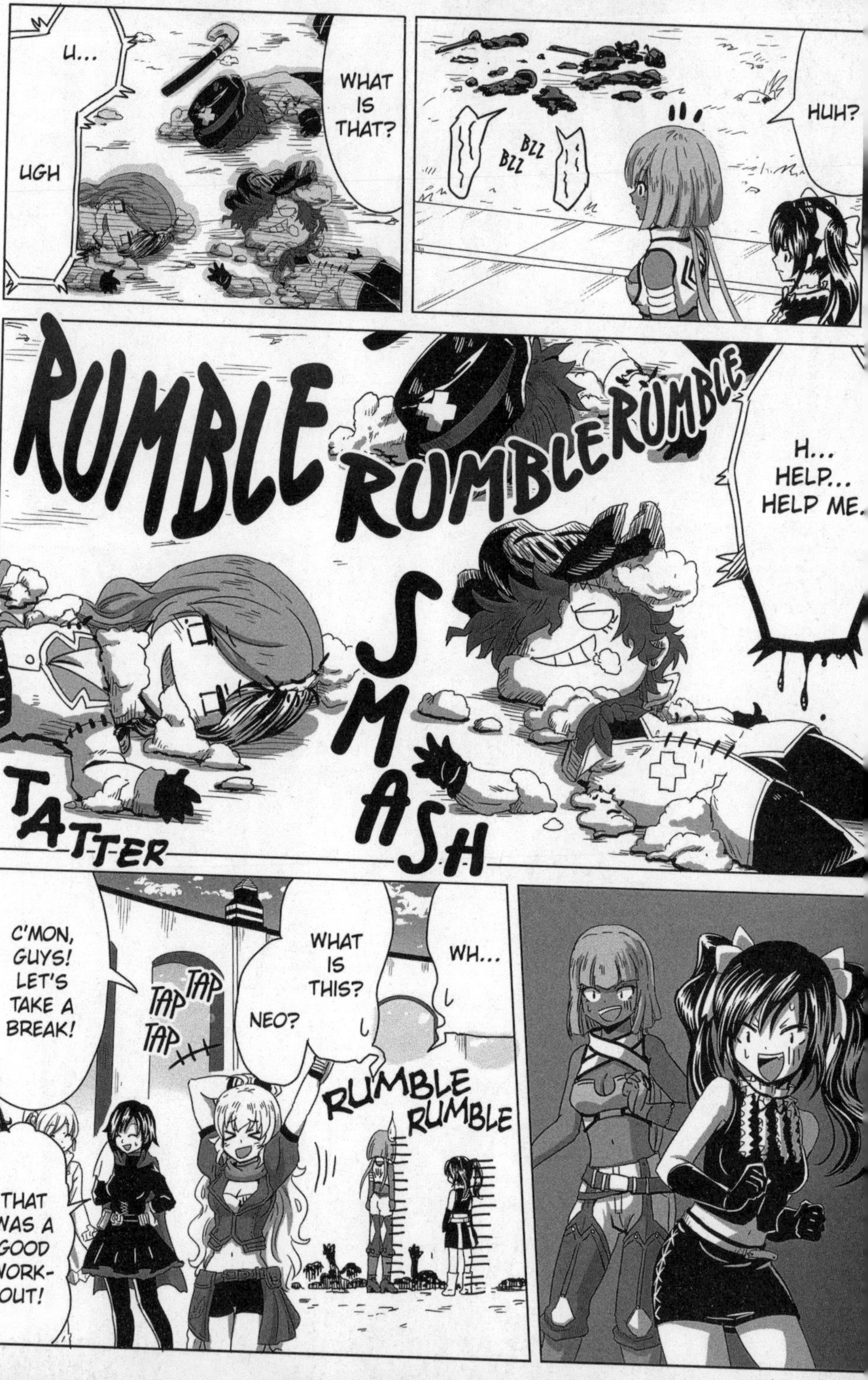
HUH?
BZZ BZZ
WHAT IS THAT?
U...
UGH
H... HELP... HELP ME.
RUMBLE
RUMBLE RUMBLE
SMASH
TATTER
WH...
WHAT IS THIS?
NEO?
C'MON, GUYS! LET'S TAKE A BREAK!
TAP TAP TAP
RUMBLE RUMBLE
THAT WAS A GOOD WORK-OUT!

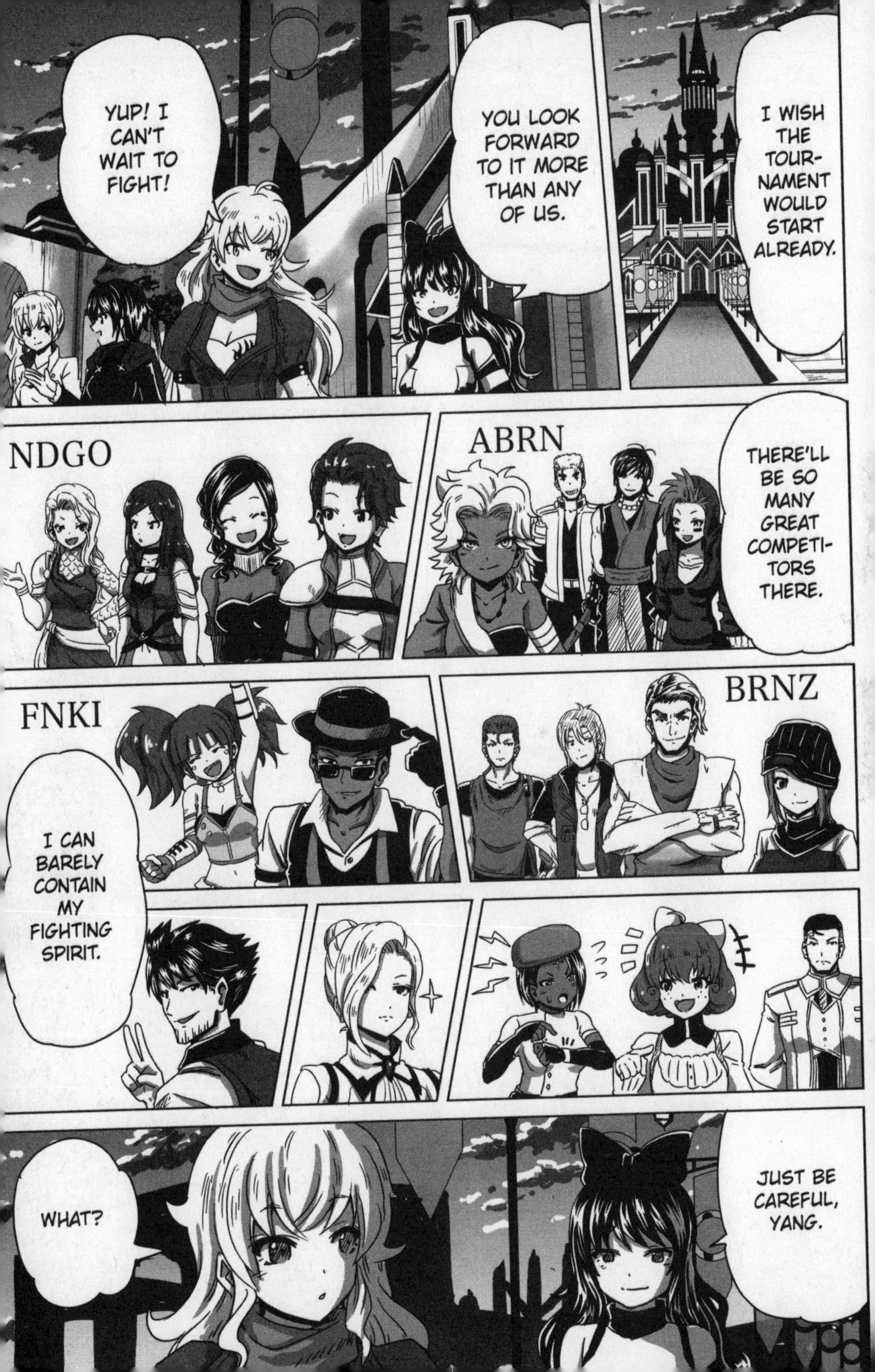
I WISH THE TOUR-NAMENT WOULD START ALREADY.
YOU LOOK FORWARD TO IT MORE THAN ANY OF US.
YUP! I CAN'T WAIT TO FIGHT!
ABRN
THERE'LL BE SO MANY GREAT COMPETI-TORS THERE.
NDGO
BRNZ
FNKI
I CAN BARELY CONTAIN MY FIGHTING SPIRIT.
JUST BE CAREFUL, YANG.
WHAT?

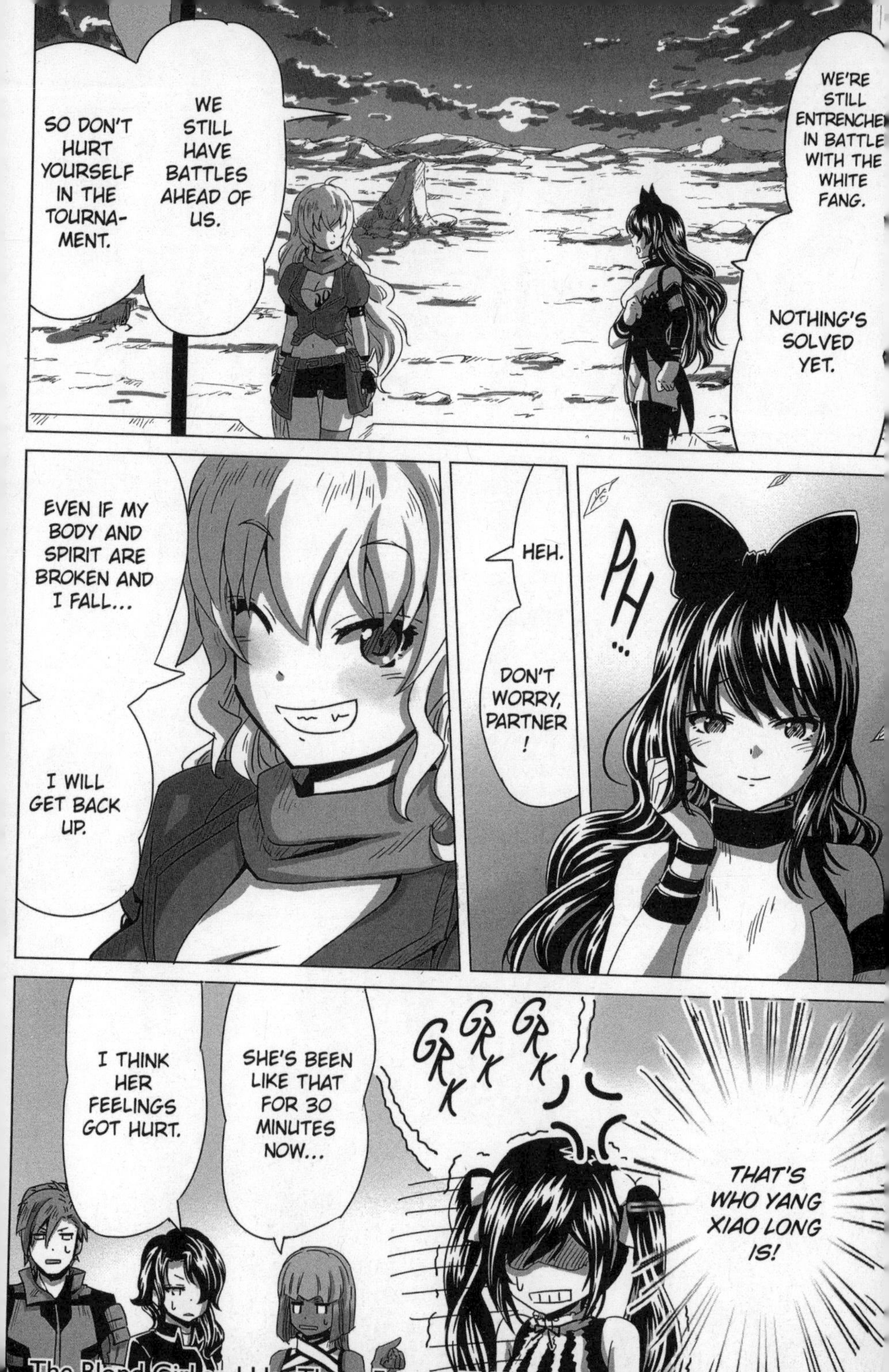
WE'RE STILL ENTRENCHE IN BATTLE WITH THE WHITE FANG.
NOTHING'S SOLVED YET.
WE STILL HAVE BATTLES AHEAD OF US.
SO DON'T HURT YOURSELF IN THE TOURNAMENT.
PH...
HEH.
DON'T WORRY, PARTNER!
EVEN IF MY BODY AND SPIRIT ARE BROKEN AND I FALL...
I WILL GET BACK UP.
THAT'S WHO YANG XIAO LONG IS!
GRK GRK GRK
SHE'S BEEN LIKE THAT FOR 30 MINUTES NOW...
I THINK HER FEELINGS GOT HURT.

The Blond Girl and Her Three Friends/END

Let's Do Something Fun Together!

Rojine Kio

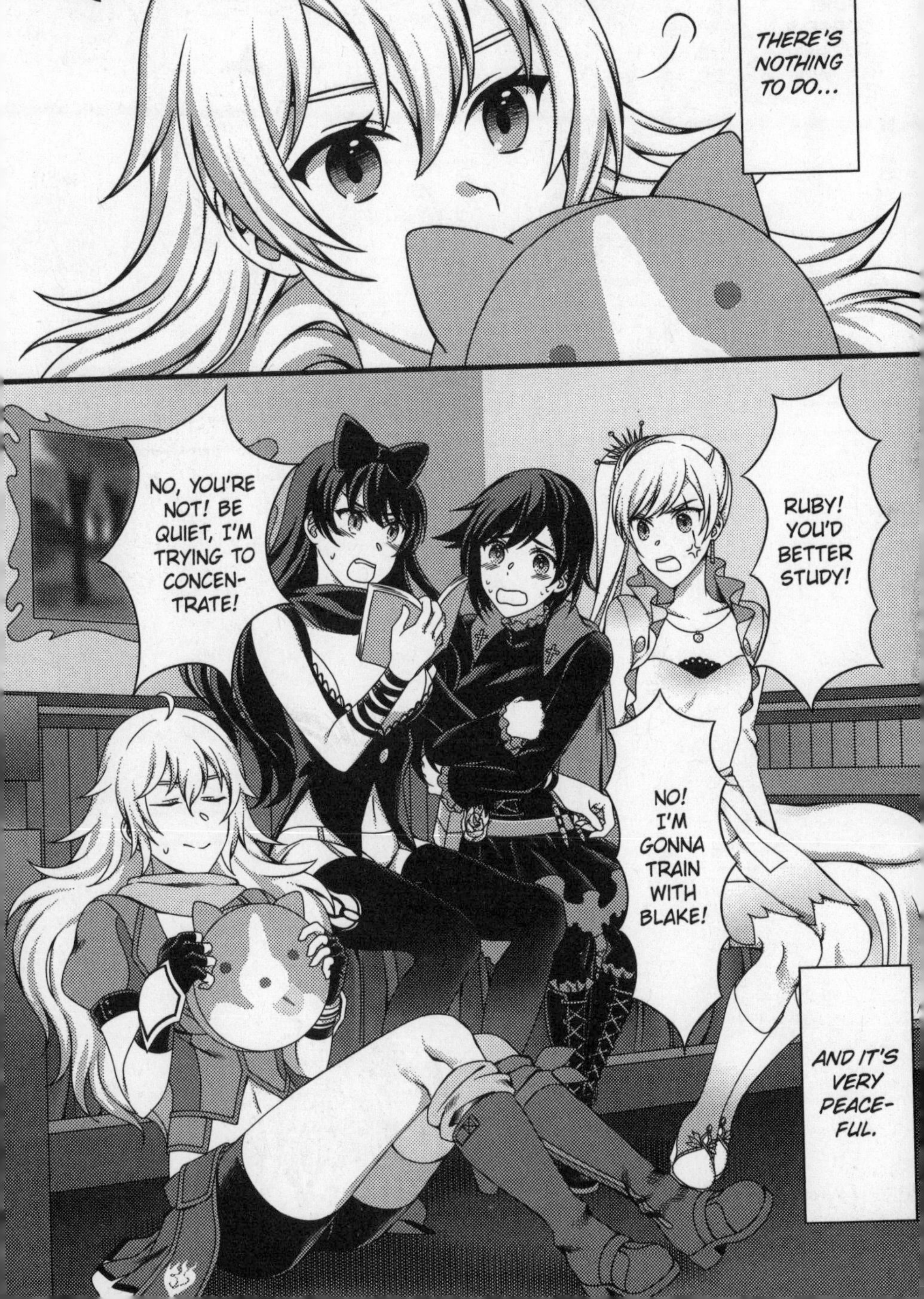
THERE'S NOTHING TO DO...
RUBY! YOU'D BETTER STUDY!
NO! I'M GONNA TRAIN WITH BLAKE!
NO, YOU'RE NOT! BE QUIET, I'M TRYING TO CONCEN-TRATE!
AND IT'S VERY PEACE-FUL.

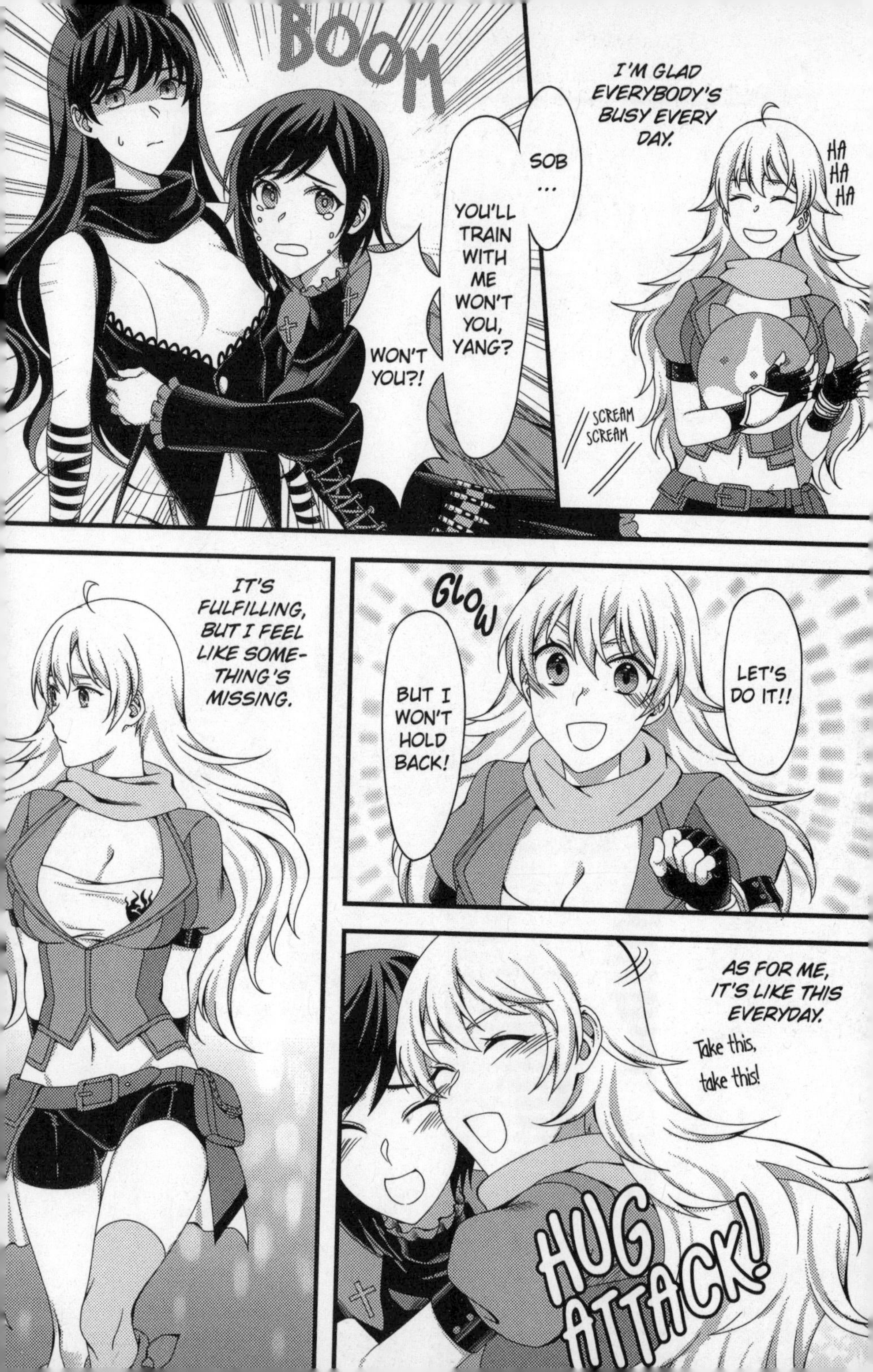
I'M GLAD EVERYBODY'S BUSY EVERY DAY.
HA HA HA
SCREAM SCREAM
BOOM
SOB ...
YOU'LL TRAIN WITH ME WON'T YOU, YANG?
WON'T YOU?!
GLOW
LET'S DO IT!!
BUT I WON'T HOLD BACK!
AS FOR ME, IT'S LIKE THIS EVERYDAY.
Take this, take this!
HUG ATTACK!
IT'S FULFILLING, BUT I FEEL LIKE SOME-THING'S MISSING.

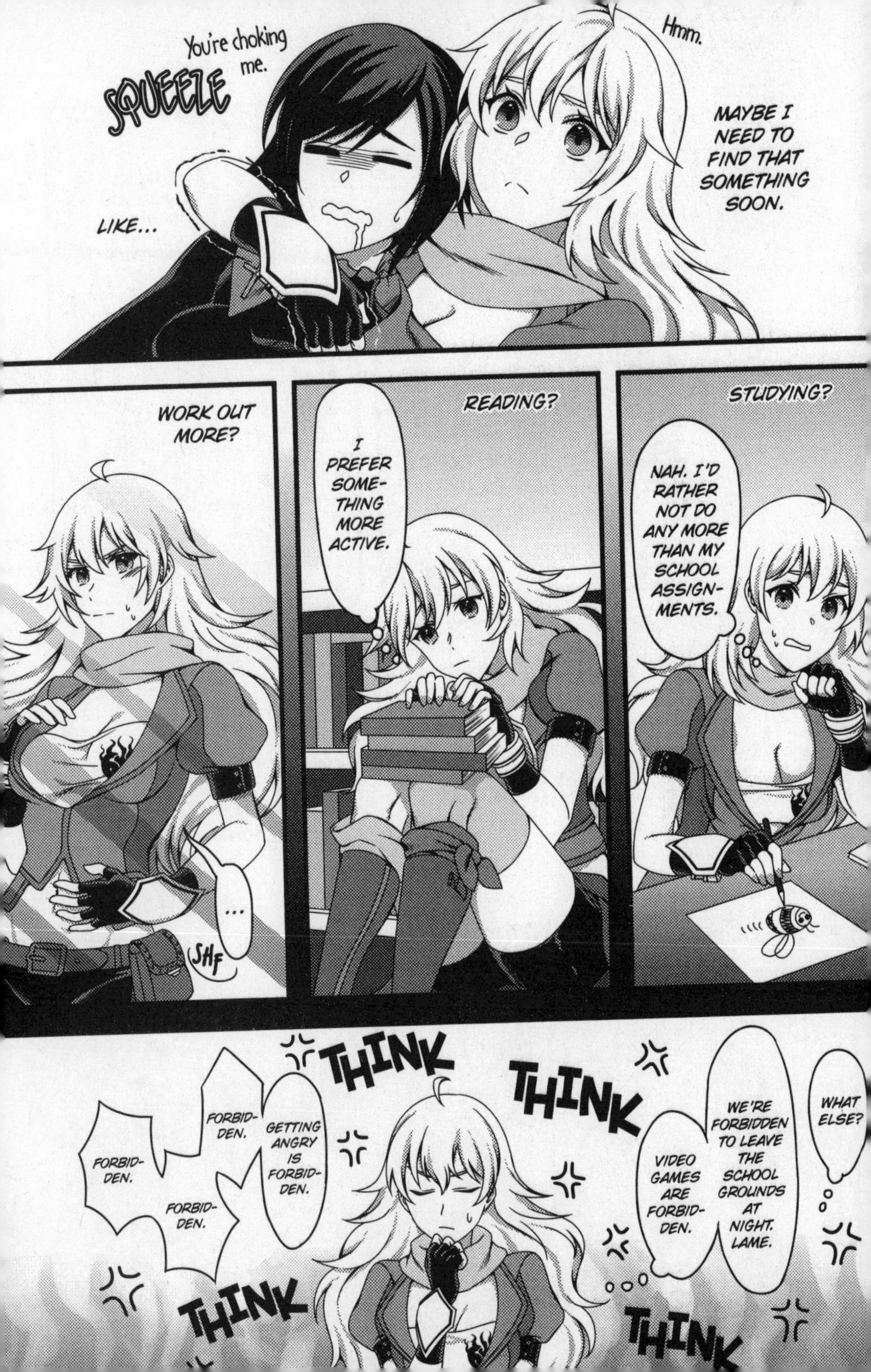
Hmm.
MAYBE I NEED TO FIND THAT SOMETHING SOON.
You're choking me.
SQUEEZE
LIKE...
STUDYING?
NAH. I'D RATHER NOT DO ANY MORE THAN MY SCHOOL ASSIGN-MENTS.
READING?
I PREFER SOME-THING MORE ACTIVE.
WORK OUT MORE?
...
SHF
WHAT ELSE?
WE'RE FORBIDDEN TO LEAVE THE SCHOOL GROUNDS AT NIGHT. LAME.
THINK
VIDEO GAMES ARE FORBID-DEN.
THINK
GETTING ANGRY IS FORBID-DEN.
FORBID-DEN.
FORBID-DEN.
FORBID-DEN.
THINK
THINK

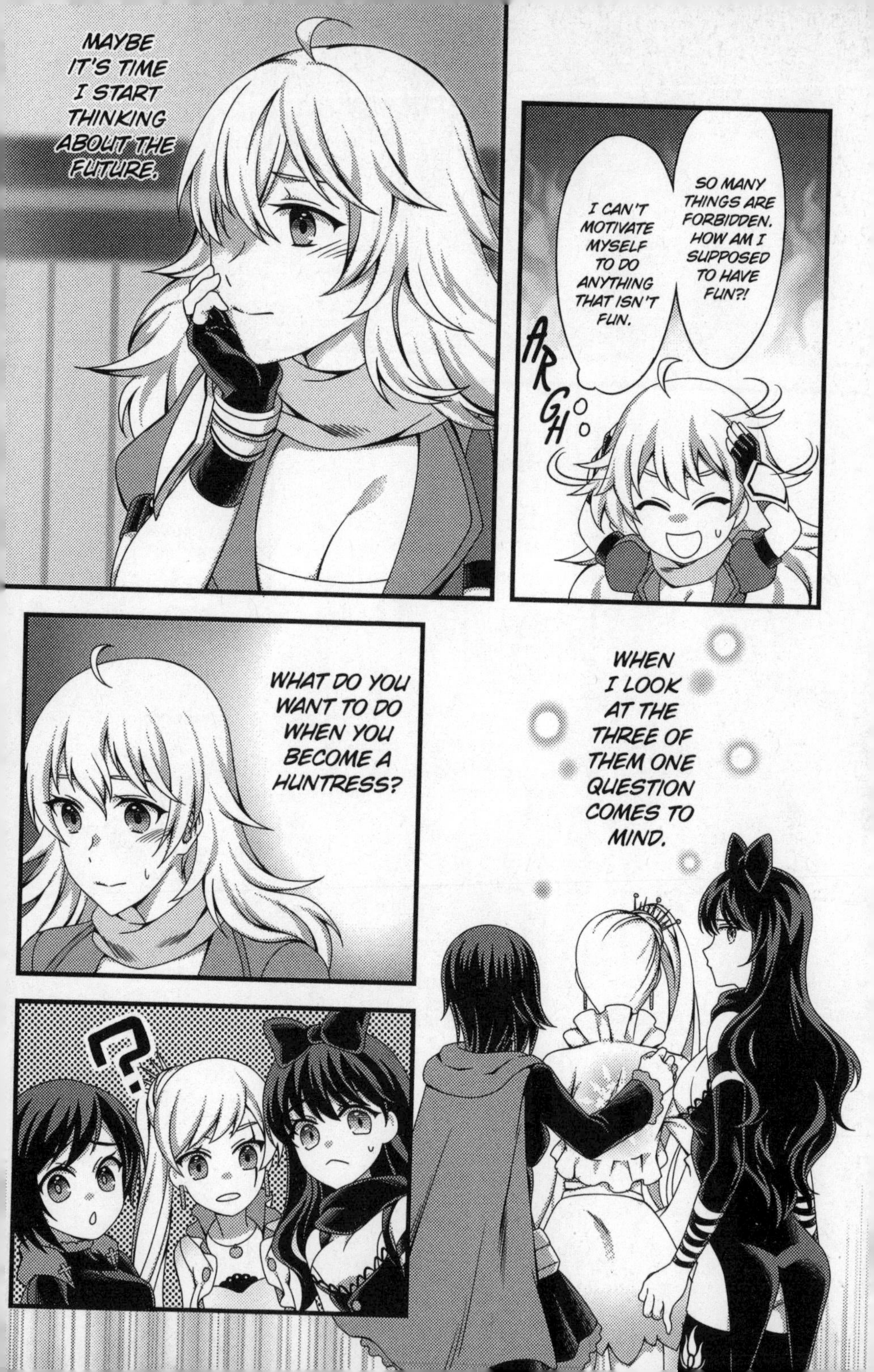
SO MANY THINGS ARE FORBIDDEN. HOW AM I SUPPOSED TO HAVE FUN?!
I CAN'T MOTIVATE MYSELF TO DO ANYTHING THAT ISN'T FUN.
ARGH
MAYBE IT'S TIME I START THINKING ABOUT THE FUTURE.
WHEN I LOOK AT THE THREE OF THEM ONE QUESTION COMES TO MIND.
WHAT DO YOU WANT TO DO WHEN YOU BECOME A HUNTRESS?
?!

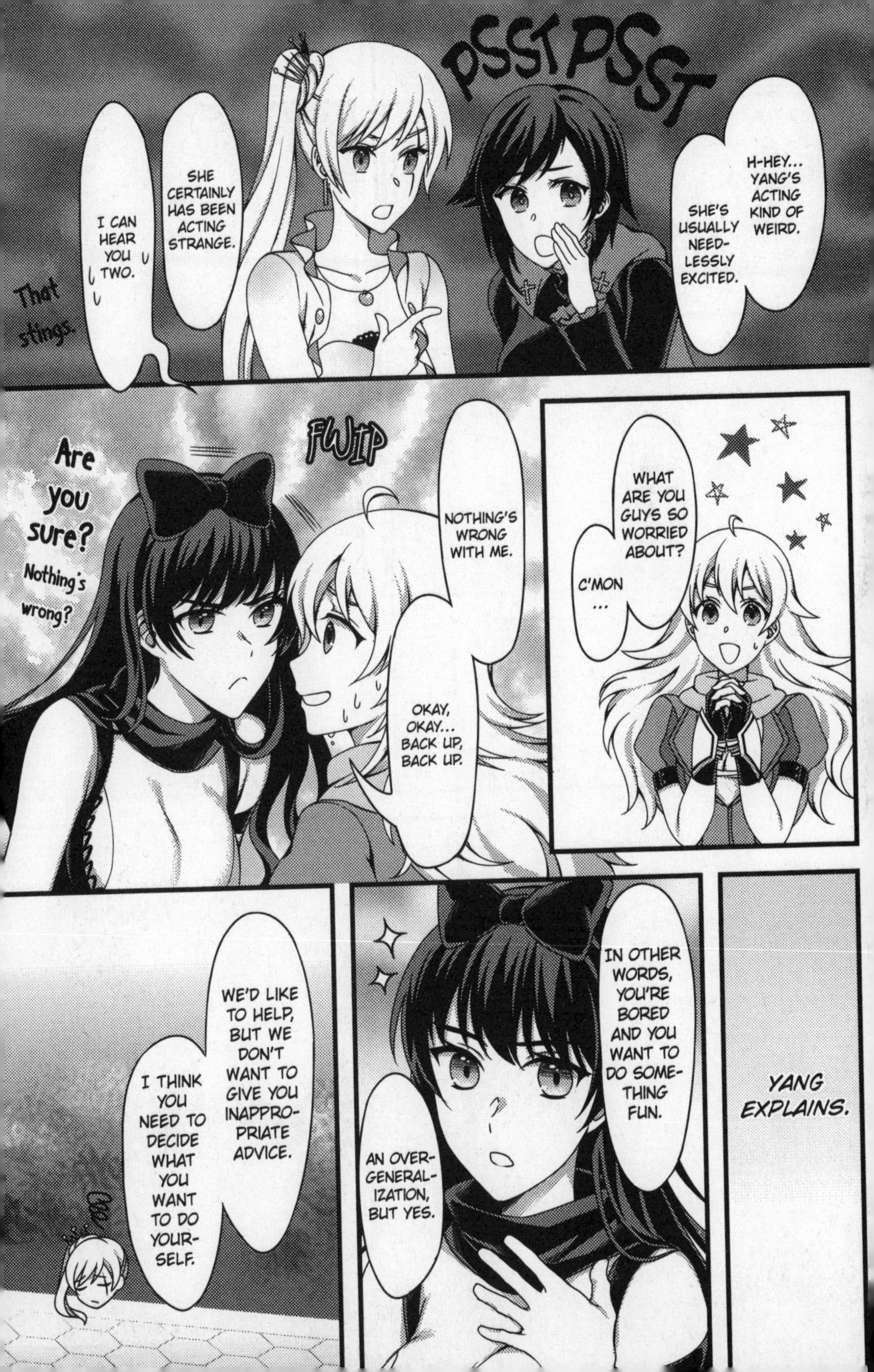
PSST PSST
H-HEY... YANG'S ACTING KIND OF WEIRD.
SHE'S USUALLY NEEDLESSLY EXCITED.
SHE CERTAINLY HAS BEEN ACTING STRANGE.
I CAN HEAR YOU TWO.
That stings.
WHAT ARE YOU GUYS SO WORRIED ABOUT?
C'MON...
FWIP
NOTHING'S WRONG WITH ME.
Are you sure? Nothing's wrong?
OKAY, OKAY... BACK UP, BACK UP.
YANG EXPLAINS.
IN OTHER WORDS, YOU'RE BORED AND YOU WANT TO DO SOMETHING FUN.
AN OVERGENERALIZATION, BUT YES.
WE'D LIKE TO HELP, BUT WE DON'T WANT TO GIVE YOU INAPPROPRIATE ADVICE.
I THINK YOU NEED TO DECIDE WHAT YOU WANT TO DO YOURSELF.

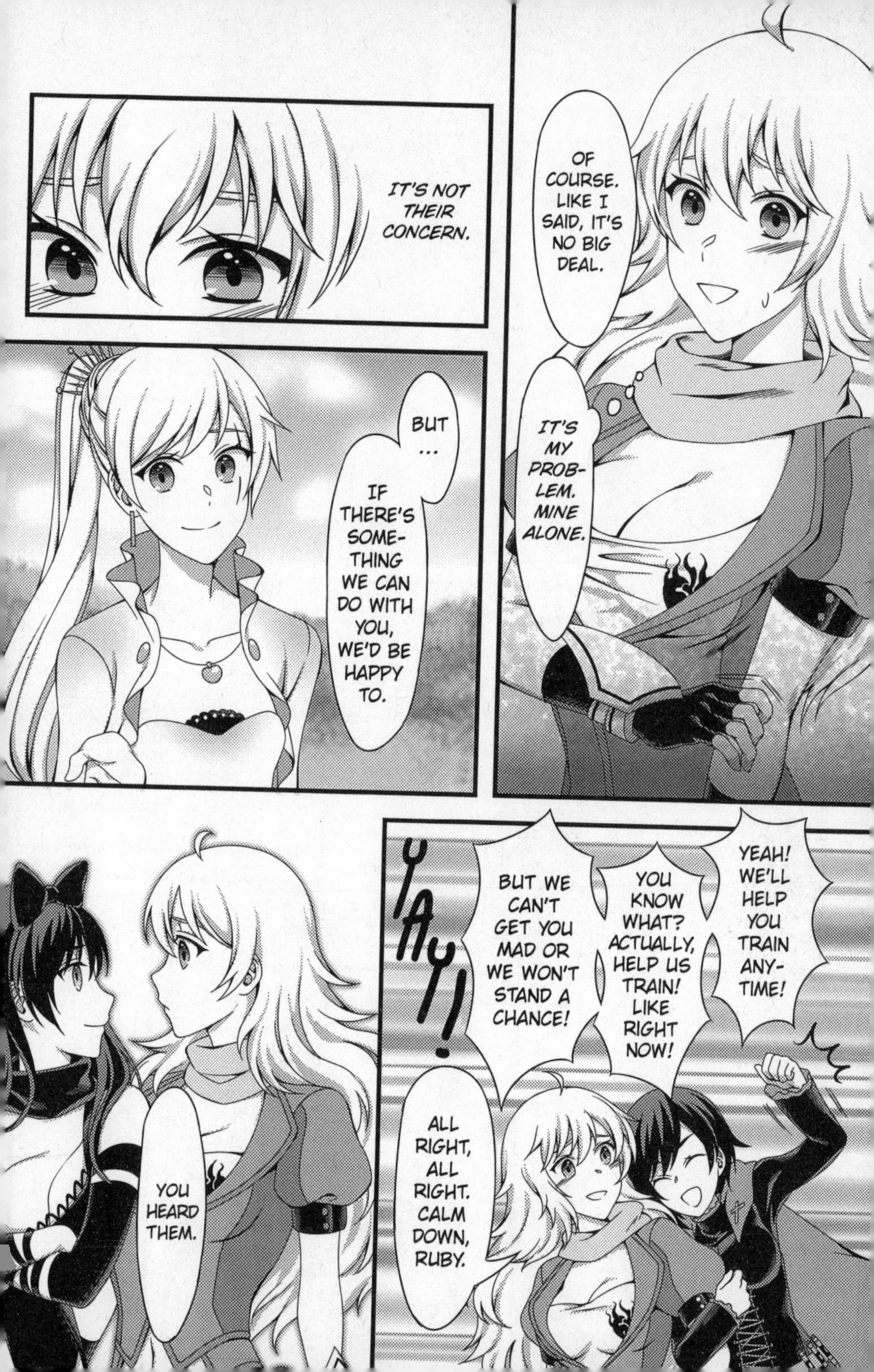
OF COURSE. LIKE I SAID, IT'S NO BIG DEAL.
IT'S MY PROB-LEM. MINE ALONE.
IT'S NOT THEIR CONCERN.
BUT ...
IF THERE'S SOME-THING WE CAN DO WITH YOU, WE'D BE HAPPY TO.
YEAH! WE'LL HELP YOU TRAIN ANY-TIME!
YOU KNOW WHAT? ACTUALLY, HELP US TRAIN! LIKE RIGHT NOW!
BUT WE CAN'T GET YOU MAD OR WE WON'T STAND A CHANCE!
YAY!
ALL RIGHT, ALL RIGHT. CALM DOWN, RUBY.
YOU HEARD THEM.

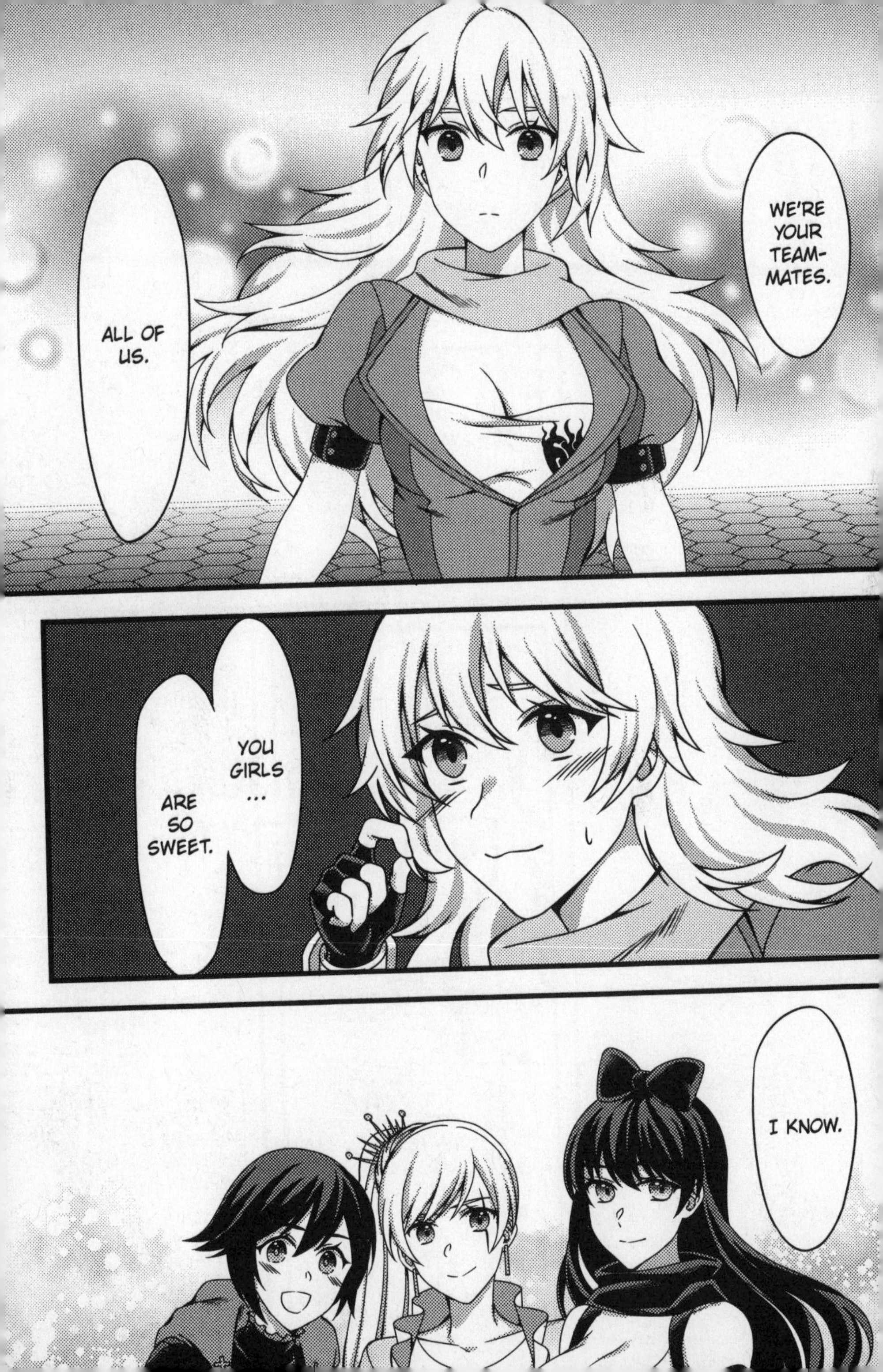
WE'RE YOUR TEAM-MATES.
ALL OF US.
YOU GIRLS ...
ARE SO SWEET.
I KNOW.

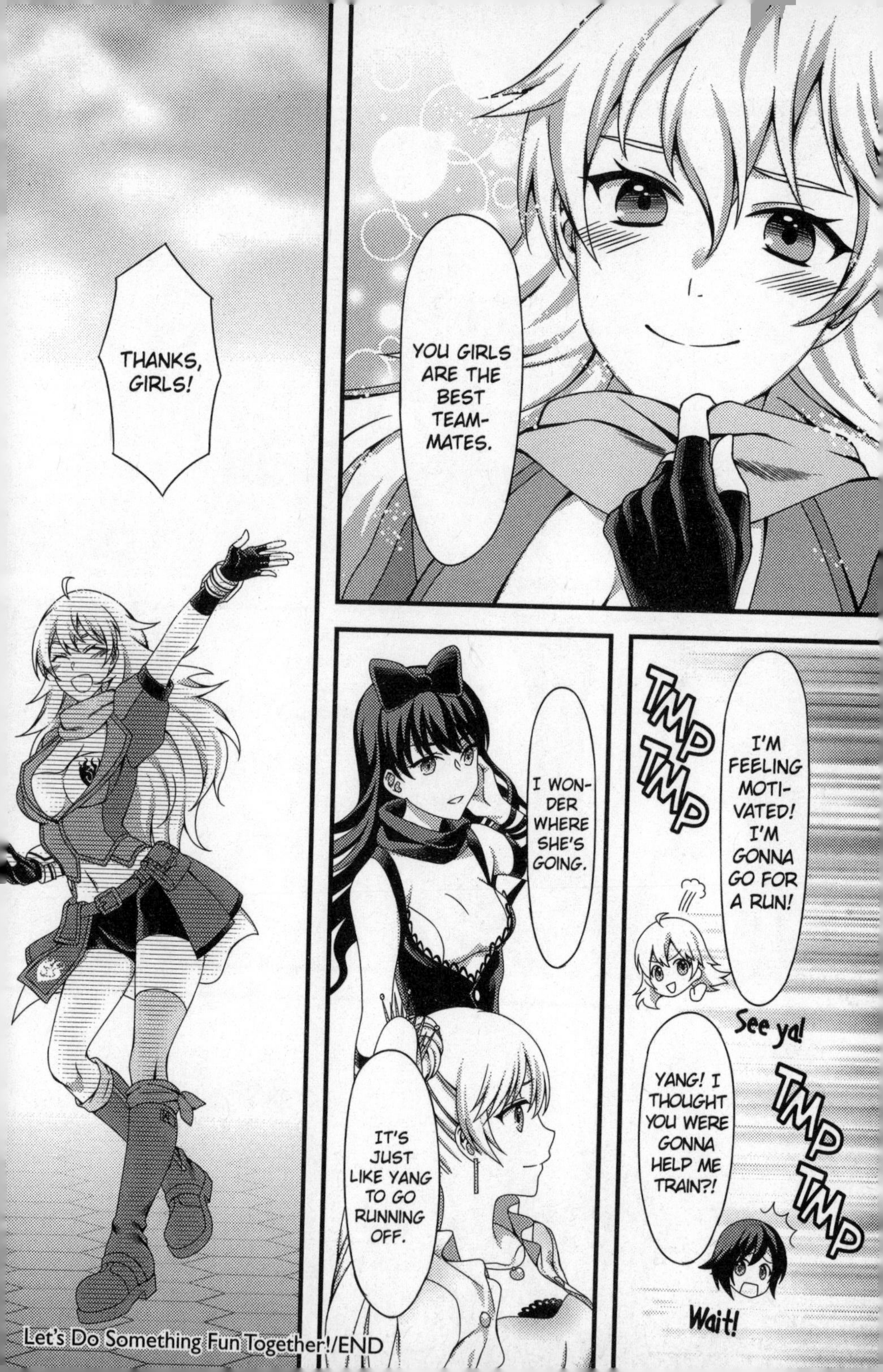
YOU GIRLS ARE THE BEST TEAM-MATES.
TMP TMP
I'M FEELING MOTI-VATED! I'M GONNA GO FOR A RUN!
See ya!
YANG! I THOUGHT YOU WERE GONNA HELP ME TRAIN?!
TMP TMP
Wait!
I WON-DER WHERE SHE'S GOING.
IT'S JUST LIKE YANG TO GO RUNNING OFF.
THANKS, GIRLS!
Let's Do Something Fun Together!/END

Team RWBY
EMO

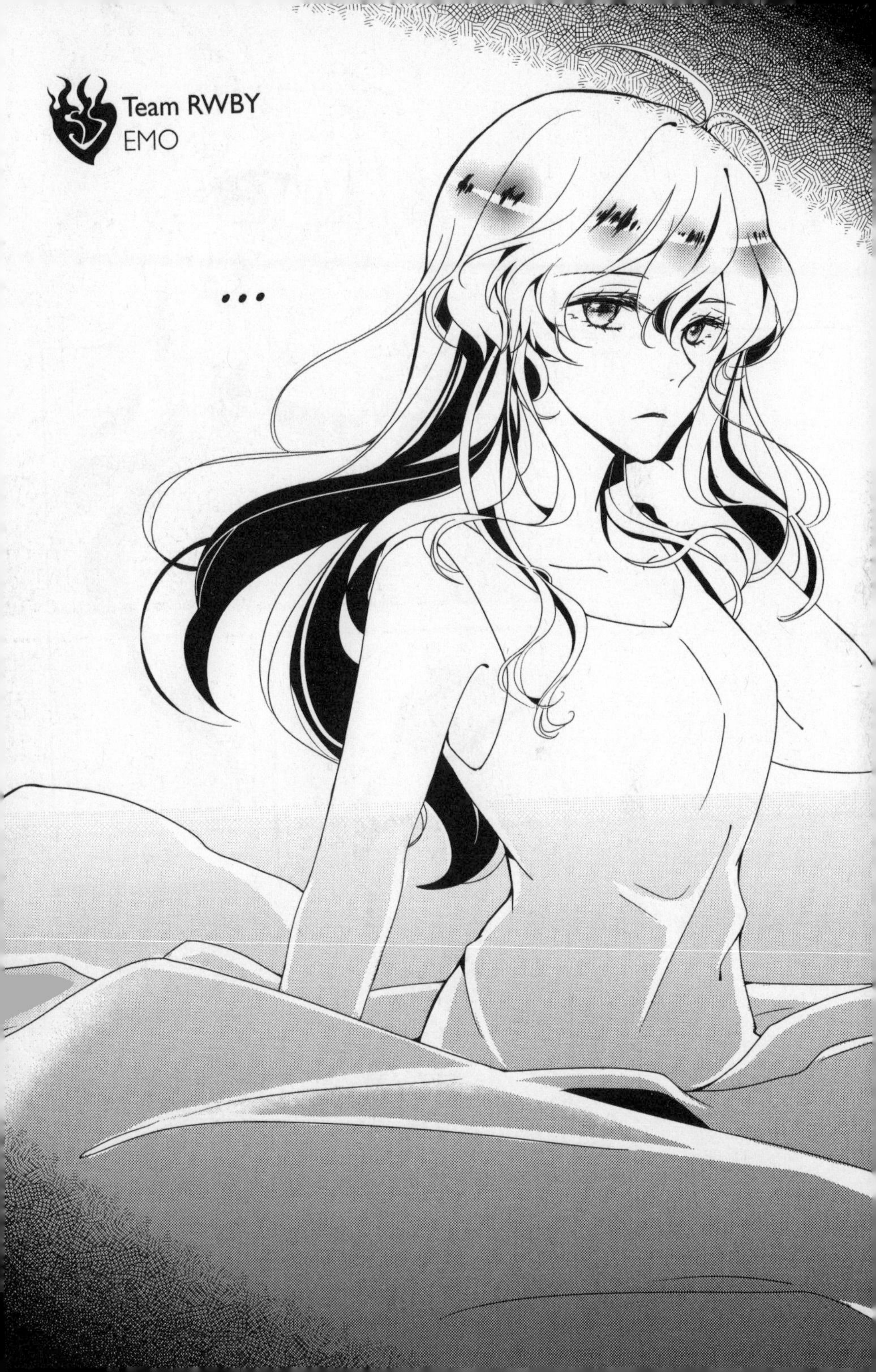
...

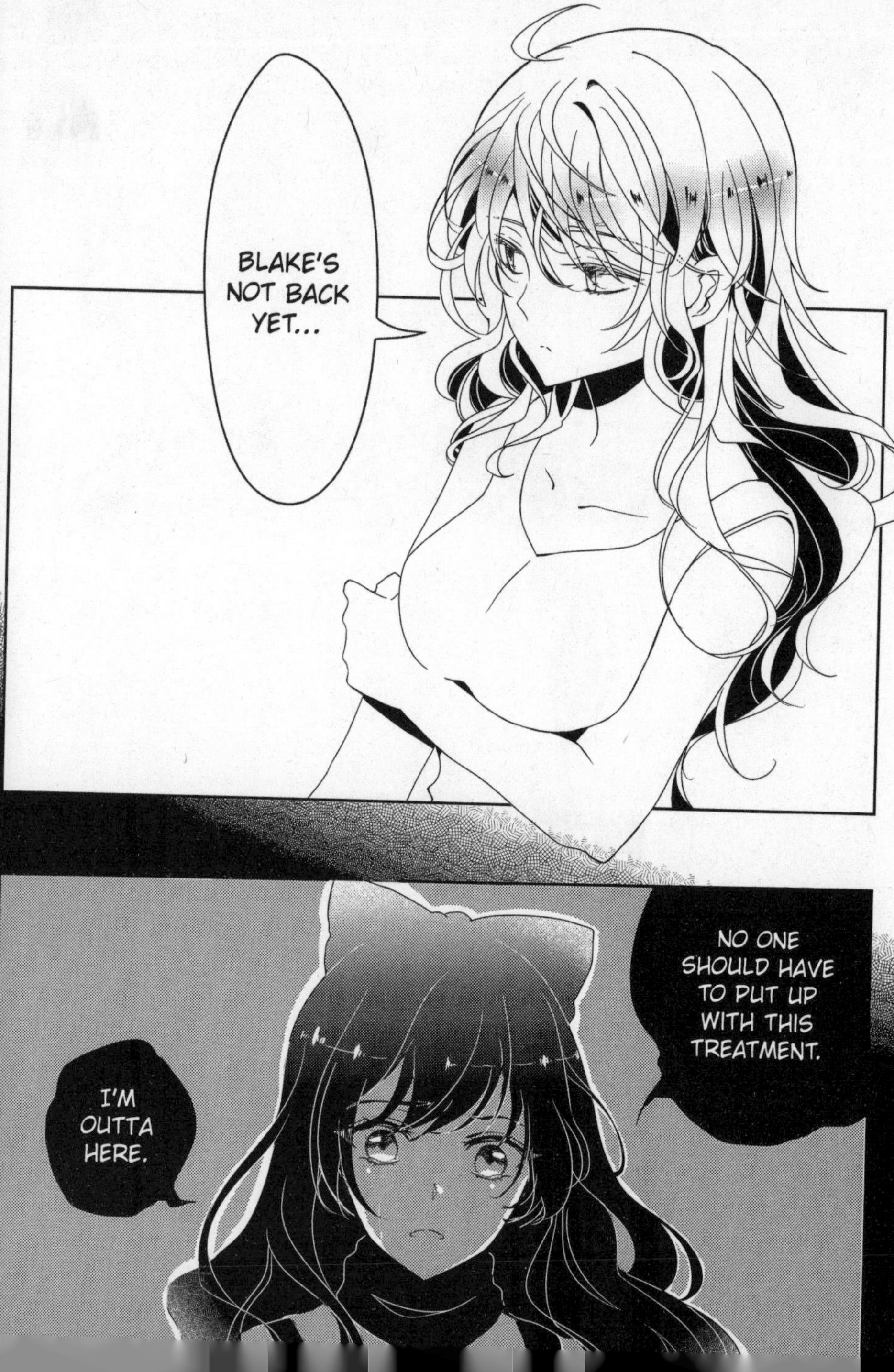
BLAKE'S NOT BACK YET...
NO ONE SHOULD HAVE TO PUT UP WITH THIS TREATMENT.
I'M OUTTA HERE.

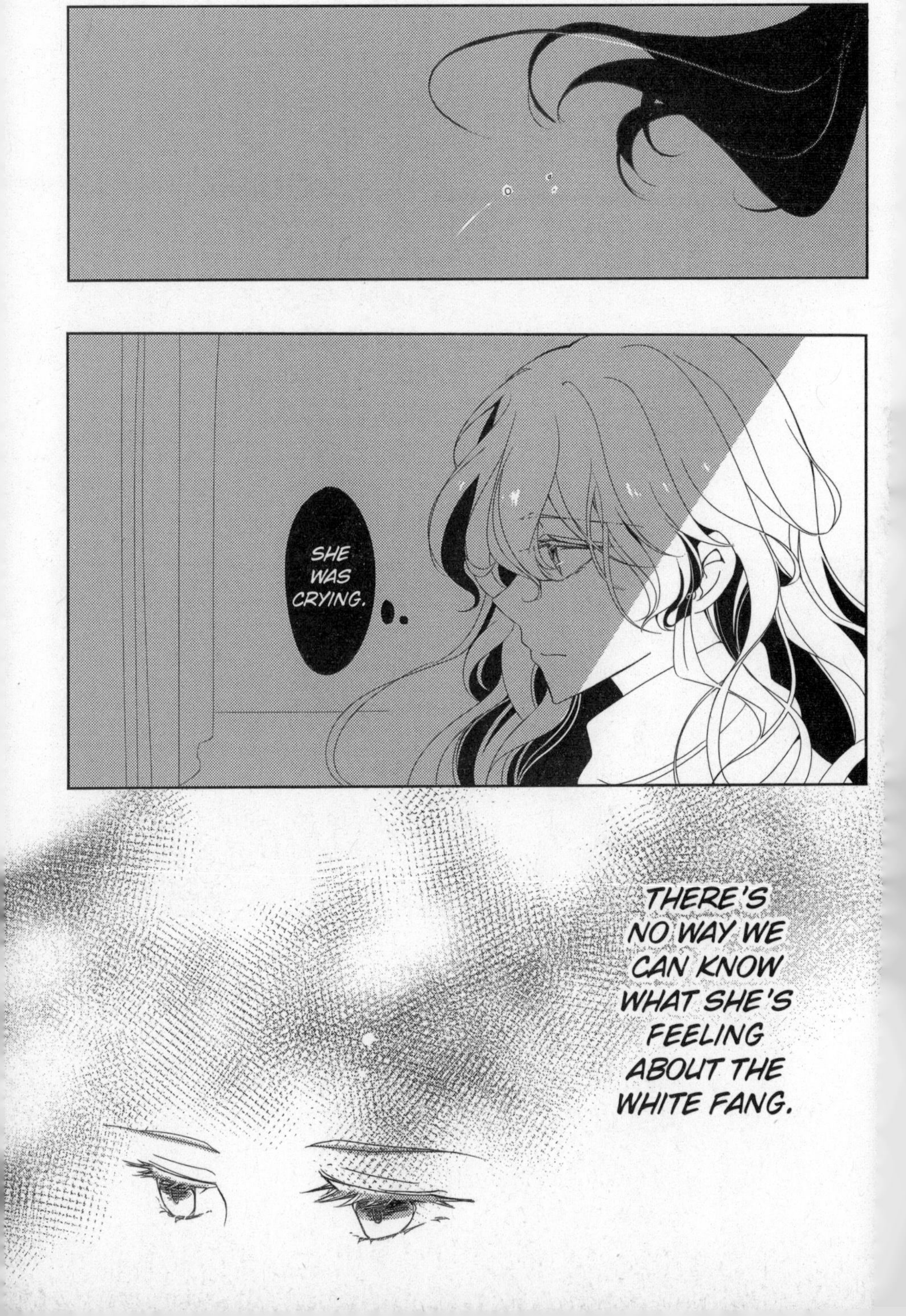
SHE WAS CRYING.
THERE'S NO WAY WE CAN KNOW WHAT SHE'S FEELING ABOUT THE WHITE FANG.

RUBY IS MY
SISTER, NO
MATTER WHAT.
BUT BLAKE IS
MY FRIEND...
EVEN IF SHE
WAS ONCE
PART OF THE
WHITE FANG.

RUBY IS
REALLY
WORRIED
ABOUT HER.

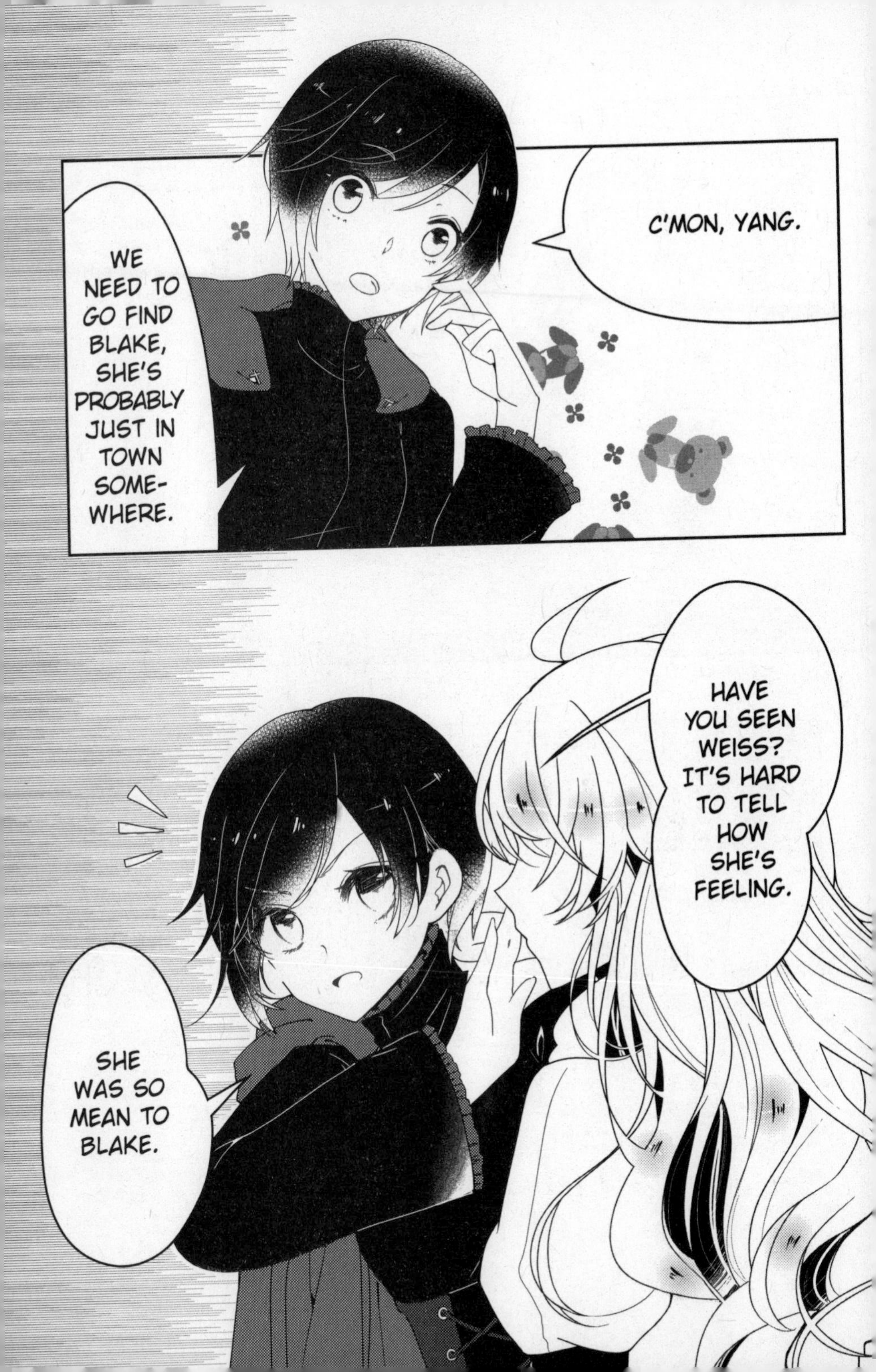
C'MON, YANG.
WE NEED TO GO FIND BLAKE, SHE'S PROBABLY JUST IN TOWN SOME-WHERE.
HAVE YOU SEEN WEISS? IT'S HARD TO TELL HOW SHE'S FEELING.
SHE WAS SO MEAN TO BLAKE.

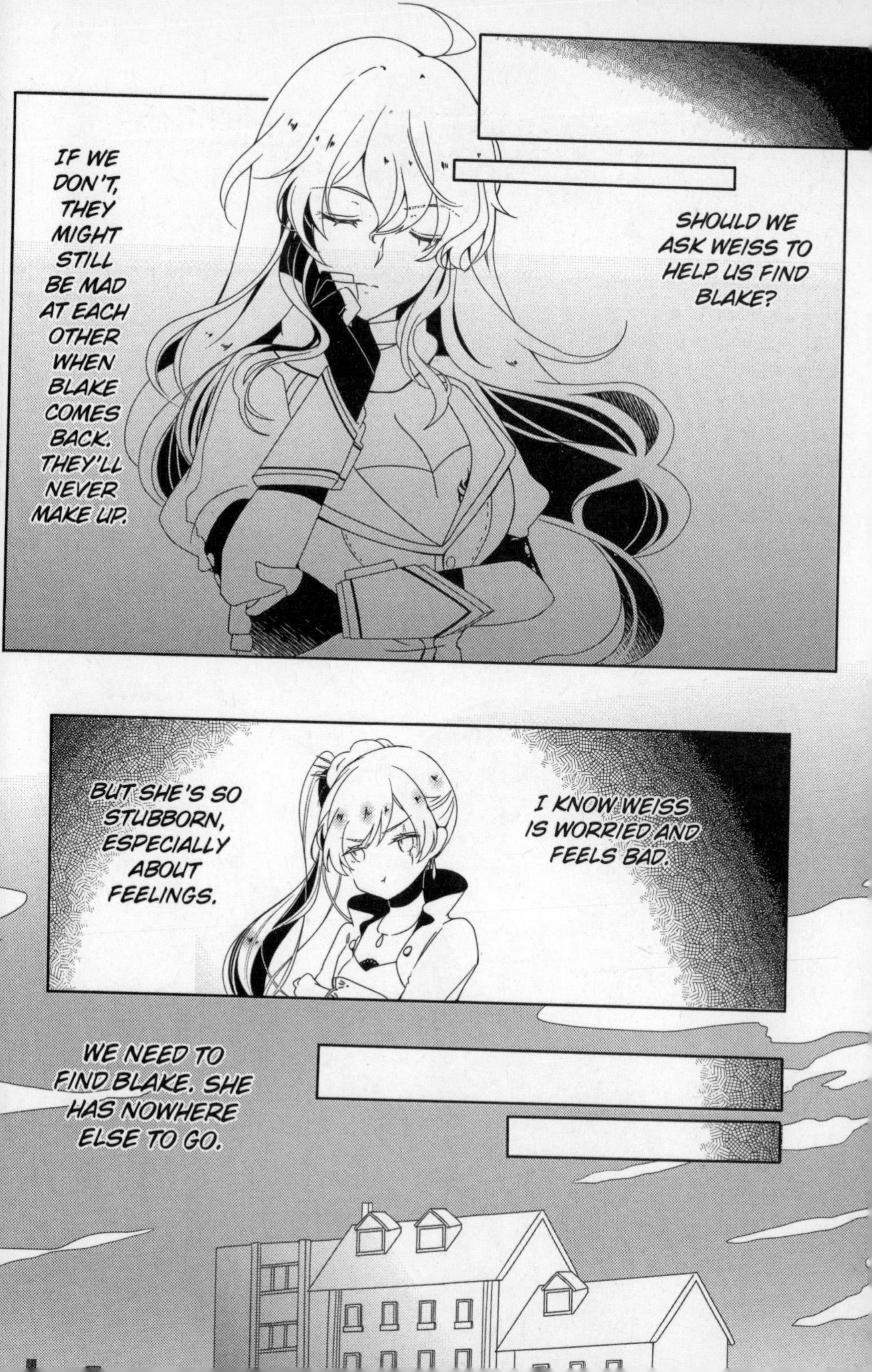
SHOULD WE ASK WEISS TO HELP US FIND BLAKE?
IF WE DON'T, THEY MIGHT STILL BE MAD AT EACH OTHER WHEN BLAKE COMES BACK. THEY'LL NEVER MAKE UP.
I KNOW WEISS IS WORRIED AND FEELS BAD.
BUT SHE'S SO STUBBORN, ESPECIALLY ABOUT FEELINGS.
WE NEED TO FIND BLAKE. SHE HAS NOWHERE ELSE TO GO.

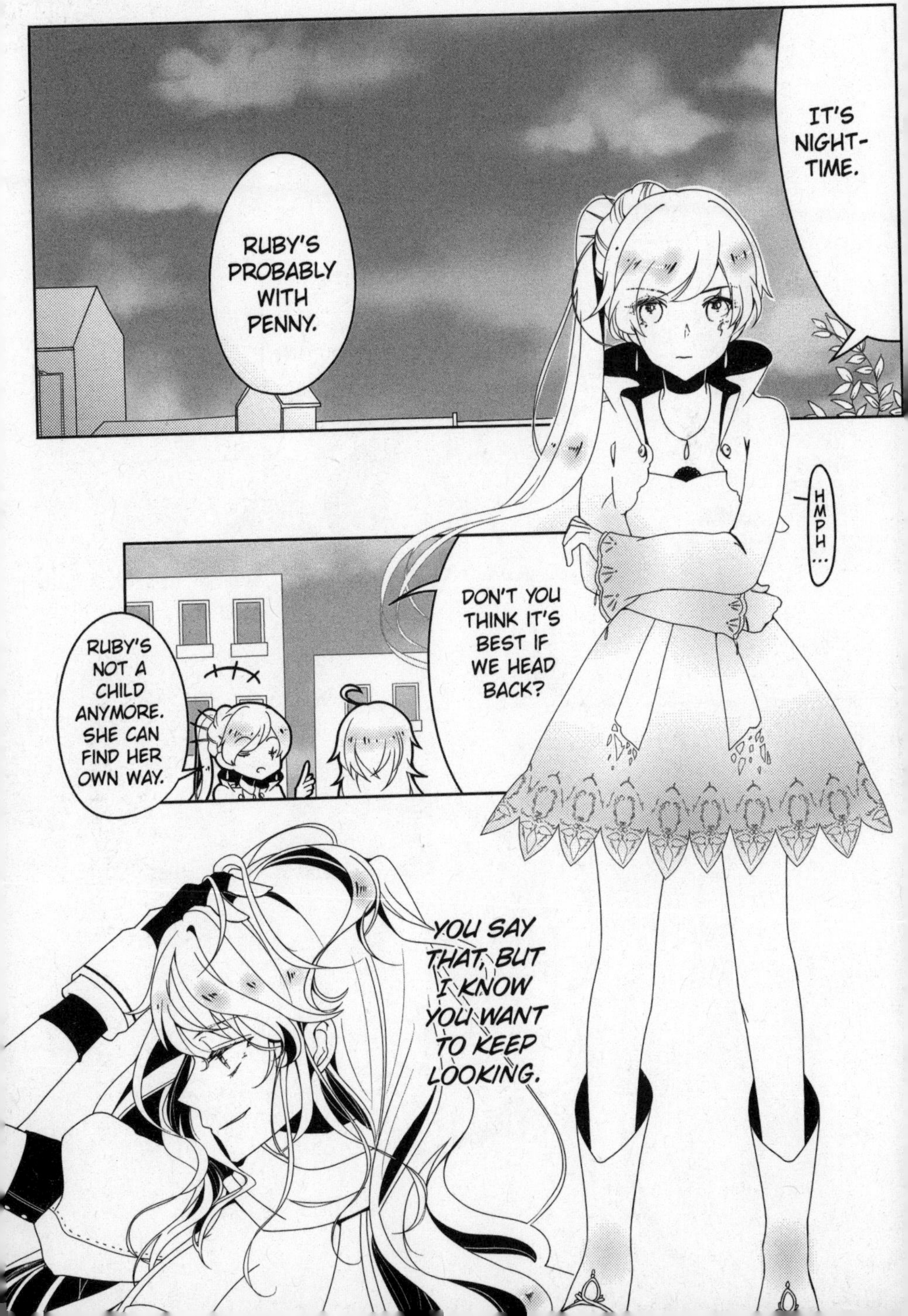
IT'S NIGHT-TIME.
RUBY'S PROBABLY WITH PENNY.
HMPH...
DON'T YOU THINK IT'S BEST IF WE HEAD BACK?
RUBY'S NOT A CHILD ANYMORE. SHE CAN FIND HER OWN WAY.
YOU SAY THAT, BUT I KNOW YOU WANT TO KEEP LOOKING.

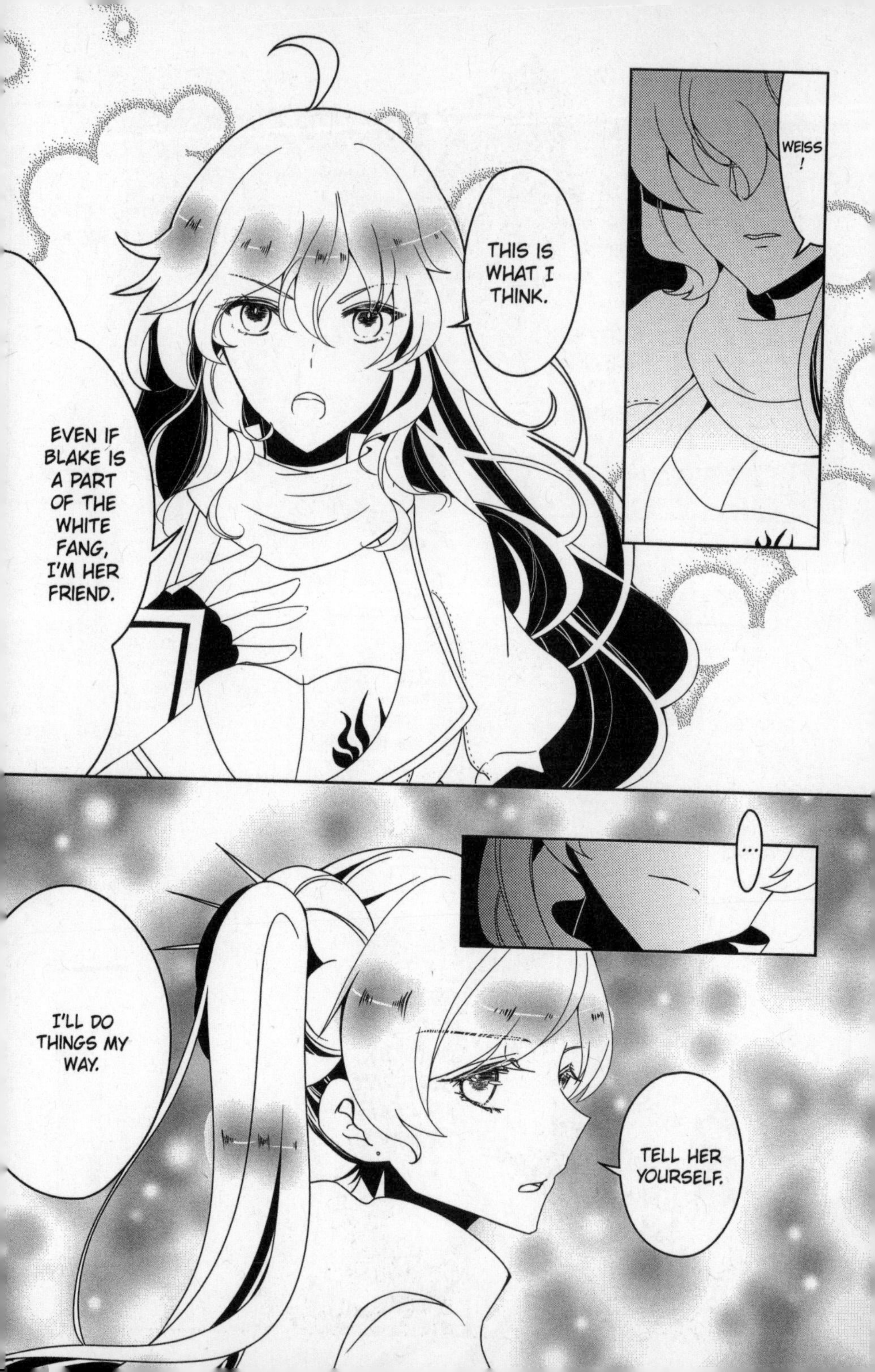
WEISS !
THIS IS WHAT I THINK.
EVEN IF BLAKE IS A PART OF THE WHITE FANG, I'M HER FRIEND.
...
TELL HER YOURSELF.
I'LL DO THINGS MY WAY.

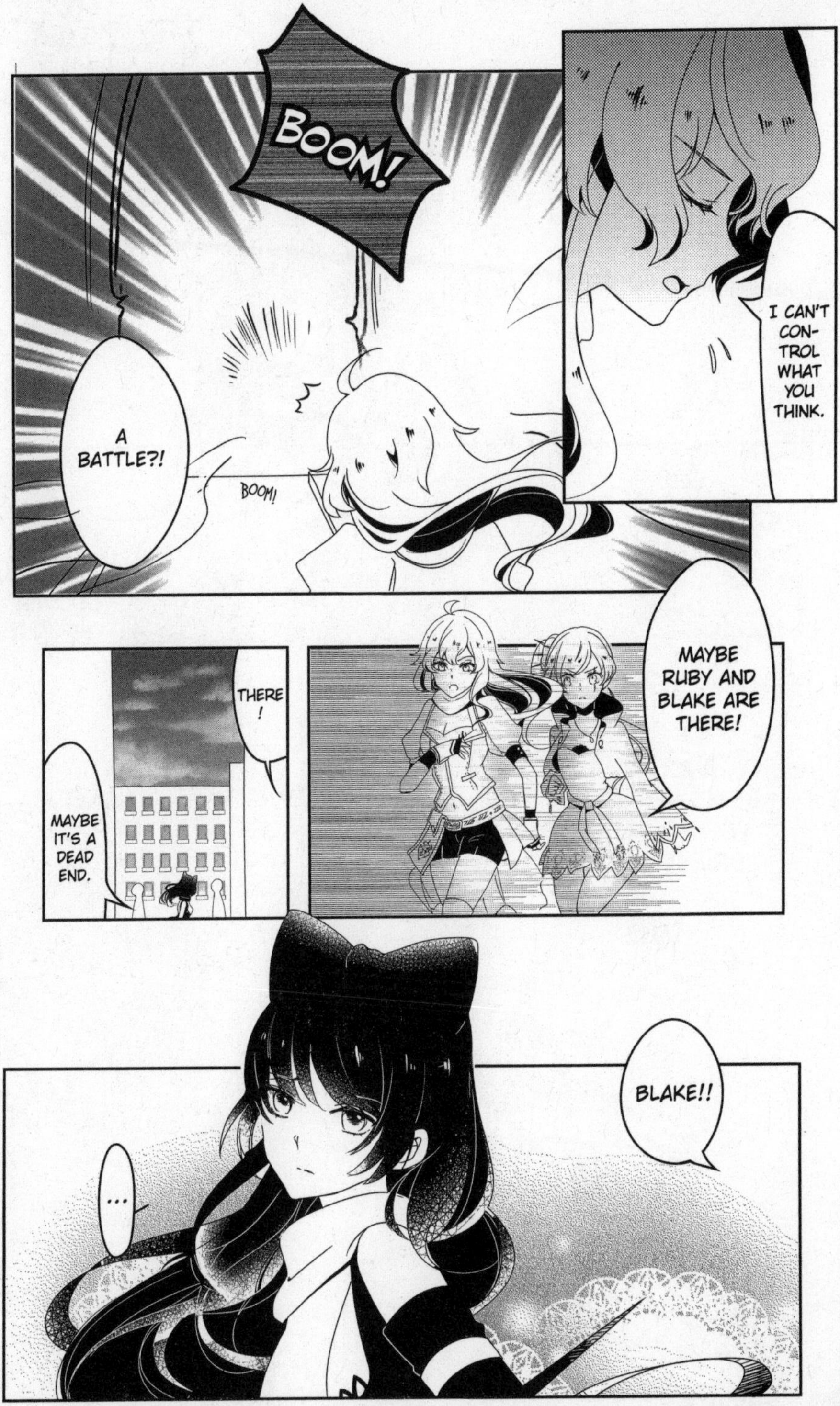
I CAN'T CONTROL WHAT YOU THINK.
BOOM!
A BATTLE?!
BOOM!
MAYBE RUBY AND BLAKE ARE THERE!
THERE!
MAYBE IT'S A DEAD END.
BLAKE!!
...

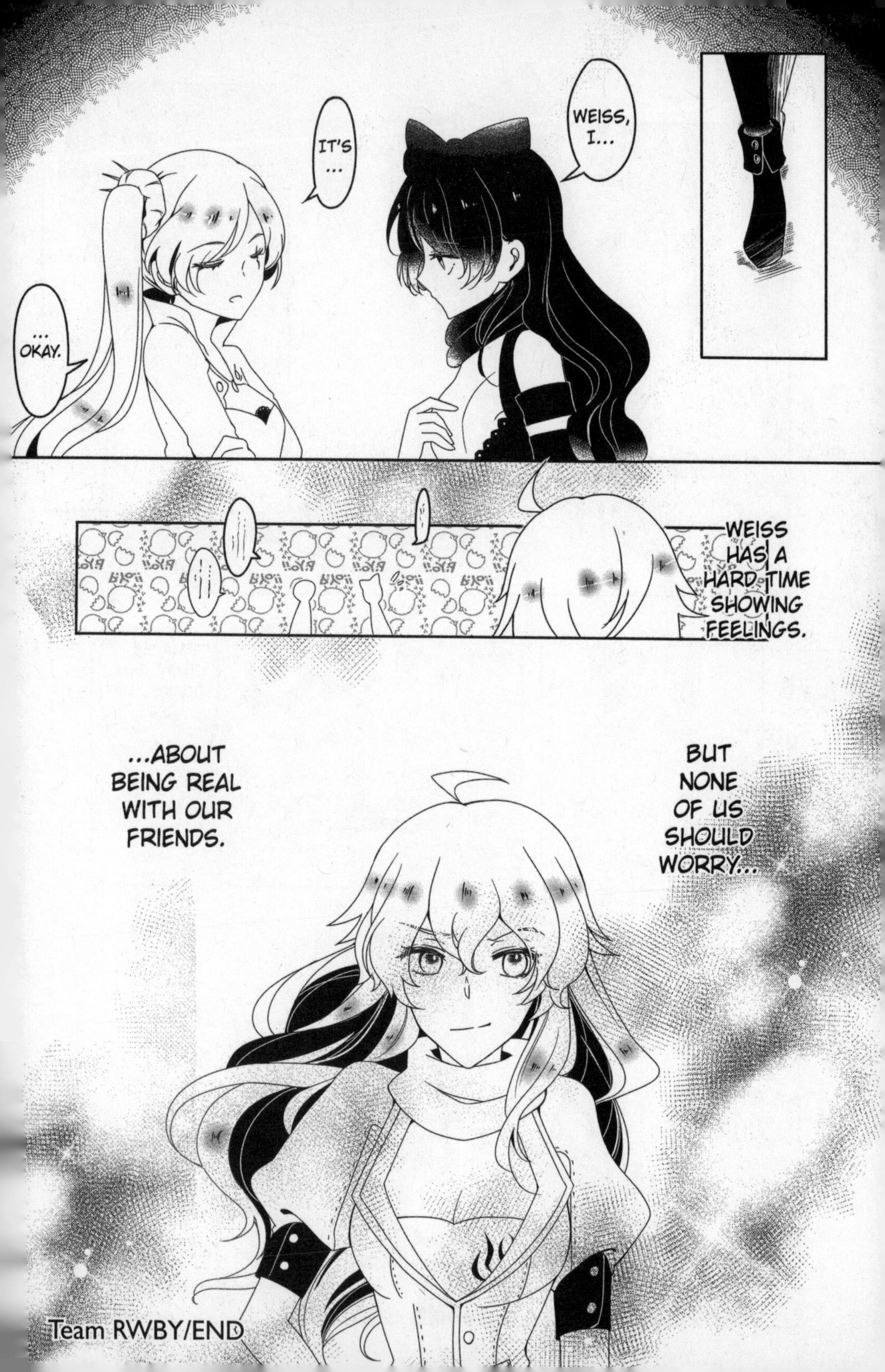
WEISS, I...
IT'S ...
... OKAY.
WEISS HAS A HARD TIME SHOWING FEELINGS.
BUT NONE OF US SHOULD WORRY...
...ABOUT BEING REAL WITH OUR FRIENDS.
Team RWBY/END

The Reader

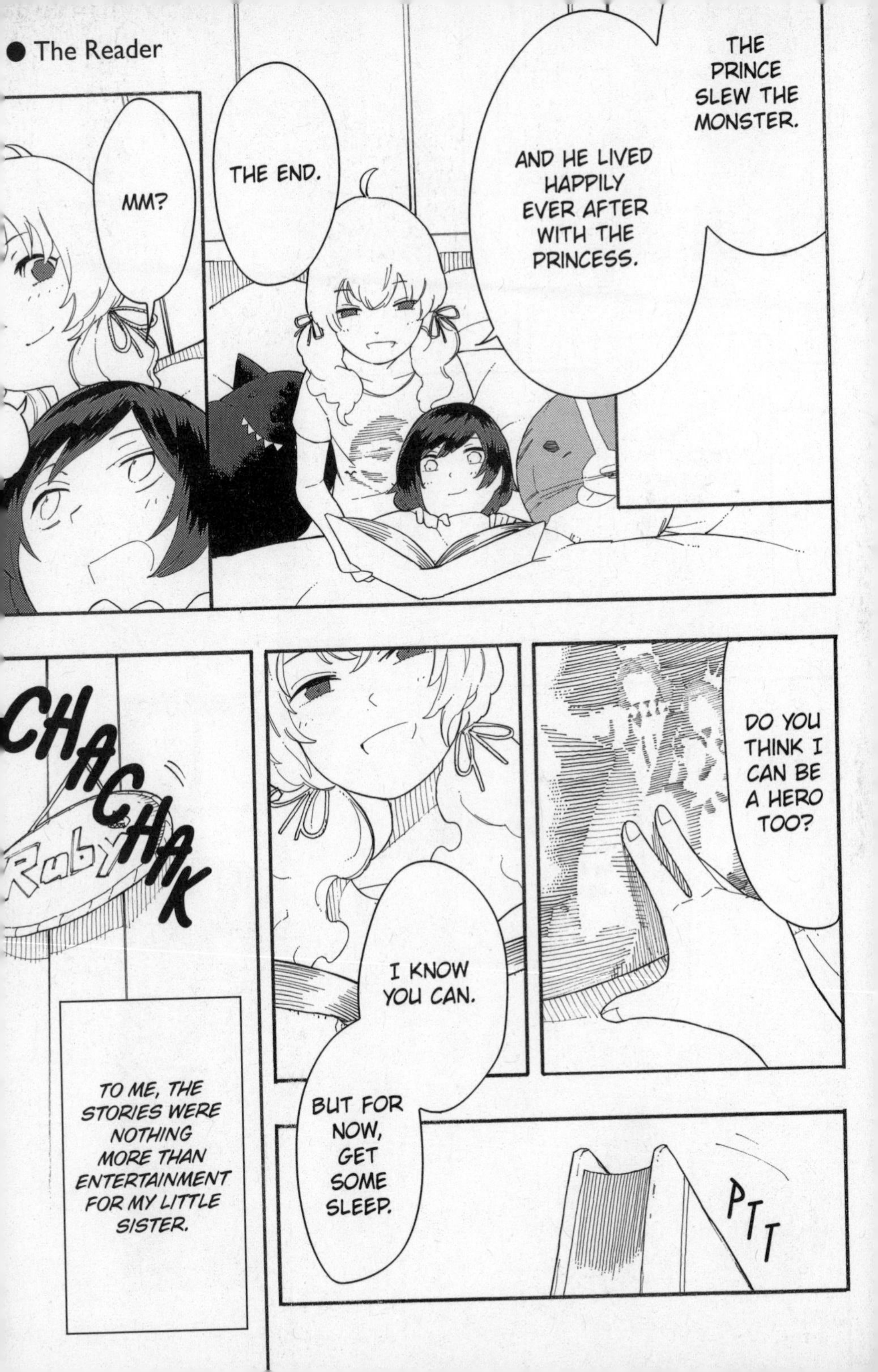
THE PRINCE SLEW THE MONSTER.
AND HE LIVED HAPPILY EVER AFTER WITH THE PRINCESS.
THE END.
MM?
DO YOU THINK I CAN BE A HERO TOO?
I KNOW YOU CAN.
BUT FOR NOW, GET SOME SLEEP.
PTT
CHACHACHAK
Ruby
TO ME, THE STORIES WERE NOTHING MORE THAN ENTERTAINMENT FOR MY LITTLE SISTER.

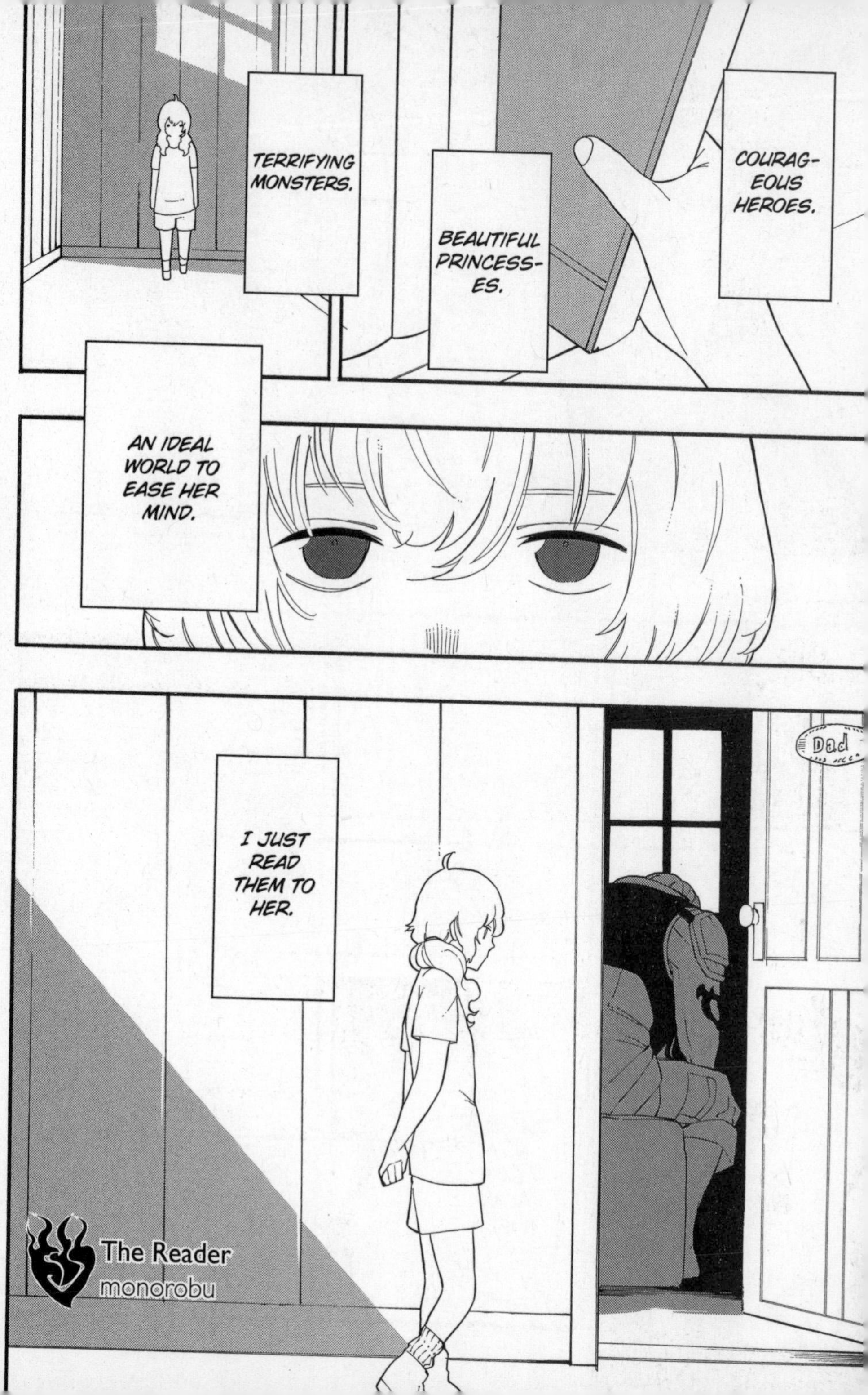
COURAG-EOUS HEROES.
BEAUTIFUL PRINCESS-ES.
TERRIFYING MONSTERS.
AN IDEAL WORLD TO EASE HER MIND.
Dad
I JUST READ THEM TO HER.
The Reader
monorobu

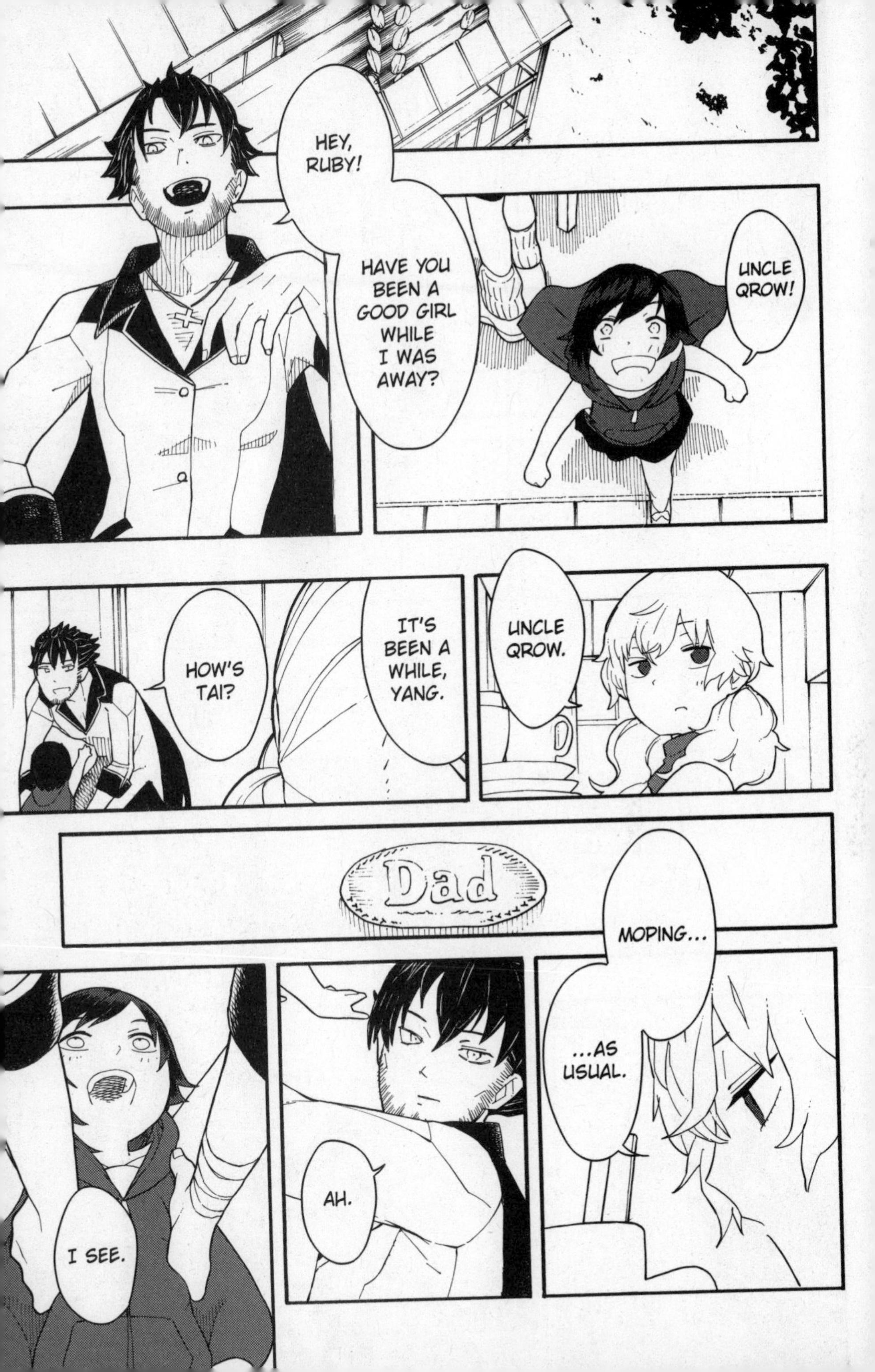
UNCLE QROW!
HEY, RUBY!
HAVE YOU BEEN A GOOD GIRL WHILE I WAS AWAY?
UNCLE QROW.
IT'S BEEN A WHILE, YANG.
HOW'S TAI?
Dad
MOPING...
...AS USUAL.
AH.
I SEE.

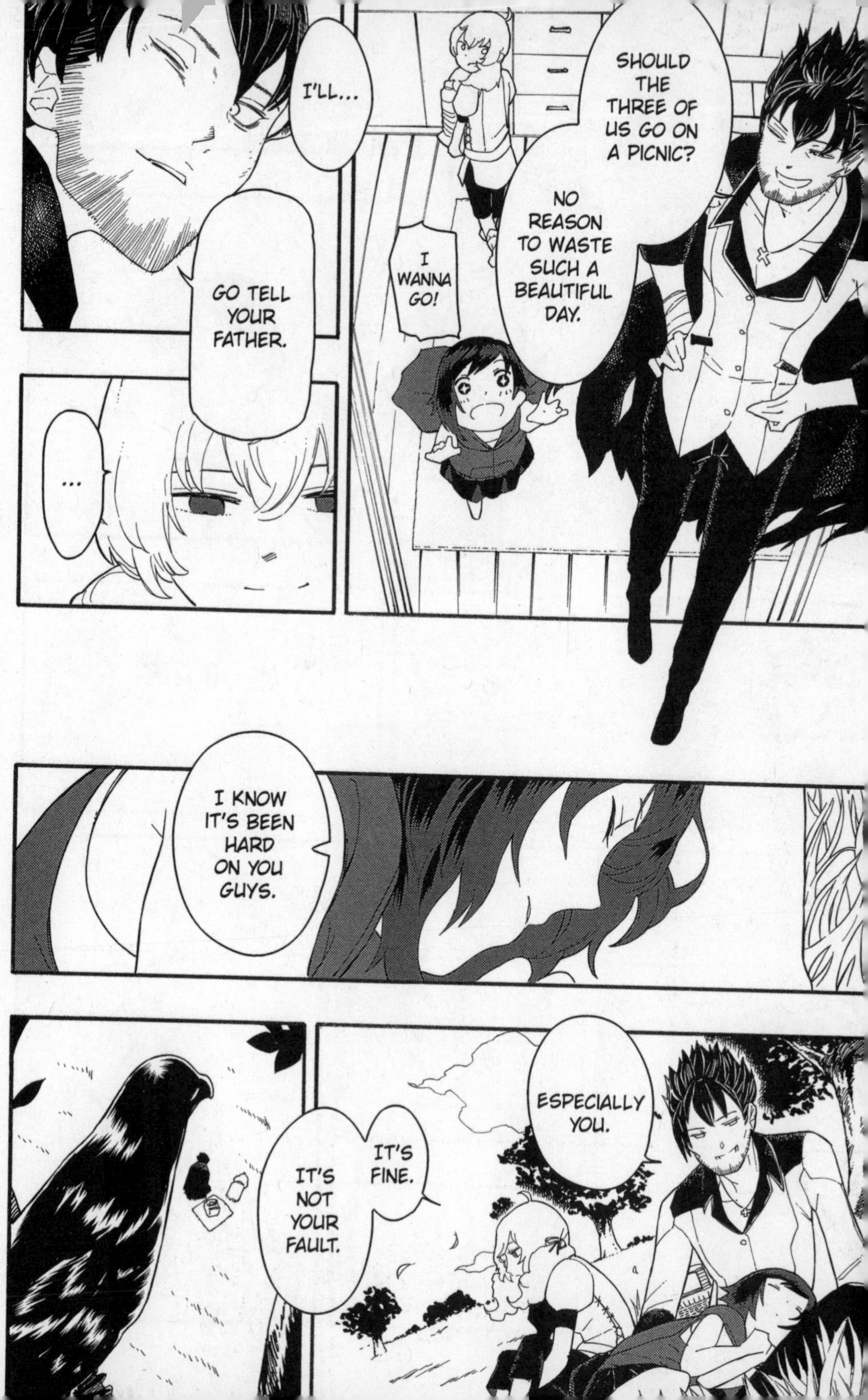
SHOULD THE THREE OF US GO ON A PICNIC?
NO REASON TO WASTE SUCH A BEAUTIFUL DAY.
I WANNA GO!
I'LL...
GO TELL YOUR FATHER.
...
I KNOW IT'S BEEN HARD ON YOU GUYS.
ESPECIALLY YOU.
IT'S FINE.
IT'S NOT YOUR FAULT.

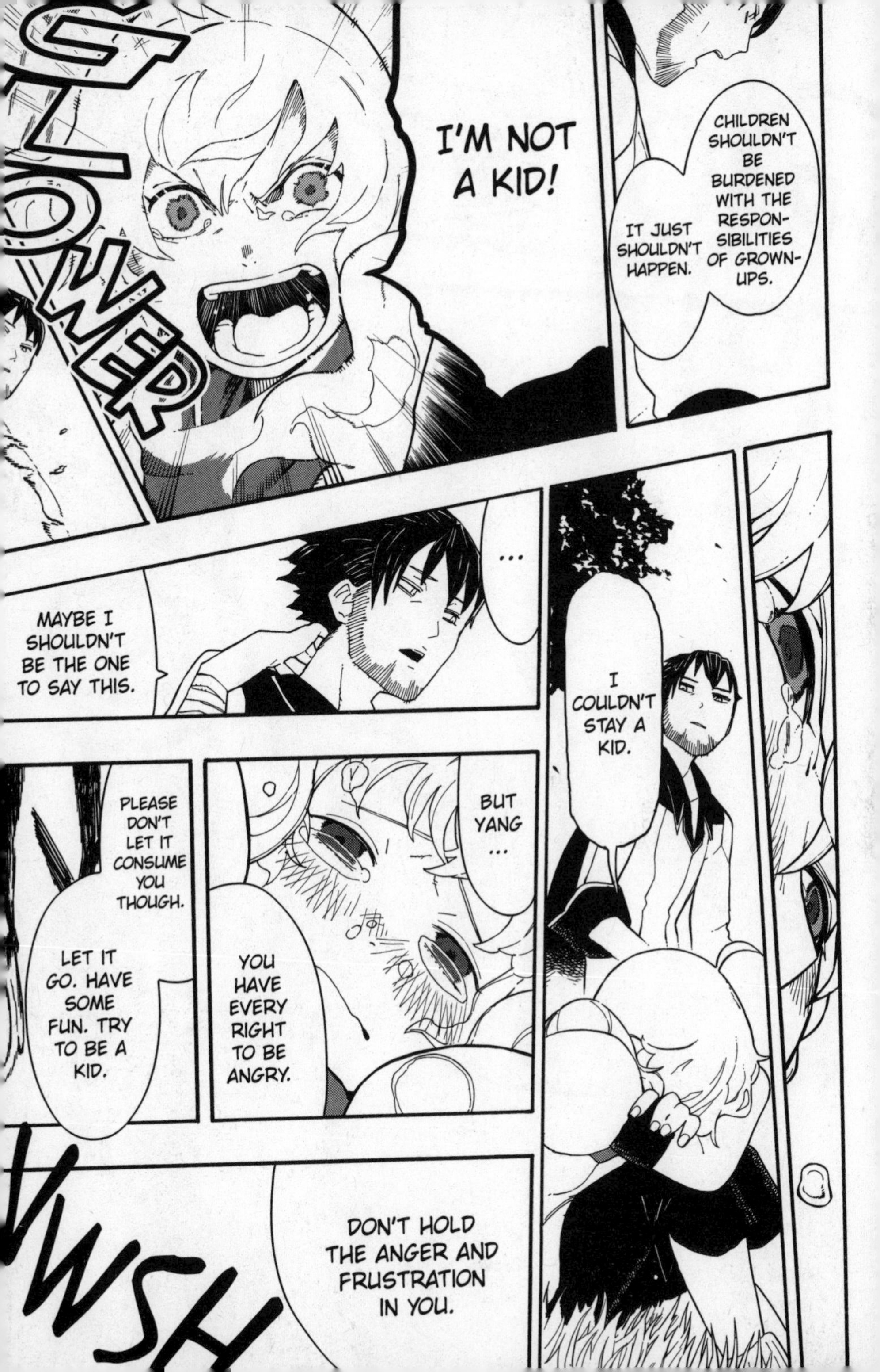
CHILDREN SHOULDN'T BE BURDENED WITH THE RESPON- SIBILITIES OF GROWN- UPS.
IT JUST SHOULDN'T HAPPEN.
I'M NOT A KID!
GLOWER
I COULDN'T STAY A KID.
...
MAYBE I SHOULDN'T BE THE ONE TO SAY THIS.
BUT YANG ...
YOU HAVE EVERY RIGHT TO BE ANGRY.
PLEASE DON'T LET IT CONSUME YOU THOUGH.
LET IT GO. HAVE SOME FUN. TRY TO BE A KID.
DON'T HOLD THE ANGER AND FRUSTRATION IN YOU.

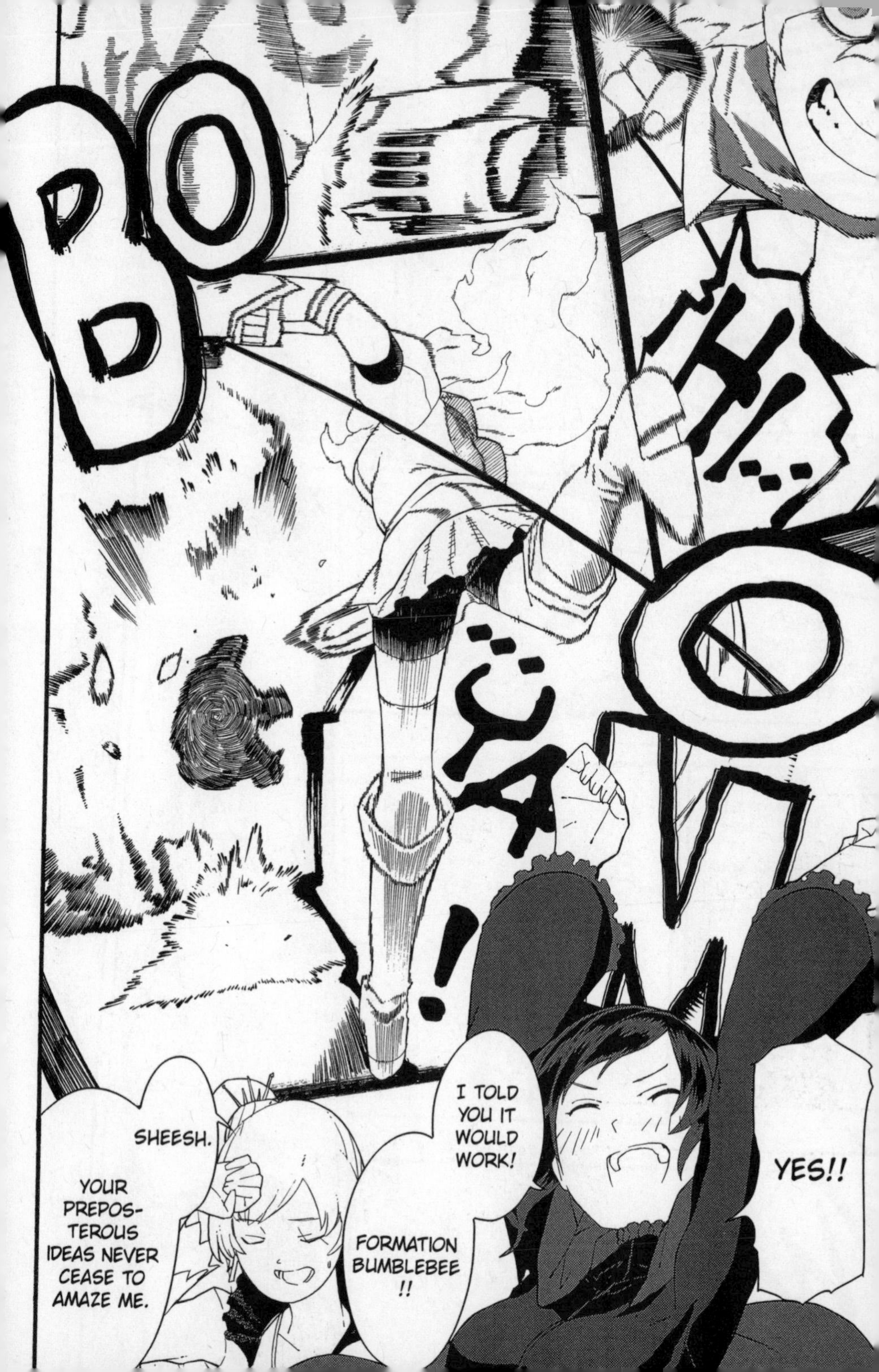
YES!!
I TOLD YOU IT WOULD WORK!
FORMATION BUMBLEBEE!!
SHEESH.
YOUR PREPOS-TEROUS IDEAS NEVER CEASE TO AMAZE ME.

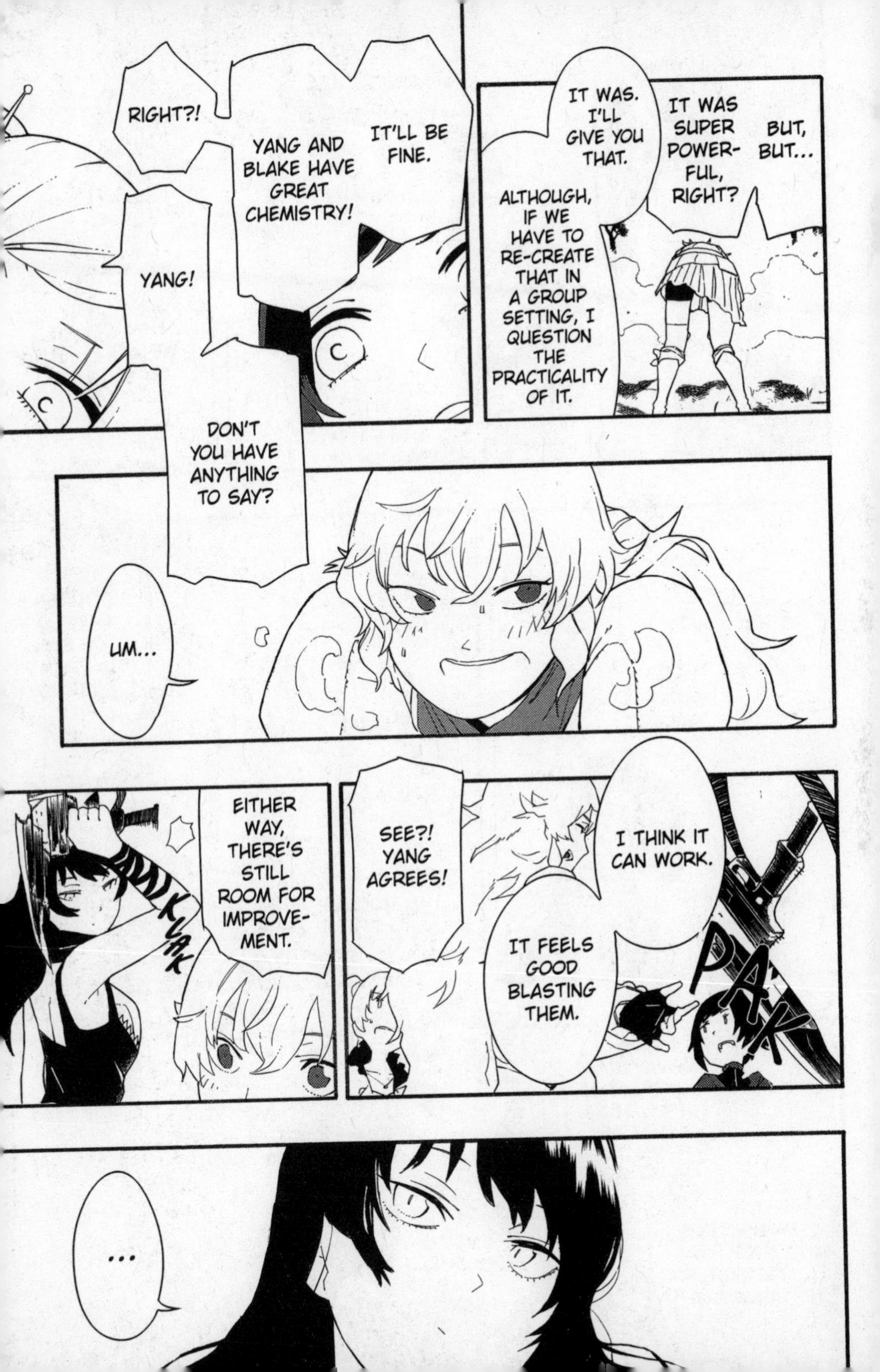
BUT, BUT...
IT WAS SUPER POWERFUL, RIGHT?
IT WAS. I'LL GIVE YOU THAT.
ALTHOUGH, IF WE HAVE TO RE-CREATE THAT IN A GROUP SETTING, I QUESTION THE PRACTICALITY OF IT.
IT'LL BE FINE.
YANG AND BLAKE HAVE GREAT CHEMISTRY!
RIGHT?!
YANG!
DON'T YOU HAVE ANYTHING TO SAY?
UM...
I THINK IT CAN WORK.
IT FEELS GOOD BLASTING THEM.
DAK
SEE?! YANG AGREES!
EITHER WAY, THERE'S STILL ROOM FOR IMPROVEMENT.
KLAK
...

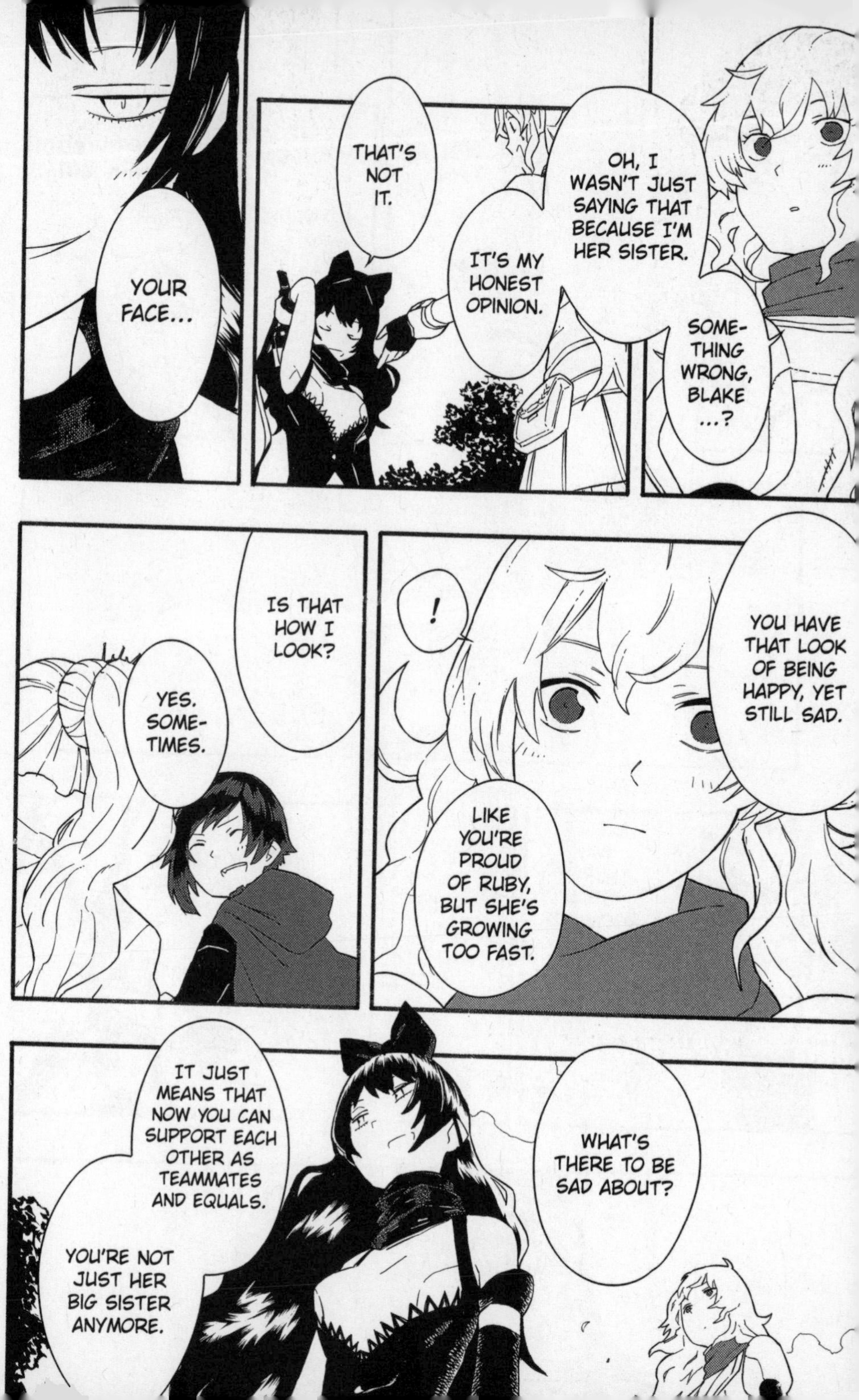
OH, I WASN'T JUST SAYING THAT BECAUSE I'M HER SISTER.
IT'S MY HONEST OPINION.
SOME-THING WRONG, BLAKE ...?
THAT'S NOT IT.
YOUR FACE...
YOU HAVE THAT LOOK OF BEING HAPPY, YET STILL SAD.
!
LIKE YOU'RE PROUD OF RUBY, BUT SHE'S GROWING TOO FAST.
IS THAT HOW I LOOK?
YES. SOME-TIMES.
WHAT'S THERE TO BE SAD ABOUT?
IT JUST MEANS THAT NOW YOU CAN SUPPORT EACH OTHER AS TEAMMATES AND EQUALS.
YOU'RE NOT JUST HER BIG SISTER ANYMORE.

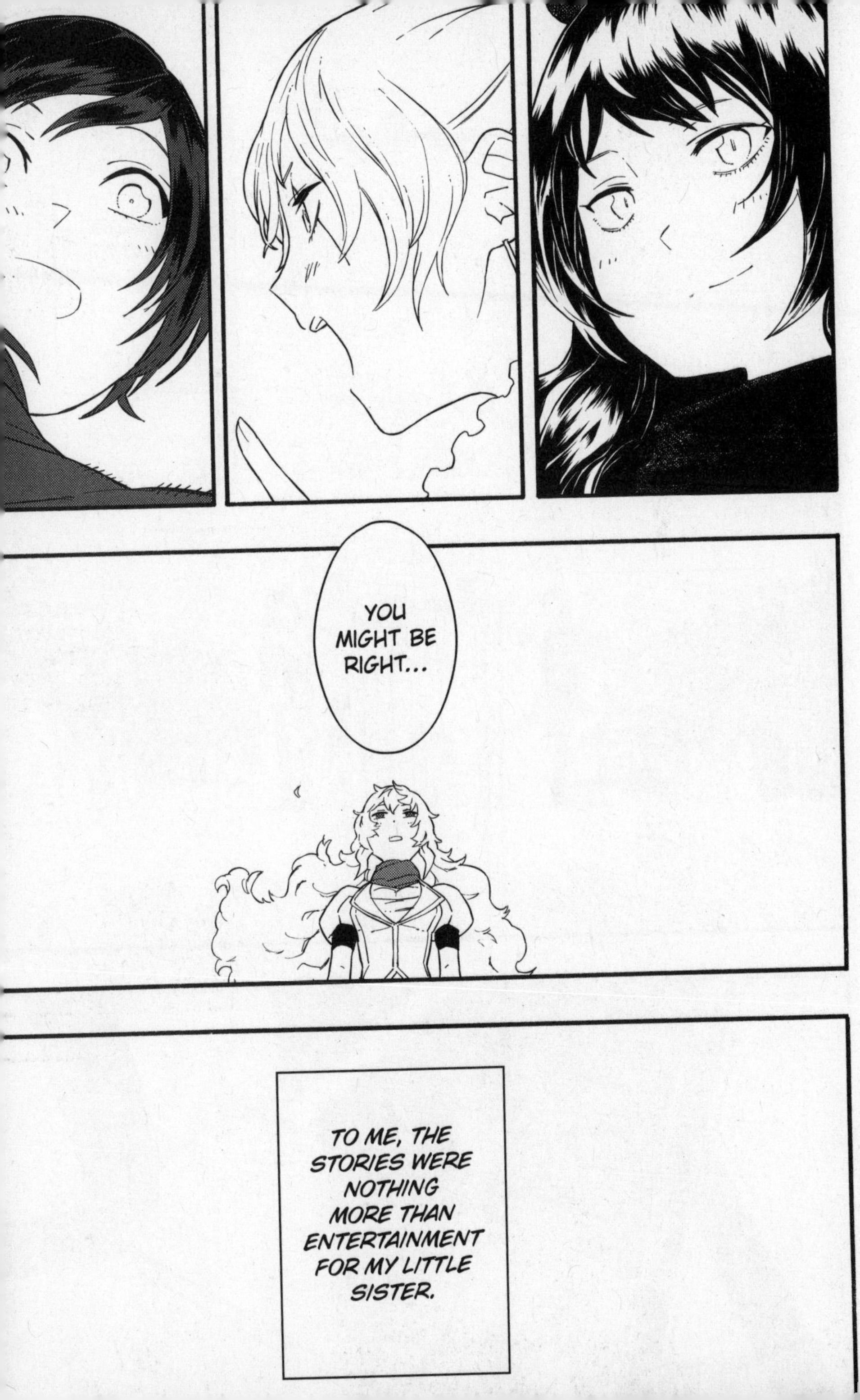
YOU MIGHT BE RIGHT...
TO ME, THE STORIES WERE NOTHING MORE THAN ENTERTAINMENT FOR MY LITTLE SISTER.

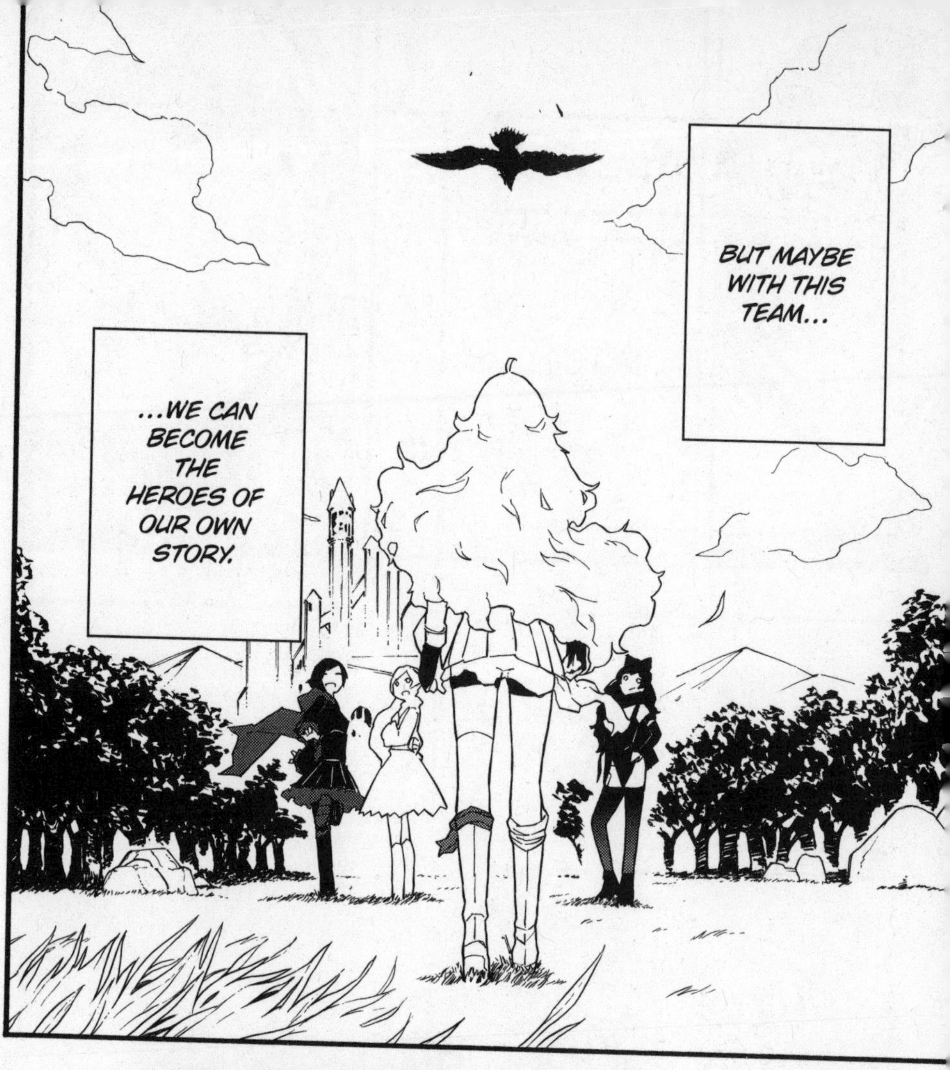
BUT MAYBE WITH THIS TEAM...
...WE CAN BECOME THE HEROES OF OUR OWN STORY.

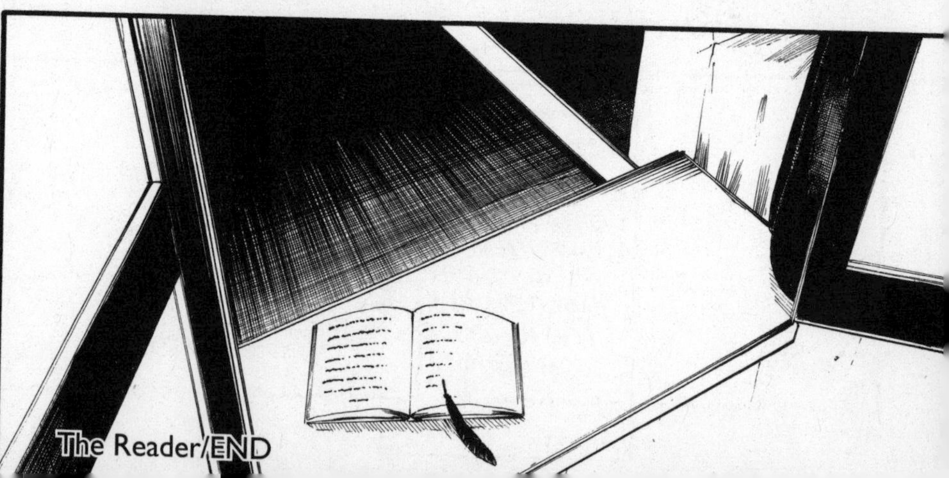
The Reader/END

RWBY No Doubt: Yang

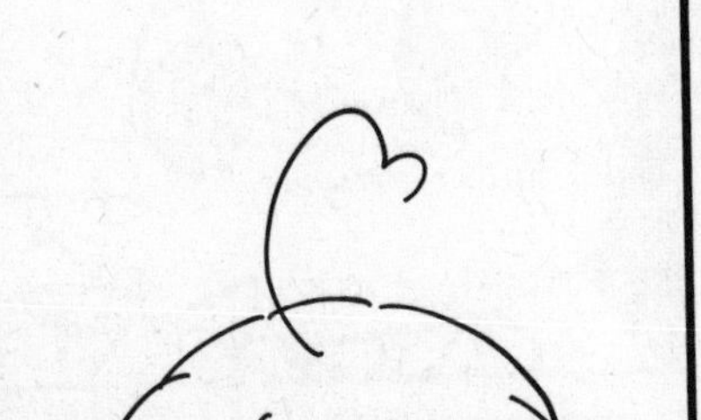
RWBY No Doubt: Yang
Umiya

Yang Appears!

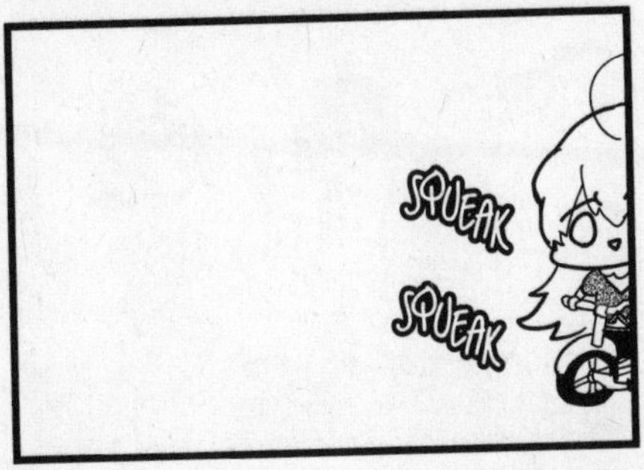
SQUEAK
SQUEAK

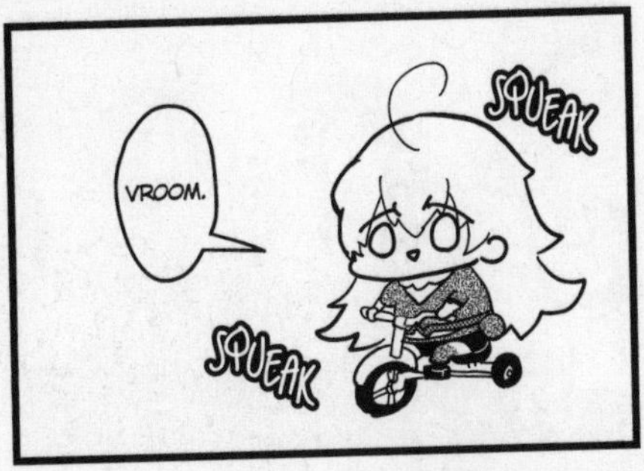
SQUEAK
VROOM.
SQUEAK

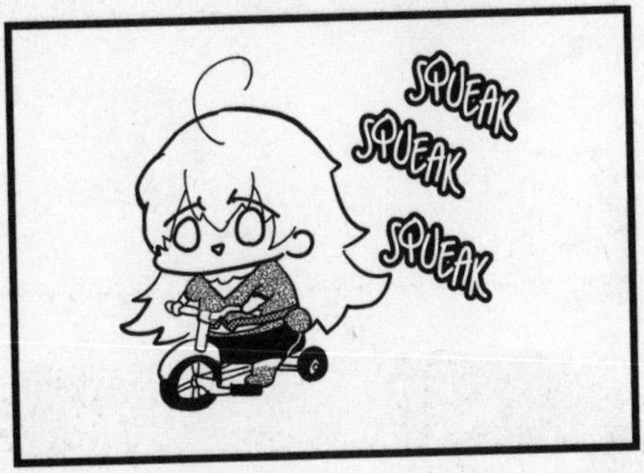
SQUEAK
SQUEAK
SQUEAK

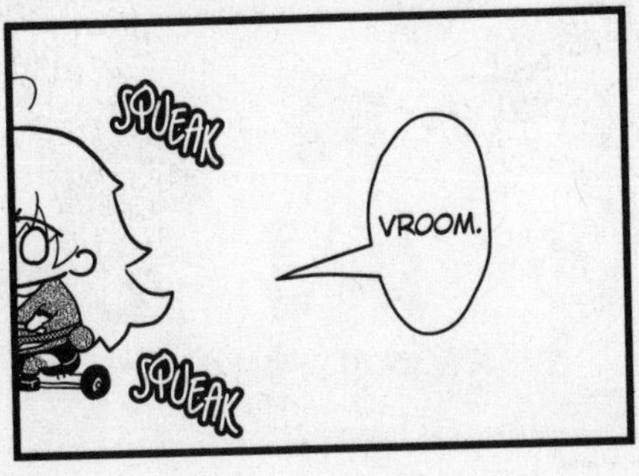
VROOM.
SQUEAK
SQUEAK

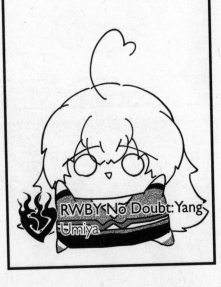

Boo at Bar

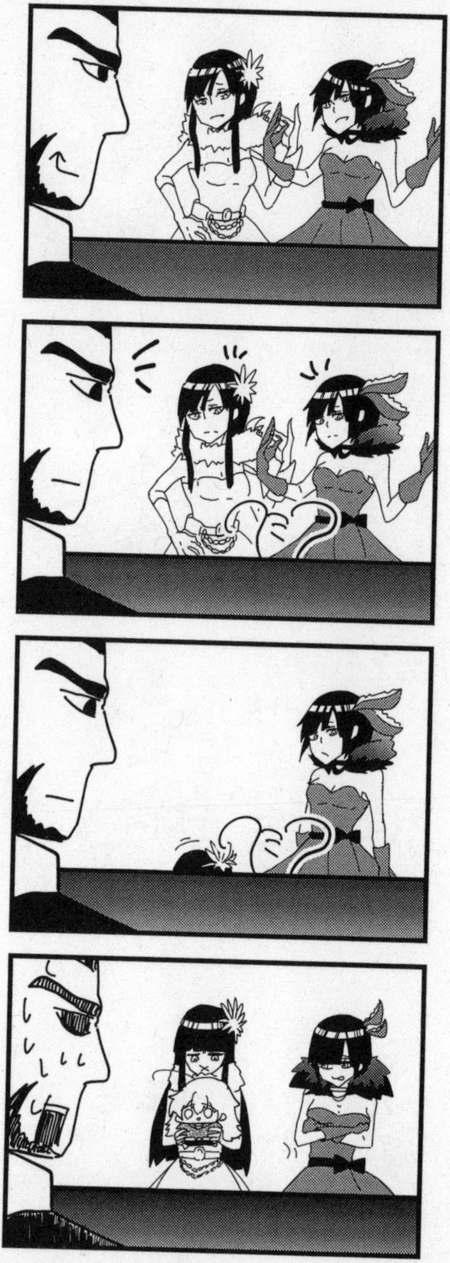

Boom at Bar

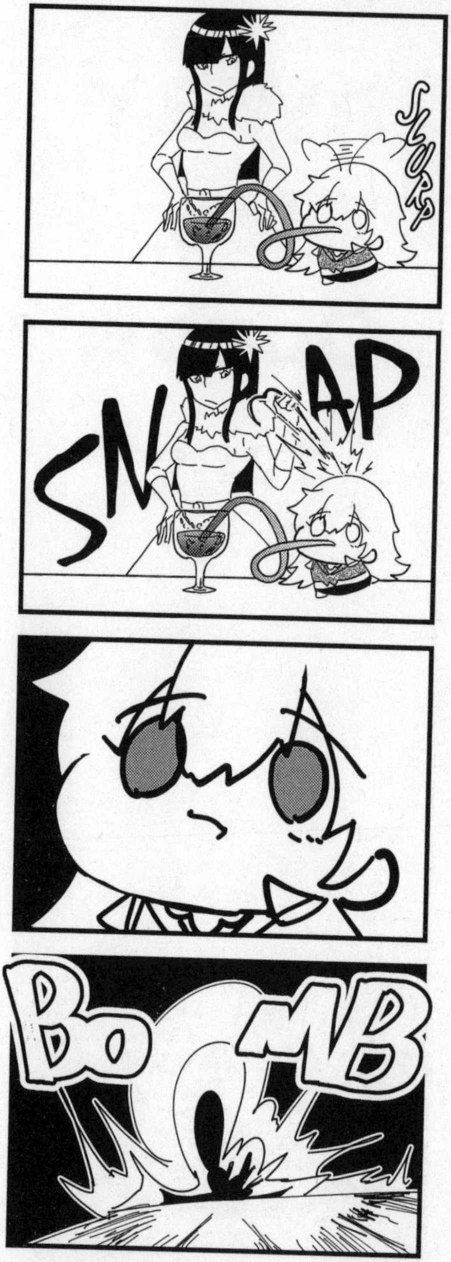
SLURP
SNAP
Bo
MB

Food Fight

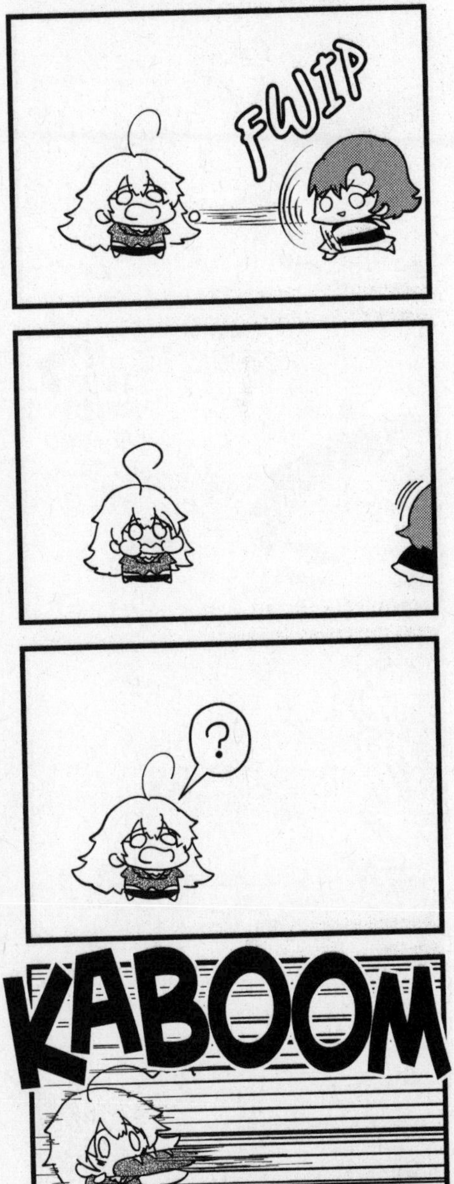
FWIP
?
KABOOM

Commence Rescue Operation

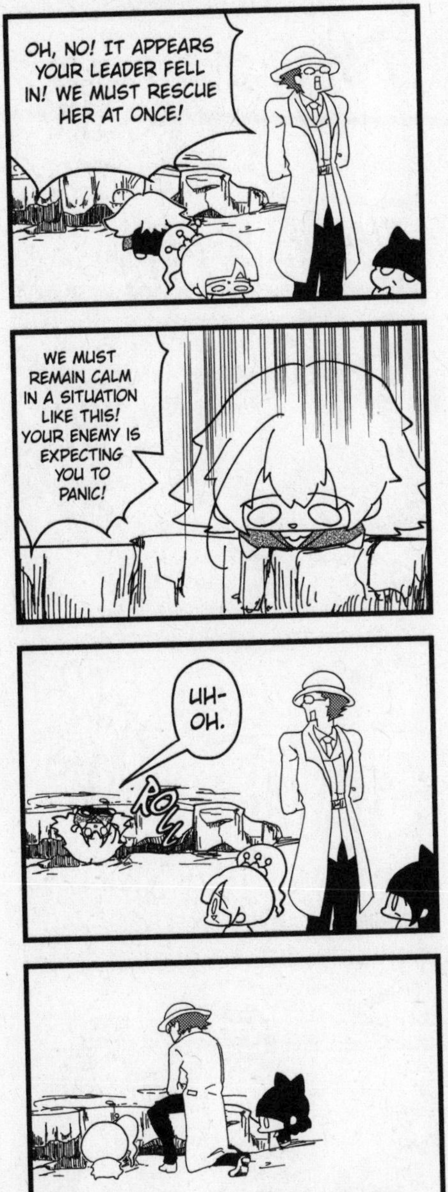
OH, NO! IT APPEARS YOUR LEADER FELL IN! WE MUST RESCUE HER AT ONCE!
WE MUST REMAIN CALM IN A SITUATION LIKE THIS! YOUR ENEMY IS EXPECTING YOU TO PANIC!
UH-OH.
POW

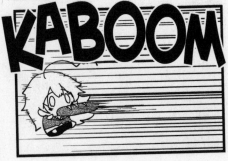

Stuck

FWIP
FWIP
FWIP
FWIP
FWIP
SHOOM
THUNK

It's Not a Game

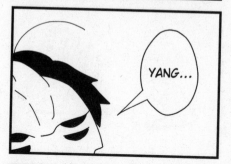

YANG...
THERE'S A LOT WE NEED TO TALK ABOUT.
DAZE
GET DOWN HERE RIGHT NOW!

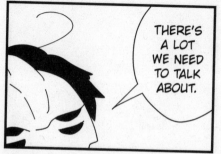

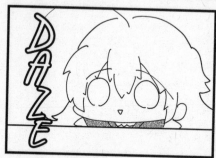

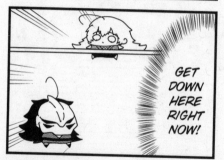

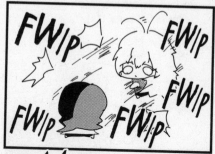

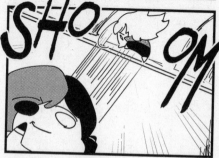

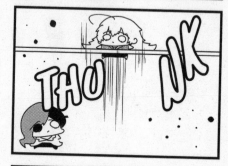

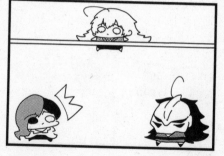

RWBY No Doubt: Yang/END

RWBY

OFFICIAL MANGA ANTHOLOGY

Volume 4

I Burn

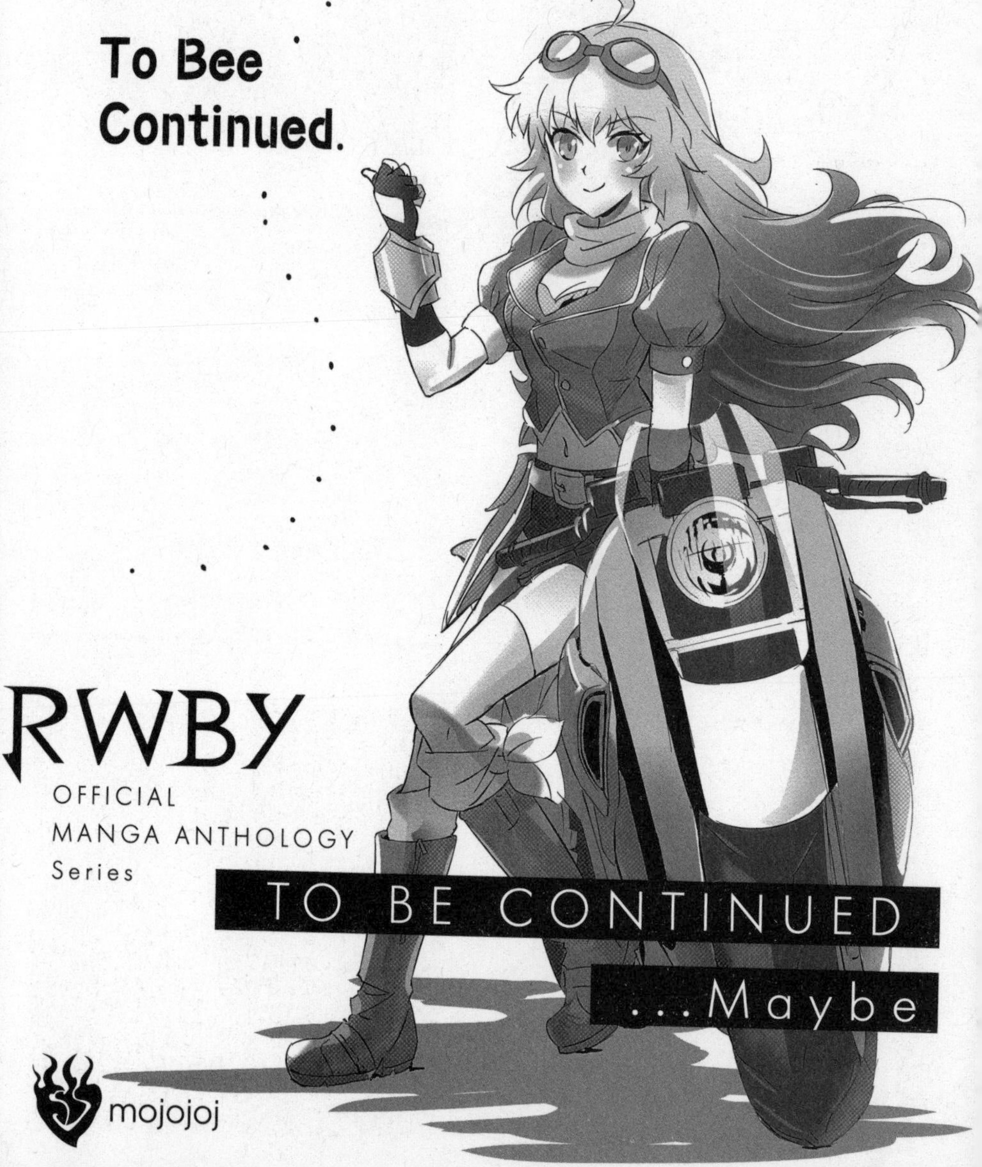
To Bee Continued.
RWBY
OFFICIAL
MANGA ANTHOLOGY
Series
TO BE CONTINUED
...Maybe
mojojoj

Messages From Illustrators and Mangaka

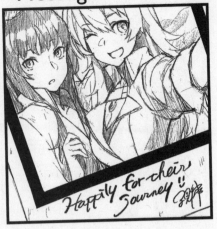

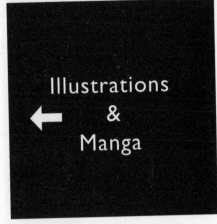

Illustrations & Manga

Happily for their Journey!!

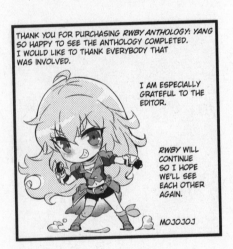

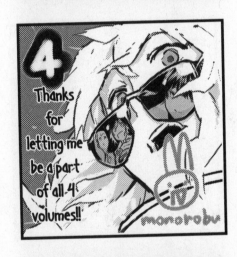

4
Thanks for letting me be a part of all 4 volumes!!
mororobu

THANK YOU FOR PURCHASING *RWBY ANTHOLOGY: YANG* SO HAPPY TO SEE THE ANTHOLOGY COMPLETED. I WOULD LIKE TO THANK EVERYBODY THAT WAS INVOLVED.
I AM ESPECIALLY GRATEFUL TO THE EDITOR.
RWBY WILL CONTINUE SO I HOPE WE'LL SEE EACH OTHER AGAIN.
MOJOJOJ

Illustrations

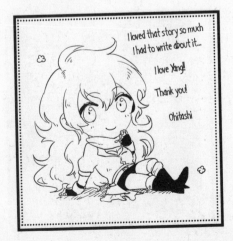

I loved that story so much I had to write about it...
I love Yang!!
Thank you!
Ohitashi

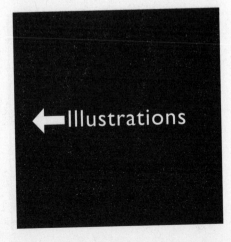

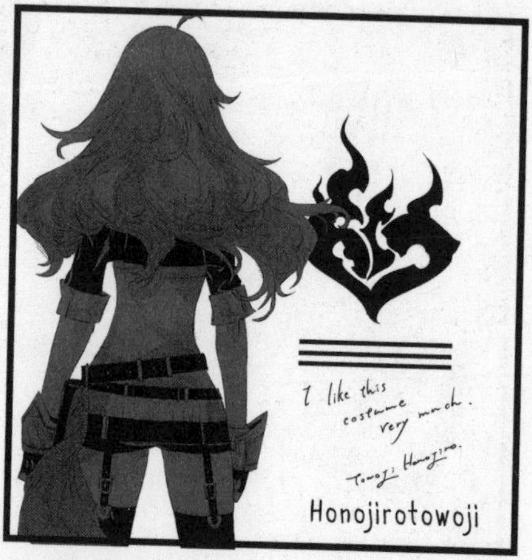
I like this costume very much.
Towoji Honojiro.
Honojirotowoji

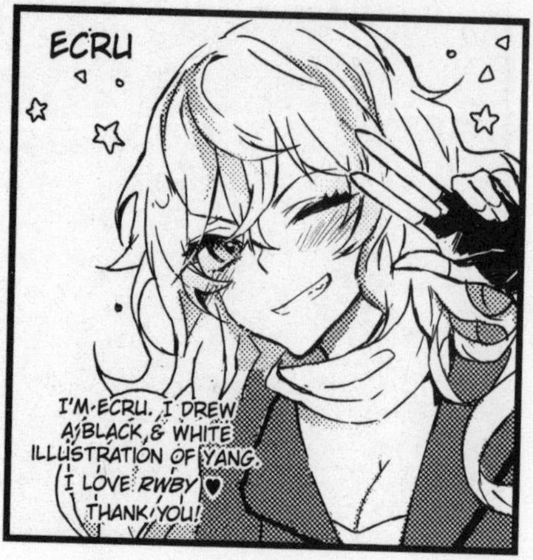
ECRU
I'M ECRU. I DREW A BLACK & WHITE ILLUSTRATION OF YANG. I LOVE RWBY ♥ THANK YOU!

← Manga

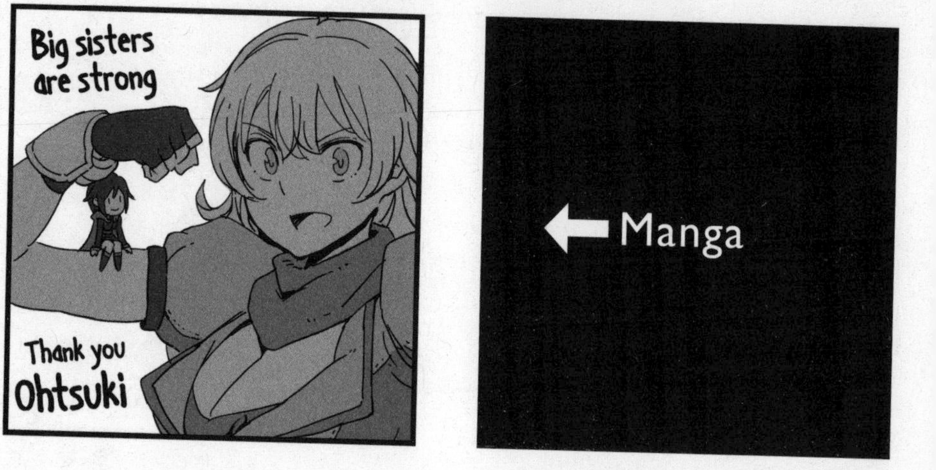
Big sisters are strong
Thank you Ohtsuki

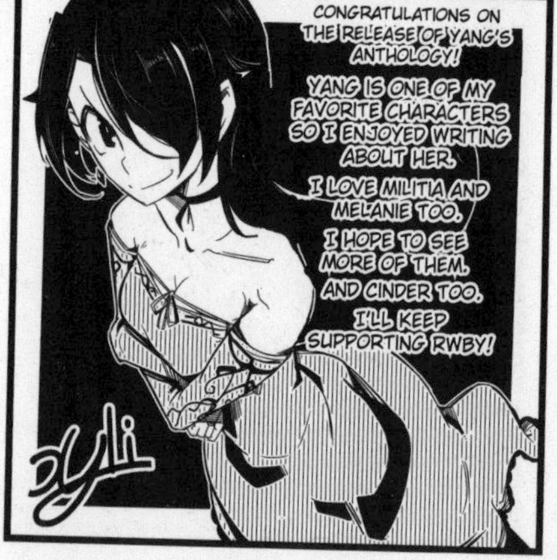
CONGRATULATIONS ON THE RELEASE OF YANG'S ANTHOLOGY!
YANG IS ONE OF MY FAVORITE CHARACTERS SO I ENJOYED WRITING ABOUT HER.
I LOVE MILITIA AND MELANIE TOO.
I HOPE TO SEE MORE OF THEM. AND CINDER TOO.
I'LL KEEP SUPPORTING RWBY!
Dyli

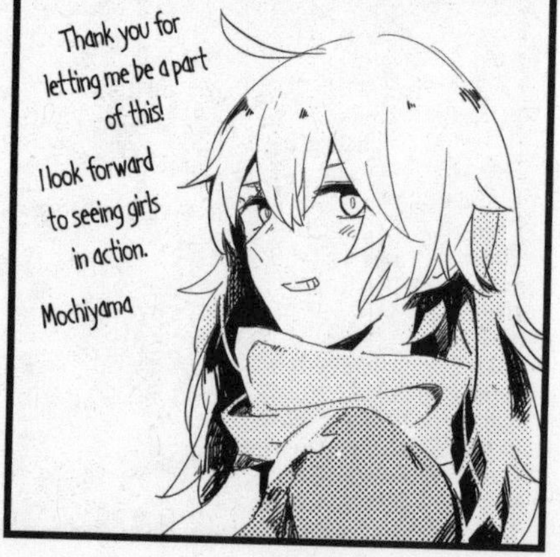
Thank you for letting me be a part of this!
I look forward to seeing girls in action.
Mochiyama

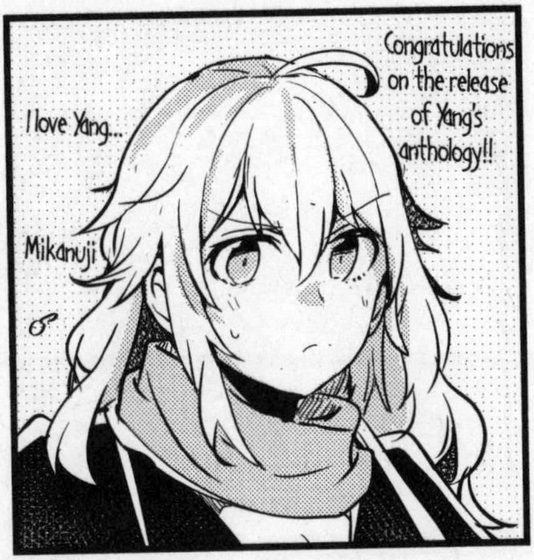
Congratulations on the release of Yang's anthology!!
I love Yang...
Mikanuji

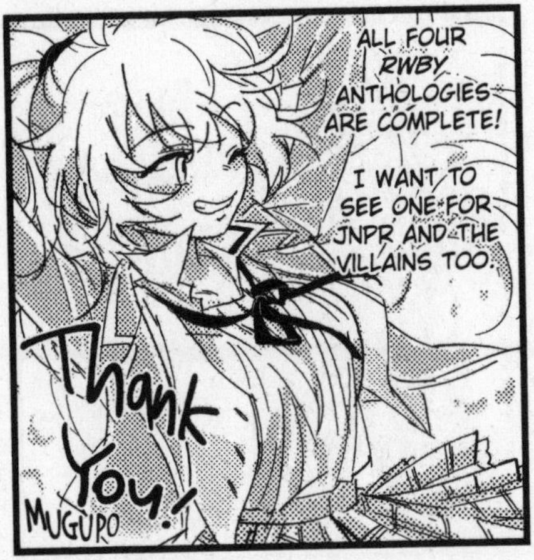
ALL FOUR *RWBY* ANTHOLOGIES ARE COMPLETE!
I WANT TO SEE ONE FOR JNPR AND THE VILLAINS TOO.
Thank You!
MUGUPO

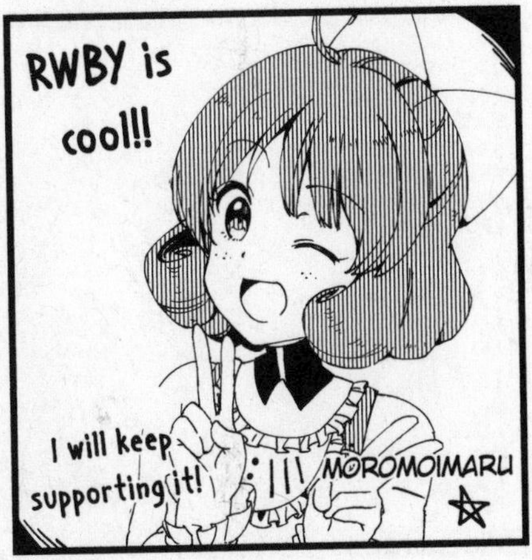
RWBY is cool!!!
I will keep supporting it!
MOROMOIMARU

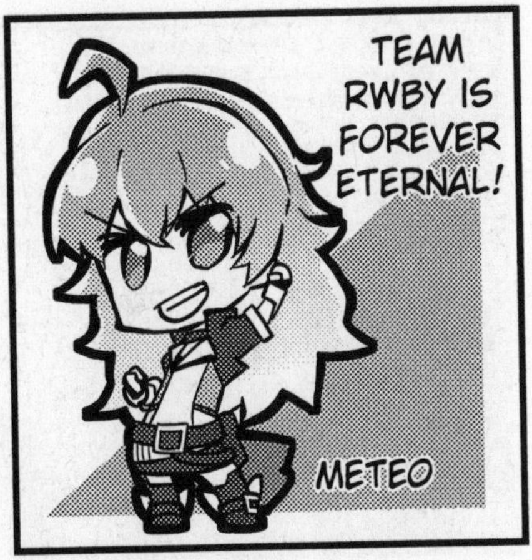
TEAM RWBY IS FOREVER ETERNAL!
METEO

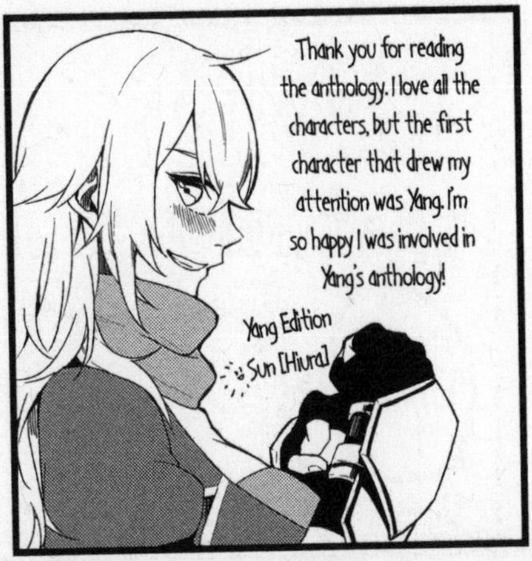
Thank you for reading the anthology. I love all the characters, but the first character that drew my attention was Yang. I'm so happy I was involved in Yang's anthology!
Yang Edition
Sun [Hiura]

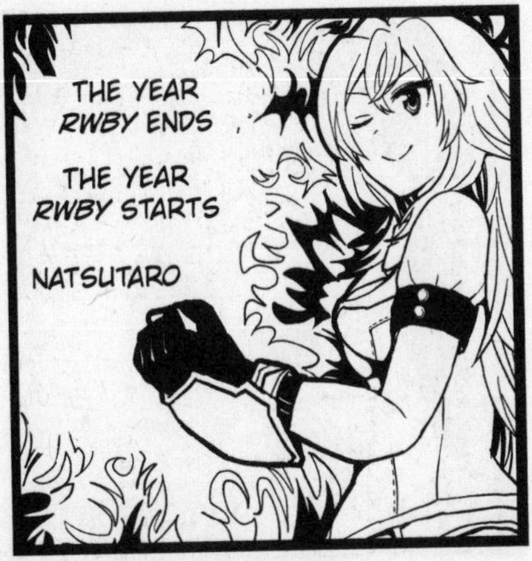
THE YEAR *RWBY* ENDS
THE YEAR *RWBY* STARTS
NATSUTARO

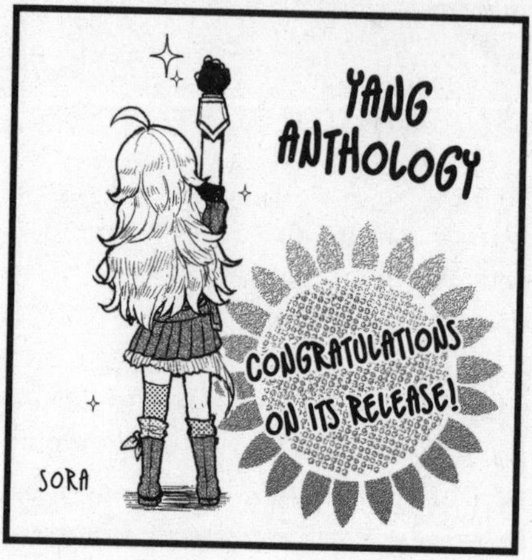
YANG ANTHOLOGY
CONGRATULATIONS ON ITS RELEASE!
SORA

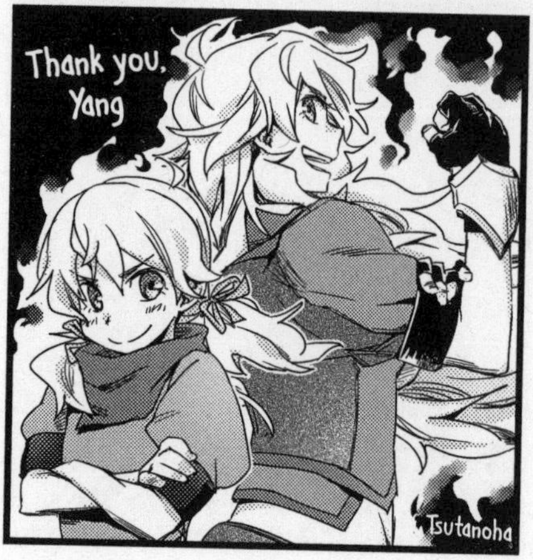
Thank you, Yang
Tsutanoha

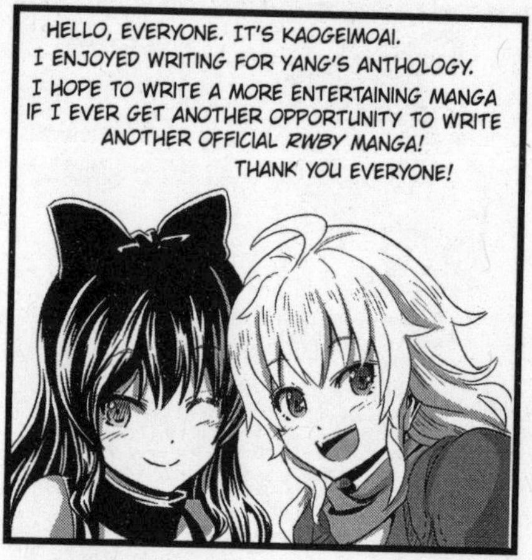
HELLO, EVERYONE. IT'S KAOGEIMOAI.
I ENJOYED WRITING FOR YANG'S ANTHOLOGY.
I HOPE TO WRITE A MORE ENTERTAINING MANGA IF I EVER GET ANOTHER OPPORTUNITY TO WRITE ANOTHER OFFICIAL RWBY MANGA!
THANK YOU EVERYONE!

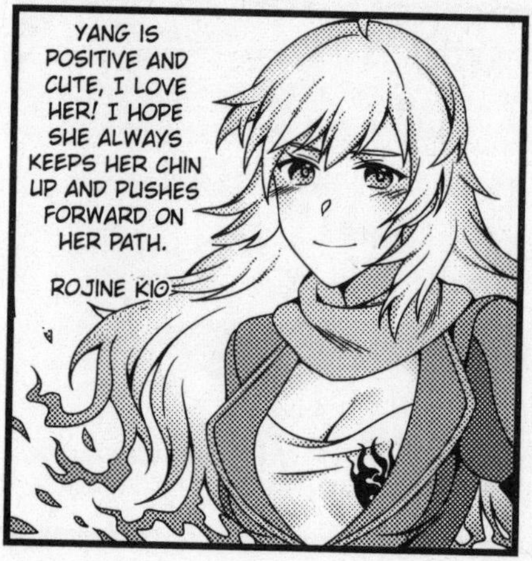
YANG IS POSITIVE AND CUTE, I LOVE HER! I HOPE SHE ALWAYS KEEPS HER CHIN UP AND PUSHES FORWARD ON HER PATH.
ROJINE KIO

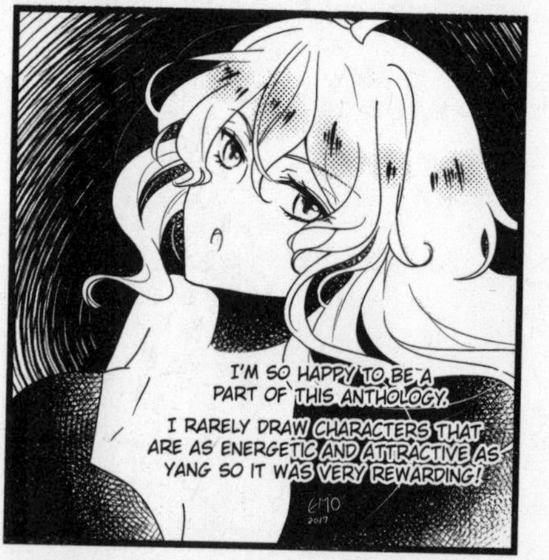
I'M SO HAPPY TO BE A PART OF THIS ANTHOLOGY.
I RARELY DRAW CHARACTERS THAT ARE AS ENERGETIC AND ATTRACTIVE AS YANG SO IT WAS VERY REWARDING!

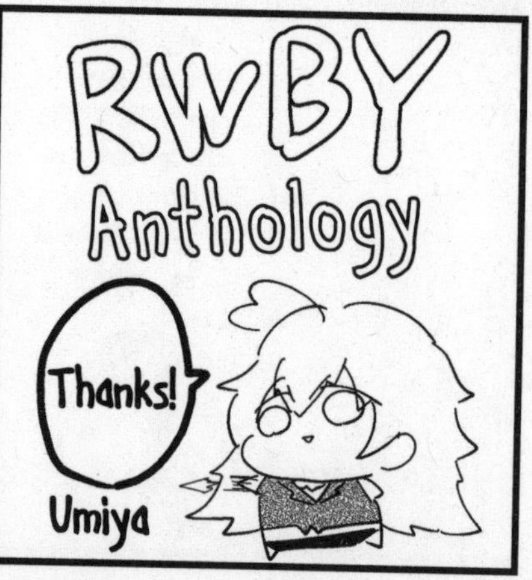
RWBY Anthology
Thanks!
Umiya

About Yang

Ein Lee

I think the mood of Yang's character design turned out the furthest from my usual designs.
I'm not dissatisfied with it (quite the contrary). The design of her skirt isn't my usual style. Her
asymmetrical skirt and the 'blade' hanging from her belt are very Monty-like. He asked me to
incorporate it into my design.

Looking at it now, maybe the details sprinkled on her clothes emphasize her confidence and slightly
precocious personality. She's a good example of a character designed by two artists with different
sensibilities coming together through the stories.

By the way, her 3-D character model, her proportions, and her facial features in volumes 1 through 3
are my favorite of the four characters. But the modeling team forgot the buttons on her jacket... It's
disappointing because I like buttons. As for the cover, I emphasized her fearlessness to make it seem
like she's actually in combat. I never drew Yang's weapon in detail in the past so I had to do some
research. *(laugh)*

The other cover idea of Yang lying on petals was designed to complement Blake's cover idea.
I'm very pleased with how her gazing contentedly at how the small flowers turned out.

Hey there, friend!

Never in a million years did I think I would be so fortunate as to be part of a show like *RWBY*. I am overwhelmed on a daily basis by your passion, love, and dedication, and am so thankful for your undying support. It has been the honor of a lifetime to be able to bring Yang Xiao Long to life. She is such an inspiration to so many people; myself included! I wish I looked that cool in aviators.

We mean it when we say that *RWBY* wouldn't exist without people like you, so thank you for watching the show and being part of our journey!

With love,

Barbara Dunkelman

RWBY OFFICIAL MANGA ANTHOLOGY 4

I Burn

VIZ Signature Edition
Official Manga Anthology Vol. 4
I BURN
Based on the Rooster Teeth Series Created by MONTY OUM.

TRANSLATION Joe Yamazaki
ENGLISH ADAPTATION Jason A. Hurley
TOUCH-UP ART AND LETTERING Evan Waldinger
DESIGN Shawn Carrico
EDITOR Joel Enos

COVER ILLUSTRATION Ein Lee/Meteo
ORIGINAL COVER DESIGN Tsuyoshi Kusano

SPECIAL THANKS
Ken Takizawa (Home-sha)
Takanori Inoue (Home-sha)
Misato Kaneko
Yoshihiko Wakanabe (Editor/Planner of RWBY OFFICIAL MANGA ANTHOLOGY)

Printed in the U.S.A.

Published by VIZ Media, LLC
P.O. Box 77010
San Francisco, CA 94107

10 9 8 7 6 5 4 3 2 1
First printing, February 2019

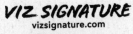

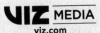

VIZ SIGNATURE
vizsignature.com

VIZ MEDIA
viz.com

ratings.viz.com
RATED T TEEN

PARENTAL ADVISORY
RWBY is rated T for Teen and is recommended for ages 13 and up. This volume contains violence and peril.

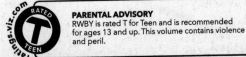

Much appreciated.

Thank you for getting this anthology.

HAVE FUN!

This is the last page.

RWBY reads right to left.